IN SEARCH OF YOUR EUROPEAN ROOTS

Angus Baxter

In Search of Your European Roots

A COMPLETE GUIDE TO TRACING YOUR ANCESTORS IN EVERY COUNTRY IN EUROPE

Third Edition

GENEALOGICAL PUBLISHING CO. INC.

First Edition 1985
Second Edition 1994
Third Edition 2001

Published by Genealogical Publishing Co., Inc.
1001 N. Calvert St., Baltimore, MD 21202
Library of Congress Catalogue Card Number 00-136383
International Standard Book Number 0-8063-1657-8
Made in the United States of America

For my daughter, Susan, with much love. Aided by
her husband, Thomas Barcsay, she has produced
the ultimate European, our granddaughter
Katherine, who can number among
her ancestors Scots, Hungarians,
English, French, Normans,
Vikings, Italians, and
Germans. She is
proud to be a
Canadian.

Pride in family is pride in ordinary
people—who in our hearts and
minds become extraordinary.
—Anon.

CONTENTS

ACKNOWLEDGMENTS

First and foremost, my love and my thanks to my wife, Nan, who read each chapter as it was produced, and helped me—as she has done with all my books—with sound advice.

I would like to express my gratitude to The Church of Jesus Christ of Latter-day Saints, an organization that shares its genealogical knowledge and vast resources with those of us who are not members of the Church. Their records are too voluminous to list, but you must be sure to check them before you start ancestor-hunting in most European countries, since many of the records of that continent are available on microfilm and microfiche. In the writing of this book and others, and in my own personal genealogical research, I am deeply in their debt.

I must also say thank you to the Everton Publishers, of Logan, Utah, for its series of "Handy Guides to Genealogical Records" in various European countries—Austria, Hungary, Italy, and Switzerland. These books are essential for any genealogist researching a family from these countries. You will find more details in the bibliography. This company also publishes *Everton's Genealogical Helper*, another excellent and valuable aid.

I acknowledge with great sincerity my obligation to leading archivists and church officials in Europe—many of whom I met personally during my research, and others who have supplied me with information by mail. I have been in every European country except Albania, Finland, Iceland, and Norway, and I cannot speak too highly of the help and cooperation extended to me by these officials. They have listened patiently to my queries, answered many questions, and pointed me in the right direction for any further help that they could not provide.

In the original edition of this book, I listed a number of names of people in Europe who had gone to a great deal of trouble to supply me with accurate information about their records—national archivists, church officials, officers of genealogical societies (where they exist), and individuals and historians in the many countries my wife and I had visited and explored in our travels over the years. Many of them are no longer holding their various offices, but I remain grateful to them. They deserve my thanks, too, for making it possible for the American Library Association to name the book as one of the top three works of reference in 1986.

For this edition I have received even greater help and friendly cooperation from their successors. I hope they will forgive me for not listing them by name because of the limitations of space. A number have thanked me for helping their tourist trade by increasing the number of visitors searching for their roots! Others have paid tribute to my knowledge of their country and its history.

Apart from thanking my friends in Europe, there are others in North America to whom I am grateful for their assistance: Nada Cunic for her help in translating Slovenian and Serbo-Croat; Dr. Jaroslav Polak, MD, for assistance with translating Czech; Marian Hoffman, my editor, who keeps an eagle eye on my prose; Susan Baxter, my daughter who, apart from her work as a Financial Director, used her "on-line" wizardry to find me Russian web sites; and, again, Nan Baxter, my wise and wonderful wife, whose advice and guidance in writing this book and all my other books is beyond praise.

ANGUS BAXTER

FOREWORD

Why are more and more people tracing their ancestors? All over the world people are in search of their roots, and there must be a reason for this. For members of The Church of Jesus Christ of Latter-day Saints, the answer is simple—they believe that if they can trace their forebears and have them baptized into their own faith, they will be reunited with them after death. But what about the rest of us? Why are we tracing our families back?

There are no easy answers, because our reasons are diverse: some hope to find a title in the family; some hope to discover they are descended from some ancient king; and some want to unlock the key to hidden wealth, to impress their friends with the social standing of a great-great-grandfather, or to find a family coat of arms.

At least two of the hopes are almost certain to be dashed: hidden wealth and a coat of arms. Almost every family has a story that has been handed down about a missing fortune—vast wealth tied up in some court battle because a birth certificate is missing. The tale is always the same, but I have never known anyone to find riches through ancestor-hunting! If you do, as a result of this book, then I shall expect the usual ten percent!

A family coat of arms is just as unlikely. The right to bear arms (heraldic ones, that is) was usually granted by a ruler of a country as a reward for services rendered by some brave soldier or great landowner. Since ninety-five percent of us are descended from farmers and farm workers, the odds against your family having a coat of arms are very great. You may come across one granted centuries ago to someone with the same surname, but there is absolutely no guarantee that there is any family connection; in any case, the right to arms almost always descended in the male line.

However, I suspect that for most of us the motives that move us are quite different and very simple. We have an inborn need to go back and find out where our ancestors came from—not just the name of the country, which we probably know already, but the exact place in that country. We want to know what they did, how they earned a living. Why did they leave? What clothes did they wear? What was happening in that country at that particular time? These are our questions and we are the people who will answer them if we are patient and determined.

Patience and determination. And there is more. You will need money, you will need skill in finding information, you will need charm and good manners in extracting it, you will need time, and you will need luck.

The cost will vary—it will depend on how much you know at the start, on the cost of postage and the cost of paying return postage, on the ease or difficulty of access to records in the "old country," and on how much you will have to pay for an occasional professional researcher. Each family is too individual for me to hazard a guess—but remember that ancestor-hunting is a pay-as-you-go affair! Whenever you think you are spending too much money, stop for a while and let your finances recover. Never, never let searching for your roots be a burden—it should be a pleasure, it should be fun!

Don't spread yourself too wide—take one side of your family at a time; otherwise you will only become confused with the hundreds of names you will acquire as time goes by. You will also find that when you are searching long lists of names (and you will be), it will be much easier to look for *one* surname and not seven or eight. Of course, if two or more sides of your family come from the same village or town, that is quite a different story— you will save time and money by looking for them simultaneously.

How do you start on this magic journey? Well, you start with *you* and with no one else. You go back in time from *you*. You do not find someone with a similar name and trace them down the centuries to you. First, it is impossible, and second, there is little likelihood of a family connection, anyway. Names can be misleading in three ways:

Even within a few generations of a family, the spelling of a name can change, usually because our ancestors could not read or write and so the name would be spelled phonetically (as it sounds). Unfortunately, there was another complication, for a name might sound differently to different people. Just as some people are tone-deaf to music, so other people are tone-deaf to words. That is why in my own family you will find Baxter, Backster, Bacster, Bagster, Bakster, and Bacaster—all the way back to the original Saxon word Bacaestre, meaning baker. So, as you trace back, be prepared for changes of name, and don't assume that because you find a different spelling of your name it is not connected with your family.

Don't assume that everyone with the same name must be related to you somewhere way back in time. Up until the early fourteenth century in almost all European countries there were no surnames. People were known by the first name, and attached to it for identification purposes was a word describing where they lived, or what they did. Then you had John of the hill, or John the baker. As the population grew, this became more than a little complicated, and so the names became John Hill and John Baker. Since almost every village had a hill (except in the Netherlands) and a baker, you can see there is no way that all the Hills and Bakers have any blood relationship.

You may find that your surname was changed a few generations back. This could happen in several ways. It could be a fool or a bigot in the immigration service of this country who might have said, "What's your name—Pryzyborsky? What sort of name is that? I'll call you Price. Next!" It could have been your own ancestor who, finding his new friends and neighbors had difficulty pronouncing his name, changed it himself. When obtaining family stories from relatives and friends, or reading family papers, keep an eye and an ear open for a name change.

Write down everything you are told about your family—where they originated, their religion, their occupations—and write down, too, the names of the persons who gave you the information. You may need to go back to them for a recheck of the details they gave you. Go steadily back from you to your parents and grandparents, and listen carefully to all the family stories—but, having listened to them, don't always believe them! Family stories often become "decorated" with the passing of time. The sergeant in the army becomes a colonel, the tiny cottage becomes a fifty-room mansion, the bricklayer becomes a master builder! If you accept the stories without question you may have created your own dead end, and you will find enough of these along the way without adding to them.

When you start to question your own family, you may meet with resistance. People may say to you, "Leave well enough alone," or "Let sleeping dogs lie," or "Don't go and stir up trouble," or "Don't you bother about our ancestors; they were a bunch of sheep stealers, anyway," and so on. Try and overcome this sort of resistance. They are probably afraid you will find out something to the discredit of the family, some rogue in your ancestry, some skeleton in the closet. Be sure you explain that it is most unlikely you will ever find out anything about the character of your ancestors. You will find out when and where they were born, married, and died—and, probably, how much money they left—but unless they were very prominent in the life of a particular area, you will not find out if they were saints or sinners. So give them the benefit of the doubt, and believe you are descended from a long line of saints!

No one can tell you how far back you can get, as so much depends on the information you find within your own family, and on the records still available in the part of Europe from which your family came. So much, too, depends on you; tracing your ancestors is not easy, and it helps to possess the combined qualities of a Job, a detective, a bloodhound, and an elephant!

Of course, if you have plenty of money and no time you can pay a professional researcher to do all the work for you. The names of researchers can be obtained from genealogical organizations or government archivists, and you will find they are reliable and hard-working. However, they will lack the two things only *you* can provide: love of your family and a deep personal dedication to the task before you. There will, however, be occasions when you will have to use a researcher for a couple of hours because some archives and record offices insist on this.

There is one other important thing you must never forget. Be sure you always send return postage when you send a letter of inquiry abroad. You can do this by buying three International Reply Coupons (IRCs) from your own post office and enclosing them with your letter. Also enclose a self-addressed *airmail* envelope; otherwise your reply may come by surface mail and that has been known to take two months! While we are on the subject of postage, if you are going to be corresponding a great deal with one country, you can save money by writing to the General Post Office in the capital of that country, enclosing whatever sum of money you wish to spend at one time, and asking them to send you a supply of their stamps of the right value for airmail postage to this country. Then you can stick a stamp on the self-addressed airmail envelope and you will have no need to spend money on the three IRCs; there is quite a saving in cost.

When you are writing to archives, or parish priests or ministers, or genealogical organizations, or local officials, remember that they are not compelled to reply to you. There is no international law that says they must. So be sure you write a nice polite letter, give them as much background information as you can about the subject of your query, offer to pay whatever fees are required, and thank them in advance for their kind assistance. You may think this advice is totally unnecessary, and I am sure it is for *you*, but you should read some of the letters—rude and demanding—that are received in Europe from ancestor-hunters overseas! The post office suggests that when writing abroad you should always include the postal code, and you should put the name of the country in capital letters on a separate line at the end of the address. For example:

Landsarkivet in Visby
Visbogsgatan 1
621 57 Visby
SWEDEN

This book is written to help you trace your ancestors in the old country; it will give you no information about records in *this* country. There are a number of books available for that purpose. We are concerned only with ancestor-hunting "over the water" in the Europe of our forebears.

Remember, you do not need to visit Europe to trace your ancestors. It can all be done by mail and the cost will not be astronomical. It will take up as much or as little of your time as you wish. Most archives and genealogical societies now have web sites and e-mail addresses, so a great deal of leg-work can be accomplished online. Of course, one day your natural curiosity will take you back to the land of your forefathers. You will want to walk the streets they walked; to visit the houses in which they lived; to stand in silence in the churchyards where they lie; and to know that where you are, so were they many, many years ago.

In actual fact, it will be to your advantage to visit the old country *after* you have traced the family some way back, because by then you will know so much more about its history and its people. You will have been corresponding with officials of various kinds, librarians, archivists, clergymen, and even newly found distant cousins. Your visit will be so much happier than if you suddenly arrive with no personal contacts, no knowledge of where the records are located, and—quite soon—no time left to do the searching you could have done before you left home.

I mentioned "newly found distant cousins." Many people have found cousins by writing a letter to a local newspaper in the old country. If your ancestor emigrated within the last one hundred years, there may be relatives he left behind whose descendants still speak of the man (or woman) who left home to make good over the ocean. So, if you know the name of the place or the district from which your ancestor came, write to the local paper and ask for information about the family. Give the full name of your ancestor and the date of departure. Keep it brief; in fact, write a letter on the following lines:

> My grandfather, Alexandru Stanescu, emigrated from Pitesti to America in 1890. He was a farmworker. His father was named Nicolae. If there are any relatives still living in Pitesti I would very much like to hear from them.

I should emphasize *local* newspapers because "big-city" ones are not likely to publish your letter, but small ones always will. How do you find out the name of the local paper? Simple; you write to the nearest consulate or embassy of the particular country and ask them. Romania, for example, has a local newspaper in each of its counties, or administrative districts, including ten in Hungarian, and two in German.

You may get letters from people who are not related, complete strangers who are going out of their way to help you. Let me give you a very recent example of kindness I received.

My family originated in a remote valley named Swindale in the Lake District of England. I have traced them back in a proven line to 1340. In fact, there were Baxters there in 1195 but I cannot *prove* descent beyond the later date, and what I cannot prove I do not claim. I visited the valley many years ago but it was a brief visit and all I was able to do was to take a quick look and travel on. I've always meant to go back and spend more time there, but somehow the years have passed and when my wife and I could have been in Swindale we were in Nepal or Tonga or Afghanistan or Egypt or any one of the many places to which our itchy feet have taken us.

So, in 1984 I wrote a letter to the *Westmorland Gazette* (the local paper), explained that my family came from the area, and asked if, by any chance, any reader had any photographs of the houses and farms in which my ancestors had lived (I listed them), and if so, could they lend me a print to be copied, or have a copy made—at my expense, of course.

I had three replies from people who did not have any photographs but who had made a special journey to Swindale to photograph the houses and the scenery of that lovely, lonely valley. In one instance they made up a complete album of pictures with a written commentary; another couple sent me lots of slides and a fifty-foot movie they had made for me; and a third correspondent discovered and photographed the ruins of a very large house reputed to have been built by my family in about 1400. I say "about" because I am in the middle of a whole new project of checking land records and tax rolls to find out more about my earliest ancestral house.

I tell you this story simply to make the point that people are good and kind and friendly, and you should always be prepared to try an unorthodox approach to your ancestor-hunting. A letter to a newspaper may bring you quite extraordinary results.

I could tell you half a dozen stories of people who have done this and have found third and fourth cousins in the old country, have been sent complete family trees and copies of photographs of great-grandparents, and have stayed with their new-found relatives when they eventually visited the country of their ancestors.

So much for these preliminary words of wisdom! With the aid of this book you are starting on an exciting journey, and no one knows where it will take you, or what treasures you will discover along the way. Searching for your roots may not bring you wealth, but the intangible rewards of discovering your own family background may make you a richer person. Good luck!

INTRODUCTION TO EUROPE

People setting out to trace their ancestors in continental Europe face major problems. If you are lacking in patience or are easily discouraged, perhaps you should forget the whole idea. If, on the other hand, you are determined to succeed and are prepared to surmount many obstacles, overcome political and personal resistance, and use charm you did not know you possessed, you have the odds in your favor and the results may exceed your expectations.

Ancestor-hunting in Europe is affected by wars and revolutions, by economic and natural disasters, by religious and political turmoil, and most of all, by four major events that changed the lives of millions of people.

These events were the following:

1. The break-up of the Austro-Hungarian Empire in 1918–19.
2. The dissolution of the Ottoman Empire between 1830 and 1913.
3. The division of Germany and the loss of its eastern territories in 1946 (and the recent re-unification of 1990).
4. The break-up of the Soviet Union, Yugoslavia, and Czechoslovakia in the early 1990s.

Nearly everyone tracing their European ancestors in eastern and central Europe will be faced with problems caused by these events and the boundary changes that followed. Indeed, only Portugal, Spain, and Switzerland of all European countries have had no boundary "rectifications" in this century. The Scandinavian countries have been relatively peaceful, but both Denmark and Finland have had their frontiers varied in recent years.

If you have only traced ancestors in this country, you will have no conception of what awaits you in Europe. Here, records are centralized, generally speaking. There, they are scattered in many different places. Here, records have been preserved in a stable society. There, you must surmount the myriad difficulties caused by wars, revolutions, rebellions, civil disturbances, partitions, plebiscites, conquest, defeat, and boundary changes. Here, we live in an open society where the job of civil servants is to serve the people. There, in many instances, civil servants serve the State and are most reluctant to disclose information of any kind.

Let me give you some examples of what is ahead of you. In France most genealogical records are kept at the local level (the town hall or the parish church), and with no central index your search will be hard unless you have a place-name with which to start. In Germany, which was divided in 1946 and re-united in 1990, some records are in state or Länder archives, others in local archives in each city, town, or village. In Hungary you will find records from Romania, because part of Hungary is now in that country. And the reverse applies; in Romania there are many Hungarian records. In Turkey you will find many records of those Balkan countries that were once a part of the Ottoman Empire.

Let us examine the four major events I have described above insofar as they affect ancestor-hunting:

1. The break-up of the Austro-Hungarian Empire in 1918–19. Eleven distinct national groups lived within the frontiers of the Austro-Hungarian Empire: Austrians, Croats, Czechs, Germans, Hungarians, Italians, Romanians, Ruthenians, Serbs, Slovaks, and Slovenes, plus a number of minor ethnic groups akin to the major races listed above.

The Austrians were found principally in the area of present-day Austria; the Croats in Croatia, Dalmatia, Slavonia, and Bosnia-Herzegovina; the Czechs in Bohemia and Moravia; the Germans in the Hungarian province of Transylvania, the Banat, and the Dobrudja; the Hungarians in Hungary proper but also in the Hungarian provinces to the east—Transylvania and the Banat; the Italians in the Bolzano area of the South Tirol and in Istria; the Romanians in Transylvania, the Banat, Bessarabia, Bukovina, Moldavia, and Wallachia; the Ruthenians in the sub-Carpatho-Ukraine; the Serbs in Yugoslavia, Bosnia-Herzegovina, and Croatia; the Slovenes in Slovenia; and the Slovaks in Slovakia.

It was never the intention of the victors in the First World War (France, Great Britain, and the United States) to destroy the Austro-Hungarian Empire. They planned to abolish the Hapsburg Dynasty, to provide some form of local autonomy for the various ethnic minorities, and to establish a Danubian Confederation. All these ideas and others were debated in the corridors of power.

However, various secret treaties had been concluded during the war between the major powers—either acting in concert or alone—and some of the smaller states such as Romania, and these restricted the freedom of the Allies to negotiate, or even to impose their professed principles of self-determination.

Simultaneously, old enmities surfaced among the national groups of the Balkans and the ethnic minorities of central and eastern Europe. The result was the complete dismemberment of the Empire; the emergence of new nations, which proceeded to treat their own minorities as they themselves had been treated by the Hapsburg regime; and the consequent displacement of millions of Europeans from their place of birth. Below you will find details of the transfers of land from the Empire:

THE BANAT: northeast part to Romania; southwest part to Yugoslavia
BOHEMIA-MORAVIA (now Czech Republic): to Czechoslovakia
BOSNIA (now independent): to Yugoslavia
BUKOVINA: to Romania
CROATIA (now independent): to Yugoslavia
DALMATIA: to Yugoslavia
GALICIA: to Poland
HERZEGOVINA: to Yugoslavia
SILESIA: to Czechoslovakia and Poland
SLAVONIA: to Yugoslavia
SLOVAKIA (now independent): to Czechoslovakia
SLOVENIA (now independent): to Yugoslavia
TIROL: southern part to Italy
TRANSYLVANIA: to Romania

This massive transfer of territory solved some problems and created others. You must be prepared for changes in place-names. Grandfather Janos may have told you he came from Nagy Becskerek, in Hungary; however, when you start your ancestor-hunting you will not be able to find it (except on old maps) because it is now named Zrenjanin, and is in Yugoslavia. Pressburg is now Bratislava, Lemberg is Lvov—the list is a lengthy one. The transfer of populations did not solve the minority problems of Europe, for millions of Hungarians were left behind in Transylvania, and millions of Germans in Czechoslovakia; thousands of Austrians found themselves in Italy; thousands of Slovenes were left in Austria; and so on.

Austria itself was reduced to the predominantly German-speaking part of the Empire, and Hungary, which had always enjoyed almost total independence within the Empire, became a small country, having lost all the rich lands to the east and southeast. In Transylvania Hungarians whose ancestors had lived there for a thousand years had to make the choice: flee to Hungary or become second-class citizens in Romania. Most chose the former course, but even today one and a half million still live in Romania.

An example of the problems existing for an ancestor-hunter as the result of boundary changes can be seen with Silesia. Teschen (Tesin in Czech, Cieszyn in Polish) is a former principality and town in the area. It has had a checkered history. It was under Bohemia from 1292 to 1625, then under

Austria until 1918. In 1920 the western part was given to Czechoslovakia and the eastern part to Poland. The town of Teschen was also divided; the eastern part became Cieszyn in Poland, and the western part Cesky Tesin in Czechoslovakia. Poland seized the latter section in 1938, Germany occupied both sections from 1939 to 1945, and then the boundaries reverted to those of 1920.

All this, genealogically, means that a Wilhelm Müller, born in Herrengasse, Teschen, in 1912 and living in the same house all his life, was Austrian at birth and Czechoslovak at his marriage in 1936, and that his children, born in 1937, 1939, and 1940, were respectively Czechoslovak, Polish, and German.

2. The dissolution of the Ottoman Empire between 1830 and 1913. Early in the nineteenth century all the territory known as the Balkans was part of the Ottoman Empire—a vast conglomerate of lands and peoples in the continents of Europe, Asia, and Africa. In Europe alone it ruled nine million people, most of whom were Christians. The area was divided into five provinces: Bosnia, Crete, Djezair (including part of Greece and the Greek islands), Rumelia, and Silistria. In addition, some areas were more loosely attached to the Empire and retained much self-government—the two provinces of Romania, Wallachia and Moldavia, for example.

Strangely enough, in view of the militancy of Islam over the centuries, the Christian subjects of the Empire were not persecuted in any obvious way. Although they could not aspire to any major part in government, they could retain their own religious beliefs (mainly Eastern Orthodox, but there were also Catholic and Jewish areas). However, the obvious power and prestige of the Muslim religion had some effect on the population, and certain areas (Albania, Crete, Bosnia, and Herzegovina) became predominantly Muslim, the converts then enjoying the privilege of first-class citizenship.

The Eastern Orthodox Church was divided along national lines. The Greeks were under the suzerainty of the Patriarch at Constantinople (now Istanbul), while the Serbs looked to their Patriarch at Péc, and the Bulgars to an archbishop at Ohrid. One disadvantage, which all non-Muslim religions suffered, was the law that no new churches could be built, and all male Christians had to pay a special head tax in lieu of military service, which was not permitted anyway for non-Muslims! The Greek Orthodox Church was the most cooperative with the Ottoman authorities, and as a result, in 1766 and 1767 the Serbian Patriarchate and the Bulgarian Archbishopric were abolished. By the early 1800s the Patriarch at Constantinople ruled over eight million Christians.

The beginning of the nineteenth century brought with it the first major rebellions against the Empire, and during the next eighty years Serbia,

Greece, Montenegro (which later joined Yugoslavia), and Romania became independent nations, and Bulgaria was granted autonomy. The latter declared full independence in 1908.

At the same time the Austro-Hungarian Empire annexed the Ottoman provinces of Bosnia and Herzegovina. In 1912 Albania proclaimed its independence. At this point the old Ottoman Empire ceased to exist and its territories in Europe were now confined to the area around Constantinople. Its remaining territories in the Middle East and Africa were lost after the First World War.

The dates of independence of the various countries mentioned above were: Albania (1912), Bulgaria (1908), Greece (1830), and Montenegro, Romania, and Serbia (1878).

In addition, under the terms of the Treaty of San Stefano (3 March 1878) Ottoman territory was ceded to Romania. In Berlin in July 1881 a conference of the Great Powers returned Macedonia and Thrace to the Ottoman Empire (previously given to Greece in 1878). Greece was consoled by the award of Thessaly and part of Epirus; Russia received Bessarabia; the Austro-Hungarian Empire was given the right to administer Bosnia, Herzegovina, and the Sanjak of Novi Pazar. Few of these awards were to be permanent and all of them provided fertile ground for the seeds of future wars.

If you work back in your research to the days of the Ottoman Empire, you may be able to obtain some information from Turkey. (The countries most affected are Albania, Bosnia-Herzegovina, Bulgaria, Greece, Montenegro, Romania, and Yugoslavia.) The National Archives of Turkey (Topkapi Palace, Istanbul) does not have records of births, marriages, and deaths, taxes, censuses, or wills. They will not provide information about their holdings but suggest you write directly to the Prime Minister's Archives (Baş-Bakanlik Arşivi Müdürlügo, Cağaloğlu, Istanbul).

3. The division of Germany and the loss of its eastern territories in 1946 (and the recent re-unification of 1990). In 1945 the Allies of the First World War—this time with the addition of the USSR—were faced with a similar problem to that of 1919: what should be done with a defeated Empire? Here again the problem was solved by events. It was decided that Germany should remain intact but should be occupied by the four Allies, with a small token occupation in the Rhineland by Belgium. Berlin itself was to be jointly administered, with each power occupying a sector of the city.

The Potsdam Agreement of 2 August 1945 contained a number of clauses that decisively influenced Germany's future. It was agreed that the final German-Polish border should be settled with a peace treaty, but until then the "former" German territories east of the Oder and Neisse rivers should be under Polish administration. It was also agreed that the USSR should get

Königsberg, the north of East Prussia, and Memel. These two decisions affected a quarter of Germany.

In addition, agreement was reached on the return of the Sudetenland to Czechoslovakia. Behind the official wording of the agreement were hidden the roots of a human suffering greater than that of the First World War, and the start of a tortuous chain of events that led to the partition of Germany.

The eastern territories lost to Poland and the USSR consisted of East Prussia, Silesia, and parts of Brandenburg and Pomerania. It was recognized that there should be a "transfer" of Germans from Czechoslovakia, Hungary, and Poland. With this provision one of the great movements of population in history started. Before the Potsdam Agreement four million Germans had fled from the eastern territories as the Russians advanced. Now another five million still living in the Polish-occupied areas were expelled by force, as were three million Sudeten Germans now living in Czechoslovakia. Altogether more than thirteen million Germans were driven from the land on which they had lived for centuries, and probably another million died during the great exodus.

In 1948 that part of Germany occupied by the Western Powers became the Federal Republic of Germany (Bundesrepublik Deutschland, or B.R.D.). This followed the de facto administration set up in the area occupied by the USSR. In 1949 the so-called Russian Zone became the German Democratic Republic (Deutsche Demokratische Republik, or D.D.R.). In 1950 the D.D.R. recognized the Oder-Neisse Line as the frontier with Poland, and in 1970 the Federal Republic followed suit. Germany's boundaries and partition were an accomplished fact, but again suffering followed. Nearly three and a half million people left the D.D.R. for the west between 1948 and 1961.

In 1990 the two parts of Germany were re-united with Berlin as the capital.

4. The break-up of the Soviet Union, Yugoslavia, and Czechoslovakia in the early 1990s. The events in Europe in the 1990s have created additional problems for those searching for records of their ancestors. With the Soviet Union, Yugoslavia, and Czechoslovakia broken up into a number of independent countries, it's not always easy to ascertain the location of genealogical records or to gain access to them.

So, the once mighty empires are no more: the Austro-Hungarian Empire of the Hapsburgs, the Ottoman Empire of the Sublime Porte, and the Third Reich of Germany. The Soviet Union and Czechoslovakia have been broken up, and Yugoslavia has been torn apart in a particularly bloody civil war.

All the problems of European research that I have mentioned, and many more that you will discover for yourself, will not make your search easy, but when you do succeed the results may be beyond your wildest dreams.

You may discover your ancestors took a leading part in freeing a country from brutal oppression; you may find a grim castle on a mountain in Ruthenia as your ancestral home; you may find a fjord in Norway from which your Viking forebears set out to explore the unknown world beyond the sea; you may tread the black soil of Ukraine from which your ancestors fled czarist oppression; you may follow the footsteps of your Huguenot and Mennonite ancestors as they fled religious persecution; you may find ancestral tombstones beside the painted churches of Moldavia; you may sail by caique to Naxos, in the Aegean Sea, and find the whitewashed cottage of your Greek great-grandfather; you will, perhaps, go back to that great estate in Transylvania where your princely ancestors held court; or to that wooden hut in Poland where your family starved and suffered through successive invasions.

You may discover a 250-year-old family portrait (my wife did); you may discover the ruins of the fifteenth-century "great house" of your ancestors (I did); you may find princes and poets and peasants, soldiers and saints and sinners; you may find diaries and letters and documents; you may find unknown cousins. All these things and more may be waiting for you back in the old country.

All this lies ahead of you on the magic and wonderful journey that takes you in search of your roots!

Computers

Since the last update of this book two important developments have taken place in the field of European genealogical research that have greatly improved opportunities for research; specifically, the emergence of the Internet as a communications and reference tool and the proliferation of CD-ROMs containing databases with information relevant to European ancestor-hunters. While neither development in any way alters the nature of the records or the research techniques described in this work, readers should be aware that the growing list of web sites devoted to European genealogy and the parallel explosion in the field of CD-ROM databases have made the task of locating your European ancestors immeasurably easier.

Whenever possible, I have included web sites and e-mail addresses for the major archives and genealogical organizations in each country. However, be prepared to discover that changes have occurred in these since this book went to press. In addition, the following web sites will be of great help to the European ancestor-hunter:

Cyndi's List (**www.CyndisList.com**)—the largest source of genealogy sites on the Internet, with approximately 83,000 links and information on all European countries.

World GenWeb (**www.worldgenweb.org**)—a project dedicated to meeting the needs of genealogists worldwide who are trying to research their ancestors online. Most European countries are represented by a web site hosted by a researcher who either lives in that country or who is familiar with that country's resources.

FamilySearch Internet Genealogy Service (**www.familysearch.org**)—a site that gives you access to the vast record collections of The Church of Jesus-Christ of Latter-day Saints.

The fantastic growth in the interest in genealogy has led to demands in each country for increased archival space and changes in addresses, phone and fax numbers, and all methods of communication—except, perhaps, in the use of carrier pigeons. This book is concerned with sources and not with methods, and not with detailed methods of access.

There are many books on the market about the application of computers to genealogical research. In addition, public libraries and family history societies now hold regular classes on the use of computers. As the result of the Internet you may make contact with other ancestor-hunters by e-mail or even in person. BEWARE: You may be in dangerous territory. The intimate and personal family information you may reveal in confidence to strangers may not be treated as such. All kinds of such information are scattered all over the Net.

The other danger is that the stranger you have "met" on the Net may feed you totally erroneous family information with no basis in fact—just the products of a wild imagination or of wishful-thinking. If you accept such information as "gospel" you may have been sent off on a false lead. There is no reliable substitute for careful personal research.

Telephone Numbers

The international telephone and fax numbers that appear in this book have been presented in such a way that readers may call from the United States. Ancestor-hunters calling from other countries will need to apply their own International Access Codes to these phone numbers in lieu of the "011."

THE LDS CHURCH RECORDS

The initials LDS stand for The Church of Jesus Christ of Latter-day Saints—whose members are sometimes referred to as "the Mormons," a name that is not as widely used as it once was. The LDS Family History Library was founded in 1894 to collect genealogical records and to help Church members trace their ancestors. Located in Salt Lake City (35 North West Temple Street, Salt Lake City, UT 84150; for information call 801-240-2331, fax 801-240-5551, or e-mail fhl@ldschurch.org), it has the greatest collection of genealogical records in the world and is open to the general public without charge. The library consists of 142,000 square feet of space on five floors. When it was designed and built in 1985, allowance was made for an additional three floors to be added at some date in the distant future. With more than three thousand people visiting the library each day, and the steady increase in records, there is no doubt that the extra space will be needed long before the original estimated date.

No one starting off to trace their ancestors should do so without checking the library's records for the country or area in which they are interested. There is no need to go to Salt Lake City to do this because there are more than 3,400 branch Family History Centers in sixty-four different countries around the world. You can find the one nearest to you by consulting your local public library or the LDS web site (**www.familysearch.org/Browse/ BrowseLibrary.asp**), or by writing to Salt Lake City at the above address for the information.

There are no strings attached to the use of the library and its wonderful collection of records by those who are not LDS Church members. No one will try to convert you, and to quote the TV commercial "no salesman will call."

The interest of the church members in genealogy is not an idle one, or to be regarded as an interesting hobby as it is by many of us. It is a deep religious need based on their theological belief that family relationships are intended to be eternal, and not limited to a short period of mortality. They believe that husband and wife and their children remain together throughout eternity as a family unit, with all their ancestors and descendants. Members trace their ancestors in order to perform "sealing" ceremonies in temples erected for this purpose. Before the families can be "sealed" together, all the ancestors must be traced so far as is possible.

The library does not have sufficient staff to do detailed research for individuals, but it will answer one or two specific questions. If more detailed information is needed, you will be mailed a list of accredited researchers. When asking for this list, be sure you specify the country in which you are interested, and the state or province if known, since the researchers are specialists in particular regions. You will then make your own financial arrangements with the researcher you have selected. Remember, you are paying for the *research* and not for the result!

Be specific—give all the information you have, distinguish between fact and belief, and give details of the research you have already done. If you are buying a computer printout of the church registers of Graz in Austria, for example, state if you want Catholic or Lutheran registers; if you want army records from Poland specify the rank of the soldier and the name of the regiment, if you know it.

The library is engaged in the most comprehensive genealogical research program ever known. Microfilming and computerization are at the heart of the operation, and every day genealogical records are being copied, filmed, and preserved on compact discs (CDs) and in computers. Documents such as church registers, censuses, civil registration, land records, army and navy lists, deeds, wills, marriage bonds, cemetery records, magazines, and newspapers are all being copied.

The statistics associated with the library are staggering in their immensity. The library contains over 2.2 million rolls of microfilm—equivalent to more than 6 million, 300-page bound volumes. These records contain nearly 2 billion names. If these figures amaze you, there is more to come! The collection grows by 5,000 rolls of film and 1,000 books a month. Ancestral File™ records over 35 million names, while the International Genealogical Index™(IGI) database contains over 600 million names and millions more are added each year (see below for more information about Ancestral File and the IGI). Visitors to the library in Salt Lake City use over 500 microfilm and microfiche viewers daily, and 100,000 rolls of microfilm are being circulated to local Family History Centers every month!

The LDS Church has updated and expanded its genealogical record systems to keep up with new developments in the computer field. Many records are now stored on compact discs, as well as the old standbys of microfilm and microfiche, and many are available online at **www.familysearch.org**.

Now let me summarize for you the most recent developments in LDS Church record-keeping and accessibility.

FAMILYSEARCH®

This is the umbrella name for all of the various records and research aids developed by the LDS Church to help its members in their search for their ancestors and is generously made available to those of us of other religions, or of no religion at all.

The various components of FamilySearch can be consulted in the Family History Library in Salt Lake City, in the local Family History Centers in cities around the world, on the Internet, and on compact discs available for purchase through the Church. FamilySearch includes the following separate segments:

- The FamilySearch™ Internet Genealogy Service
- The International Genealogical Index™ (IGI)
- Personal Ancestral File® (PAF)
- Ancestral File™
- The Social Security Death Index—U.S. only
- The Military Index—U.S. only
- The Family History Library Catalog™ and Publications List
- The Periodical Source Index (PERSI)
- The Parish and Vital Records List (PVRL)
- TempleReady
- The Pedigree Resource File™
- Vital Records Indexes
- The Family History SourceGuide

The FamilySearch Internet Genealogy Service

The largest and most exciting component of FamilySearch is the Internet Genealogy Service at **www.familysearch.org**. This site allows you to search the following sources for family history information: Ancestral File; the International Genealogical Index; the Pedigree Resource File; the Family History Library Catalog; the Family History SourceGuide; and a guide to useful web sites. In addition, you can browse a category list to find information about a specific family history topic or person; collaborate with others by sharing your family history information; submit GEDCOM files of ancestral information to the Church for preservation; recommend a web site to be included in the FamilySearch Internet Genealogy Service; purchase items produced by the Church; and download the newest edition of Personal Ancestral File. The web site has been phenomenally successful, averaging roughly 8.5 million hits a day. New information is always being included—at the end of 2000, 240 million new names were added to the FamilySearch Internet genealogy database, culled primarily from Western Europe, Scandinavia, and Mexico.

The International Genealogical Index (IGI)

The IGI remains an integral part of the FamilySearch network, because it is vital to your success in tracing your ancestors. Its base is also widely misunderstood by those just starting their search. It consists of information copied from church registers, censuses, wills, and other sources. So far as church registers are concerned it only contains information from those that have been copied. There are a number of church authorities in various countries that do not allow the LDS Church any access to their registers, and so the IGI is not 100 percent complete and probably never will be. For example, the United Church of Canada (which was formed from a merger of Methodists, Congregationalists, and some Presbyterians) is opposed to any copying of its registers in the church archives, and there are other ecclesiastical bodies or individual churches in other countries that share its views. Its attitude is simple to understand. It does not believe its members should be baptized or sealed into another religion after they are dead.

Often, on my lecture tours around the world, people will come up to me and express their worry that they cannot find an event listed in the IGI that they know occurred. "I can't find great-grandfather's baptism in the church in Blanktown though I know it took place." I explain to them that the reason is because the church registers there have not been copied, and that they must get their information from the original church or, in many cases, the local record office, archives, or church headquarters. They are astonished because no one told them the IGI is based on available sources only.

There can be another problem with the IGI. Records are only as good as the accuracy of the copier. Let me tell you a personal story to illustrate what I mean.

A good many years ago I was tracing my CALEY ancestors. I know they came from a particular place in the north of the county of Lancashire, in northern England, called Cockerham. My wife and I visited the parish church (at that time it still held the original registers) and took careful note of all the Caley entries. The earliest entry was the marriage of Henry Caley and Ellen Webster in 1798. Some years later I bought a printout of the Caley entries for Lancashire in the IGI. I was still searching for the birthplace of Henry Caley. As I read through the list I was astonished to find no mention of his marriage, although the Cockerham registers had been copied and the information included in the IGI. I did find, however, a mention of the marriage of a *Thomas* Caley to Ellen Webster on the same day in the same place! I could not believe I had made a silly mistake. So I wrote to the Archivist of Lancashire who, by then, had custody of the registers of Cockerham, and asked him to check the entry. He replied, telling me that I was correct. Henry had married Ellen and there was no mention of a Thomas. I notified the LDS Church in Salt Lake City, sending them a photocopy of the letter. It took six years for the correction to be made in the IGI.

I do not tell this story in any spirit of carping criticism of the LDS Church, but it illustrates the fact that errors can be made in spite of the double checking of the IGI. I, of course, had copied the registers *before* the LDS did and so the error caused me no problem. However, if I had not, the entry of the fictitious Thomas would have brought me to a dead end. So the moral is to take full advantage of the information included in the IGI but still check the original source if you run into a situation that is creating a problem for you.

Most of the names in the IGI come from the period 1500–1875 and do not include death details. Apart from civil and church sources it also includes information submitted by church members and other individuals. You will find copies of the IGI in the Family History Library in Salt Lake City, in local Family History Centers, in many public libraries, and in the libraries of genealogical societies. The IGI is also searchable on the LDS web site. You can buy printouts of entries from particular areas, or diskettes with information from these areas or complete countries. Each event recorded in the IGI is coded as follows:

A   Adult christening
B   Birth
C   Christening
D   Death or Burial
F   Birth or Christening of first known child (in lieu of marriage date)
M   Marriage
N   Census
S   Miscellaneous
W   Will or Probate

The individual entries in the IGI include the name and surname, and in the case of births or christenings, the names of the parents. It also gives the region or locality, the date and place of the event, and the source of the information. Remember that deaths and burials are rarely recorded.

As I mentioned above you should also check the original sources wherever possible. If you are fairly certain, from information within the family, that great-grandfather Frank Baker was born in Laindon, Essex, England, on May 12, 1865, and you cannot find the event in the IGI, there may be any one of several reasons for the omission:

1. The register of the church or chapel where the baptism occurred has not been microfilmed by the LDS. Some ecclesiastical authorities do not allow this.

2. The first name you have for him may not be correct. Although he was known in the family as Frank he may have been christened Francis, or he may have been baptized as Zachariah Frank and dropped off the first name because he did not like it.

3. His baptism may not have been recorded in the church register for some reason, or the register may have been destroyed.

4. Although his parents were Protestant he may have been baptized in the church of another religion for some family reason, and the minister of that church may have refused permission to the LDS Church to copy the entries.

5. The LDS Church worker may have missed copying the entry, or entered a wrong name.

There are other obstacles looming ahead of you! If you are searching for an ancestor from the Scandinavian countries, Wales, and certain areas of the Netherlands and Germany you should remember that surnames often changed with each generation (the use of patronymics or creating a surname from the first name of the father—Erik Johansen, for example, or Erik, son of Johan). In Iceland there were also matronymics, and in Norway surnames were taken from the family farm, and changed as the individual moved from one place to another. Fortunately, most Lutheran registers included both kinds of names.

Surnames appear in the IGI as spelled in the original registers, wills, or census returns, but they can be grouped together if they *sound* the same. My own simple name of Baxter, for example, appears over the years as Backster, Bacaster, Bacchuster, and a dozen others.

In its computerized form the IGI has been greatly improved. Originally, it was indexed within a country by county or province (usually the former). If you had no idea of the area of origin within the country you had a lengthy search ahead of you. Now, there is an index for the whole country. There is also a parent index feature. You can search for the parents' names, and so obtain the names of all their children. This often leads to the discovery of hitherto unknown brothers and sisters of your direct ancestors.

Explanatory leaflets available from the LDS Church include:

IGI (on compact discs)
IGI (on microfiche)
IGI (Finding a source)
IGI (Order form for microfiche)

Some microfiche sets are available for purchase, such as Germany (1554 fiche) and Iceland (49 fiche). Contact the LDS Church for prices. An order form is available from the Church Family History Library or your local center.

Personal Ancestral File (PAF)

This section of FamilySearch contains the world's best home computer genealogical program. PAF allows you to organize your family history records. It provides a wide variety of printouts such as family group sheets, pedigree charts, descendants charts, and other lists. It also includes in its program the ability to submit your information to Ancestral File and the IGI. The latest version is Windows-based and includes multimedia capabilities and a number of enhanced features. PAF is available on 3¹/₂-inch diskette for Macintosh or PC; on compact disc; or as a free download from the FamilySearch Internet Genealogy Service (**www.familysearch.org**).

Ancestral File

This is one of the several files in the FamilySearch system and is available on compact disc and on the LDS web site. It consists of genealogies of families from around the world and links individuals with their ancestors and their descendants. It differs from the IGI, which records single events, because it can show all the family information in one entry—birth, marriage, and—in most cases—death. It contains information about many millions of individuals, and also contains the names and addresses of people who have submitted the information. The file is updated from time to time.

This is one of the first sources you should check. You can see individual records, family group records, and family trees on the screen. The LDS has three important pieces of advice for those using these records:

1. Some people may have submitted incorrect information.
2. More than one person may have submitted information about an individual you are searching for, and this may cause duplication or discrepancies.
3. Errors may have been made when data was typed into the computer.

You are encouraged to contribute information about your family but try and make sure your information is accurate and not already recorded in the system. By contributing your family information you will help other ancestor-hunters. You can also search the file free of charge, and print copies of records and charts for a small fee, or copy them on a diskette for use in a personal computer.

In addition, you can correct erroneous information you find in the file. For full details of the procedure for doing this you should consult the FamilySearch leaflet _Correcting Information in Ancestral File_, obtainable from the Family History Library in Salt Lake City or from your nearest Family History Center. Other useful leaflets from the same source are _Using Ancestral File_ and _Contributing Information to Ancestral File_.

Social Security Death Index (USA only)

This contains the names of over 63 million people in the United States whose deaths were reported to the Social Security Agency mainly between 1962 and 2000. The index gives full date of birth, month and year of death, the Social Security number, the state where the number was issued, and the last residence. There are also _some_ records as early as 1937.

The records are from the Social Security Administration and became available through the Freedom of Information Act. As the records are of dead people no rights of privacy are involved.

The index is on compact disc and is updated at intervals. The details of the last place of residence may help you find an obituary in a local newspaper, and the place to which the death benefit payment was sent may enable you to find living relatives.

The Military Index (United States Only)

This is a list of 100,000 men and women who died while serving in the Armed Forces in the Korean and Vietnam wars between 1950 and 1975. It gives birth and death dates, place of residence, place of death, rank and service number, and in the case of the Vietnam War, religion, marital status, and race. The Korean Index covers the period 1950–57 and Vietnam 1957– 75. (Deaths in the latter index may have been in Cambodia, China, Laos, North Vietnam, South Vietnam, and Thailand.)

Please note that the index only provides information about the two wars mentioned. It gives no family details or information about place of birth.

Family History Library Catalog and Publications List

The Catalog is available on compact disc and on the LDS web site, and describes the records, books, microfilms, and microfiche in the Family History Library. It does not contain any records but does describe them in detail. They come from around the world, and include church registers, birth records, marriage records, census returns, wills, family histories, etc. It is also available on microfiche and is updated at regular intervals. It lists over 3 million books, and other materials. You can search by locality or family name, and the call number will bring into your local Family History Center copies of records from around the world. More information can be obtained from the leaflet *Family History Library Catalog on Compact Disc*, obtainable from Salt Lake City or your nearest Family History Center.

The Publications List (also obtainable as above) lists all the LDS Church publications designed to help the ancestor-hunter. These are far too numerous to list but are fully described in the leaflet *Family History Publications List*.

Periodical Source Index (PERSI)

This is a subject index to thousands of articles in genealogical periodicals and journals. It is available on microfiche, compact disc, and in printed form. PERSI can help you find articles very quickly and save you a great deal of time in searching through periodicals for a particular subject. It indexes articles from more than 5,000 periodicals and provides access to more than a million articles. It includes all English language genealogical periodicals, plus those written in French about French-Canadian roots. It indexes articles by locality and family surname, as well as generalized subjects. It does not index every name mentioned in the articles or include the actual articles; it also doesn't index queries, family trees, or book reviews. PERSI can be consulted at Family History Centers, and a compact disc version is now available from Ancestry.

PERSI contains two separate indexes that are updated annually. The 1847–1985 Index (FHL fiche 6016863) indexes articles in journals in that period, and it is not complete. The Annuals Index (FHL fiche 6016864) covers virtually all genealogical journals from 1986 onwards.

Here again, you can obtain full details of accessibility from the leaflet *Periodical Source Index on Microfiche.*

Parish and Vital Records List (PVRL)

This list, which is on microfiche, shows which records have been extracted and indexed and listed in the IGI for each geographical area and time period. It also shows which records are being indexed at present. This is being done by church volunteers and is updated several times a year.

The list can help you to decide which records to search. If you do not find mention of a particular record it means it has not been extracted yet. The records are listed alphabetically by country, and the United States, Canada, and Germany are subdivided into states or provinces. You can use a microfiche printer in the Family History Library in Salt Lake City or in a Family History Center to copy a page. If your nearest center does not have a printer you can order a copy from the library for a small fee. More information can be found in the Resource Guide leaflet *Parish and Vital Records List.*

TempleReady

This system is primarily of interest to LDS Church members, enabling them to put the names of their ancestors on a computer diskette that can be taken to a temple to provide temple ordinance for ancestors. For more information you should obtain an explanatory leaflet entitled *Introduction to TempleReady.*

The Pedigree Resource File

This is a new lineage-linked database on compact disc. It contains family history records that individuals have submitted through the FamilySearch Internet Genealogy Service. The family information is organized in family groups and pedigrees and may include notes and sources. New names are constantly being added to this file. You can search the index to this database on the FamilySearch Internet Genealogy Service (**www.familysearch.org**).

Vital Records Indexes

These are part of a series entitled Family History Resource Files, which is available on compact disc. The Vital Records Index of North America contains more than 4.6 million christenings, births, and marriages in the United States and Canada for the years 1631 to 1888. The Vital Records Index of the British Isles contains birth, christening, and marriage records from England, Wales, Scotland, and Ireland. Approximately 5 million names were transcribed from original parish registers, civil registration records, and other collections of records from the British Isles. Some of these records date back to 1538, while others are as recent as 1888. Recently, the LDS Church released the Vital Records Index for Western Europe, which covers the Alpine, BeNeLux, French, German, Italian, and Spanish regions.

Family History SourceGuide

SourceGuide is designed to help individuals find the original records of their ancestors. Available on compact disc and on the LDS web site, the SourceGuide includes lists of sources to find records of birth, marriage, occupation, immigration patterns, and military service; a glossary of terms defining unfamiliar research and genealogical terms; searchable outlines describing records and research strategies for finding ancestors in various locations throughout the world; letter-writing guides, blank forms, and census worksheets; and a Catalog Helper to identify the best subjects to search in the Family History Library Catalog.

All the above information in this chapter will have made it clear to you how far the LDS Church has gone toward simplifying our search for our ancestors. Just pause for a moment and think what our hunt for our family past would be like if the LDS Church did not exist! I am old enough to remember when our searching took place in damp and drafty old churches, crouched in a tiny vestry, or kneeling on a stone floor, or standing up in an unlit corner of a tower. There were also occasions when I sat with the minister in front of a roaring fire drinking his whiskey but they were few and far between!

We have many reasons to thank the LDS Church and its members for opening so many doors for us!

JEWISH RECORDS

The Internet has made the task of searching for your Jewish ancestors immeasurably easier. The web site *JewishGen: The Home of Jewish Genealogy* (**www.jewishgen.org**) is a comprehensive guide to information sources, databases, and other researchers of Jewish genealogy worldwide. Some of its most popular features are the JewishGen Discussion Group; the *JewishGen Family Finder*, a database of over 200,000 surnames and towns; InfoFiles, a directory of information resources organized by both topic and country; JewishGen Databases, offering all kinds of genealogical information; interactive databases such as *ShtetLinks*, where users can share their knowledge; and the *Family Tree of the Jewish People*, which contains data on over one million people. JewishGen should be your first stop for the most accurate and up-to-date information on Jewish genealogy.

In most European countries over the years, people of the Jewish faith were required to register their vital events with a priest or minister of the State church, whether it was Catholic or Lutheran. Of course, the records were also maintained by the rabbi in the synagogue of the community. Because many Jewish records have been destroyed, it is always wise to check church registers on the appropriate date, at least up to the middle of the last century.

Until recently many people of Jewish descent were convinced of the absolute impossibility of tracing their ancestors. Most certainly there are major problems because of the Diaspora and persecutions, pogroms, and death camps. However, many "lost" records have been rediscovered, a concerted effort is being made to bring all the records together, and the possibility of a successful ancestor-hunt is improving. Remember, too, that you will find your Jewish ancestors recorded in many of the general genealogical records of European countries.

The Jews in Europe were divided into two main groups: the Sephardim (an old Hebrew word meaning Spaniards), who lived in Spain and Portugal;

and the Ashkenazim (Germans), who lived in the Rhineland, central and eastern Europe, and Russia. The differences between the two are minor, consisting mainly of a variation in Hebrew pronunciation and some differences in religious practice.

The first Jews to emigrate from Europe went from Portugal to England in the sixteenth and seventeenth centuries, though there had been much individual migration over the English Channel from the time of the Norman Conquest. There was further emigration to the United Kingdom in the eighteenth century from Poland, Germany, France, the Netherlands, and eastern and central Europe. The main migration to North America started in the early 1800s, although the first Jewish immigrants actually arrived as early as 1654.

ISRAEL

In Israel itself a tremendous amount of information has been collected about European Jews and Jewish communities on that continent. These collections are not in any one place, and if you are planning a visit to Israel be sure you know just where to look for the information you need.

The Central Archives for the History of the Jewish People
Hebrew University Campus, Sprinzak Bldg., P.O. Box 1149,
  Jerusalem 91010
Phone and Fax: 011-972-2-5635716
E-mail: archives@vms.huji.ac.il
Web site: www.sites.huji.ac.il/archives

These archives, founded in 1938, have the largest collection of Jewish documents and records in the world. Many of the records are of Jewish communities in Europe, or of microfilmed documents in national and local archives there. The Central Archives also maintain an up-to-date record of all items of Jewish interest in archives in other countries.

For example, the archives in Jerusalem include nearly all registrations of births, marriages, and deaths in Jewish communities in Germany, dating back to about 1800 (with some going back much further) and continuing up to 1876, when state civil registration was started. There is also the Diamant collection. This is the result of the lifelong labors of an Austrian genealogist and contains the genealogies of some three hundred families from Austria, Czechoslovakia, Germany, Hungary, and Poland. However, some of the information is fragmentary, so do not expect to find a complete family tree dating back some three hundred years.

The Central Archives are understaffed, and if you visit the building you must not look for anything that resembles our own public archives. If you are writing for information, please don't expect the impossible. They cannot produce a name out of a hat. You must be able to supply them with specific dates and places, and be prepared to wait. The archives are lacking in funds because Israel is a poor country with its own list of priorities on which to spend its money, and these do not include the Central Archives. When you write, be sure to cover the return airmail postage (include at least three International Reply Coupons) and offer to pay whatever fee is required.

Finally, the most complete records are from Austria, France, Germany, and Italy, whereas those from eastern Europe, such as Poland and Russia, are fragmentary. This is because the western countries have maintained good records and their governments are cooperative, while in eastern Europe this has not always been so.

The Jewish National and University Library
Givat Ram Campus, Hebrew University, Jerusalem 91341
Phone: 011-972-2-6586228
Web site: www.sites.huji.ac.il/jnul

This is located quite near the Central Archives but is a separate organization. The Jewish National and University Library serves a threefold purpose: it is the National Library of the State of Israel; the National Library of the Jewish People; and the Central Library of the Hebrew University. It has a large collection of birth and death registers (pinchassim) from Austria, France, Germany, Greece, Hungary, Italy, Poland, Romania, Turkey, and the former USSR (including the Baltic countries of Estonia, Latvia, and Lithuania). Here again the records from eastern Europe are very limited but they can certainly tell you if the records of a specific Jewish community are in their collection.

The Douglas E. Goldman Jewish Genealogy Center
P.O. Box 39359, Tel Aviv 61392
Phone: 011-972-3-6462020. Fax: 011-972-3-6462134
E-mail: bhgnlgy@post.tau.ac.il
Web site: www.bh.org.il/Genealogy/index.htm

Located on the Tel Aviv University Campus, the Center has family trees from around the world, and registers them in their computerized database to preserve the information for future generations and to help people find links with other families. Two other organizations—The International Association of Jewish Genealogical Societies and JewishGen—have agreed to combine their family tree information with the more than 1,200,000 names already entered in the Douglas E. Goldman's database, bringing the total of names available to more than two million. The database is accessible at the museum and search orders can be placed through the web site.

The Center also has a small but important reference library with over 500 family books and genealogy reference books, and a collection of 1,200 microfilms of vital records from Jewish communities in Poland.

Ghetto Fighters' House
Western Galilee M.P., 25220
Phone: 011-972-4-9958029
E-mail: yshavit@gfh.org.il
Web site: www.gfh.org.il

The Ghetto Fighters' House was founded in April 1949 by Holocaust survivors, ghetto fighters, and partisans, who settled in the Western Galilee. Initially conceived as a documentation center, it now functions as a museum, a research institute, and a center for education. The Ghetto Fighters' House contains thirteen major archives, collections, and bequests: The General Archives; The Dutch Archives; The Pioneering Youth Movements Archive; The Art Collection (art created in the Holocaust and after the war); The Film Archives; The General Archives of Photographs; The "Hehalutz" Archives of Photographs; The "Jewish Children of Unknown Identity" Department; The Russian Archives; The Korczak Archives; The Jewish Fighters Database; the Collection of Exhibits; and The Ghetto Fighters' House Archives.

Yad Vashem, Har Hazikaron
P.O. Box 3477, 91034 Jerusalem
Phone: 011-972-2-6443400. Fax: 011-972-2-6443443
E-mail: info@yad-vashem.org.il
Web site: www.yadvashem.org.il

If you're on a visit to Israel, this museum will be high on your list because it exists as a perpetual reminder of the Holocaust. It is on the schedule of every organized tour. However, if you have the time, you should go back on your own, and this time avoid the main museum and go to the building on the right, the archives building. This is the largest and most comprehensive repository of books and manuscripts dealing with the period from 1933 to 1946. It includes 55 million pages of documents, more than 80,000 titles in many languages, thousands of periodicals, nearly 100,000 still photographs, and thousands of videotaped testimonies of survivors of the Holocaust. There are a great many accounts of Jewish communities destroyed by the Nazis, particularly in Eastern Europe. If you know the exact community from which your ancestors came, your visit may be well worthwhile. You can also, of course, check their information by correspondence. Your main source will be the very large collection of memory (yizkor) books from eastern European communities in some six hundred towns. These books came into existence after the Second World War when survivors of a community had a reunion and produced a yizkor book, which listed details of the area and the names of victims and survivors.

There are copies of most of these books in the YIVO Institute for Jewish Research (15 West 16th Street, New York, NY 10011; Phone: 212-246-6080; Fax: 212-292-1892; E-mail: yivomail@yivo.cjg.org; Web site: www.yivoinstitute.org); the Hebraic Section of the Library of Congress; the New York Public Library; the Hebrew Union Colleges in Cincinnati and Los Angeles; and the Robarts Library, Toronto, Canada. Many of them can be obtained through inter-library loan. They can also be bought from Eichler's Books (1401 Coney Island Avenue, Brooklyn, NY) or online at **www.eichlers.com**.

Two recent developments at Yad Vashem are a computerized list of 204,000 residents of the Łódź ghetto (the second largest in Europe) and the list of half a million Hungarian victims of the Holocaust.

A recent addition to the museum is the Hall of Names. This tribute to the victims concentrated not on anonymous numbers but on the individual human beings. It contains millions of names and personal details about the martyrs, as recorded on pages of testimony given by family members and friends.

One problem you will encounter when researching in Israel is that of a change of name. Kanofsky became Kane, Moses became Morris, Martinez became Martin, and so on. Another complication is the literal translation of a name, so that Zevi, in Hebrew, became Hart in English and Hirsch in German. It would be wise to talk to older members of your family, and to examine all family papers, to see if you are going to be affected by a name change.

EUROPE

There are, of course, sources of information in the different countries in Europe and we should also talk about these. First and foremost, if your immigrant ancestor sailed from Europe, particularly from Germany or central or eastern Europe, then you should check the Hamburg Passenger Lists. You will find full information about them in the chapter on Germany.

Austria

The Jewish records are in a variety of places, such as provincial and municipal archives, and magistrate's courts. Although you may be only interested in Austria as it now exists, you should bear in mind that Austria was joined with Hungary (The Austro-Hungarian Empire) until 1919 (see page 26).

Also remember that the Austrian province of Burgenland was part of Hungary until 1919. However, in this section we are, of course, mainly concerned with present-day Austria and nowhere else.

Undoubtedly the main course of information to start you off is the active and growing organization known as Israelitische Kultusgemeinde (Seitenstettengasse 4, 1010 Vienna; Phone: 011-431-531-040; E-mail: h.weiss@ikg-wien.at; Web site: http://www.ikg-wien.at). Do your best to discover your main sources by your own efforts and not overload the organization with unnecessary queries. Remember it only has the records of Vienna, and not those of Austria as a whole. The organization's Department of Records has supplied me with a list of addresses to which you can write for information before writing to the Department:

If you want to know who lived in Vienna in this century (espec. before 1954): Town Hall (Rathaus), department M.A. 8, Mr. Koch.

If you want to know if a family really was from Vienna (beginning with 1870): Town Hall (Rathaus), department M.A. 61, Mr. Kunkl or Mr. Huemer.

If you are looking for a grave (beginning with 1880): Cemetery Zentralfriedhof, Simmeringer Haupstrasse 224, 1110 Vienna, Mr. Kohut (Phone: 011-431-767-62-52)

If you are interested in deportations (only from Vienna directly): Dokumentationsarchiv, Altes Rathaus, Wipplingerstrasse 8.

If you want to have a birth/death/marriage certificate (and you have exact dates): Phone: Vienna 011-431-531-04-29. Fax: 011-431-533-15-77 (Jewish Community).

Bulgaria

It has not been possible to obtain any definite information about Jewish records in this country. There are reports that some documents are in the National Archives (Centralen Darzaven Arhiv Na Narodna, ul. Slavjanka, Sofia), so you might try writing there for information.

The Czech Republic and Slovakia

There is Jewish genealogical material in the Czech National Archives that dates from the early 1600s. It will be necessary for you to follow the procedure set out in the chapter on the Czech Republic. Remember that this new country consists of the former areas of Bohemia and Moravia. The main archive is located in Prague (Archivní Správa, Milady Horákové 133, 16621 Prague).

There are also some Jewish records in Obvodní Narodní Výbor, Vodičkova 18, Prague. For more information about Jews in this country, please read the chapter on the Czech Republic.

Because Slovakia was joined to the Czech Republic until 1993, some Slovakian records may still be in Prague. The main archive for Slovakia is located in Bratislava (Odbor archívnictva a spisovej služby, Križkova 7, 81104 Bratislava).

For more information about this country, read the chapter on Slovakia.

Estonia

Jewish records from 1918–1946 are located in the National Archives (Maneeži 4, 15019 Tallinn). More information can be obtained from the Jewish Cultural Society (P.O. Box 2385, Tallinn).

France

The Jewish people have been in France since the first or second centuries. There is quite a lot of genealogical material about Jews scattered around various archives in France. Most of it has been microfilmed by the Central Archives in Jerusalem. If your ancestors came from a specific area of France, I suggest you should first find out from them whether the nearest archives have Jewish material. If so, then you can deal directly with that particular French archive. In any case, remember that Jews were subject to the normal civil laws. Civil registration, for example, started in 1792 and affected all citizens of France. Read the chapter on France to find out what general records there are of use to you. Be sure, too, that you check the passenger lists for emigrants leaving the port of Le Havre between 1750 and 1898. You will find information about these valuable lists in the same chapter.

Germany

In this area, Jews were affected by the same civil laws as were all citizens of the various German states, both up to the unification of the country in 1871 and since then. Civil registration started in 1875 for the country as a whole but had existed long before that year in many of the individual states. You will find full details in the chapter on Germany.

The Weissensee Cemetery in Berlin is the largest Jewish cemetery in Europe. In the offices, there are over 115,000 index cards that give full details of each person buried there for over a century. You can obtain more details from Zentralarchiv zur Eforschung der Geschichte der Juden in Deutschland (Bienenstrasse 5, 69117 Heidelberg; Phone: 011-49-6221-164141; Fax: 011-49-6221-181049; Web site: www.uni-heidelberg.de/institute/sonst/aj/). Be sure you send three International Reply Coupons with your letter.

If your Jewish ancestors came from Germany, be sure to read the German chapter, which gives full details of genealogical records in this country, and, of course, remember the Hamburg Passenger Lists. If your ancestor emigrated during the nineteenth century, he or she almost certainly left from either Hamburg or Bremen. The lists for the latter port were destroyed by the authorities or, later, by British bombing, but those of Hamburg survive. They usually list not only the names of the passengers but also their place of origin.

If you are dealing directly with the various German archives you will find the staffs very helpful. You should also check with local libraries (Bibliotheken) because very many of the larger ones have Jewish collections referring to that particular area. These include quite detailed histories of Jewish communities. For example, the Hamburg Staatsarchiv has a register of Jews in the city from 1769.

Other sources of possible information are as follows:

Jüdische Presse
Rüngdorfer Strasse 6
53173 Bonn
Phone: 011-49-2-28361499

Jüdisches, Kulturmuseum
Halderstrasse 8
86150 Augsburg
Phone: 011-49-8-21513658

Jüdisches, Dokumentationszentrum
Valentin-Becker-Strasse 11
97072 Würzburg
Phone: 011-49-9-3118275

Jüdisches, Museum Westfalen
Julius-Ambrunn-Strasse 1
46282 Dorsten
Phone: 011-49-2-36245279

Hungary

If your ancestors came from this country, don't forget that present-day Hungary is a fraction of its original size. Parts of the old Hungary are now in Croatia, the Czech Republic, Romania, Slovenia, and Slovakia. However, if your forebears did come from a place within the present boundaries you may be very lucky. The Hungarian National Archives, located at Magyar Országos Levéltár, Bécsi kapu tér 2-4, 1014 Budapest (Mailing address: Postafiok 3, 1250 Budapest; Phone: 011-36-1-356-5811; Fax: 011-36-1-212-1619; E-mail: mail@natarch.hu; Web site: www.natarch.hu), have on microfilm the registers of over three hundred Jewish communities. Most of these date from the mid-1800s but some go back much further—for example, Apostag (1825), Budapest-Nagytétény (1760), Csurgó (1776), Kaposvár (1771), Marcali (1774), Székesfehérvár (1776), and Zsámbék (1769). The final date in all the registers is 1895, when civil registration commenced. The microfilms are also in the various county archives (Megyei Levéltárak) serving each particular area. All this information is listed in the Hungarian chapter. Yad Vashem (see above) has a computerized list of half a million Hungarian victims of the Holocaust.

Italy

Jews have taken an active part in the life of Italy since 100 A.D. and there are extensive collections of Jewish records and documents in many of the major archives and libraries. Unfortunately, there is no one collective list of all this material. Until just over a century ago Italy consisted of a great number of small principalities and states, and nearly all historic documents are still in the various individual archives. The Italians have been meticulous about keeping every possible record, but no one seems to know where they all are. However, the Central Archives in Israel have been active in microfilming many of the Italian Jewish records and if you write, giving the place of origin of your ancestors, they will give you the name and address of the local archive or library if one exists.

Netherlands

All the various records in the Netherlands chapter (except church records) will be of interest to you. In fact, you may even need to check these records as well because in certain places at certain times it was necessary to register the vital events of a Jewish family with the local priest or minister! Jewish people have been in the Netherlands (which then included Belgium) since the Middle Ages. Amsterdam was a main center of Sephardic Jews in Europe, and there are very large Jewish collections in the university library there. The Israel Central Archives also have a very fine collection of Netherlands Jewish records, including marriage contracts and deeds from 1787 (with a number of gaps). Also try contacting the Jewish Family Archive (Nederlands Joods Familienarchief, Postbus 51140, 1007 EC Amsterdam; Phone: 011-31-20-675-0596; E-mail: GAASECR@xs4ALL.nl).

Poland

This country in its days of grandeur included all the main areas of Jewish settlement in Europe: Ukraine, Galicia, Lithuania, and White Russia (present-day Belarus). So far as modern Poland is concerned, the various regional archives have some Jewish material, and this also has been microfilmed for the Central Archives in Jerusalem. It is mainly from Białystok, Kielce, Kraków, Łodź, Lublin, Poznań, and Warsaw. There is a Jewish Historical Institute in Warsaw (Zydowski Instytut Historiczny, ul. Tlomackie 3/5, Warsaw; Phone: 011-48-22-827-9221). There are two museums in Poland with index cards on concentration camp victims. The Państwowe Muzeum (Droga Meczennikow Majkenska 67, 20325 Lublin) has about 100,000 cards of victims of the Majdanek concentration camp. As you can imagine, there has been a great deal of destruction of Jewish records in Poland, and what could have been a tremendous source of information on eastern European Jewry is, in fact, a genealogical desert.

Romania

I have no information about Jewish records in this country. Under Communism, there appeared to be a policy of total lack of cooperation with genealogical researchers. The Hungarian province of Transylvania was ceded to

Romania in 1919 and it is possible that the Hungarian National Archives may have some Jewish records. You can certainly try a letter to the Romanian National Archives in Bucharest (Archivelor Statului, Bulevardul M. Kogălniceanu 29, 706021 Bucharest), but don't hold your breath!

Russia

The government is now cooperating with Jewish organizations on a limited scale. Hebrew manuscripts in the National Library in St. Petersburg are now being catalogued (17,000 file cards) and photocopied. The microfilms are being sent to the Hebrew University in Jerusalem. They are of very limited genealogical interest but—at least—are an example of developing cooperation. Unfortunately, the Russian archives contain masses of uncatalogued material, no adequate financing, and few finding aids. A listing of Russian archives, with information on their holdings is available on the web at **www.iisg.nl/~abb**

Before 1772 the Russian government discouraged Jews from living or settling in the country. Then, when Poland was partitioned (see the chapter on Poland), whole areas were included in Russia that had large Jewish populations—eastern Poland, Lithuania, White Russia (Belarus), Galicia, and Ukraine. They were not allowed to move into Russia proper. There were four million Jews in this new area, which stretched from Kovno and Vitebsk in the north to Bessarabia and the Crimea in the south, and from Warsaw in the west to Chernigov in the east. Even within the region, Jews could not live in the cities of Kiev, Nikolaev, Sebastopol, or Yalta without special residence permits.

Over the following years the government forcibly moved Jews who had been living in old Russia into the acquired area. It was this inhumane treatment and the constant harassment, poverty, and population pressures that led to the massive emigration of Jews from Russia to other countries in the 1800s—some two million in all.

Before 1918 there was no civil registration in Russia. Jewish communities kept their own records but few of them survived the pogroms and the various displacements. Perhaps many more exist in the archives of Russia; we do not know. The answer is not *Nyet*. There is just no answer at all.

Yugoslavia, Croatia, and Macedonia

Very little information is available about Jewish records in these countries. You will find details of the general genealogical sources in the Yugoslavia, Croatia, and Macedonia chapters. The main areas so far as the Jewish population was concerned were in Croatia and the Vojvodina (in Yugoslavia), both of which were part of Hungary until 1919. You may well find some Jewish community records in the Hungarian National Archives or in the Hungarian microfilms held by the LDS Church. There is also a Jewish Museum in Belgrade, the capital of Yugoslavia, and the Central Archives in

Jerusalem has full details of the genealogical material held there. It covers the period from the mid-1700s to 1952.

There are also some Jewish registers (1750–1832) in the State Archives of Macedonia (G Prlichev 3, Skopje 91000).

THE UNITED STATES AND CANADA

The most dramatic development in Jewish record-keeping in North America in recent years has been the creation of the Center for Jewish History at 15 West 16th Street, New York, NY 10011. Five organizations have joined together to establish what is destined to be the world center for research into Jewish history—including, of course, Jewish genealogical research. Conceived in 1994 and opened in 2000, it cost $52 million. All but $4 million of this was raised by individuals, family trusts, and income from various events over the years of construction. The remaining money was a grant from the federal government.

The building encompasses 125,000 square feet of space in this five-section, multi-level complex. Online access will be available to the holdings of the Center, which include documents, art, and artifacts, as well as a library. The computer system will provide worldwide access to the treasures that are being accumulated from Israel, archival treasures of the member organizations, and individual collections.

The organizations concerned with this great achievement are given below, with the telephone and fax numbers:

Center for Jewish History. Phone: 212-294-8301. Fax: 212-294-8302
American Jewish Historical Society. Phone: 212-294-6160. Fax: 212-294-6161
American Sephardi Federation. Phone: 212-294-8350. Fax: 212-294-8348
Leo Baeck Institute. Phone: 212-744-6400. Fax: 212-988-1305
Yeshiva University Museum. Phone: 212-960-5390. Fax: 212-960-5406
YIVO Institute for Jewish Research. Phone: 212-246-6080. Fax: 212-292-1892.

(The Leo Baeck Institute specializes in the German-speaking areas of Europe; the YIVO Institute specializes in East European Jewry.)

Other sources of Jewish genealogical information in North America are:

The American Jewish Archives
Hebrew Union College, 3101 Clifton Avenue, Cincinnati, OH 45220

The American Jewish Archives has collected every available record of Jews in the United States before 1900. They will not undertake any individual searches, but they will tell you if they have the records for a specific community.

Avotaynu, The International Review of Jewish Genealogy
PO Box 99, Bergenfield, NJ 07621
Phone: 201-387-7200. Fax: 201-387-2855. E-mail: info@avotaynu.com
Web site: www.avotaynu.com

This excellent journal is really a MUST for anyone searching for their Jewish roots. Avotaynu also publishes books, including several that are mentioned in the bibliography at the end of this book, as well as a series of microfiche indexes to a variety of Jewish records. There are always new discoveries of ancestral sources, and a subscription to the journal will keep you up-to-date with these.

The publisher is Gary Mokotoff, without any doubt the leading figure in Jewish genealogical research here in North America. He has written many books, including the classic *Where Once We Walked* (co-authored by Sallyann Amdur Sack)—a gazetteer that provides information about more than 22,000 towns in central and eastern Europe where Jews lived before World War II. He is also the co-creator of the Daitch-Mokotoff Soundex code, and the compiler of the JewishGen Family Finder—a database of ancestral towns and surnames being researched by some 14,000 Jewish genealogists throughout the world—and the Consolidated Jewish Surname Index.

The Canadian Jewish Genealogical Society
PO Box 446, Station A, North York, Toronto M2N 5T1
Phone: 416-638-3280

This is one of the most active Jewish genealogical societies in North America.

Sephardic Jews in the United States

Before we leave North America I must tell the tale of this little known epic of Jewish settlement here on our own doorstep. In 1492 all Jews in Spain were ordered to convert to Catholicism or leave the country. Half did leave and are known to us as the Sephardic Jews—based on the place name *Sepharad* in the Bible, which scholars identify with Iberia. Those who remained and became Catholics (at least on the surface) were known as *Conversos*. The majority assimilated over the years, but a stubborn few kept the faith. When the first Spanish settlers left for the Americas, some of the Conversos managed to obtain passage and settled in what we now know as New Mexico. Their descendants are still there and still regard themselves as Jews. In various scattered cemeteries you will find tombstones dating from the early years of the nineteenth century until the present day. The inscriptions do not mention the Jewish faith, but they contain symbols that identify them as Jews quite clearly.

ALBANIA

The Albanians are supposed to be descended from the ancient Illyrian and Thracian tribes. After the end of the Roman Empire in 395 the area passed to the Byzantines. During the next six centuries the northern part was invaded by the Serbs and the south was taken by Bulgaria. In 1014 the Byzantines reconquered the area, but by 1204 it had passed to the control of Epirus. Then followed invasions over the years by Venetians, Normans, Neapolitans, and Serbs.

In the fifteenth century the Turks of the Ottoman Empire arrived on the scene and stayed for the next five centuries. The First Balkan War (1912) gave the Albanians the chance to proclaim their independence, but during the Second Balkan War (1913) the Serbs occupied the country. A peace conference later in the year ended Albania's dreams of glory when large areas were given to Greece, Montenegro, and Serbia.

With the start of the First World War in 1914 Albania became a battleground for contending armies from Serbia, Montenegro, Greece, Austria, Bulgaria, and Italy. In 1920 the Congress of Lushnje gave Albania complete independence. In 1939 Italy invaded, and a pro-Italian puppet regime declared war on the Allied powers, but guerrilla groups within the country continued the fight against the invaders. In 1946 Albania became a Communist republic.

Albania existed in almost complete isolation from its fellow Communist countries and the rest of the world until 1991. We know little about genealogical sources in the country. Civil registration started in 1929, but before that, records were kept in the mosques and churches. The population was mainly Muslim, but the country is now officially atheist. There was a census in 1921. Until 1929 only religious marriages were allowed. Since 1946 the reverse has applied; only civil marriages are allowed.

It appears that most church records in the country, as well as the churches, have been destroyed. There is a new spirit stirring there, and perhaps some registers will come to light in the future. Meantime, I can offer very little encouragement to anyone of Albanian descent who hopes to trace ancestors.

ANDORRA

This is a very tiny state (population about 64,000) high in the Pyrenees between France and Spain. It is believed to have been first settled by stragglers from the rear guard of Charlemagne's army in 779 when it was returning to France after an unsuccessful campaign in Spain. Deserting soldiers intermarried with local Catalan girls and set up a small community. In the ninth century the Emperor Charles II made the Bishop of Urgel, in Spain, the overlord of Andorra. This led to protests by the counts of Foix, in France, who actually owned the valley of Andorra. The dispute lingered on, but in 1278 the two countries agreed that the Bishop and the Comte de Foix should be joint rulers. The rights of the Comte passed to the King of France by inheritance, and, in due course, from the kings to the presidents of France. So in the present day we still have the Bishop of Urgel and the President of France as co-rulers.

In actual fact, the control is minimal and the country is completely independent. It is governed by a council of twenty-four members, elected from the seven villages that make up the country. The council appoints a secretary-general to administer the affairs of the nation. The seven villages, or parishes, are the following: Andorra la Vella (the capital), Canillo, Encamp, Escaldes-Engordany, La Massana, Ordino, and Sant Julià de Lòria.

There is no form of civil registration, but the parish registers of births and baptisms, marriages, and deaths and burials serve the same purpose. These records are maintained in the church of each parish. Baptismal records started in 1614, and marriages and deaths in about 1694.

Wills are in the custody of the two notaries public (Notaires Publics des Vallées) in the capital and date back to the sixteenth century.

Censuses are conducted intermittently on a parish basis and the returns are located in the town hall (mairie) of each village. The population is almost entirely Catholic and the language a mixture of French and Catalan.

All correspondence should be addressed to Secretaire-General, Andorra la Vella, Andorra. More information on Andorra is available at **www.andorra.ad/**

AUSTRIA

I must start this chapter by emphasizing that it refers to present-day Austria and its existing boundaries. If your ancestors are "Austrian," be sure you know they came from a place within an area covered by the provinces of Burgenland, Carinthia, Lower Austria, Upper Austria, Salzburg, Styria, Tirol, Vorarlberg, and Vienna (in German: Burgenland, Kärnten, Niederösterreich, Oberösterreich, Salzburg, Steiermark, Tirol, Vorarlberg, and Wien).

One major difficulty ahead of you may be that immigration and census records in this country simply describe your ancestor as "Austrian" without giving the exact place of origin. If this is the case, you will have to depend upon either getting more information from within your own family, or basing your research on the apparent ethnic origin of your surname. Of course, the name may not help you at all; your surname, for example, may be Hungarian but your family may have lived in the German-speaking part of the old Austro-Hungarian Empire for centuries!

The following examples show you typical names from the different parts of the "old" Austria, but are only given to illustrate the point I am making:

AUSTRIA:	Müller
CROATIA:	Yankovic
THE CZECH REPUBLIC:	Formanek
HUNGARY:	Szabo
ITALY:	Scarlatti
POLAND:	Pryzyborski
ROMANIA:	Tatarescu
SLOVAKIA:	Lucachko
UKRAINE:	Yaremko

If your "Austrian" ancestors did, in fact, originate in any of the above areas of the Empire, you will have to trace them in the records of that country.

Now let us talk about the main sources of genealogical information to be found within the boundaries of present-day Austria. You must remember that all records are not centralized in one location, so there is no single archive in which you can discover all the information you want. There are state archives located in Vienna (Wien), provincial archives in each of the nine provincial capitals, city archives in the main population centers, family archives in some castles, and other specialized archives in various places.

Present-day Austria is often thought of as a homogenous language unit speaking only German, all the other races of the old Austro-Hungarian Empire having been happily settled in their own independent countries after the First World War. This is not true. Nor is the reverse true: all Austrians are not within Austria's present boundaries—in the South Tirol there are many thousands of Austrians living under Italian rule.

The Province of Carinthia has between 22,000 and 45,000 Slovenes. The Slovenian people originated in what is now Russia and settled in their present area in the sixth century. The majority of Slovenes were incorporated into the new country of Yugoslavia in 1919 and then into the independent country of Slovenia in 1991.

The Province of Burgenland contains about 8,000 Hungarians in the areas of Unterwart, Siget-in-der-Wart, and Oberpullendorf. There are some 25,000 Czechs in the same province in an area stretching from Kittsee in the north to Reindersdorf in the south.

The names and addresses of the state and provincial archives are given below:

State Archives (Österreichisches Staatsarchiv)

The following archives are located in Vienna:

Österreichisches Staatsarchiv
Nottendorfergasse 2, 1030 Vienna
Phone: 011-431-79540-504. Fax: 011-431-79540-109
Web site: www.oesta.gv.at/

These are the main state archives.

Finanz- und Hofkammerarchiv,
Johannesgasse 6, 1010 Vienna
Phone: 011-431-51254-3417. Fax: 011-431-51254-3414

The most important genealogical records located here are the lists and records of the German colonization of the Banat and Transylvania in the seventeenth and eighteenth centuries. The archives contain reports of the administration of the German colonies and are alphabetically indexed with names of the settlements, but are not indexed with individual surnames. Quite often the place of origin of the family in Germany is given.

Allgemeines Verwaltungsarchiv
Nottendorfergasse 2, 1030 Vienna
Phone: 011-431-79540-354. Fax: 011-431-79540-109

This is the Archival Administration Office, where you will find administrative and government records, including those pertaining to the Imperial Court and noble families.

Kriegsarchiv
Nottendorfergasse 2, 1030 Vienna
Phone: 011-431-79540-452. Fax: 011-431-79540-109

The military archives are located here too. They are of major genealogical importance and will be referred to later in this chapter.

Provincial Archives (Landesarchiv)

The provincial archives are located in the capital city of each province and in the capital city of Austria (Wien), which in this case—for archival purposes—is treated as a province:

BURGENLAND
Burgenländisches Landesarchiv
Freiheitsplatz 1, 7001 Eisenstadt
Phone: 011-43-2682-600-2347. Fax: 011-43-2682-61884
E-mail: norbert.frank@bgld.gv.at

KÄRNTEN
Kärntner Landesarchiv
St. Ruprechter Strasse 7, 9020 Klagenfurt
Phone: 011-43-463-56234-0. Fax: 011-43-463-56234-20
Web site: www.buk.ktn.gv.at/landesarchiv/

NIEDERÖSTERREICH
Niederösterrichisches Landesarchiv
3109 St. Pölten, Landhausplatz 1
Phone: 011-43-2742-200-6264. Fax: 011-43-2742-200-6550
E-mail: post.k2archiv@noel.gv.at
Web site: www.noel.gv.at/service/k/k2/landesarchiv.htm

OBERÖSTERREICH
Oberösterreichisches Landesarchiv
Anzengruberstrasse 19, 4020 Linz
Phone: 011-43-732-655523. Fax: 011-43-732-655523-4619
E-mail: landesarchiv@ooe.gv.at
Web site: www.ooe.gv.at/einrichtung/kultur/larchiv.htm

SALZBURG
Salzburger Landesarchiv
Michael-Pacher-Strasse 40, 5020 Salzburg
Phone: 011-43-662-8042-4527. Fax: 011-43-662-8042-4661
E-mail: post@land-sbg.gv.at
Web site: www.land-sbg.gv.at/archiv/

STEIRMARK
Steiermärkisches Landesarchiv
Karmeliterplatz 3, 8010 Graz
Phone: 011-43-316-877-2363. Fax: 011-43-316-877-2954
E-mail: post@stla.stmk.gv.at
Web site: www.stmk.gv.at/verwaltung/stla/

TIROL
Tiroler Landesarchiv
Michael-Gaismar-Strasse, 6010 Innsbruck
Phone: 011-43-512-508-3502. Fax: 011-43-512-50813505
E-mail: landesarchiv@tirol.gv.at
Web site: www.tirol.gv.at/

VORARLBERG
Vorarlberger Landesarchiv
Kirchstrasse 28, 6901 Bregenz
Phone: 011-43-5574-511-4511. Fax: 011-43-5574-511-4545
E-mail: landesarchiv@vlr.gv.at
Web site: www.landesarchiv.at/

WIEN (VIENNA)
Wiener Stadt- und Landesarchiv
Rathaus, 1082 Vienna
Phone: 011-431-4000-84815. Fax: 011-431-4000-7238
E-mail: post@m08.magwien.gv.at
Web site: www.magwien.gv.at/ma08/

It is impossible to list in any great detail the records in each of the above provincial archives. There is great variation from province to province.

Generally speaking, the provincial archives contain records dating back to the seventeenth century and including internal passports (Passkontrollen); orphans' lists (Waisenbücher); citizens' lists (Bürgerbücher); tax rolls (Steuerbücher); wills (Testamente); city directories (Adressbücher); certificates of domicile (Heimatscheinlisten); labor book registration (Arbeitsbuch-Protokolle); poorhouse records (Armen- und Versorgungshäuser); foundling books (Findelbücher); house records (Abhandlungsakten über Hausbesitz); land and property registers (Bürger Kataster); land records

(Grundbücher or Kaufbücher). Please note that not all the provincial archives have all the above records.

Certain of the provincial archives, however, do have very specialized records which can be of great value to you:

Niederösterreich

The archives here hold the Feudal Tenure Books (Lehenbücher) from the sixteenth to the eighteenth centuries for the whole of Lower Austria. These list the names of the serfs, their location, and the names of their noble masters.

Salzburg

In 1731–32 the Prince-Bishop of Salzburg expelled some 30,000 Protestants from his province. Some went overseas but the majority settled in North Germany. The provincial archives have records of those expelled, and there are other sources in Germany (see that chapter).

Styria

Very early censuses were held in this province between 1707 and 1853 and the returns are in the archives. Of course, you need to know an approximate address, but generally speaking, if you know the name of the village, that is sufficient. Larger towns such as Graz may present problems, but even there the address should be obtainable.

Tirol

The provincial archives can put you in touch with the local genealogical organization (Tiroler Matrikel-Stiftung) in Innsbruck, and for a small fee its members will search for a particular surname listed in the standard book about Tiroler families (*Tiroler Namenkunde* by Karl Finsterwalder, 1978).

City Archives (Stadtarchiv)

Limited sources of information are also available in the city, town, and village archives (Stadtarchiv). Most of them have some records of genealogical value. The main city archives are listed below, followed by details of those with good genealogical records. The address in each case is Stadtarchiv, Rathaus, followed by the name of the place.

The Stadtarchiv exist in all the main cities and towns and in most villages. The contents vary considerably, from the vast resources of Vienna to a handful of material in such places as Leoben, in Styria. Because of this great variation, no general list of records will be of value, but to give you some guide to the type of records you will find I list below the main items in the Vienna City Archives and then, by contrast, the material in two much smaller places:

The Vienna City Archives are combined with the provincial archives for Vienna and are located at the same address: Rathaus, 1082 Vienna.

Conscription Lists (Konskriptionsregister), 1740–1820

These give name, date and place of birth, and often, names and addresses of next of kin.

Passport Controls (Passkontrollen), 1795–1901

These are the records of people who left Vienna for overseas, or for another part of the Empire. They give names, dates, and destinations.

Citizen Books (Bürgerbücher), 1600s–1900s

These list names and addresses of people becoming *citizens* of the city and not merely inhabitants. There was a major difference between the two.

Tax Books (Steuerbücher), 1600–1905

These list taxpayers, giving address and occupation. There is an index by name from 1600 to 1748 and by profession or occupation from 1749 to 1812.

Guild Records (Zunftbücher), 1600s–1800s

These are only partially complete but they do give names of masters and their apprentices. The trade guilds were the equivalent of modern trade unions but exercised more power over their members and their occupations. The "closed shop" was invented in Europe in the Middle Ages! These records may be very valuable to you.

Wills and other Probate Records (Testamente)

These run from the early sixteenth century to the present and are indexed.

Certificates of Domicile (Heimatscheinlisten), 1850–91

These are records of identity documents issued; they give place of birth, occupation, and address.

Labor Book Registers (Arbeitsbuch-Protokolle), 1820–91

Everyone who worked had to carry a small book listing his name and address, age, and occupation, and employers for whom he had worked.

City Directories (Adressbücher), 1797 to date

These give name, address, and occupation and are invaluable if you are trying to trace an exact address in order to search census records.

Pedigrees (Abstammungskartei von Personen Jüdischer Abstammung)

These records contain nearly half a million names and are the family trees of Austrians with Jewish blood. The information was collected in 1938–39, and in many cases family information was given dating back to the early nineteenth century.

There are many other sources of information in the Vienna City Archives: poorhouse records, orphans' lists, court records, inquests, mortgages, and a partially indexed list of deaths in the city from 1648 (with some gaps between 1657 and 1677).

Here are some examples of records available in smaller places:

Enns (in Upper Austria): Miscellaneous family documents, 1366–1653

Wels (in Upper Austria): Censuses (Volkszählunglisten) from 1830

Now that you know the main locations of miscellaneous, but important, genealogical records in Austria, let us talk about the major and more obvious sources.

Civil Registration (Standesamt Register)

This is the compulsory registration of births, marriages, and deaths—a vital source of information in this country but of less value in Austria because it did not start until 1938, with the exception of Wiener Neustadt (1872) and Burgenland (1895). The records are in the Standesamt in Wiener Neustadt and Eisenstadt in Burgenland. Before 1938 the only similar records were baptisms, marriages, and burials recorded by the local churches. You will find the civil registration records of each district in the office of the local registrar (Standesamt).

Church Registers (Pfarr Register)

The religions that were officially authorized to keep records of vital events before civil registration were:

1. The Catholic Church
2. The Lutheran Church (Protestant). This was divided into two sects, the Augsburg Confession and the Helvetic Confession.*
3. The Old Catholic Church
4. The Eastern Orthodox Church (Holy Trinity)
5. The Eastern Orthodox Church (St. George)
6. The Romanian-Greek Orthodox Church (Holy Resurrection)
7. The Serbian-Greek Orthodox Church (St. Sava)
8. The Jewish Cultural Community

The great majority of Austrians are Catholic, but until 1849 Catholic priests also had to include in their registers the records of all other denominations. So, even though your ancestors were Lutheran or Jewish, you must search Catholic registers up to 1849. From 1878 until 1917 the Lutherans had to send a duplicate copy of all register entries to the church headquarters: Oberkirchenrat, Severin Schreiber-Gasse 3, 1180 Vienna. From 1870 onward other religions, and also people with no religion, registered their names in local magistrates' courts, where the lists are still located.

Catholic Registers

The Catholic Church headquarters are located at Erzbischofliches Sekretariat, Wollzelle 2, 1010 Vienna. These are, generally speaking, still in the original churches or in city and town archives. A few are in church and provincial archives. There is no point in listing every Catholic parish in Austria since this would, in effect, be a gazetteer listing the name of every city, town, and village in the whole country, including thirty churches for Vienna alone. The starting date of the parish registers varies considerably, but in general, you will find that most of them go back to 1750 and many to the early 1600s. At least one (Thalgau) dates back to 1580.

The following places have parish archives (Pfarrarchiv) in which church records are located. Not all of them contain church registers, for often these have been lost. You will have to write to the parish priest (Pfarrer) to find out just what he has in his custody. Quite apart from the registers, check to see if he has any of the following records:

> Grave Registers (Grabregister)
>
> Church Receipt Books (Einnahme Bücher)
>
> Confirmation Records (Konfirmation Bücher)
>
> Funeral Sermons (Leichenpredigten)

Of course, when you do write be sure you enclose at least three International Reply Coupons and a self-addressed airmail envelope. Also, make it clear you will pay whatever fees are required. Finally, and I know this should be unnecessary advice, be friendly and polite. He does not have to give you any information and a terse, demanding letter won't produce results. Try to write in German, but good English is better than bad German, and if you do write in English you can always end your letter with the magic words "Mit freundlichen Grüssen"—"With friendly greetings."

In this list of parish archives the parishes are given alphabetically under each province:

BURGENLAND: Eisenstadt (Diocesan Archives—Diözesanarchiv).

CARINTHIA: Bad St. Leonhard, Klagenfurt (Diözesan).

LOWER AUSTRIA: Aggsbach, Emmersdorf, Friedersbach, Gmünd, Gresten, Haag, Krems/Donau, Krumau, Laa an der Thaya, Langenfeld, Maria Taferl, Neustadl, Oberleis, Pitten, Ruprechtshofen, St. Egtden, Spitz/Donau, Tribuswinkel, Walterskirchen, Weiten, Weitra, St. Pölten (Diözesan).

SALZBURG: Abtenau, Adnet, Aigen, Alm, Altenmarkt, Badgastein, Bergheim, Berndorf, Bischofshofen, Bramberg, Bruck, Dienten, Dorfbeuern, Elizhausen, Embach, Fusch, Golling, Hallein, Hallwang, Henndorf, Bad Hofgastein, Köstendorf, Krimml, Kuchl, Lend, Leogang, Mariapfarr, Neumarkt, Pfarrwerfen, Piesendorf, Radstat, Ramingstein, Rauris,

Saalbach, Saalfelden, St. Georgen, St. Johann/Pongau, St. Veit, Siezenheim, Strasswalchen, Strobl, Stuhfelden, Tamsweg, Taxenbach, Thalgau, Uttendorf, Wagrain, Wald, Werfen, Zederhaus, Zell am See, Salzburg (Diözesan).

STYRIA: Anger, Eggersdorf, Fehring, Feldbach, Gaal, Gleisdorf, Gröbming, Gröming, Grosslobming, Hartberg, Haus, Judenburg, Knittelfeld, Köflach, Krieglach, Kumberg, Leibnitz, Lind, Obdach, Oberzeiring, Paldau, Pols, Purgg, Radkersburg, Ranten, Ratten, Riegersburg, Rottenmann, St. Georgen/Murau, St. Marein/Knittelfeld, St. Marein/Mürztal, St. Oswald, St. Peter/Judenberg, St. Radegund, Spital, Voitsberg, Weizberg, Graz (Diözesan).

TIROL: Innsbruck (Diözesan).

UPPER AUSTRIA: Enns, Freistadt, Grieskirchen, Östermiething, Uttendorf, Wartberg, Windhaag/Perg.

VORARLBERG: Feldkirch (Bishop's Archive—Bistumarchiv).

In addition to the above archives there are many others in various places concerned with religious institutions—nunneries and monasteries, markets, government departments, guilds, etc.

The Lutheran Church

The main archives are at Severin Schreiber-Gasse 3, 1180 Vienna (Phone: 011-431-4791523-34).

Lutheran Registers

These, also, are still in the churches, and since the numbers are far fewer than the Catholic ones, it is possible to list those parishes with registers dating back before 1900:

BURGENLAND: Bernstein, Deutsch Jahrndorf, Deutsch Kaltenbrunn, Eltendorf, Gols, Grosspetersdorf, Holzschlag, Kobersdorf, Kukmirn, Lutsmannsburg, Markt Allhau, Moerbisch-am-See, Neuhaus/ Klausenburg, Nickelsdorf, Oberschutzen, Oberwart, Pinkafeld, Pöttelsdorf, Reichnitz, Rust, Sziget, Stadt Schlaining, Stoob, Underschutzen, Weppersdorf, Zurndorf.

CARINTHIA AND EAST TIROL: Arriach, Bleiberg, Dornbach/Gmünd, Eggen/ Kraigerberg, Eisentratten, Feffernitz, Feld-am-See, Fresach, Gnesau, Klagenfurt, St. Ruprecht/Villach, Trebising, Tressdorf/Kirchbach, Tschörau/Bodensdorf, Völkermarkt, Waiern/Feldkirchen, Weissbriach, Wolfsberg, Zlan.

LOWER AUSTRIA: Baden, Mitterbach, Mödling, Nasswald, St. Pölten, Wiener Neustadt.

SALZBURG AND NORTH TIROL: Innsbruck, Salzburg.

STYRIA: Graz, Gröbming, Murzzuschlag, Ramsau am Dachstein, Schladming, Stainach/Irdning, Wald/Schober.

UPPER AUSTRIA: Attersee, Bad Goisern, Braunau-am-Inn, Eferding, Gall-neukirchen, Gmunden, Gosau, Hallstatt, Linz-Innere Stadt, Neukematen, Rutzenmoss, Scharten, Steyr, Thening, Vöcklabruck, Wallern/Trattnach, Wels.

VIENNA: Gumpendorf, Landstrasse, Vienna, Währing.

Many of the above registers date back to the early eighteenth century.

Registers of the Old Catholic Church date back to 1870 when this sect broke away from the main Catholic Church in a dispute over the infallibility of the Pope. The Orthodox Churches started to keep records in 1790.

Wills (Testamente)

These date back to 1600 and can be found in three different locations: provincial archives (Landesarchiv), city archives (Stadtarchiv), and in local courts.

Census Returns (Personenstandsgesetz)

These have been held in Austria since the eighteenth century with the actual dates varying from province to province. The first nationwide census was held in 1869 and since then eleven censuses have been held. The first four were for the whole Austro-Hungarian Empire, and the last seven for present-day Austria (1869, 1890, 1900, 1910, 1923, 1934, 1951, 1961, 1971, 1981, and 1991). The records are kept at the Central Statistics Office (Österreiches Statistisches, Zentralamt), Hintere Zollamtstrasse 2b, 1030 Vienna. Don't forget, of course, the early censuses in the province of Styria mentioned earlier in this chapter.

Movement Registration (Einwohnerlisten)

These records date from the early eighteenth century up to the present day and record all movement within the Empire up to 1918 and in the country from then on. Their location, unfortunately, varies between the National Archives (Staatsarchiv, Nottendorfergasse 2, 1030 Vienna); the various provincial archives (Landesarchiv); and the different city archives (Stadtarchiv).

Marriage Contracts (Eheverträge)

These were necessary whenever the bride owned, or was heiress to, property. They date back to the late 1300s and can be found in city archives (Stadtarchiv).

University Registers (Universitätsmatrikeln)

If your ancestor attended a university, you will find full information about him or her in the archives of each university, or in the archives of the city in which the university is located. Records started in the 1300s.

Genealogical Organizations (Familienverbände)

By far the most important organization in Austria is Heraldisch-Genealogische Gesellschaft "Adler," Universitätsstrasse 6/9b, 1096 Vienna. It is a small private organization with a dedicated membership, but without a government subsidy or any paid staff. The members in general are working on their own family tree as you are, but some of them are prepared to undertake searching for an overseas inquirer for a reasonable fee. The territory of operation is that of the old Empire and not just of modern Austria. All inquiries should be accompanied by three International Reply Coupons and a self-addressed airmail envelope. The organization will give you the name of a member willing to do research and you will agree on the fee with him or her. You must remember there is never any guarantee of success with research, and you must be prepared for this.

You may be sure that the member suggested will be familiar with the records in the place in which you are interested, and the charges will be on a par with what you would pay in this country.

There are three other genealogical organizations—in Gaz, Linz, and Tirol. Address changes are likely, so I suggest you write for the new addresses to the provincial archives for the three areas mentioned.

MILITARY RECORDS

I have left this part of genealogical research toward the end of this chapter because it is very important and deserves your special attention. You may well ask, "What use are military records to me? My ancestors were farmers, not soldiers!" The answer is simple. In 1868 universal conscription came into effect in the Austro-Hungarian Empire and every male had to serve three years in the army or navy (this was reduced to two years in 1912).

Every conscript was fully documented from his date and place of birth, and all the records exist, they are readily available, and many of them are indexed. They are located in the Kriegsarchiv War Archive: Nottendorfergasse 2, 1030 Vienna (Phone: 011-431-79540-452. Fax: 011-431-79540-109. Web site: www.oesta.gv.at/ebestand/ekv/efr1_kv.htm). There is not the space to list all the records, but at least I can tell you about the main ones.

First of all, I should mention that the records do, in fact, cover the period from the sixteenth century up to 1919. In other words, regular soldiers are included (long before the days of conscription a man enlisted for life).

In the armed forces there was no racial discrimination, and if your ancestors were Jewish you may well find a great deal of information about your soldier or sailor forebears, information which, in the civilian records, has been destroyed.

Commissions (Bestallungen)

These contain biographical and personal information about all officers serving in the army from the middle of the fifteenth century.

Muster-Rolls (Musterunglisten)

These contain full information about officers and other ranks serving in particular regiments. You do need to know the regiment in which your ancestor served in order to use these records, but quite often regiments were drawn from a particular area. In that case, if you know the place, you should be able to find out what the regiment was. For example, if your ancestor came from Graz, the odds are that he served in the 62nd Infantry. The regiments usually stayed close to home except in the case of war or rebellion.

The muster-rolls are available for the period 1740–1820 and contain the following: name, age, place of birth, religion, occupation before enlistment, names and places of birth of wife and children, and next of kin. They are indexed for officers.

Enlistment Orders (Stellungslisten)

These separate records give the exact birth date and the names of the enlistee's parents.

Discharge Books (Abgangsprotokolle)

These only cover a period of sixty years from 1859 but list all those discharged from the services.

Conscription Lists (Konskriptionsregister)

These records list the men conscripted for service each year in each particular area, giving the usual personal details and the name and address of the next of kin.

Other records available in the archives include wills (Testamente), 1639–1771, and foundation books (Grundbuchblätter und Stellungslisten). The latter list each soldier on a separate page, with full details of his movements with his regiment, and cover the years 1820–1918. There are also records of the navy organized on similar lines to that of the army.

It should be noted that many of the records for areas no longer in Austria have been transferred to the archives of their present-day countries.

LOCAL ARCHIVES

The various city and town archives in Austria that will be of possible use to you are listed below, alphabetically province by province. However, keep in mind that many small towns and villages, while not possessing archives, do have records in the Rathaus that may contain genealogical information:

BURGENLAND: Eisenstadt, Mattersburg, Neusiedl am See, Pinkafeld, Rust.

CARINTHIA: Friesach, Bad St. Leonhard, Oberdrauberg, Wolfsberg.

LOWER AUSTRIA: Amstetten, Baden bei Wien, Bruck, Drosendorf, Dürnstein, Eggenburg, Gmünd, Gross Enzersdorf, Gross-Siegharts, Haag, Hainburg an der Donau, Herzogenburg, Hollabrun, Hollenstein, Horn, Kloster-neuberg, Korneuburg, Krems/Donau, Laa an der Thaya, Langenlois, Litschau, Mautern, Mistelbach, Mödling, Neunkirchen, Perchtoldsdorf, Pöchlarn, Poysdorf, Retz, St. Pölten, Schwechat, Stockerau, Traiskirchen, Traismauer, Tulln, Bad Voslau, Waidhofen/Thaya, Weitra, Wiener Neustadt, Wolkersdorf, Ybbs an der Donau, Zistersdorf, Zwettl.

SALZBURG: Hallein, Radstadt, Salzburg, Wald, Zell am See.

STYRIA: Bierbaum, Bruck an der Mur, Gaal, Gleisdorf, Hainfeld, Judenberg, Leoben, Murau, Radkersburg, Voitsberg, Weiz.

TIROL: Innsbruck, Kitzbühel, Kufstein, Rattenberg, Solbad Hall.

UPPER AUSTRIA: Braunau am Inn, Eferding, Enns, Freistadt, Gaflenz, Gallneukirchen, Gallspach, Gmünden, Grein/Donau, Greinburg, Haag/Hausbruck, Bad Ischel, Kematen, Neufelden, Neumarkt/Grieskirchen, Ried, Rohrbach, Scharding, Steyr, Vöcklabruck, Wels.

VORARLBERG: Bludenz, Bregenz, Dornbirn, Feldkirch.

ESTATE AND FAMILY ARCHIVES

Many of the old Austrian families (and some new ones!) have maintained estate records over the years. These either are in the original family house (usually a castle or *schloss*) or have been handed over to local archives. If you are descended from one of these families or your ancestors worked on the estate, you may find useful information in these archives. Those known to be available for research are listed below. For further information you should write to, for example, Archiv Kripp, Absam, Tirol:

Place	*Province*	*Family Name*
Absam	Tirol	Kripp
Aistersheim	Upper Austria	Aistersheim
Bleiburg	Carinthia	Thurn
Eberau	Burgenland	Erdödy
Eferding	Upper Austria	Starhemberg
Eisenstadt	Burgenland	Esterházy
Feilhofen	Styria	Liechtenstein
Forchenstein	Burgenland	Esterházy
Grafenstein	Carinthia	Orsini-Rosenberg
Güssing	Burgenland	Battyány
Halbenrain	Styria	Stürgkh
Helfenberg	Upper Austria	Revertera
Himmelberg	Carinthia	Lodron
Hoch Flachau	Salzburg	Plaz
Hohenems	Vorarlberg	Waldburg-Hohenems
Hollenegg	Styria	Liechtenstein
Horn	Lower Austria	Hoyos-Sprinzenstein
Klam bei Grein	Upper Austria	Clam-Martinitz
Murau	Styria	Schwarzenberg
Neulengbach	Lower Austria	Liechtenstein
Patsch	Tirol	Thurn and Taxis
Reideben	Carinthia	Donnersmark
Rosenburg	Lower Austria	Sprinzenstein
Starhemberg	Upper Austria	Starhemberg
Thannhausen	Styria	Gudenus
Waidhofen/Thaya	Lower Austria	Gudenus

GLOSSARY

These are the German words you are most likely to find useful in your search through Austrian records:

Abhandlungsakten über Hausbesitz	House Records
Abstammungskartei von Personen Jüdischer	Jewish Pedigrees
Adressbücher	City Directories
Arbeitsbuch-Protokolle	Labor Book Registration
Armen- und Versorgungshäuser	Poorhouse Records
Auswanderer Listen	Emigration Lists
Bezirk	District
Bezirksgerichte	District Courts

Bistum	Bishopric or Diocese
Bürgerbücher	Citizens' Lists
Bürgerkataster	Land and Property Registers
Eheakten	Marriage Deeds
Eheverträge Verlassenschaften	Marriage Contracts
Einwohnerlisten	List of Inhabitants
Erbverträge	Inheritance Contracts
Findelbücher	Foundling Books
Grundbücher, Kaufbücher	Land Records
Heimatscheinlisten	Certificates of Domicile
Herrschaftsarchiv	Landlord Archives
Kirchenbücher	Church Registers
Konskriptionsregister	Conscription Lists
Land	Province
Lehensbücher	Feudal Tenure Books
Magistratisches Zivilgericht	Magistrate's Court
Musterunglisten	Army Muster Rolls
Passkontrollen	Passport Controls
Personenstandsgesetz	Census Returns
Pfarr	Parish
Rathaus	City or Town Hall
Regierungsgebäude	Government Office
Sonderstandesämter	Special Registers
Staatsarchiv	State Archives
Stadtarchiv	City Archives
Standesamt	Registrar's Office
Steuerbücher	Tax Books
Taufen	Baptisms
Testamente	Wills and Probate Records
Totenbücher	Burial Lists
Trauungen	Marriages
Verfachbücher	Court Records
Volkszählunglisten	Census Returns
Waisenbücher	Orphans' Lists
Zunftbücher	Guild Records

BELARUS

Belarus was formerly known as White Russia or Byelorussia. From the ninth to the twelfth centuries the country consisted of two large principalities—Polotsk and Turov—and a number of smaller ones—Gorodno, Slonim, Dainova, and Naishany. In the middle of the thirteenth and fourteenth centuries Belarus became part of Lithuania. At that period of history Lithuania was a mighty country that dominated eastern Europe, but it is now a small Baltic republic. *Sic transia*!

A federal state, Rzecz Pospolita, was established, which included Lithuania, Poland, and the Belarus area. However, there were three partitions of the federal state in 1772, 1793, and 1795 and, as a result, Belarus became part of the Russian Empire. In 1919 the Byelorussian Socialist Republic was created, and in 1920 it became an independent republic within the Soviet Union. In 1990 the republic became completely independent. However, it remained closely allied with Russia because of economic ties and many mutual interests.

The capital of Belarus is Minsk, and that is where the National Historic Archive is located. Because of the destruction of most of the genealogical and statistical records and registers by fire in World War II, this is not the great repository it could have been. The archival staff are extremely helpful—in contrast to those in Russia—but you must not count on a successful end to your search. Birth, marriage, and death records of people born before 1939 are practically non-existent. It might be possible for you, on a personal visit, to travel to the village of your ancestors (if it still exists) and obtain information from older people still living there. Unless you speak Russian fluently you will need an interpreter, and this will not be easy.

The Belarus National Archives are prepared to search all available records, and if necessary send an archivist to visit the town or village of your ancestors to make local inquiries. A charge will be made with an initial fee of $80 US, which must be paid in advance and is not returnable. This is not unreasonable since you are paying for the time spent by the archivist, and a successful result cannot be guaranteed.

In order to arrange a search you must contact a Belarus embassy in the capital of the country in which you live. The National Archives of the country in Minsk have asked me to include the following message:

> First of all you have to recall names, second names, the place of birth, and the occupation of your grandfather and grandmother. Please also enumerate their brothers, sisters, and children. Do not get disappointed if you find you do not know some things. Probably you have some additional information on this subject. All the information should be included in the request for genealogical search. It is made in the form of a letter that you can send to the Belarussian or consular mission in your country.

The addresses and phone numbers of the archives of greatest interest to genealogists are:

The National Historical Archives of Belarus
55 Kropotkina, 220002 Minsk, Belarus
Phone: 011-375-17-268-65-22. Fax: 011-375-17-268-65-20
Web site: www.president.gov.by/gosarchives/eindex.htm

National Historical Archives in Grodno
2 Tizengauza Sq., 230023 Grodno, Belarus
Phone: 011-375-152-44-94-66
Web site: www.president.gov.by/gosarchives/eindex.htm

You can write directly to these archives if you wish. They will inform you of the terms and conditions of the search, and the cost. You will be asked to transfer the sum of $80 US to a bank in Minsk or Grodno as the advance payment.

One final word: If you are of Jewish descent, I am happy to tell you that if your ancestors are from Belarus you may be lucky because the records in the archives in Minsk are reasonably good. You can obtain more information from some of the Jewish organizations listed in the chapter on Jewish records, which starts on page 19.

BELGIUM

This country is known as *Belgique* in French and *Belge* in Flemish. Since both languages are official in Belgium, I have tried as far as possible to give names of organizations and addresses in the language used in that particular part of the country. In bilingual areas, such as the capital of the country, I have tried to give organization names and addresses in both languages, with French first and Flemish second, for example Brussels appears as Bruxelles (Brussel). I should, perhaps, explain to my readers of Flemish descent that no slur is intended in placing the Flemish word after the French in this way. It is simply that one has to be first and I have made an arbitrary decision.

The Low Countries (what is now Belgium and the Netherlands) have had a very checkered history and it is quite astonishing that so many genealogical records have survived. Because of the strategic position of the area they were in a constant state of war over many centuries. Originally the Low Countries belonged to the Empire of Charlemagne; later the major part belonged to one of the minor German kings. After 1384 the various provinces were ruled by the Duke of Burgundy, who got them by purchase, marriage, blackmail, threats, and cession—the classic steps on the road to dynastic power in the Middle Ages. In 1548 they passed by marriage into the possession of Spain.

From 1568 to 1648 there was a succession of revolts against the Spanish, and in 1581 the northern provinces of the Low Countries became the country of Holland (the Netherlands). Belgium remained under Spanish rule until 1810 when Napoleon incorporated the whole area into France. In 1815, at the Congress of Vienna, it was decided that both areas should be united in one country. The Belgians did not approve (they had anticipated their freedom for too long) and in 1831 they declared their independence.

Genealogical records in the country are scattered about in many archives, and before we talk about major sources of research we should perhaps think about their locations.

The archives in Belgium are divided into the General State Archives in Brussels and eight provincial archives, four in the Walloon Provinces (Les

Provinces Wallonnes) and four in the Flemish Provinces (De Vlaamse Provinciën). Generally speaking, the northern provinces are Flemish, the southern ones are French, and Brussels is bilingual.

The General State Archives (Phone: 011-32-2-513-7680; Fax: 011-32-2-513-7681. E-mail: Persoons@arch.be; Web site: arch.arch.be) are located in the capital, at the address given below in both French and Flemish:

Archives Générales de l'État	Algemeen Rijksarchief
rue de Ruysbroeck 2	Ruisbroekstraat 2
1000 Bruxelles	1000 Brussel

These central archives include those of the Province of Brabant, of which Brussels is the center. They also contain the government archives; records of contested estates, involving land and/or money; and the parish registers of the Catholic churches in the Province of Brabant. There are also many family archives and genealogical collections donated by families or individual researchers.

The provincial archives contain such items as conscription records dating from 1796; population registers from 1796 (these record births and deaths of family members, addresses, and details of internal migration, and are usually indexed); records of passports issued and destination of emigrants; wills and probate records; civil registration of births, marriages, and deaths from 1795 (many of these are also indexed); parish registers and other church records from the early 1600s, or earlier; census returns where they exist; notarial records (lawyers' notes, papers, property sales or transfers, marriage contracts); genealogical collections and family papers; court records from 1341; guild records (members, date of admission, details of families); burgess rolls (details of people becoming citizens of a city, and not just inhabitants); and tax records.

As you can see, the genealogical material is enormous in quantity and excellent in quality. Not all the provincial archives have all this material, but most of them do, and some have records that are unique to a particular one. Antwerp (Anvers-Antwerpen), for example, has a record of every emigrant from the port in 1855, complete with place of origin, family members, and destination.

The provincial archives are located as follows:

Walloon Provinces (Provinces Wallonnes)
Archives de l'État à Arlon (Aarlen)
Parc des Expositions
6700 Arlon
Province du Luxembourg
Phone: 011-352-63-22-0613
E-mail: Archives.Arlon@skynet.be

Archives de L'État à Liège (Luik)
rue de Chéra 72
4000 Liège
Province de Liège
Phone: 011-32-4-252-0393. Fax: 011-32-4-229-3350
E-mail: Archives.Liege@skynet.be

Archives de l'État à Mons (Bergen)
place du Pparc 23
7000 Mons
Phone: 011-32-65-35-4506
E-mail: Archives.Mons@skynet.be

Archives de l'État à Namur (Namen)
rue d'Arquet 45
5000 Namur
Province de Namur
Phone: 011-32-81-22-3498
E-mail: Namur@skynet.be

Flemish Provinces (Vlaamse Provinciën)

Rijksarchief Antwerpen (Anvers)
Door Verstraeteplein 5
2018 Antwerpen
Provincie Antwerpen
Phone: 011-32-3-236-7300
E-mail: Rijksarchief.Antwerpen@skynet.be

Rijksarchief Brugge (Bruges)
Academiestraat 14
8000 Brugge
Provincie West Vlanderen
Phone: 011-32-0-50-33-7288
E-mail: Rijksarchief.Brugge@skynet.be

Rijksarchief Gent (Gand)
Geraard de Duivelstraat 1
9000 Gent
Provincie Oost Vlanderen
Phone: 011-32-9-225-1338
E-mail: Rijksarchief.Gent@skynet.be

Rijksarchief Hasselt
Bampslaan 4
3500 Hasselt
Provincie Limburg
Phone: 011-32-11-22-1766
E-mail: Rijksarchief.Hassel@skynet.be

Note: In certain of the above provinces the archives do not include a part of the province that has its own archives. These are shown below:

Walloon Provinces (Provinces Wallonnes)
Archives de l'État à Huy (Hoei)
rue Vankeerberghen 20
4500 Huy
Province de Liège
Phone: 011-32-85-21-5395

Archives de l'État à Saint-Hubert
Place de l'Abbaye
6870 Saint-Hubert
Province de Luxembourg
Phone: 011-32-61-61-1455

Archives de l'État à Tournai (Doornik)
Place Paul-Emile Janson 3
7500 Tournai
Province de Hainaut
Phone: 011-32-69-22-5376

Flemish Provinces (Vlaamse Provinciën)
Rijksarchief Beveren
Kruibekesteenweg 39
9120 Beveren
Provincie Oost Vlanderen
Phone: 0011-32-3-775-3839
E-mail: Rijksarchief.Beveren@skynet.be

Rijksarchief Kortrijk (Courtrai)
G. Gezellestraat 1
88500 Kortrijk
Provincie West Vlanderen
Phone: 011-32-56-21-3268. Fax: 0011-32-56-20-57-42
E-mail: Rijksarchief.Kortrijk@skynet.be

Rijksarchief Ronse (Renaix)
Vanhovestraat 45
9600 Ronse
Provincie Oost Vlanderen
Phone: 011-32-55-21-19-83
E-mail: Rijksarchief.Ronse@skynet.be

Saint-Hubert and Beveren, although functioning as district archives, are primarily only temporary resting places for archival material destined for other major archives, but for which there is no space available for the time being.

Parish Registers (Registres Paroissiaux— Parochierregisters)

Belgium is one of the few countries in Europe where the early church registers (up to at least 1796) have been handed over to the state archives, and either originals or copies of many of the more recent ones have also been deposited. What is even more exciting is that almost every register has been indexed. They really are a joy to work with and I wish many more countries would follow the example of Belgium. With the limitations of space it is not possible to list all the registers in the archives—although I have been supplied with full details by the Archivist-General of Belgium. However, this presents no problem, because if you have a place and a date, the various provincial archives can very quickly find the particular entry you need.

The archives at Liège have the registers from the former German area of Eupen-Malmedy. Both Catholic and Protestant registers are available for Blegny, Dalhem, Eupen, and Olne. A few years are also available for Bassenge (1770), Eisenborn (1807), Meyrose (1783, 1785), Reuland (1808), Richelle (1813), Saint-André (1813), Saint-Remy (1813), Sourbrodt (1807), Visé (1813, 1814), Waimes (1806, 1807), and Wévercé (1807).

In the archives at Antwerp you will find that many of the parishes have deposited registers as recently as 1885. The same applies to Hasselt but only up to 1870, and to Ronse to the same year.

So far as the Province of Brabant (which includes Brussels) is concerned, its parish registers are in the custody of the General State Archives (Archives Générales de l'État, rue de Ruysbroeck 2, 1000 Brussels).

Civil Registration (Registres de L'État Civil— Registers van de Burgerlijke Stand)

Civil registration started in 1796 under the French occupation. One copy of the records is held in the local municipality and the registrar will provide a photocopy for a small fee (inquiries should be sent to M. l'Officier de l'État

Civil—M. Officier van de Burgerlijke Stand). The registers are indexed from 1802 onwards. It should be noted that surnames with the prefix "de" are under D and those with the prefix "van" are under V.

There are also population registers, starting in 1850, in the municipal offices. For some reason they are not open to public inspection, but information from them will be given quite freely by the official named above.

Wills (Testaments)

Except for more recent ones these are in the custody of the provincial archives. More recent ones are in the local courts.

Emigration Records

As mentioned above, many of the provincial archives have records of passports issued, and also of police records that show the removal of a family or an individual from one place to another within Belgium. Some police records are in municipal archives and if you do not find anything in the provincial archives you should check locally.

In addition, the provincial archives in Antwerp have the 1855 register for all persons emigrating through the port of Antwerp. Records of other years were destroyed during the First World War. The registers have been indexed by the LDS Church and give the name of the ship, the name of the captain, the destination, the date of departure, the full names of the passengers, and their age and place of birth.

Hotel Registers

These are in the Antwerp Municipal Archives (Stadsarchief Antwerpen, Venusstraat 11, 2000 Antwerpen; Phone: 011-32-3-231-54-11; E-mail: stadsarchief@antwerpen.be; Web site: www.antwerpen.be/efloris) and can be very useful indeed. The emigrant vessels did not adhere to a regular schedule and would wait in port until the very last passenger could be packed into an already overcrowded ship. The result was that emigrants would arrive in the port to find that the sailing was delayed. They would have to find a small hotel and, usually, a temporary job until they could board the ship. The available hotel registers date from 1679 to 1811 for foreigners from other parts of Europe, and from 1858 to 1898 for all nationalities.

Genealogical Organizations

L'Office Généalogique et Héraldique de Belgique
Musées Royaux d'Art et d'Histoire
10 avenue des Nerviens
1040 Brussels

This organization is devoted to research in the Walloon areas of Belgium, but failed to answer my inquiries.

Service de Centralisation des Études Généalogiques et Démographiques de Belgique
Maison des Arts
Chaussée de Haecht Schaerbeck 147
1030 Brussels

This is a centralized referral service for genealogical research inquiries in Belgium. It also did not respond to my inquiries.

Vlaamse Vereniging voor Familiekunde
Van Heybeeckstraat 3
2170 Antwerpen-Merksem
Phone: 011-32-3-646-99-88
Web site: win-www.uia.ac.be/u/pavp/sdv/vvf.htm

This excellent and helpful organization is a credit to any country. If your ancestors from Belgium are of Flemish descent or from the Flemish section of the country, you are lucky to have the V.V.F. to help you. It is staffed entirely by volunteers, and for service and efficiency there is no comparison between the V.V.F. and other organizations with a paid staff.

The organization was set up in 1964 and publishes a monthly magazine called *Vlaamse Stam*, which goes out to each of the 4,500 members. In every Flemish province the V.V.F. has a *gouw* or district branch, with sub-branches in each important town.

At the national headquarters in Antwerp the staff answer all written, telephone, and personal-call questions, totaling over 4,500 a year. They will try to answer your simple queries without charge (if you cover the return postage with three International Reply Coupons), but if your inquiry is more complicated you will be referred to one of their members, who will do research for you for an agreed fee. You will find the association particularly willing to help overseas inquirers. Donations will be welcome, of course. Your query can be sent in English.

The V.V.F. library is growing by 800 books a year from all over the world, and by 100 genealogical magazines a month. The V.V.F. also holds seventy-five percent of all indexes and inventories of genealogical sources from all over the world; the electoral registers of nearly all the Belgian municipalities; over 100,000 obituaries; half a million "In Memoriam" cards; a growing collection of press clippings; family and local histories in both published and manuscript form; and a large collection of genealogical manuscripts from 1500 to the present day.

Obviously the V.V.F. is fast becoming a document collection center for all genealogical material. It also has access to an on-line computer. In Belgium, as in many other countries, this is a very visible part of genealogical research.

If you join the organization, you can also make use of the Question and Answer Section (Vraag en Antwoord) of *Vlaamse Stam*. Use of this section could well put you in touch with distant relatives, or with other members who are expert and knowledgeable about a particular district in Belgium.

Belgian Minorities

There are over 100,000 people of German descent living in the Province de Liège. This is the result of the transfer of the Eupen and Malmedy districts to Belgium after the First World War. Church and civil records for this area are located in the provincial archives at Liège (for address, see earlier in this chapter).

Census Returns

Censuses are held every tenth year (starting in 1846) with occasional gaps. The returns are not normally available for public search, but consideration will be given to a special application on legal grounds, accompanied by proof of descent. Application can be made to the Institut National de Statistiques (Nationaal Instituut voor Statistiek), Brussels (Web site: www.statbel.fgov.be). The odds, however, will be against you.

There are some early census returns that are open for search. There were censuses in the city of Namur in 1745, 1766, 1775, 1784, 1794, 1804, and 1812 that are in the state archives there. Censuses also took place in the Province of Brabant in 1693, 1709, and 1755, and these are in the General State Archives in Brussels.

The Low Countries

If you get back far enough you will enter the period when Belgium and Holland were controlled by either Austria or Spain. Some records exist in the National Archives of both countries, but in Spain you may have trouble in running them to earth. In this area the V.V.F. (see above) can be very helpful.

In Antwerp V.V.F. has an inventory of sources of information about men from the Southern Netherlands (Belgium) who served in the Austrian army. It also has inventories of genealogical material from the occupation period, most of which is now located in the archives at Dijon, Lille, and Paris, in France, and also in the Simancas Archives in Spain.

Details of the holdings in the archives at Lille are very important as it was once part of the Earldom of Flanders, which included the Flemish areas of Belgium. The archives at Lille have a great deal of genealogical material for Flanders during that period. So far as French Flanders is concerned, the V.V.F. holds a great deal of material from Bergues St. Winoque, which was a Flemish-speaking district in a Walloon area.

BOSNIA AND HERZEGOVINA

I suppose this part of Europe has known some periods of peace and happiness—a few years of normal life between invasions by Turks and Germans, and civil wars when neighbors killed each other in the name of religion. If they ever did, it is not obvious to those of us who are not Bosnians.

The country consists of the two regions of Bosnians and Herzegovinians—united in name, partners politically and economically, and bitter enemies because of religion—neighbors who fight and kill each other because they are Muslims, Catholics, or Greek Orthodox.

The two countries joined together in a protective alliance to ward off threats of invasion by Turks. Catholics and Protestants united in an uneasy friendship because of fear. They were subjugated by the forces of the Ottoman Empire, then lived peaceably for three centuries, were both absorbed by the Austro-Hungarian Empire for some seventy years. They were partners, apparently peacefully, in a Yugoslav kingdom for twenty years, fought together against German invaders for six years, and joined the Yugoslav Republic for twenty-five years. They left the Republic to become independent, and started fighting each other once again. Only intervention by the United Nations brought an uneasy peace and a deeply divided country.

Thousands were killed; churches, mosques, and synagogues were burned; religious relics were destroyed; and precious records that could have helped you trace your family back over the centuries were stolen or thrown away. You Bosnians and Herzegovinians will not have an easy search, but be determined, be patient, and never give up. Eight years have passed since the civil war. Many records that were hidden to keep them safe have been returned to archives, and many dedicated archivists are working under difficult conditions to repair books about local history.

Here are the details of archives that still exist. There are a number of archives in the two countries, and their locations are given below (the cities of Banja Luka and Mostar are damaged):

BOSNIA
Archives of Bosnia and Herzegovina (Arhiv Bosne i Hercegovine)
Dzemaludina Reisa Causevica 6
Sarajevo

Federal Archives of Bosnia and Herzegovina
Dzemaludina Reisa Causevica 6
Sarajevo

Archives of Bosnia (Arhiv Sredje Bosne)
Skolska bb
Travnik

Regional Historical Archives (Regionalni istorijski arhiv)
Franje Ledera 1
Travnik

Archives of Unsko-Sanskog Canton
UL bosanskih banova 7
Bihac

Archives of Sarajevo Canton (Kantonalni arhiv)
Koturova 3
Sarajevo

Archives of Srpske
Svetog Save 1
Banja Luke

HERZEGOVINA
Archives of Herzegovina (Arhiv Hercegovine)
Trg 1 maja 17
Mostar

BULGARIA

Bulgaria occupies the area of ancient Thrace and Moesia, which was settled by Slavic peoples in about 600 and later by the nomadic Bulgars. It is believed they originated in the Volga area of what is now Ukraine. Sofia was taken from the Byzantines in 811. By this time the Bulgars and the original Slavs had merged into one race, speaking a Slavic language.

In 1018 the Byzantines reconquered the country and it remained under their control until a rebellion in 1186. During the next century Bulgaria reached its period of greatest expansion, controlling nearly all the Balkan area with the exception of Greece. At the end of two centuries of grandeur it was conquered by the Ottoman Empire. There were frequent unsuccessful revolts during the next five centuries until the country was liberated by Russia in 1878. The Bulgarians you meet in your visit to the homeland of your ancestors will be quick to tell you that they have twice been liberated by their "Russian brothers" from the "Imperialists" (the other time being in 1944).

After the Congress of Berlin in 1878, North Bulgaria became a vassal state of Turkey, while South Bulgaria (then known as Eastern Rumelia) and Macedonia were ruled directly from Constantinople. In 1885 Eastern Rumelia was reconquered by the Bulgars, and in 1908 Bulgaria declared the complete independence of the reunited country.

Bulgarian claims to Macedonia led to the Balkan Wars of 1912–13 in which Bulgaria made wide conquests of Balkan territory. In 1915 the country, led by its German-born king, "Foxy Ferdinand," joined the First World War on the side of Germany and the Austro-Hungarian Empire. It was a disastrous move, because in the Peace Treaty of Neuilly that followed the Allied victory, Bulgaria lost its outlet to the Aegean Sea to Greece, the South Dobrudja to Romania, and some territory to Yugoslavia.

In 1940 Bulgaria reclaimed the South Dobrudja and joined the Axis powers in 1941. The USSR declared war on Bulgaria in 1944—belatedly because in 1941 the Bulgarians had declared war on the United States and Great Britain, and had occupied parts of Greece and Yugoslavia. Since the population of Bulgaria was very pro-Russian, no action was taken against the USSR at that time. However, the USSR did declare war in due course, and this was followed by an immediate armistice. Bulgaria then declared war on Germany. In 1945 a republic was declared and in 1947 a peace treaty allowed Bulgaria to retain the South Dobrudja.

The capital of the country is Sofia and the administrative districts are Blagoevgrad, Burgas, Gabrovo, Haskovo Choumen, Iamdol, Kakdjali, Kustendil, Lovetche, Michailovgrad, Pazardjik, Pernik, Pleven, Plovdiv, Razgrad, Russe, Silistra, Sliven, Smolian, Sofia (city), Sofia (district), Stara Zagora, Targovichte, Tolbouhin, Varna, Veliko-Tarnovo, Vidin, Vratza.

Each of the above-mentioned districts has its own archives. For information about a particular area you should write to the Director, Dăržaven Istoričeski, followed by the name of the city. For more general information contact the National Archives (Centralen Dăržaven Arhiv, ul. Slavjanka, Sofia).

Civil Registration

This started in 1893 for births, marriages, and deaths. The records are kept in the various districts in the People's Council Office, which acts as the local registration office. Birth, marriage, and death certificates may be obtained for a small fee.

Church Registers

These appear to have started as recently as 1800 in most places and are kept in the local churches. It was at this time that the Bulgarian Orthodox Church broke away from the Eastern Orthodox Church. Eighty-five percent of the Bulgarians belong to this church, the remainder being Muslims. The churches can supply certificates of marriage and baptism. Be sure you ask for the full details, including names of witnesses or godparents.

Wills

These are limited in number, because very few Bulgarians owned enough property or real estate to make a will necessary. They are in the custody of the Ministry of Justice, in Sofia.

Censuses

These took place in 1881, 1893, 1905, 1920, 1926, and 1934. It is not known what information is contained in the census returns; whether any have been held since 1934; where the returns are located; or whether anyone tracing their Bulgarian ancestors may have access to them.

There must surely be other records of genealogical value in the various archives, but under Communism the Bulgarian government was totally non-informative about its records. I failed to obtain any details during my visit to the country, nor was I any more successful by correspondence with Sofia. However, the Cultural Attaché of Bulgaria in Ottawa, Canada, was most helpful in answering a few questions. I suggest you try writing directly to the National or District Archives first, and if that fails, try your nearest Bulgarian Embassy.

One result of the disappearance of Communist regimes in Eastern Europe has been greater cooperation with the LDS Church. This is particularly true of Bulgaria. The LDS has recently concluded agreements to microfilm civil registration and church records of all denominations for the period from 1800 to 1945.

Note: The above was written for the 1986 edition of this book. It is regretted that the National Archivist of Bulgaria was unwilling to supply any further information.

CROATIA

Croatia includes within its borders such areas of historical renown as Dalmatia, Slavonia, and parts of Istria. The majority of Croats are Catholic, but there are minority groups—including Serbs, Slovenes, Hungarians, Germans, Czechs, and Italians—who belong to other religions.

Croatia became an independent kingdom in the tenth century but became linked with Hungary in 1091. However, it continued to elect its own rulers and retained its own *Diet*, or Parliament. In 1526 it came under Turkish rule, and this forced the Croats to accept the Hapsburgs as their kings in return for military assistance in expelling the Turks.

When the Austro-Hungarian Empire was first established in 1867, Croatia and Slavonia were included in Hungary, and Dalmatia and Istria in Austria. The following year Croatia was granted local autonomy but was restless under Hungarian control and efforts to Magyarize it. In 1918 the country joined with Serbia and Slovenia in creating Yugoslavia—the kingdom of the Serbs, Croats, and Slovenes as it was called. It was not long before sporadic uprisings occurred because of Serbian efforts to centralize government in Belgrade.

In World War II Croatia was granted limited independence under joint German-Italian control. Civil war followed with the majority of Croats under Tito (himself a Croat) fighting the Germans. In 1945 it became one of the founding states in a reconstituted Yugoslavia. Croatia declared its independence in 1991, and this was recognized by the United Nations and the European Community (EC).

Croatian State Archives

These consist of the National Archives in Zagreb and various archives in the major centers throughout the country:

National Archives (Hrvatski Državni Arhiv)
Marulićev trg 21
10000 Zagreb

Phone: 011-385-1-48-01-999. Fax: 011-385-1-48-29-000
E-mail: hda@arhiv.hr
Web site: zagreb.arhiv.hr

Regional archives are located in various provincial centers throughout the country. Be prepared for a difficult search for documents that may no longer exist. There was much destruction of records in World War II and also in the recent civil war, which led to Croatian independence. The locations of regional archives are given below:

Opatićka 79	V. Nazora 3
10000 Zagreb	52400 Pazin
Trsteńakova 7	Glagoljaška 18
42000 Vara in	21000 Split
Trg Fugena Kvaternika 3	Sv Dominika 1
43000 Bjelovar	20000 Dubrovnik
Kamila Firingera 1	Park Nikole Hosta 2
31000 Osijek	51000 Rijeka
Augusta Cesarca 1	Lj. Šestića 5
35000 Slavonski Brod	47000 Karlovac
Frankopanska 21	Ljetnikovac Hanibala Lucića
44000 Sisak	21450 Hvar

Civil Registration

This started in 1946. Before that year vital events were recorded in the churches.

Church Registers

The religion of Croatia is mainly Catholic, but there are also Greek Orthodox, Muslim, Lutheran, and Jewish places of worship. All of these may possess early or current records.

Censuses

Most of the early censuses are missing, but fragments do exist in various archives for 1516 and later.

General Records

Many of the older registers are on microfilm in both the national and regional archives. There is no complete list of these, and for more detailed information you should consult the archives for the area from which your ancestors came. Be sure to enclose three International Reply Coupons to cover the cost of return postage. These can be obtained from your local post office.

Croatians are proud of their heritage, and you will find the archives more helpful than many others. It will help if you can write in Serbo-Croat, but if this is not possible, try and find a local translator or, at least, type your letter in simple English.

CYPRUS

Cyprus has been inhabited since 8500 BC. Greeks settled the island between 1500 and 1000 BC, followed by Phoenicians and many other temporary or permanent invaders such as Assyrians, Egyptians, Persians, Romans, Byzantines, Venetians, and Turks—its position on trade roots and its rich copper deposits attracted a wide variety of settlers. It acquired its Greek language and character in the second century BC—primarily in the southern two-thirds of the island. Later invaders from the Ottoman Empire made the northern part develop Turkish ethnically and politically. In modern times the country became 82 percent Greek and 18 percent Turkish.

In 1974 after many years of tension between the Greek and the Turkish communities, the country was invaded by Turkish forces, which occupied the predominantly Turkish-speaking north of the island. As a result, many Greeks in the north fled to the south, and many Turks in the south fled to the north. Although peace talks have continued sporadically since then, the situation is basically unchanged. Access to the Turkish-controlled one-third of the island is generally obtained by entry from Turkey (visitors may obtain day-passes to this part, or may enter for longer periods directly from Turkey). However, recently there has been some traffic allowed between the south and the north. If you are proposing to visit Cyprus, be sure you check the present situation and obtain all the necessary travel documents before you leave home. You should obtain information from both the Turkish and Cypriot embassies if you plan to travel between the two parts of the country. Entry to the south only, including the capital of Nicosia, can be obtained from any of the nearby countries such as Greece, Italy, Egypt, and Israel.

It is not easy to obtain genealogical information from Cyprus, but your best sources of information are the Ministry of the Interior (Dem. Severis Avenue, Ex-Secretariat Offices, 1453 Nicosia; Fax: 011-3572-671465) or the Archbishop of Cyprus, both located in Nicosia. Other local offices are listed below.

Religions

Islam is the predominant religion in the north, Christianity in the south. The latter is mainly Greek Orthodox, but there are also small numbers of Catholics, Armenian Gregorians, and Maronites. The church registers are still in the original churches and have not been centralized.

Civil Registration

This commenced in 1895 for births and deaths, and in 1923 for marriages. The records are kept in local registration offices in each district. For information before these dates you will be dependent on church registers, which date back to about 1870 in the Christian churches and to 1850 in the mosques.

Censuses

These were held at ten-year intervals from 1881 to 1931. Since then there have been censuses in 1946 and 1960, the last full censuses to be taken on the island. However, there was a partial census in 1973 for certain areas, and in 1976 for the non-Turkish part of the country. Information from the census returns can be obtained by writing to the Ministry of the Interior, Nicosia.

Wills

These are in the custody of the probate registrar in each district. If you do not know the exact address of your ancestor, you should write to the Ministry of the Interior in Nicosia.

Information about conditions in Cyprus so far as travel is concerned can be obtained from a travel agent or from the government:

Press and Information Office, Apellis Street, 1456 Nicosia
Phone: 011-3572-801198. Fax: 011-3572-666123
E-mail: pioxx@cytanet.com.cy
Web site: www.pio.gov.cy

THE CZECH REPUBLIC

Until 1993 the Czech Republic was joined with Slovakia to form Czecho-slovakia. Although Czechoslovakia was only created as a separate country in 1919, its historical roots go deep into central Europe. After the Treaty of Versailles the new country consisted of four provinces: Bohemia (Cechy), Moravia (Morava), Silesia (Slezsko), and Slovakia (Slovensko). The area of Ruthenia (Podkarpatská Rus) was also included.

The name Bohemia originated after the area was first populated by the Boii, a Celtic tribe, under the leadership of Boiohemus. However, the name is not used in the present-day Czech Republic. The official name is Cechy and the people are called Cechové or Czechs.

By the seventh century the four provinces mentioned had joined with Austria and Poland to form the Moravian Empire. The Magyars invaded in the tenth century and Slovakia became a part of Hungary. When the Moravian Empire disappeared, the Czechs and Moravians joined together in the Duchy of Bohemia and Moravia, and—together with Silesia—became part of the Holy Roman Empire. In 1198 the area became the Kingdom of Bohemia, and this survived until 1620, when the area came under the control of the Hapsburg Dynasty.

After the First World War, Czechoslovakia was created out of the ruins of the old Austro-Hungarian Empire. Although its creation was hailed as a great victory for democracy in central Europe, all was not sweetness and light. Many Slovakians would have preferred to remain within Hungary rather than join with a people with whom they shared neither religion nor language, and the boundaries of the new country included large numbers of Germans and Hungarians now separated from their homelands.

In 1938 the German-speaking areas, the Sudetenland, were incorporated into Germany, and in 1939 a German protectorate of Bohemia and Moravia was proclaimed. Slovakia became nominally independent under German control.

After the Second World War, there was a total and drastic expulsion of all Germans from the country, followed by a mass exodus of Hungarians.

Ruthenia was seized by the USSR and is now known as the Oblast of Zakarpatskaya, an administrative district of Ukraine.

In 1949 the original system of provincial administration was abolished and administrative districts (oblasti) were set up. The lower division is a county (okresy) and several okresy together form an oblast. An alternative name for an oblast is a kraj.

The seven oblasti are listed below, together with the name of the chief administrative city in each oblast:

> Západočeský (Plzeň)
> Severočeský (Ústi nad Labem)
> Středočeský (Prague)
> Jihočeský (České Budějovice)
> Východočeský (Hradec Králové)
> Jihomoravský (Brno)
> Severomoravský (Ostrava)

When dealing with place-names it may be helpful to know that North is Severo, East is Východo, South is Jiho, West is Západo, and Central is Středo.

The seven oblasti listed above each contain the following counties (okresy):

ZÁPADOČESKÝ: Cheb, Domažlice, Havlíčkův Brod, Karlovy Vary, Klatovy, Plzeň (Jih), Plzeň (Sever), Rokycany, Sokolov, Tachov.

SEVEROČESKÝ: Česká Lípa, Chomutov, Děčín, Jablonec nad Nisou, Liberec, Litoměřice, Louny, Most, Teplice, Ústí nad Labem.

STŘEDOČESKÝ: Benešov, Beroun, Kladno, Kolín, Kutná Hora, Mělník, Mladá Boleslav, Nymburk, Praha (Východ), Praha (Západ), Příbram, Rakovnik.

JIHOČESKÝ: České Budějovice, Český Krumlov, Jindřichův Hradec, Pelhřimov, Pisek, Prachatice, Strakonice, Tábor.

VÝCHODOČESKÝ: Chrudim, Hradec Králové, Jičín, Náchod, Pardubice, Rychnov nad Kněžnou, Semily, Svitavy, Trutnov, Ústí nad Orlici.

JIHOMORAVSKÝ: Blansko, Břeclav, Brno Město, Brno Venkov, Gottwaldov, Hodonin, Jihlava, Kroměříž, Prostějov, Třebíč, Uherské Hradiště, Vyškov, Žďár nad Sázavou, Znojmo.

SEVERMORAVSKÝ: Bruntál, Frýdek-Mistek, Karviná, Nový Jičín, Olomouc, Opava, Přerov, Sumperk, Vsetin.

A very useful book, if you can find a copy, is *Die Deutschen in der Tschechoslowakei, 1933–1947* by Vacloc Kral. It lists place-name changes from German to Czech and Slovak. Luckily the people of the various parts of the former Czechoslovakia have always been great record-keepers, either with oral histories passed down through many generations, or in family papers lovingly preserved within families over centuries.

The Czech government is reasonably helpful to ancestor-hunters and does now permit individuals to make personal searches in the various archives—providing that application is made through the nearest consulate, and details of reasons for search and of relationship are given. However, the government does encourage you to let it organize the searching for you. The reason given is that problems of language will make it hard for you to do your own research. This is very probably true, but you will be charged for this kindly gesture!

At any rate, let me explain the system. You give the name of the person whose ancestry is being searched, place of birth, marriage, and death, and dates of the same; in the case of a birth certificate the names of the parents (including the mother's maiden name); and the religion.

The minimum fee per certificate, at this moment of writing, is $10, but it may be higher if the search is difficult or the information you gave was not exact. The cost of what they call a "running account"—tracing back from the records over several generations—is based on time spent on the project. The government states that it is not possible to quote a figure in advance and you should be aware that the fee you pay is for research and not for results.

Some lines can be traced back to the seventeenth century; in other cases no records can be located. It may be several months before a report can be sent to you. You must apply to the nearest consulate for a request form, and when completed it should be mailed to the following address: Department of Archives, Archivní Správa, Milady Horákové 133, 16621 Prague 6. (It is essential that you give the religion of your family and the name of the district in Prague.)

However, it seems likely you may be spared all this official form-filling. The LDS Church has now concluded an agreement with the government that will enable it to microfilm all church registers of all religions from 1599 to 1896. Check with your nearest LDS Family History Center for up-to-date information.

Language

Try to buy a good Czech dictionary and study it. You should also buy a very good book about ancestor-hunting in the area. *Genealogical Research for Czech and Slovak Americans* by Olga Miller (Gale Research Co.: Detroit, 1978) has first-rate information about the language and a very good bibliography of books in Czech about records.

Church Records (Matriky)

These are your most valuable sources of information in both the Catholic and Protestant churches. Even if you are using the records of the LDS Church it is always wise to check original sources, and so you should read the following paragraphs with care—particularly if you are planning a personal visit to your ancestral homeland.

Catholic

Some of these registers date back to the early 1500s in Bohemia, and to 1600 in Moravia. Officially, the registers started in 1563 after the Council of Trent, but only for baptisms and marriages. Deaths or burials were listed after 1614. When the Hapsburgs took over in 1620, only the Catholic Church was permitted to record vital events.

The original matriky were loose sheets of paper which were bound together later. The entries could be from several widely scattered villages, but all within the same parish, and often included other events not normally found in church registers such as accounts of murders, floods, civil disturbances, and feasts and galas.

In the mid-1700s a new law ordained that in future the matriky should include in the baptismal entries the full names of the parents and all four grandparents, together with their addresses and occupations. Latin or German were to be the languages used instead of Czech. In the early 1800s priests started to include dates of birth and death.

In 1790 the indexing of the matriky was ordered and in 1802 the new law was made retrospective to include all earlier entries back to the beginning. This was not a very popular idea with the hard-worked priests, and the retrospective indexing was done in a very half-hearted way and is not at all reliable. I suggest you can trust the indexing after 1802 but before that you should check the entries themselves one by one around the dates in which you are interested. Even though you may find some family members in the index, there is no guarantee there are not more unindexed.

In 1799 the practice of duplicate entries was started so that an extra copy could be sent to the bishop. This was good because in many cases the originals have been lost and the duplicates are available. On the other hand, the duplicates are not always as reliable as the original—there was no carbon paper in those days!

Protestant

In 1771 the Protestants (mainly Evangelicals and Lutherans) were allowed to keep their own matriky for the first time, but they had to give copies to the Catholic priests, who included them in their own registers. At this time the Protestants did not have their children baptized, so you will find few of these entries.

Other Religions

Jews had to report their vital events to the Catholic priest in most parts of Bohemia. However, the matriky information was also used as a basis for conscription, and since the Jews did not welcome military service they often registered the birth of a son as that of a daughter. As they lived within their own enclosed community, there was little chance the false entry would be discovered. I suppose the local Gentiles might have done the same thing if it were not for the certainty of speedy discovery!

Jews were subjected to many restrictions on registration and religious observances, and there are a number of surviving records of these from various parts of Bohemia. They can be found in the Obvodní Narodní Výbor, Vodičkova 18, Prague.

The other religions in the Czech Republic were Bohemian and Moravian Brethren, Hutterite, Greek Orthodox, and Anabaptist. Most of their records have been lost over the years, but those that survive are in the District Archives. However, you may also find their vital events recorded in the Catholic Registers, as at various times these sects were not allowed to perform their own ceremonies.

One problem with the matriky is the naming system. Surnames could be based on the father's first name, on the name of the family farm, or on normal surname descent. The surname could change if the father changed farms, and if he inherited a farm through his wife he could even change his name to hers. It was all very complicated, but such changes are usually recorded in the matriky by hyphenating the names together (the family and any other) or by use of the word Kdysi or Vulgo, which roughly translated means "also known as."

Archives

The decision of Slovakia in 1993 to secede from Czechoslovakia added complication to the archival records of both countries. It was impossible to divide many of the records and for that reason your search for your ancestors—whether you are of Czech descent or Slovak—is almost certain to make a visit to the archives of both countries a necessity. Research for those of you of Czech descent will certainly be the easiest, but research in the border area will be complicated by both sides. This does not apply to church records or census returns, which were fairly easy to divide.

An additional complication for Czech ancestors will be the attitude of the National Archives of the Czech Republic in Prague. You will find a long delay if you write in English and almost as long a delay if you write in Czech. The authorities may well reply to you in Czech whether you write to them in English or Slovak. They also quite obviously prefer you to leave matters in their hands rather than visit the country to do your own research, and even if you wish to do this you will be hedged around with many restrictions.

I do not know why this should be so, but I suspect they need the money, are understaffed, and still have a hang-over from the days of Communism, where non-cooperation was official policy. The National Archivist in Prague will issue detailed instructions as to how you should apply, the minimum you must be prepared to pay, and the length of time you must be prepared to wait. All very necessary, no doubt, but very cold and impersonal. The same remarks apply if you wish to do your own research by mail or personal visit. A far cry from countries like Denmark, Italy, or even Slovakia.

National Archives (Archivní Správa)
Milady Horákové 133, 16621 Prague
Phone: 011-420-2-321173. Fax: 011-420-2-3121049
E-mail: arch@mvcr.cz

The instructions of the Archives—which I have abbreviated—state that research of civil registers of birth, marriage, and death will be restricted to the period before 1900. (This is not explained, but I assume it is intended to preserve the privacy of individuals since that date.) You should enclose photocopies of any documents you already have that may assist the archivists to obtain the information you require. The results of the search will be sent to Archivex Praha, PO Box 38, 18200 Prague (Phone or Fax: 011-420-2-6890970). Search charges will be based on time employed at $10 to $14 US an hour, plus an administrative fee of $8. A charge will also be made for documents reproduced (photocopies). You will be billed by Archivex, and when you have paid, the documents will be sent to you. You may pay by International Money Order, a check payable to Praha, or cash in US dollars.

If you wish to make personal search in the Czech Archives, or regional archives in Brno, Litoměřice, Opava, Plzen, and Zamrsk, you must apply for permission to the Archives above. Application to visit other archives (municipal, etc.) may be addressed directly to the archive concerned. No admission charges will be made at the present time.

The district archives for each of the seven districts (oblasti) listed earlier in this chapter are known at Státní Oblastní Archívy. They contain all documents connected with the history and administration of a district and are the most valuable from an ancestor-hunter's point of view.

In addition there are county archives (Okresní Archívy) and municipal archives (Městské Archívy). The latter exist in all cities, towns, and large villages.

The three administrative districts that now constitute Slovakia are listed below, together with the name of the chief administrative city in each district:

Západoslovenský (Bratislava)
Středoslovenský (Bánská Bystrica)
Východoslovenský (Košice)

The three districts listed above each contain the following counties:

ZÁPADOSLOVENSKÝ: Bratislava-Mesto, Bratislava-Venkov, Duhajská Streda, Galanta, Komárno, Levice, Nitra, Nové Zámky, Senica, Topol'čany, Trenčin, Trnava.

STŘEDSLOVENSKÝ: Bánská Bystrica, Čadca, Dolní Kubín, Liptovský Mikulaš, Lučenec, Martin, Považská Bystrica, Prievidza, Rimavská Sobota, Stara, Ždiar nad Hronom, Žilina, Zvolen.

VÝCHODOSLOVENSKÝ: Bardéjov, Humenné, Košice, Michalovce, Poprad, Prešov, Rožňava, Spišská Nová Ves, Trebišov.

Civil Registration

This began in 1918 but was only compulsory for those people not belonging to a church. Church members, both Catholic and Protestant, registered all vital events with their priest or minister as they had always done. In 1950 all registers were taken over by the state. A copy of a certificate will be issued for a small fee by the National Committee (Místní Národní Výbar) in the place where the event occurred.

Before 1869 only the church registers recorded baptisms, marriages, and burials. In some registers you may find that dates of birth and death are recorded, but don't count on it!

In 1869 some priests refused to marry people who were not Catholic. For this and other reasons, the recording of vital events was taken over by local municipal officials. The churches still had the right to keep records, but only official registration was accepted as legal proof that the event had occurred. These records are also held by the National Committee mentioned above.

In 1920 a law was passed authorizing central civil registration records. Births and deaths had to be reported to the Central Statistics Office and consisted of doctors' reports on baptisms and burials, and details of marriages and divorces received from the civil authorities.

Birth records will give the name, date and place of birth, full names of parents, occupations, ages, names of their parents, witnesses and/or godparents, and their relationship to the child.

Marriage records include date and place, full names of bride and groom, their ages and place of birth, occupations, and full names of all parents and their addresses.

Death records give date and place, full name, age at death, and name of surviving spouse and parents (whether living or dead).

These civil registers are kept in the offices of the local municipality, and there is no central index, or even a local one.

Census Returns (Sčitání Lidu)

Censuses in the Czech provinces have been held intermittently since the seventeenth century, but many returns were destroyed after the heads had been counted. Many were used as a basis for conscription and only males were recorded. In any case, the government does not at present make them available for genealogical research. I hope this policy will change, since the census records are almost as valuable for an ancestor-hunter as the church registers. The argument is used that since the matriky records are so complete there is no need to make census records available. I question this, but we have to accept the policy as it now stands.

The 1651 Census of Population for Bohemia (Soupis Obyvatelstva v Čechách, 1651) has survived for many villages and towns. The object was to check the number of Catholics, and so the religion is noted, as are numerous personal details of all family members. No indexes are available, but you should check with the nearest embassy or the district archives in the county to find out if the census is available for your ancestral village.

In case circumstances change in the future, I will describe in very general terms what may one day be available. In Bohemia censuses have been held at intervals ever since the 1651 census mentioned above, and the surviving documents can be found in the National Archives in Prague (Archivní Správa, Milady Horákové 133, 16621 Prague). The last one taken under Austrian rule was in 1910, and the first since independence was in 1921. Since then they have been held every ten years.

If you know where an ancestor was living in a particular year, and can send evidence of your descent from that person, it is worth taking a chance and writing to one of the above addresses. Maybe you will be lucky! The 1869 census has been microfilmed by the LDS Church and is available through your nearest Family History Center.

The information in the more recent censuses includes name, sex, relationships, age, place and date of birth, religion, occupation, name of employer, and length of residence in that place. However, you cannot search the census returns in person but must apply to the state archives for the information you need.

Wills (Poslední Vůle)

These date back to the fourteenth century but are limited in value, since only people with substantial wealth or property needed to make a will. They are lodged with the State Notary (Státní Notářství) in the nearest main city or town, and are then transferred to the district archives. Application for any information from them must be made through the Archívní Správa in Prague. Be sure to include proof of your descent. Wills were originally kept in the office of the notary concerned, but were all passed to the archives in 1949.

Tax Lists (Berní Ruly)

These date to about 1654, and many have been published for various villages by the archives, and many more are in preparation. Here again you must consult with the state archives in Prague.

Land Records (Pozemkové Knihy)

These date back to the 1500s and are one of the best sources of information if you are descended from someone who owned land. They are in the district archives but only available to you through governmental search at a fee.

Military Records (Vojenské Zaznamy)

Many have been lost but a few date back to 1630. The records of Czechs conscripted into the armed forces in the days of the Empire were transferred from the Military Archives in Vienna when the new country was born. They are in several different places, and you should check with the Archívní Správa in Prague. So far as recent military records are concerned, these are not available for you to search, although the archives may do so for you.

The Calendar

Before searching records, do not forget the changes in the calendar. The original Julian Calendar was introduced by Julius Caesar in 325 and divided the year into 365 days, plus an extra day every fourth year. However, astronomers later calculated that this system meant that the calendar year exceeded the solar year by eleven minutes. By 1582 there was a difference of eleven days. Since this had an effect on the calculations for Easter, Pope Gregory XIII ordained that ten days be dropped from the calendar. He also changed the beginning of the year from March 25 to January 1. The new calendar became known, of course, as the Gregorian Calendar. Catholic churches observed the change almost immediately; Protestant ones were slower to follow. In Bohemia the year started on 6 January 1584, in Moravia on 4 October 1584, and in Silesia on 12 January 1584.

Other Records

In the district archives you will find records of the ancient craft guilds, particularly from Prague and other major cities; early newspapers and directories; passport records (mainly internal); and many records of the noble estates, which contain lists of tenants and employees.

Newspapers can be particularly important. Obituaries were a great feature (very often paid advertisements, which went to great lengths to eulogize the late departed). You should check for the existence of newspapers with the district archives for your area.

Emigration

No lists have survived, except in a few unrelated places, but don't forget that most Czechs emigrated overseas through the German ports of Hamburg and Bremen. Although the latter records were destroyed during the Second World War, the Hamburg records exist for the period 1850 to 1934 (except for the early part of 1853 and the years 1915 to 1919). You will find many more details about these records in the chapter on Germany.

Finally, remember it is essential you know the place in the Czech Republic from which your family came. Dig deep into your family memories and papers. Then you have three ways to go: use the facilities and records of the LDS Church so far as they go; do your research through the state archives in Prague; or go to the country and do it yourself. Personally, I would try the first one, then the second, and, finally, the third. By then you may have enough preliminary information to make your journey really pay off.

The German genealogical society concerned with researching ethnic Germans in the former Czechoslovakia is: Vereinigung sudetendeutscher Familienforscher (VSFF), Juttastrasse 20, 90480 Nürnberg, Germany. All letters should be in German or clear non-idiomatic English, and three International Reply Coupons must be enclosed.

If your ancestors were Germans you should bear in mind that although they were mainly in the northern and western areas of the country, there were also many German enclaves in other purely Slavic areas. They were mainly Catholic, but many registers were destroyed in World War II. There are some duplicates for 1780 to 1820 for western Bohemia in the custody of the Bishop of Regensburg, Germany (see page 120).

DENMARK

Denmark is now a peaceful country but once upon a time the Danes were feared from Ireland to Russia and south to the Mediterranean. With their neighbors the Norwegians and the Swedes they formed the brave, warlike race known as the Vikings. From 1018 to 1035 Denmark, England, and Norway were united under King Canute (Knut). The south part of Sweden was part of Denmark (with some interruptions) until 1658, as was Iceland until 1944. Today Greenland and the Faeroe Islands are part of Denmark, but have local autonomy. In 1397 Denmark, Norway, and Sweden were united under the Danish Crown. The union was dissolved in 1523, but Denmark's union with Norway lasted until 1814. In that year Denmark lost Norway to Sweden.

In 1848 Denmark, with some disregard for reality, started a war with her larger and much more powerful neighbor, Prussia, over the status of the two duchies of Schleswig and Holstein. These two areas were ruled by the Danish kings on a personal basis, and were not an integral part of the kingdom itself. Since the majority of the inhabitants were German-speaking, Prussia kept an eye on their interests. Denmark won this war and included the duchies in her territory. A long period of confusion followed. In 1852 Denmark agreed that the status of the duchies should, after all, remain as in 1847; in 1855 Denmark reincorporated them; in 1858, under pressure, she canceled this; in 1863 they were incorporated once again; in 1864 Prussia and Austria declared war on Denmark, and won. Schleswig went to Prussia and Holstein to Austria. In 1867 these two countries fought over the spoils and Austria lost. Both the duchies were then included in Prussia.

If all this is confusing to you, you are not alone. The British Foreign Secretary at that time said, "Only three people understand the Schleswig-Holstein question: Prince Albert, who is dead; a professor who is now insane; and myself, and I have forgotten."

After the First World War Denmark regained north Schleswig after a plebiscite in 1920. Some 23,000 German-speaking people still remain in that area (which is now South Jutland, or Sønderjylland). Roughly speaking, the present frontier between Denmark and Germany is a horizontal line across the Jutland Peninsula just north of the city of Flensburg, in Germany. Records for the part of Schleswig that remained German after the 1920 plebiscite are in the custody of the Landesarchiv Schleswig-Holstein (Prinzenpalais, 24837 Schleswig, Germany; Phone: 011-49-4621861800; Fax: 011-49-4621861801; E-mail: LASH-SL@t-online.de; Web site: www.schleswig-holstein.de/archive/lash/index.html). An exception is the census records of the area, which are still in the Danish National Archives (Rigsarkivet). See below for address.

You should also know that in 1970 the number of counties in Denmark was reduced and many changed their names. The original counties were Aabenraa-Sønderborg, Aalborg, Aarhus, Assens, Bornholm, Frederiksborg, Haderslev, Hjørring, Holbaek, København s, Maribo, Odense, Praestø, Randers, Ribe, Ringkøbing, Roskilde, Skanderborg, Sorø, Svendborg, Thisted, Tønder, Vejle, and Viborg.

The new counties are Aarhus, Bornholm, Frederiksborg, Fyn, Københavns, Nordjylland, Ribe, Ringkøbing, Roskilde, Sønderjylland, Storstrøm, Vejle, Viborg, and Vestsjaelland.

It may be useful to you to know the areas covered by the counties before that date. The mainland of Jylland included the counties of Hjørring, Thisted, Aalborg, Ringkøbing, Randers, Viborg, Skanderborg, Aarhus, Ribe, Vejle, Haderslev, Tønder, and Aabenraa-Sønderborg.

The island of Fyn had two counties—Odense and Svendborg. The islands of Sjaelland and Møen included the counties of Frederiksborg, Holbaek, Københavns, Sorø, and Praestø. The two islands of Lolland and Falster formed the county of Maribo. The island of Bornholm formed a county of the same name.

Possible Problems

If you are researching by use of printed material—books, Internet, fax, or correspondence by mail, you will probably not be troubled by the fact that up to the later years of the nineteenth century handwriting in Denmark was in what is known as Gothic or Danish script. All official documents used this method. This applies particularly to entries in church registers (births, marriages, and deaths or burials) and to census returns and wills.

The other problem—for which you must be prepared—is the fact that the majority of the population (outside of the few large cities) did not have a family name before the middle 1880s; in other words, patronymics were used, so that the letters *sen* were added to the father's name for use by sons, and *dotter* added for daughters.

Archives

The National Archives (Rigsarkivet) are at Rigsdagsgården 9, 1218 Copenhagen K (Phone: 011-45-33922341; Fax: 011-45-33153239; Web site: www.sa.dk/ra). In addition to the censuses mentioned above, they hold records of administration and government, but generally, you will find your major sources of genealogical information in the four provincial archives. These are known as Landsarki*ver*. The individual archives are known as Landsarki*vet* and are in the following locations:

Landsarkivet for Sjælland, Lolland-Falster og Bornholm
Jagtvej 10, 2200 Copenhagen N
Phone: 011-45-31393520. Fax: 011-45-35390535
Web site: www.sa.dk/lak

Landsarkivet for Fyn
Jernbanegade 36, 5000 Odense C
Phone: 011-45-66125885. Fax: 011-45-66147071
Web site: www.sa.dk/lao

Landarkivet for Nørrejylland
Lille Skt. Hansgade 5, 8800 Viborg
Phone: 011-45-86621788. Fax: 011-45-86601006
E-mail: mailbox@lav.sa.dk
Web site: www.sa.dk/lav

Landsarkivet for Sønderjylland
Haderslevvej 45, 6200 Åbenrå
Phone: 011-45-74625858. Fax: 011-45-74623288
E-mail: mailbox@laa.sa.dk
(This archive has North Schleswig records and also copies of census returns for Holstein.)

Of course, you will want to know which particular state archive covers the area from which your ancestors emigrated. If you do not already have a map of Denmark, or cannot find one in a local library, I suggest you (a) write to your nearest Danish embassy or consulate or (b) write to the National Archives mentioned above. By all means write in English. It is a generality to say all Danes speak English, but certainly English is a required language in the schools. You will find Danes are extremely helpful and patient in dealing with your queries.

Civil Registration

This does not exist in the form that applies to most other European countries. The Lutheran Church (which is the official state church) is responsible for the registration of vital events, as births, marriages, and deaths are called, and so it is in the church registers and other ecclesiastical records that you will be searching for your ancestors.

However, there are certain civil records that exist outside of the churches:

1. The civil registration of births, marriages, and deaths for the counties of Aabenraa-Sønderborg, Haderslev, and Tønder exist from 1876 and are located in the state archives (Landsarkivet) at Aabenraa.

2. Death certificates up to 1913 are in the state archives, and from 1914 are in the National Archives.

3. Some civil marriages were recorded from 1851 and these can be found in state or city archives.

4. Records of marriage licenses for the city of Copenhagen only (1735–1868) are in the city archives (Byarkiverne) in Copenhagen. They are called Kopulations-protokoller.

Church Records

Before we examine church records in any detail, there are several things to be said. A major problem in ancestor-hunting in Denmark is the duplication of personal names and place-names. It is essential that you find out all you can about the location from which your emigrant ancestor departed for his or her new country. There are some emigration records available and we will talk about them later, but the multiplication of place-names is the major problem. In fact, there are problems within problems, because you must also consider farm names as well. In addition, you must be concerned with patronymics, which is a surname taken from the given name of the father; the system was widespread in Denmark up to the closing years of the last century.

So, if all you know is that your ancestor Jens Nielsen came from a place named Skovlund in Denmark, you have a problem. Nielsen is an extremely common name and there are 114 places in Denmark named Skovlund.

However, even if you do have this problem, there is an excellent organization in Denmark that will help you solve it. I will tell you more about this later, but in the meantime let us assume you know the exact location of your ancestors in Denmark and want to know what you can find out in the church records.

Registers (Kirkebøger)

Although the state church is Lutheran, there are other church registers available. The *recognized* non-Lutheran churches were the Roman Catholic Church (Romersk Katolske Kirke); the Reformed Churches (Reformerte Menigheder); the Episcopal Methodist Church (Biskoppelige-Metodistiske Trossamfund); and the Jewish Communities (Mosaiske Trossamfund). These recognized churches were permitted to record vital events in their own registers. Any other religion or sect was not recognized and the members of those churches were compelled to register their family events in the registers of the Lutheran Church. No other religious organizations were recognized until early in this century.

In 1645 a law was passed requiring the Lutheran ministers on the island of Sjaelland to record all births, marriages, and deaths in their parishes. Some ministers had begun keeping such records even earlier. As a matter of fact, some seventy-five parishes have entries pre-dating 1645. In many cases the ministers did not conform exactly with the civil law, preferring to record baptisms rather than births, and burials rather than deaths.

Many of the earlier registers have been lost to fire, damp, and rats; many are beautifully written, others almost impossible to decipher. Before 1814 many ministers recorded the events as they occurred in chronological order; others kept separate sections in the registers for the different events. In addition, the sexes were not separated, After 1814 there were separate lists of male and female christenings, confirmations, and burials.

All the church registers of all denominations up to 1891 are located in the state archives (Landsarkivet) covering the particular district. Since 1891 a copy of the parish register has been sent to the state archives thirty years after it has been completed. Generally speaking, registers or copies of registers up to 1925 are now in the archives.

So far as birth or baptism is concerned, the entry lists the name of the child, the date of birth and/or baptism, the names of the parents (the mother's name is often left out or she is identified by her maiden name), and the names of witnesses and their relation to the child. The baptism took place within a few days of the birth, usually on a Sunday.

Before 1814 the marriage register often recorded only the names of the bride and groom and the date. After 1814 the registers give the date and place of birth of each, details of any previous marriages, and names of witnesses.

Most death or burial records give name, address, date, and age. After 1814 the cause of death is usually included.

Betrothal (Trolovelse)

These are the equivalent of the banns of other churches. Not all the ministers recorded them, but it is worth checking for them because quite often they give more information than the marriage register.

Confirmation (Konfirmation)

In 1736 a law was passed requiring that every child be confirmed at the age of fourteen. Most parishes recorded all confirmations from that year on but often listed only the name and age of the child. After 1814 it was customary to list the names of the parents.

Introduction (Introduktion)

After each child was born, the mother was regarded as "unclean." After a period of several weeks she was regarded as cleansed and the minister then introduced her to the congregation and she was able to take her place in church again. After 1814 the date of the woman's "introduction" was usually included in the birth or baptism records.

Communion (Kommunion)

These records date back to 1645 in many places and usually include name and address.

Absolution

These records started in the mid-1600s and were discontinued in 1767. They give the name of the person absolved for transgression and, often, details of the transgression.

Vaccination

Strangely enough, these records were also regarded as a matter of church business. They started in 1800, and though the records are still kept, they are now found included in the confirmation or marriage records. They give the child's name and address, and the name of the doctor.

Lutheran Parish Register Extracts (Kirkebogsuddrag)

These cover some two hundred years between the seventeenth and nineteenth centuries. The entry is identical with that in the parish register but is usually confined to prominent or noble families. If you find that a particular parish register has been lost or destroyed, and if you think the above description fits your own family, it will be worthwhile to check the extracts.

Arrival Lists (Tilgangslister)

From 1814 to 1875 the minister was required to record arrivals and departures from the parish. He noted the name of the person concerned, his or her age and address within the parish, and the name of the parish from which he or she came. I should mention that the law was never enforced in cities but only in rural areas.

Removal Lists (Afgangslister)

The details in the previous paragraph apply here, except that the parish to which a person was moving was listed, instead of the one from which he or she had arrived.

General Schematic Register (Almindeligt Jevnførelse Schema)

These registers were started in each parish in 1814. Although intended to be a register of every person recorded in the church records, with reference to the page of the book in which the original entry was listed, many of these registers were never kept, and many are incomplete. However, they are in the state archives and you may just find some vital fact not recorded elsewhere.

So much for all the church records in Denmark. My own reaction to this formidable list is that a conscientious minister would have to make a choice between his records and his parishioners. I really can't see how he could possibly look after both!

There are, of course, a number of other available records, many of which will be essential to you:

Police Census (Politiets Mandtalslister)

This covers the period from 1869 to 1923 and lists the names of residents of Copenhagen and their children over ten, with place of birth, occupation, and address. The records from 1869 to 1900 are in the city archives, and those from 1901 to 1923 in the Statistical Office, Copenhagen.

Censuses (Folketaellinger)

These have been held from as early as 1787 and the returns from all of them are in the custody of the National Archives (Rigsarkivet, Rigsdagsgården 9, 1218 Copenhagen K). The questions asked by the census-takers varied greatly over the years. The returns available for search are 1787, 1801, 1834, 1840, 1845, 1850, 1860, 1870, 1880, 1890, 1901, 1911, 1921, 1925, 1930, 1949 (those for 1921 onwards require special permission). There are also many local censuses that were taken in various years and for these you should check with the municipal archives for the particular place in which you are interested. Check with the LDS Church for microfilm copies. Census lists from 1787 to 1916 can be accessed online at **ddd.sa.dk/kiplink_en.htm.**

Emigration (Udvandrings-journaler)

These records were kept from 1868 to 1959 and are in the Landsarkivet for Sjaelland. The Danish Emigration Archives maintains a computerized database of emigrants from 1869 to 1904 (see page 86 for details).

Passport Records (Pasprotokoller)

These are to be found in the various Landsarkiver for the period 1780–1920.

Marriage Licenses (Kopulations-protokoller)

These are for the city of Copenhagen only for 1720–1868 and are in the city archives (Rådhuset, Rådhuspladsen, 1550 Copenhagen V).

Army Service (Stambøger)

The military records are in the Haerens Arkiv, Copenhagen. There are lists of officers and men serving in the army from the mid-1700s to the present date (some muster-rolls dating back to 1693), and also lists of men liable for service in the local units of the militia. These Military Levy Rolls (Laegsdsruller) are on a parish basis and date from 1789. There are similar records for the navy from 1802 and these are in the National Archives.

Deeds and Mortgages (Skøde og Panteprotokoller)

These date from 1580 and contain names and addresses of the contracting parties and descriptions of the property involved. They are in the state archives and also in the nearest municipal archives.

Trade Guilds (Lavsprotokoller)

In Denmark, as in most European countries, the trade guilds were powerful organizations very similar to present-day trade unions except that they were concerned with skilled crafts rather than with general industry. The records date from 1527 and give personal details of all applying for membership including place of birth, age, and names of parents. The guilds were usually established only in principal cities unless a small town was the center of a major craft. The records are in several locations, but the National Archives will help you locate the records for a specific guild in a particular place. You will find them in state and city archives, in museums, and in some cases, still in the possession of a guild.

Servants (Tyendeprotokoller)

These records were kept from 1828 to 1923 and are in the state archives. They give the names of domestic employees, dates and places of birth or baptism, and changes of address.

Trade Licenses (Rådstue og borgerskabs protokoller)

These are to be found in city archives and date from 1596. They should not be confused with guild records. They are, in effect, a license to operate a business in a particular municipality. They give the usual personal details of name, address, occupation, and place and date of birth.

Schools (Skoleprotokoller)

These records are either in the state archives or in the original schools. They go back to 1584 and list pupils, matriculations, endowments and scholarships, and the probate records of the teaching staff.

Probate Records (Skifteprotokoller)

These records go back to the fourteenth century in a few cases, but in general they start in the second half of the sixteenth century. They are located in the state archives, with more recent records in the custody of the local courts. Details are given of the deceased, family members, and the inventory and disposition of his or her property.

Court Records (Tingbøger eller retsprotokoller)

These records are in the National Archives and state archives and can often be of great value, since they are concerned not only with crime, but with real estate transfers, marriage settlements, mortgages, and guardianship applications.

You will find that the various archives will usually undertake a quick search (i.e., when you can supply exact date, name, and place) without charge. However, a fee will be charged for anything more general. The archive may undertake the work itself, or may refer you to a list of approved researchers.

Genealogical Organizations

There is one major genealogical organization in Denmark, with twenty-one local branches. One of them may well be in the particular area in which you are interested, but as addresses change often I suggest you write to the parent organization for guidance (remember the three IRCs for return postage): Samfundet for Dansk Genealogi og Personalhistorie (Society for Danish Genealogy and Personal History), Grysgaardsvej 2, 2400 Copenhagen NV; Web site: www.genealogi.dk.

The Emigration Archives (Det danske Udvandrerarkiv)

This is not a genealogical organization, but the greatest source of help! In the first edition of this book in 1985, I referred to a small collection of books and documents about emigration from Denmark as follows: "It has the potential to become a major source of assistance to people of Danish descent tracing their ancestors." How far-seeing I was! Let me tell you about this magnificent organization—Det danske Udvandrerarkiv (The Danish Emigration Archives).

Det danske Udvandrerarkiv
Arkivstraede 1, PO Box 1731, 9100 Aalborg, Denmark.
Phone: 011-45-99314220. Fax: 011-45-98102248
E-mail: bfl-kultur@aalborg.dk
Web site: www.emiarch.dk/home.php3

The official Danish Emigration Records from 1868–1940 are on micro-fiche. The Archives have also produced a CD-ROM with records listed by the Copenhagen Police 1869–1904. This contains about 350,000 records and includes a free text-searching facility, which will enable you to search all the listings made by the Copenhagen police. You can buy it by sending a $40 US check together with your name and address to the address above.

The Danish Emigration Archives was established to record the history of Danes who emigrated. They have published a number of booklets to assist ancestor-hunters and also possess a large collection of books, letters from emigrants, photographs, biographies, and diaries. They also provide access to official records containing information about emigrants' place of origin and their planned destination.

No other country in Europe has such complete records, and all honor is due to the men and women—officials and volunteers—who labored so long and hard to unearth these genealogical treasures and make them available.

The records are in date order, and a computerized database from 1869 to 1904 is available on the Internet. They are currently working on including the years up to 1940.

For a search in the emigration records, the Archives charges a fee of $40 US. No extended search will be undertaken, but you will be referred to other archives or genealogical organizations. In addition, special books have been written about emigration to the United States, Canada, Australia, and New Zealand, and these may be purchased from the Archives.

Other Records

There are a number of Danish records that may be vital to you, depending on your personal background, but due to space limitations they cannot be included.

Military records in the National Archives; records of wills in the provincial archives; the Danish records in the collections of church records (of all religions) in the Family History Library of the LDS Church in Salt Lake City—and, of course, available to you in your nearest Family History Center—and, finally, local history archives all across Denmark (usually found in local public libraries) are among the resources available.

ESTONIA

The Estonians, who are ethnically close to the Finns, were conquered in 1219 by the Danes and a German military order named the Livonian Brothers of the Sword, or the Livonian Knights. The Danes took the northern part of Estonia and the Knights the southern part. In 1346 the Danes sold their share to the Knights, under whose control Estonia remained until 1561, when the northern part was taken by Sweden and the southern by Poland. In 1629, after a war between the two countries, Sweden took control of the whole country. In 1710 Russia seized control of Estonia and Livonia.

Estonia declared its independence in 1918 but under the German-Soviet Pact of 1939 all three Baltic states, including Estonia, were absorbed by the Soviet Union. In 1991 Estonia declared its independence once again.

Archives

Until 1999 there were two national archives—one in Tallinn, the capital, and the other in Tartu. Although one was supposed to contain pre-1918 records and the other later material, the rules were not always followed, and there was a certain amount of confusion. However, a new system went into effect on January 1, 1999.

The new system was explained to me by the national archivist. "The former Historical Archives and the State Archives are united and now form a new institution—the Estonian National Archives (Eesti Rahvusarhiv), with the center in Tartu. At the same time, materials are stored as before— the records up to 1918 are in Tartu, and those from 1918 to the present day in Tallinn."

The addresses are:

National Archives of Estonia, J. Liivi 4, 50409 Tartu (Phone: 011-372-7-422-336. Fax: 011-372-7-421-482).

National Archives of Estonia, Maneeżi 4, 15019 Tallinn (Phone: 011-372-441-118).

Civil Registration

The records of births, marriages, and deaths up to 1926 are in the State Registry Office (Lossi plats la, 15163 Tallinn). Records since that year are in local municipal offices.

Church Registers

Registers up to 1926 are in the State Registry Office mentioned above, but there are also copies in the National Archives in Tartu (see above) and the City Archives (Tolli 4, 200001 Tallinn). There are also copies in many of the churches.

The addresses of the headquarters of the various churches are:

CATHOLIC:	Rev. Rein Òunapuu
	Vene 18, 200001 Tallinn
ORTHODOX:	Rev. Kornilius
	Pikk 64-4, 200001 Tallinn
LUTHERAN:	Archbishop K Oajula
	Kiribu 8, 200001 Tallinn
BAPTIST:	Presbyter U. Meriloo
	Pargi 9, 200016 Tallinn
ADVENTIST:	Rev. R Kalmusm
	Nere pst 3, 200001 Tallinn
METHODIST:	Rev. O Pärnamets
	Apteegi 3, 200001 Tallinn

Ancestor-hunters of Estonian descent are welcome to visit the archives and do their own research. At present, there is no charge for this. Written applications for information will be answered—provided that return postage is covered by three International Reply Coupons. A fee will be charged for a search—the amount will depend on the type of inquiry.

People of Jewish descent will find records for the period 1918–1946 in the State Archives in Tallinn. More information can be obtained from the Jewish Cultural Society (P.O. Box 2385, 200036 Tallinn).

FINLAND

The capital city of Finland is Helsinki (or Helsingfors, in Swedish). Both Finnish and Swedish are official languages of the country, even though only eight percent of the people are Swedish-speaking. The main Swedish areas are in the west and in the south. Until 1809 Finland was part of Sweden. In that year it was annexed by Russia and ruled by the Czar in his capacity as Grand Duke of Finland. It declared its independence in 1917 at the time of the Russian Revolution. In 1939 Finland was attacked by the USSR and quickly subdued. By the treaty of Moscow (1940) Finland ceded part of the Karelian Isthmus (including Vyborg), and an area on Lake Ladoga. In addition, the USSR was granted a thirty-year lease of the port of Hango.

When Germany attacked the Soviet Union in 1941, Finland allied itself with Germany in the hope of regaining the lost territories. It was forced to sign an armistice with the USSR in 1944, and the terms confirmed the cession of territory in 1940, except that in place of the lease of Hango the USSR was given a fifty-year lease of the Porkkala Peninsula, near Helsinki. In the 1947 Peace Treaty, which followed, Finland also ceded Pechenga (Petsamo) in the far north of the country, and also some additional border districts in the east. About half a million Finns left the ceded areas and were resettled in Finland. In 1956, after some years of tactful relations with the USSR, Porkkala was returned to Finland. Over 90 percent of the population is either Lutheran or Greek Orthodox.

The country is divided into twelve provinces. These are listed below with the name of each provincial capital in parentheses: Uudenmaan Lääni (Helsinki), Turun JA Porin Lääni (Turku), Hämeen Lääni (Hämeenlinna), Ahvenanmaan Lääni (Mariehamn), Kymen Lääni (Kouvola), Mikkelin Lääni (Mikkeli), Kuopion Lääni (Kuopio), Pohjois-Karjalan Lääni (Joensuu), Keski-Suomen Lääni (Jyväskylä), Oulun Lääni (Oulu), Lapin Lääni (Rovaniemi), Vaasan Lääni (Vaasa). A number of these provinces have their own archives. The National Archives (Kansallisarkisto) are located in Helsinki (Rauhankatu 17, 00170 Helsinki; Phone: 011-358-09-228521; Fax: 011-358-09-176-302; Web site: www.narc.fi).

Provincial archives are located at the following addresses:

Hämeenlinnan maakunta-arkisto
Arvi Kariston katu 2A
13100 Hämeenlinna
Phone: 011-358-3-656-460. Fax: 011-358-13-251-4606
E-mail: hameenlinna@narc.fi

Joensuun maakunta-arkisto
Yliopistokatu 2
PL 146
88101 Joensuu
Phone: 011-358-13-251-4602; Fax: 011-358-13-251-4606
E-mail: joensuu@narc.fi
(There is a possibility that the archives of the Lost Provinces will be transferred here from the archives at Mikkeli [address below].)

Jyväskylän maakunta-arkisto
Pitkäkatu 23
40700 Jyväskyla
Phone: 011-358-14-338-1000. Fax: 011-358-14-338-1049
E-mail: jyvaskyla@narc.fi

Mikkelin maakunta-arkisto
PL 2
50101 Mikkeli
Phone: 011-358-15-321-310. Fax: 011-358-15-321-3157
E-mail: mikkeli@narc.fi

Oulun maakunta-arkisto
PL 31
90101 Oulu
Phone: 011-358-8-514-5800. Fax: 011-358-8-514-5850
E-mail: oulu@narc.fi

Turun maakunta-arkisto
PL 383
20101 Turku
Phone: 011-358-2-2760-818. Fax: 011-358-2-2760-810
E-mail: turku@narc.fi

Vaasan maakunta-arkisto
PL 240
65101 Vaasa
Phone: 011-358-6-317-3912. Fax: 011-358-6-312-0392
E-mail: vaasa@narc.fi

Church Registers

Although it should not be necessary to write for information in any language but English (the Finns are excellent linguists), I think I should give the Finnish and Swedish descriptions that you may need to make certain your request is clearly understood:

English	Finnish	Swedish
Catholic Records	Katolisen Kirkon Luettelot	Katolska Kyrkans Böcker
Lutheran Registers	Luterilaisen Kirkon Historialliset Aikakirjat	Historieböcker
Greek Orthodox	Kreikkalaiskatolisen Kirkon Luettelot	Grekisk-Katolska Kyrkans Böcker
Lutheran Main Books	Luterilaisen Kirkon Pääkirjat	Kommunion-Eller Huvudböcker

The Lutheran church registers date back to 1648 in some cases, the Greek Orthodox to about 1779, and the Catholic to 1800. There are over 500 parishes in Finland, and over 300 have now transferred their records to the National Archives and provincial archives. The more recent registers from 1860 onward are still in the original churches (an exception to this is that the registers from the areas ceded to the USSR are all in special archives; more about these later). I have not listed all the parish registers now in the archives because the list would be out of date very quickly. The transfers are being speeded up and should be completed within a year or so. This transfer of registers applies to all religions.

The inclusion of civil registration in the church records (Pääkirjat, or Main Books) began between 1650 and 1700 depending on the decision of the church authorities in different parts of the country. The records are fairly complete from 1700 and are on microfilm in the National Archives. Entries since then are normally closed to public search, but special exceptions can be made if there is a valid reason (including genealogical research or evidence for inheritance), and application should be made to the National Archives (address on page 90). Microfilming has now been completed up to 1900.

Lutheran Church Registers

These contain the following information:

BIRTHS: Names, dates of birth and baptism, parentage, occupations of parents, names of witnesses at baptism, places of residence.

MARRIAGES: Names, ages, dates of banns and marriage, addresses, and sometimes, names of parents.

DEATHS: Names, ages, cause of death, occupations, dates of death and burial, and place of death.

MISCELLANEOUS: Church accounts, minutes of meetings, and details of absolutions and misdemeanors.

There are also transcripts of the entries that contain the above information, with some variations, and these are also in the National Archives on microfilm, with copies in the possession of the Genealogical Society of Finland (Liisankatu 16 A, 00170 Helsinki; Phone: 011-358-9-278-1188; Fax: 011-358-9-278-1199; E-mail: samfundet@genealogia.fi; Web site: www.genealogia.fi). The Genealogical Society also has an online database with lists of christenings, marriages, burials, and moves, as well as online information about all parishes in Finland.

Lutheran Membership Movements (Luterilaisen kirkon muuttaneiden luettelot)

These give names of persons arriving in the parish or leaving it, with previous or future locations, marital status, and sometimes, date and place of birth. They date from about 1800 to the present and are in the local church. There are a few of these records that go back to the early eighteenth century. There are also Certificates of Movement (Muuttokirjat), which give similar information but often in greater detail and dating from 1800. They are also in church custody and also on microfilm in various provincial archives.

Lutheran Pre-Confirmations (Luterilaisen kirkon luettelot lapsista)

Some of these lists start as early as 1696 and give details of children eligible for confirmation with full personal details of age, address, and parentage.

Tombstone Inscriptions (Hautakivien muistokirjoitukset)

These have been recorded from the early eighteenth century and the records are in local churches and cemeteries, and also in the custody of the Genealogical Society of Finland.

Lutheran Main Books (Luterilaisen kirkon pääkirjat)

These are probably the most important and comprehensive records you will find in your ancestor-hunting in Finland. They are also known as Population Registers and contain a tremendous amount of information about each parish. They started in about 1667, but were not widespread until 1700. Details are given of the whole population of a parish, grouped by families, including not only family members, but servants, lodgers, and estate workers, with every personal record you can possibly imagine.

You will find dates of all vital events, changes of address, origins and later destinations, standards of religious knowledge, relationships with other families, legitimacy of children—the list is endless. It certainly suggests that Big Brother was watching—or at least the Lutheran minister was, or is, because the records continue right up to the present! From a genealogical point of view the system is terrific. The records are in local church custody with microfilm copies in the various archives. Here, again, access to recent information is restricted, but special permission may be granted for you to obtain some information, provided that you prove descent.

The Greek Orthodox Church was also permitted to maintain Main Books from 1779, but some are available from earlier dates. The oldest ones are in the archives in Kuopio and Mikkeli, but most are still in church custody.

Greek Orthodox Church Registers

The registers for birth, marriage, and death give names, parentage, address, occupations, ages, dates, and godparents and witnesses. Copies are also in the provincial archives at Mikkeli.

Catholic Registers

These give the same information as above.

Church Organizations

The following addresses are not the headquarters of the various religions but of the biggest bishoprics, which are more likely to answer your queries:

Evangelical Lutheran: PL 60, 20501 Turku
Greek Orthodox: Unioninkatu 39 A 18

Civil Registration

Records under this heading, as we know them in this country, only started in 1922 and registration is only required from non-members of the Evangelical-Lutheran Church. Each community keeps its own register, which is located in the municipal offices.

Head-Tax Registers

This tax was first imposed in 1634, and was abolished in 1924. Until 1652 the records of taxes paid were kept by the ministers of the church, and from then until 1779 by state list writers. Up until that date only males between eighteen and sixty were listed, but after 1780 everyone was listed. One copy is in the National Archives, one in the provincial archives, and one in local municipal offices. The lists are alphabetical within each village or town.

Property Taxes

The provincial archives have copies of these lists from 1539 onward.

Guilds (Ammattikuntaluettelot)

These records are in some of the provincial archives, since the guilds, in the main, were only established in major towns. They were craft guilds similar to modern trade unions and the records give details of apprenticeship, qualifications, personal information, place of birth, and parentage. The period covered is from the early eighteenth century to the late nineteenth.

Wills and Probate Records (Perukirjat)

These start in about 1650 and are in various locations. Up until 1809 they are in the National Archives, from 1809 to 1860 in the various provincial archives, and since then in either the National Archives, the provincial archives, the district courts, or even local libraries. Bear in mind that wills are not too common in Finland because of the widespread use of estate inventories (Bouppteckningar).

Census Returns (Henkikirjat)

Census lists have been microfilmed up to 1920. The first census (for tax purposes) was held in 1634 and a census has been held each year since then. However, before 1925 only the taxpayer (normally the head of the family) was named. Since 1925 all members of the household have been listed by name. The returns are in the National Archives. In actual fact, they are not so vital in Finland as in other countries because of the wealth of documented information available about almost everyone from several other sources.

Land Records (Maakirjat)

If your ancestors owned or leased land, these records may provide you with some extra information. They cover a period from 1630 to 1758 and are in the National Archives.

Court Records (Oikeuden päätokset)

Don't assume that these records will be of no interest to you because your very respectable ancestors would never have appeared in court! Don't be so sure; not only did the courts deal with the usual criminal cases, but they approved the transfer of real estate, mortgages, leases, tenancies, marriage settlements, guardianship records, etc., and all these records can contain a great deal of genealogical information. The records are in the National Archives, the provincial archives, and in local courthouses.

Register of the Inhabitants of Finland (Suomen asukasluettelot)

This is yet one more record designed to keep tabs on the Finns and provide work for bureaucrats. This ambitious project was started in 1539 and discontinued in 1809, although it is still being added to as new information about individuals is discovered. Basically, it is genealogical data collected from churches. It lists addresses and names and refers you to the locations of records on file for a particular person. The register is in the National Archives.

Military Records (Sotilasasiakirjat)

These are muster-rolls of various regiments from 1537 to the present. All these military records, and others, up to 1809 are in the War Archives in both Helsinki and Stockholm (Sweden); records after that date are in the National Archives.

Don't overlook the fact that records of military interest can also be found in odd places. For example, in the provincial archives at Mikkeli you can find church registers and Main Books for various military installations in the area, or for regiments stationed there:

EVANGELICAL LUTHERAN:	Military Academy in Hamina (1821–1902)
	5th Sharpshooter Battalion (1855–69)
GREEK ORTHODOX:	8th Russian Sharpshooter Battalion (1908)
	Infantry Regiment of Lesnoi (1914)
	Military Parish on the Journey (1872–1904)
	Infantry Regiment of Novotorzski (1873–1912)
	Finnish Sharpshooter Regiment (1892–1914)
	Military Parish in Tuusula (1856–1918)
	Russian Military Hospital, Tuusala (1856–60)
	Garrison in Viipuri (1802–1924)

Genealogical Organizations

The name and address of the national organization is listed earlier in this chapter, but there are also local organizations throughout Finland. I list them below and you can obtain the current address of the secretary by writing to the national headquarters:

Forssa, Hamina, Helsinki, Hyvinkää, Ilmajoki, Jakobstad, Jyväskylä, Kerava, Kokkola, Kuopio, Lahti, Lapua, Mariehamn, Oulu, Pargas, Pori, Riihimäki, Salo, Tampere, Turku, and Vaasa.

Passports

All passports issued from 1820 to 1920 have been listed and are on microfilm in the National Archives. There are plans to make later lists available.

THE LOST TERRITORIES

These are the parts of Finland taken by the USSR. The church registers and Main Books of the Evangelical Lutheran churches (and two Orthodox ones) are in the custody of a special archives *within* the provincial archives at Mikkeli (Mikkelin maakunta-arkisto, PL 2, 50101 Mikkeli; Phone: 011-358-15-321-310; Fax: 011-358-15-321-3157; E-mail: mikkeli@narc.fi). There is, however, a chance that these archives will be transferred to the Joensuun provincial archives (Joensuun maakunta-arkisto, PL 146, 88101 Joensuu; Phone: 011-358-13-251-4602; Fax: 011-358-13-251-4606; E-mail: joensuu@narc.fi). Those of you whose family members fled from Soviet-held Finnish territory during and after the Second World War will find these books and registers of major importance.

The parishes are as follows:

EVANGELICAL LUTHERAN: Antrea, Äyräpää, Harlu, Heinjoki, Hiitola, Ihantala, Ilmee, Impilahti, Inkerin (Viipuri), Jaakima, Jääski, Johannes, Käkisalmi, Kanneljärvi, Kaukola, Kirvu, Kivennapa, Koivisto, Korpiselkä, Kuolemajärvi, Kurkijoki, Lavansaari, Lumivaara, Metsäpirtti, Muolaa, Pälkjärvi, Persamo, Pyhäjärvi, Räisälä, Rautu, Ruskeala, Säkkijärvi, Sakkola, Salmi, Seiskari, Soanlahti, Sortavalan, Suojärvi, Suursaari, Terijoki, Tytärsaari, Uusikirkko, Vahviala, Valkjärvi, Viipuri (rural parish), Viipuri (cathedral parish), Vuoksela, and Vuoksenranta.

Note: The starting dates vary considerably for both the church registers and the Main Books. The rural parish of Viipuri dates back to 1686, but the majority start about 1750, and all of them end in the period 1949–53 (except Ilmee, which ends in 1900).

GREEK ORTHODOX: Korpiselka, Petsamo, Salmi, Viipuri.

FINNISH ORTHODOX CHURCH: Viipuri (1930–50)

As you will have gathered by now, Finland is a genealogist's dream, at least for the last 250 years. Before that, the going gets tough, but at least the odds are heavily in your favor that you will get off to a very good start.

If necessary, you can also make contact with the Institute of Migration, Piispankatu 3, 20500 Turku.

FRANCE

Little is known of the area we call France before the Roman Conquest in the first century B.C. During several centuries after the Roman occupation, France, then known as Gaul, was torn apart by dynastic wars. In 800 the Emperor Charlemagne brought order to France and other areas under his rule. However, his son Louis could not maintain the order established by his father, and when he died the three sons he left behind divided the lands among them (Treaty of Verdun, 843). Charles, King of the West Franks, was recognized as ruler of the area that is now France.

From then until the end of the sixteenth century, France had to contend with Viking and English invasions, the rise to power of great feudal nobles, wars against the Hapsburgs, questions of succession, religious rebellions, assassinations, strong and weak kings, honest and venal administrators, and long-suffering peasants.

In 1789 the inevitable revolution occurred, and since then France has been a republic with strong central control located in Paris.

Archives

The address of the National Archives (Archives Nationales) is 60 rue Francs Bourgeois, 75003 Paris (Phone: 011-33-1-40-27-67-00; Fax: 011-33-1-40-27-66-06; Web site: www.archivesnationale.culture.gouv.fr). With the decentralization of so many French records in the various départements and cities this is not of such major importance to ancestor-hunters as in other countries but it does hold Protestant records, records of wills, some notarial records, and nationalization lists.

There are ninety-five départements in France, each administered by a préfet responsible to the government in Paris. A département is roughly equivalent to a county, and is divided into districts (arrondissements), municipalities (communes), and cantons. Each département has its own archives (Archives Départementales), and since you will most certainly be corresponding with them, I list all the addresses below. If you are already familiar with the départements, and perhaps have a map showing their locations, you should be warned that in 1964 there were some major changes in boundaries in the Paris area. The Départements of the Seine and Seine-et-Oise were abolished. The twenty arrondissements of Paris were formed into the Département des Paris, and the remaining eighty communes of the Département de Seine were redistributed among the Départements of Hauts-de-Seine, Seine-Saint Denis, and Val-de-Marne.

The Département of Seine-et-Oise was broken up and formed to the west of Paris the Département des Yvelines and the Département de l'Essonne, and to the north that of Val-d'Oise. Its remaining communes joined with the eighty from the Seine mentioned above to form the three new départements.

Note: Correspondence for each of the following Archives Départementales should be addressed to La Préfecture, followed by the city and the postal code given below:

Ain, 01000 Bourg-en-Bresse
Aisne, 02000 Laon
Allier, 03016 Moulins
Alpes de Haute-Provence, 04000 Digne
Alpes (Hautes-), 05000 Gap
Alpes-Maritimes, 06000 Nice
Ardèche, 07000 Privas
Ardennes, 08000 Charleville-Mézières
Ariège, 09000 Foix
Aube, 10000 Troyes
Aude, 11000 Carcassonne
Aveyron, 12000 Rodez

Bouches-du-Rhône, 13000 Marseille

Calvados, 14000 Caen
Cantal, 15000 Aurillac
Charente, 16000 Angoulême
Charente-Maritime, 17000 La Rochelle
Cher, 18000 Bourges
Corrèze, 19000 Tulle
Corse, 20000 Ajaccio
Côte-d'Or, 21000 Dijon
Côtes d'Armor, 22000 Saint-Brieuc
Creuse, 23000 Guéret

Dordogne, 24000 Périgueux
Doubs, 25000 Besançon
Drôme, 26000 Valence

Essonne, 91010 Evry
Eure, 27000 Évreux
Eure-et-Loir, 28000 Chartres

Finistère, 29000 Quimper

Gard, 30040 Nîmes
Garonne (Haute-), 31000 Toulouse
Gers, 32000 Auch
Gironde, 33000 Bordeaux

Hérault, 34000 Montpellier

Ille-et-Vilaine, 35000 Rennes
Indre, 36000 Châteauroux
Indre-et-Loire, 37000 Tours
Isère, 38000 Grenoble

Jura, 39000 Lons-le-Saunier

Landes, 40000 Mont-de-Marsan
Loir-et-Cher, 41000 Blois
Loire, 42000 St. Etienne
Loire-Haute, 43000 Le-Puy-en-Velay
Loire-Atlantique, 44000 Nantes
Loiret, 45000 Orléans
Lot, 46000 Cahors
Lot-et-Garonne, 47000 Agen
Lozère, 48000 Mende

Maine-et-Loire, 49000 Angers
Manche, 50000 St. Lô
Marne, 51000 Châlons-en-Champagne
Marne (Haute-), 52000 Chaumont
Mayenne, 53000 Laval
Meurthe-et-Moselle, 54000 Nancy*
Meuse, 55000 Bar-le-Duc
Morbihan, 56000 Vannes
Moselle, 57000 Metz*

Nièvre, 58000 Nevers
Nord, 59000 Lille

Oise, 60000 Beauvais
Orne, 61000 Alençon

Paris, 75004 Paris
Pas-de-Calais, 62000 Arras
Puy-de-Dôme, 63000 Clermont-Ferrand
Pyrénées-Atlantiques, 64000 Pau
Pyrénées (Hautes-), 65000 Tarbes
Pyrénées-Orientales, 66000 Perpignan

Rhin (Bas-), 67000 Strasbourg*
Rhin (Haut-), 68000 Colmar*
Rhône, 69000 Lyon

Saône (Haute-), 70000 Vesoul
Saône-et-Loire, 71000 Mâcon
Sarthe, 72000 Le Mans
Savoie, 73000 Chambéry
Savoie (Haute-), 74000 Annecy
Seine (Haute-), 92500 Nanterre
Seine-Maritime, 76100 Rouen
Seine-et-Marne, 77000 Melun
Seine-Saint-Denis, 93000 Bobigny
Sèvres, 79000 Niort
Somme, 80000 Amiens

Tarn, 81000 Albi
Tarn-et-Garonne, 82000 Montauban
Territoire de Belfort, 90000 Belfort

Val-de-Marne, 94011 Créteil
Val-d'Oise, 95010 Cergy-Pontoise
Var, 83000 Toulon
Vaucluse, 84000 Avignon
Vendée, 85000 La Roche-sur-Yon
Vienne, 86000 Poitiers
Vienne (Haute-), 87000 Limoges
Vosges, 88000 Épinal*

Yonne, 89000 Auxerre
Yvelines, 78000 Versailles

Since many of you will be affected by the changes in the départements in the Paris area, and the consequent transfer of records of arrondissements and communes from one département to another, it may be helpful to list these transfers:

From the former Département of Seine-et-Oise to:

HAUTS-DE-SEINE: Bagneux, Bourg-la-Reine

SEINE-SAINT DENIS: La Courneuve, Île-Saint-Denis, Noisy-le-Sec, Romainville, Rosny-sous-Bois

VAL-DE-MARNE: Arcueil, Bonneuil-sur-Marne, Champigny-sur-Marne, Choisy-le-Roi, Thiais, Villejuif

---

*The archives marked with an asterisk are of interest to people of Alsace-Lorraine descent.

From the former Département of the Seine to:

HAUTS-DE-SEINE: Antony, Asnières, Bois-Colombes, Boulogne-Billancourt, Châtenay-Malabry, Châtillon, Clamart, Clichy, Colombes, Courbevoie, Fontenay-aux-Roses, La Garenne-Colombes, Gennevilliers, Issy-les Moulineaux, Levallois-Perret, Malakoff, Montrouge, Nanterre, Neuilly-sur-Seine, Le Plessis-Robinson, Puteaux, Sceaux, Suresnes, Vanves, Villeneuve-la-Garenne

SEINE-SAINT-DENIS: Aubervilliers, Bagnolet, Bobigny, Bondy, Le Bourget, Drancy, Dugny, Épinay-sur-Seine, Les Lilas, Montreuil, Pantin, Les Pavillons-sous-Bois, Pierrefitte-sur-Seine, Le Pré-Saint-Gervais, Saint-Denis, Saint-Ouen, Stains, Villemomble, Villetaneuse

VAL-DE-MARNE: Alfortville, Brie-sur-Marne, Cachan, Charenton-le-Pont, Chevilly-Larue, Créteil, Fontenay-sous-Bois, Fresnes, Gentilly, L'Hay-les-Roses, Ivry-sur-Seine, Joinville-le-Pont, Le Kremlin-Bicêtre, Maisons-Alfort, Nogent-sur-Marne, Orly, Le Perreux-sur-Marne, Rungis, Saint-Mandé, Saint-Maur-des-Fossés, Saint-Maurice, Vincennes, Vitry-sur-Seine

So much for the locations of the archives. Their holdings are immense, incredibly ancient, uncountable, and in many cases not catalogued and indexed. The volume of documents continuously arriving is not merely a flood but a total inundation at times. If you have wandered, as I have done, in some of the remote storage areas of some of the archives, you would not credit that any particular document could ever be found in the mass of records. Yet, thanks to the memories and the energies of the wonderful and hard-working men and women of the archives, the document you need will be produced with speed and efficiency.

The system of genealogical record-keeping in France differs from those of most other European countries. Once you understand it, you will find it very easy and reasonably inexpensive. The key to ancestor-hunting in France is the system used to maintain a permanent record of an individual during his or her life. For example, in the registers of birth, marriage, and death kept in the local town halls (or mairies) are wide margins. These margins are used for notes to be added later in order to update the information about the individual.

Since 1897 the birth certificate has shown in the margin the date and place of the subsequent marriage of the infant, and his or her divorce or remarriage. Since 1922 it has also shown the date and place of the marriage of the infant's parents. Since 1945 the marginal notes have given details of the eventual death of the infant. The marriage certificate includes full details of witnesses. The death certificate includes details of the date and place of birth of the deceased.

It is important, too, that you remember there is a "100 years law" governing the information that may be given to an inquirer. Information within the last 100 years will not be divulged in full so far as birth certificates are concerned unless (a) you are the person named on the certificate, or (b) you can prove your descent from him or her. These restrictions are simply to protect the privacy of people who may still be alive. However, even when you write for a certificate copy more than 100 years old, you should always specify that you want a *full* copy—in English, "an exact copy of the birth certificate"; in French, "Extrait des Registres des Actes de Naissance (Copie littérale)." If you do not specify this, you will receive an abridged copy without any details except the date and place of birth. Be sure you send three International Reply Coupons.

The government of France has issued a very clear and concise explanation of the method of keeping vital records in the country. The keeping of these records originated with two customs started by the Catholic Church:

Baptismal Records

These enabled a priest to discover a person's family background, and he could therefore avoid performing a marriage ceremony between a man and woman related to a degree prohibited by canon law.

Marriage and Death Records

These were types of account books in which the priest entered the gifts and offerings to the church received at the time of these sacraments.

It is generally accepted that baptismal records date back to the beginning of the thirteenth century and marriage and death records to the fourteenth century.

The parish records maintained by the clergy became increasingly useful to the state for the purposes of taxes, land disputes, military service, etc., and the government began to regulate them. In 1539 baptismal records were made compulsory by state law, and in 1563 a similar ordinance was issued for marriage records. Finally, in 1579 death records were also included under the Ordinance of Blois.

The records, of course, were only maintained by Catholic clergy, but in 1791, at the time of the Revolution, it was ordered that public officials would be responsible for the keeping of all such records. The Catholic records continued to exist alongside the civil records, but only those records kept before 1792 by the clergy could be used as legal documents.

The civil records are maintained in each commune in two separate registers. At the end of each year the second copy is sent to the registrar of the civil court of the first instance, while the first copy remains in the town hall. The law requires that any changes in the civil status of the individual (marriage, separation, divorce, adoption, death, and the birth of children) be entered in the margin of the original birth entry. Each document contains the date information was received and the names, ages, occupations, and addresses of everyone named.

The mayor is the registrar of each commune, but he may delegate his authority to a named local official.

French nationals living abroad, whether temporarily or permanently, may either use the forms used in their country of residence and register them with a French consul, or have the French official documents completed by the consul.

There is one final thing to remember before we leave the subject of French vital records and their systems. The death certificate will not record the place of burial. To find this, you will need to write to the parish priest of the district giving him the date and place of death. This may cause you some difficulties because many churches have been closed and a local priest may not exist in that particular parish. The registers may have been transferred to an adjoining parish, but there may be several of these. If you run into this difficulty, you should write to the Archives Départementales (addresses listed above), give them the story, and ask for their assistance.

So much for French records and record-keeping. Now let us talk—finally—about the various sources of information you may need in your search for those missing French ancestors.

Civil Registration

As you already know, this was established under French law in 1791, and the records start in 1792. This is the most important source of genealogical information in France since that date. The records are located in the town or village of origin, with a copy in the Archives Départementales up to the year 1870 approximately, and since then in the local court of the first instance (Greffe du Tribunal de Prèmiere Instance) located in the chief city of the préfecture or département (see above for address). Both the town hall and the provincial archives have yearly and ten-year indexes to births, marriages, and deaths, so there is no problem in tracing an entry as long as you have a name, date, and place to start with. If you require information about French citizens living overseas,you should write to Civil Registers of French people overseas (Direction des Affaires Administratives, Ministère des Affaires Étrangères, Boîte Postale 1056, 44035 Nantes).

If you are checking the indexes in person and not by correspondence, you should be aware that names such as De Lussac are indexed under D and not L, and you will find Leclerc under L and not C, even if the name is divided as le Clerc. Finally, bear in mind that the ten-year index I mentioned is not made up at the end of each ten-year period but is rewritten at odd intervals, so that though a name is listed by its initial letter, each letter is in chronological order:

    L. 1876 5 Mars   Lavoie, Jean
    L. 1876 4 Avril   Lacoste, Charles

L. 1876 7 Avril   Luétte, François
L. 1876 6 Mai   Lenoir, Marcel

Church Registers

These are in the Archives Départementales up to 1792 and since then in the individual churches, or in adjoining churches to which they have been transferred. Many of them have been indexed. The information in the registers includes not only baptisms, marriages, and burials but also confirmations and banns. Confirmation usually took place when a child was about twelve years old. Witnesses to baptisms are also listed, usually with addresses, and relationship, if any, to the child being baptized. These remarks apply, of course, to Catholic church registers only.

Protestant Registers

These are usually Lutheran from 1525 and Calvinist from 1559. The records are similar to the Catholic, except that confirmation usually did not take place until a child was sixteen years of age. The location of the registers is, unfortunately, scattered. Some are still in the local church, some in town halls, some in the Archives Départementales, some in the Library of the Protestant Historical Society (Société d'Histoire du Protestantisme Français, 54 rue des Saints-Pères, 75007 Paris; Phone: 011-33-1-45-48-62-07), and for part of southern France, the Archives Départementales du Gard, 30040 Nîmes.

Huguenot Records

The majority of French Protestants were Huguenots, many of whom fled the country because of religious persecution. They are fairly well documented in various places.

1. The Huguenot and Walloon Research Association (Mailmaison, Church Street, Great Bedwyn, England SN8 3PE) and the AngloGerman Family History Society (14 River Reach, Teddington, London TW11 9QL) have many documents giving details of place of origin in France.

2. The Centraal Bureau voor Genealogie (Postbus 11755, 2502 AT, The Hague, Netherlands) indexed records of Huguenots who lived in some cities of France, Germany, Belgium, and the Netherlands.

3. Both the Archives Nationales and the Archives Départementales also have some Protestant records.

4. The City Archives (Stadtarchiv) of Frankfurt-am-Main, Germany, has records of financial and other assistance given to Protestant refugees. These include names of family members, relationships, places of origin, and intended destination.

5. Consistorium der Französischen (Friedrichstrasse 4, 10711 Berlin) holds many records of Huguenot refugees in Germany.

The Calendar

For a short period from September 1792 to December 1805 the Gregorian calendar was replaced by the French Revolutionary calendar. You may find dates that include such months (or periods) as Pluviôse, Ventôse, Germinal, Floréal, Prairial, Messidor, Thermidor, Fructidor, Vendémiaire, Brumaire, Frimaire, and Nivôse. Although the names as I have given them correspond roughly with the months January to December, they do not match up exactly. There are methods of conversion from one to the other, but I doubt if I could explain them clearly, quite apart from the complications of three leap years in the period. I suggest you write down the dates you come across in the above period, and then gently persuade a friendly French archivist to convert them for you to the existing calendar.

Censuses (Recensements)

The first of these was held as far back as 1590 in at least one area; the Archives Départementales of Bas-Rhin have these on file for their area. There were other censuses in various places over the centuries, but often only the head of the family was named, and sometimes only the number of people in the house. Check with the Archives Départementales and also with the town hall. Censuses have been held regularly since 1836 at intervals of five years. Some have been lost in various wars, but those that survive are in the Archives Départementales, often with copies in town halls. The returns usually named complete families in the house, with age, occupation, and religion. The actual place of birth was not included before 1872.

In addition to the national censuses there were many local or municipal censuses, and here again you must check with the town hall. Since 1795 the municipal censuses have included the place of birth of all those present in the house.

Notarial Archives (Les Archives des Notaires)

These are probably the next most important source of genealogical information in France. Notarial documents are in existence as far back as the twelfth century, but to all intents and purposes you cannot rely on finding notarial records before the middle years of the sixteenth century. What is a notarial record? It is a document drawn up by a lawyer. These documents come under literally hundreds of headings, but as ancestor-hunters we are mainly concerned with marriage settlements, land sales, wills, inventories after death, and the division, or partition, of inheritances of land and property.

In 1928 a state law authorized notaries to deposit their documents older than 125 years in the Archives Nationales or the Archives Départementales. Papers less than 125 years old remain in the possession of the notaries. The problem has been that all the notarial records are regarded as the personal property of the notary concerned. The state recognized this claim in 1928 by allowing the notaries to retain ownership, even though the documents themselves were deposited in the archives. An example of the immense burden suddenly placed on archival resources is that of the Département de Seine (now defunct), which received documents from 144 existing notarial offices, for a total of nearly ninety million documents. That is just one département out of ninety-five!

The **marriage settlements or contracts** give us the full names of the contracting parties, their parents, the witnesses (with the relationship to the parties), and the date and place of the projected marriage.

The **inventories after death** are just that, a description of the personal papers of the deceased, the principal events of his or her life—birth, marriage, military service, children living and dead (and their marriages), property bought and sold, houses occupied, and, finally, death. Almost the whole of a man's or woman's life is set out on paper.

The **inheritances of land and property** give full details of the heirs and descendants of the deceased.

Wills and probate records are in the Archives Nationales and the Archives Départementales. Donations to heirs are records in this same general area (Donations entre vifs) and are usually gifts of property from old parents to their family. They date from the fifteenth century and are in the Archives Nationales, Départementales, and Municipales, or if filed within 125 years, in notaries' offices.

Administration of Estates (Partages de Succession)

These give names and addresses of deceased persons, their legal heirs, and the date and place of death. They can be found in the three levels of archives (national, departmental, municipal) and in notaries' offices. They date from about 1450, generally speaking.

Land and Property Records (Achats et Ventes de Terres)

These date from the mid-1400s in most localities and include details of renters, buyers, and sellers of land and buildings, with names, dates, addresses, and relationship (if any). They are in the three levels of archives or in notaries' offices.

Court Records (Archives Judiciares)

These exist from the early 1400s in many areas and are in the three levels of archives. They record not only crimes but also all civil actions involving land and property disputes, administration of estates, marriage contracts, and the buying and selling of real estate and buildings.

Schools and Universities (Écoles et Universités)

There are many records of pupils at educational institutions dating back to the fourteenth century and they give names, ages, and addresses, and names of parents. They are to be found in the three levels of archives, and also in the National Library (Bibliothèque Nationale, 58 rue de Richelieu, 75002 Paris; Phone: 011-33-1-47-03-81-26; Web site: www.bnf.fr).

Cemetery Inscriptions (Inscriptions Mortuaires)

These date from the twelfth century and are located in cemetery offices (Bureaux des Cimetières) in larger cities, or in churches, or in various archives. In the latter case they are likely to be indexed.

Burgess and Guild Records (Registres des Citoyens et des Corporations de Métiers)

These records apply only to major cities and are in one of the three levels of archives. They date from the twelfth to the eighteenth century and list those being accepted as burgesses or citizens of a city (much more important than being a mere inhabitant!), or those granted membership in a trade guild.

Electoral Lists (Listes Électorales)

These date from the early nineteenth century and list names, addresses, ages, and occupations of males only (until 1945) in each electoral district. (Women were granted the vote after the Second World War.) The records are in town halls and Archives Départementales.

Internal Passports (Passeports pour l'Intérieur)

These were in use from about 1800 to 1870 and were needed for movement between one location and another within France. They include the usual personal details, plus a physical description, and are in a certain number of Archives Départementales.

Conscription Lists (Registres de Conscription)

Since 1800 every French male has been liable for military service. These records show those who served, those who were exempted from service for one reason or another, and those who deserted either to avoid service, or while serving. Males over twenty-one years of age are included, and are listed by cities, towns, and communes or cantons. They are often indexed in alphabetical order of personal names, and are in the Archives Départementales.

Emigration Records (Registres d'Émigrés)

These date from 1788 to the present and list all those granted permission to emigrate. The records give place and date of birth, address, occupation, physical description, and names of family members traveling with the person listed. The intended destination is also included.

Passenger Lists (Rôles des Passagers)

These date mainly from the early eighteenth century and are listed under the names of the ships. They list the usual personal information, including country of origin since many passengers through French ports were from other European countries. The records for Le Havre (1750–1898) are in the Archives Départementales de la Seine-Maritime, 76100 Rouen. The archives are prepared to make a search if you can give precise information—name of vessel, name of passenger(s), and date of sailing. Similar records for Bordeaux (1713–87) are in the Archives Départementales de Gironde, 33000 Bordeaux.

Naturalization Records (Lettres de Naturalisation)

These date from 1635 to the present and, of course, give the country of birth of those becoming French citizens by naturalization. They are in the custody of the Archives Nationales and the Archives Départementales.

Military Records (Registres Militaires)

These are extensive and it is only possible to list some of the items available.

The records start in the seventeenth century and continue to the present day. Details are available at the Army Historical Service (Service Historique de l'Armée de Terre, Château de Vincennes, 94300 Vincennes) of all officers and most men serving in the army during that time. So far as the navy is concerned, the address is Service Historique de la Marine, Pavillon de la Reine, Château de Vincennes, 94300 Vincennes. The records list all personal details including next of kin and their address, dates of marriage and birth of children, children's names and ages, name and address of wife, injuries and death, and personal description.

Army records in most countries, including France, are your only source of information about the physical appearance of your ancestors. They are very detailed, listing height, weight, color of hair and eyes, "wart on chin," and so on. The description had only one purpose: to make it easier to catch a deserter from the armed forces. Conditions, up to modern times, were so bad for serving soldiers, particularly those in the ranks, that desertions were common.

There are also records from 1817 of disability pensions paid to ex-servicemen and pensions paid to widows. These are indexed.

I should, perhaps, mention at this point that if you intend searching archives personally on a visit to France, you should be sure to bring with you (a) proof of descent from the original emigrant from France, (b) a letter of introduction from a priest, minister, lawyer, or doctor translated into French, (c) half a dozen passport-size photographs. If you visit the National Archives first, you will be issued with an identity card, and this is usually sufficient to also give you admission to archives at a lower level—département, ville, commune. However, some local archives insist on checking your bona fides and issuing you with their own archival identity card.

Genealogical Societies

There are one or more genealogical societies or associations in each of the ninety-five départements. It is pointless to list the names and addresses of the secretaries of each of these because they change so often. If you are interested in a particular area, I suggest you write to the Federation (Fédération des Sociétés Françaises de Généalogie, d'Héraldique et de Sigillographie, 3, rue de Turbigo, 75001 Paris; Phone: 011-33-1-40-13-00-88; Fax: 011-33-1-40-13-00-89; E-mail: Genealfede@aol.com; Web site: www.Genefede.org) —which includes among its members most of the regionl organizations in France—and ask for the address for your location, or check the list of associations on their web site.

In case you are wondering, *Sigillographie* means the study of seals— not the cuddly kind, but the big blobs of red wax that appear on ancient documents!

Be a little careful in your dealings with professional researchers and be sure they are on the approved list of an archive or a genealogical organization. There are many people in France who check the probate records, discover someone who died without a known heir but with a large estate, and try to trace a descendant, or near relative. Once found, the inheritance is split fifty-fifty. These inheritance searchers call themselves genealogists and advertise as such in newspapers and magazines.

The usual final word: **Don't forget the return postage!**

GERMANY

It is probably harder to trace your ancestors in Germany than in any other European country. It can also be said that if you are of German descent your roots may not be in Germany at all, at least may not have been for centuries. I don't want to discourage you in any way, but you must arm yourself for the fray with patience, determination, a sense of order, and an infinite capacity for hard work—in fact, with all those admirable characteristics associated with your German ancestors.

Let me set out for you the causes of the problems you will face:

1. Germany as an undivided nation existed only from 1871 to 1945, a brief period of seventy-four years. By comparison, such countries as France and England have been unified since the thirteenth and fourteenth centuries. In the seventeenth and eighteenth centuries the area we know as Germany consisted of 1789 kingdoms, principalities, grand duchies, dukedoms, electorates, free cities, right down to tiny personal estates of only a few acres. Each political unit had its own laws, archives, and systems of record-keeping. You cannot say, for example, that "censuses were first taken in Germany in 1871." That is true for the unified country of Germany, but censuses were taken in Württemberg in 1821, in Prussia in 1831, and so on. The only unifying and centralizing force in the Germanic area was the church, first the Catholic Church and later the Lutheran Church as well.

2. In the first half of the nineteenth century, because of the Congress of Vienna and growing German nationalism, the number of states was reduced to thirty-four. Some of these formed the German Confederation and in 1867 the North German Federation (Norddeutscher Bund) came into existence under the leadership of Prussia. In 1871 Prussia defeated France, and the south German states then joined with the Federation to form the German Empire (Deutsches Reich). Suddenly, in the very center of Europe, a powerful new country existed.

3. The new empire included the following territory:

(a) Kingdoms of Bavaria, Prussia, Saxony, and Württemberg

(b) Grand Duchy of Baden

(c) Free Cities of Hamburg, Bremen, and Lübeck, and Anhalt, Brunswick, Darmstadt, Hesse, Lippe, Mecklenburg, Oldenburg, Reuss, and the various states comprising Thuringia. (Justice, education, health, and police were left under the control of the individual states.)

4. The unification of Germany ended in 1945 when parts of it were given to Czechoslovakia, Poland, and the USSR. What was left was then divided between East Germany (Deutsche Demokratische Republik, or D.D.R.) and West Germany (Bundesrepublik Deutschland, or B.R.D.). This division of Germany into two countries lasted until 1990. You may be dealing with six countries as well as Germany—if you include Belgium, Denmark, and France, which obtained German territory in 1919. All this may be ahead of you, plus the fact you may be dealing with the records of some of the original German states!

5. During the period when Germany was unified, little or no attempt was made to centralize records in one place such as Berlin; instead, they remained in the capital cities of the original states. In retrospect, this was a blessing to ancestor-hunters because the destruction of records in Germany during the Second World War was surprisingly small. Imagine what would have happened if everything had been in Berlin!

6. Even though you are of German descent, your roots may not be in Germany. Over the centuries, Germans from the Germanic area settled in other parts of Europe. Many tens of thousands settled in Ukraine and the area of the Volga Basin, others established themselves in Transylvania (Hungarian until 1919, Romanian since then), and still more are to be found in parts of Hungary and Yugoslavia. There were also nearly four million Germans in Czechoslovakia, but they were expelled by force after the Second World War.

7. The postwar dismemberment of Germany mentioned in (4) above is set out below:

TO CZECHOSLOVAKIA: Part of Silesia (Schlesien)

TO POLAND: The eastern parts of Brandenburg and Pomerania (Pommern), the southern part of East Prussia (Ostpreussen), Posen, Silesia (Schlesien), and West Prussia (Westpreussen)

TO THE USSR: The northern part of East Prussia (Ostpreussen)

The remaining part of Germany was then divided into the eastern part occupied by the USSR and the western part occupied by Britain, Belgium, France, and the United States. These two parts later became the German Democratic Republic or East Germany (Deutsche Demokratische Republik, or D.D.R.) and the Federal Republic of Germany or West Germany (Bundesrepublik Deutschland, or B.R.D.). Details of this division were:

EAST GERMANY (D.D.R.): Anhalt, Brandenburg (western part), part of Brunswick (Braunschweig), Mecklenburg-Schwerin, Mecklenburg-Strelitz, Reuss, Sachsen-Altenburg, Sachsen-Meiningen, Sachsen-Weimar, Schwarzburg-Rudolstadt, and Schwarzburg-Sondershausen. Also four provinces of the State of Prussia (the parts remaining after territory taken by Czechoslovakia, Poland, and the USSR).

WEST GERMANY (B.R.D.): Baden, Bavaria (Bayern), part of Brunswick (Braunschweig), Coburg, Lippe, Oldenburg, Schaumberg-Lippe, part of Thuringia (Thüringen), Waldeck, Westphalia (Westfalen), and Württemberg; and five provinces of the State of Prussia—Hanover (Hannover), Hessen-Nassau, Rhineland (Rheinland), Schleswig-Holstein, and Sigmaringen.

After the division in 1945, various changes were made within each of the two Germanys and they were then divided as follows:

EAST GERMANY (D.D.R.): Originally this consisted of five Länder or provinces. These were then abolished and replaced by fifteen districts (Kreise). However, the D.D.R., unlike the B.R.D., was not a federal state, and all power was centered in the capital (East, or Ost, Berlin).

WEST GERMANY (B.R.D.): The country consisted of ten federal states (Bundesländer or just Länder): Baden-Württemberg, Bavaria (Bayern), Bremen (city-state), Hamburg (city-state), Hesse (Hessen), Lower Saxony (Niedersachsen), North Rhine-Westphalia (Nordrhein-Westfalen), Rhineland-Palatinate (Rheinland-Pfalz), Saarland, and Schleswig-Holstein. The city-state of Berlin (West) was also integrated into the legal and economic system of the Federal Republic.

Following unification in 1990 the fifteen districts of East Germany (D.D.R.) mentioned above were replaced by the five original provinces or Länder. All the states of the unified Germany are listed below with the name of their capital cities:

Baden-Württemberg (Stuttgart)
Bayern (Munich)
Berlin
Brandenburg (Potsdam)*
Bremen
Hamburg
Hessen (Wiesbaden)
Mecklenburg-Vorpommern
   (Schwerin)*

Niedersachsen (Hannover)
Nordrhein-Westfalen
   (Düsseldorf)
Rheinland-Pfalz (Mainz)
Saarland (Saarbrücken)
Sachsen (Dresden)*
Sachsen-Anhalt (Magdeburg)*
Schleswig-Holstein (Kiel)
Thüringen (Erfurt)*

The Länder marked * are the political divisions of the old East Germany, which replace the fifteen districts. The names of these districts or Bezirkes now within each of the five Länder are:

BRANDENBURG: Berlin, Cottbus, Frankfurt, Potsdam

MECKLENBURG-VORPOMMERN: Neubrandenburg, Rostock, Schwerin

SACHSEN: Dresden, Karl-Marx-Stadt, Leipzig

SACHSEN-ANHALT: Halle, Magdeburg

THÜRINGEN: Erfurt, Gera, Suhl

Note: Karl-Marx-Stadt has now reverted to its original name of Chemnitz.

We can now start to talk about the main German sources of genealogical information, beginning with the various church registers. However, there will be a slight delay at this point because it is essential you know all about the organization and archival policies of the various churches before you hear about the registers and other church records.

In your search of records remember that it was common in Germanic areas in the middle 1700s to use only the *second* baptismal name in official records later in life. The first name was that of a parent or grandparent and was given as a compliment, but never used officially. So Oskar Georg Weber would only appear as Georg Weber.

THE EVANGELICAL CHURCH

The Evangelical Church in Germany (Evangelische Kirche in Deutschland) is a union of independent territorial Lutheran, Reformed, and United churches. The various sections are not yet officially unified, but there is very close co-operation. There are eight United Evangelical Churches; five more are members of the World Federation of Lutheran Churches; others belong to the Evangelical Lutheran Church; and others to the Federation of Reformed Churches, the two branches of the Moravian Church, and other completely independent sects. In the words of a church official who gave me much information, "I understand that from an outside perspective our German structure looks pretty difficult—I hope you will find a way through."

I hope so too! If you find errors, blame me. You will find web sites, e-mail addresses, and phone and fax numbers, when available, listed in this new edition for the first time. However, be warned that these are constantly changing. You may use the Evangelical Lutheran Church web site (**www.velkd.de/**) or the e-mail address (zentrale@velkd.de).

Evangelische Landeskirche Anhalts
Friedrichstrasse 22, 06844 Dessau
Phone: 011-49-34025260. Fax: 011-49-3402526130
E-mail: lkanhalt-presse@t-online.de
Web site: www.landeskirche-anhalts.de/

Evangelische Landeskirche in Baden
Blumenstrasse 1-7, 76133 Karlsruhe
(Postfach 2269, 76010 Karlsruhe)
Phone: 011-49-7219175550. Fax: 011-49-7219175444
Web site: www.ekiba.de/

Evangelische-Lutherische Kirche in Bayern (Bavaria)
Meiserstrasse 11-13, 80333 Munich (München)
Phone: 011-49-8955950. Fax: 011-49-895595444
E-mail: poep@elkb.de
Web site: www.bayern-evangelische.de/

Evangelische Kirche in Berlin-Brandenburg
Georgenkirchstrasse 69-70, 01249 Berlin
Phone: 011-49-30243440. Fax: 011-49-3024344500
E-mail: ekibb.com
Web site: www.ekibb.com

Evangelisch-Lutherische Landeskirche in Braunschweig (Brunswick)
Dietrich-Bonhoeffer-Strasse 1, 38300 Wolfenbüttel
Phone: 011-49-53318020. Fax: 011-49-5331802707
Web site: www.luth-braunschweig.de/

Bremische Evangelische Kirche
Franziuseck 2-4, 28199 Bremen
Phone: 011-49-42155970. Fax: 011-49-4215597265
E-mail: bek@magicvillage.de
Web site: www.kirche-bremen.de/bek/index.htm

Evangelisch-Lutherische Landeskirche Hannovers (Hanover)
Rote Reihe 6, 30169 Hannover
Phone: 011-49-51112411
Web site: www.evlka.de/

Evangelische Kirche in Hessen und Nassau (Hesse and Nassau)
Paulusplatz 1, 64285 Darmstadt
Phone: 011-49-6151405291. Fax: 011-49-6151405441
Web site: www.ekhn.de/

Evangelische Kirche von Kurhessen-Waldeck
Wilhelmshöher Allee 330, 34131 Kassel
Phone: 011-49-56193780. Fax: 011-49-5619378400
Web site: www.ekkw.de/index.html

Lippische Landeskirche
Leopoldstrasse 27, 32756 Detmold
Phone: 011-49-523197660. Fax: 011-49-5231976850
E-mail: LKA@Lippische-Landeskirche.de
Web site: www.lippische-landeskirche.de/

Evangelisch-Lutherische Landeskirche Mecklenburgs
Münzstrasse 8, 19055 Schwerin
Phone: 011-49-3855185147. Fax: 011-49-3855185162
Web site: www.ekd.de/kirche/mecklen.html

Nordelbische Evangelisch-Lutherische Kirche
Dänischestrasse 21/35, 24103 Kiel
Phone: 011-49-4319797999. Fax: 011-49-4319797999
E-mail: info.nka@nordelbien.de
Web site: www.nordelbien.de/

Evangelisch-Lutherische Kirche in Oldenburg
Philosophenweg 1, 26121 Oldenburg
Phone: 011-49-44177010. Fax: 011-49-4417701299
Web site: www.ev-kirche-oldenburg.de/

Protestantische Landeskirche der Pfalz (Palatinate)
Domplatz 5, 67346 Speyer
Phone: 011-49-62326670. Fax: 011-49-6232667199
Web site: www.evpfalz.de/kern.htm

Pommersche Evangelische Kirche (Pomerania)
Bahnhofstrasse 35, 17489 Greifswald
Phone: 011-49-3834554799. Fax: 011-49-3834572512
Web site: ekd.de/kirche/pommern.htm

Evangelische Kirche im Rheinland (Rhineland)
Hans-Böckler Strasse 7, 40476 Düsseldorf
Phone: 011-49-21145620. Fax: 011-49-2114562444
E-mail: pressestelle@ekir.de
Web site: 195.20.244.80/ekir/

Evangelische Kirche der Kirchenprovinz Sachsen (Saxony)
Am Dom 2, 39104 Magdeburg
Phone: 011-49-3915346225. Fax: 011-49-3915346226
Web site: www.ekd.de/kps/welcome.htm

Evangelische-Lutherische Landeskirche Schaumburg-Lippe
Herderstrasse 27, 31675 Bückeburg
Phone: 011-49-57229600. Fax: 011-49-572296010
E-mail: LKA-Bueckeburg@t-online.de
Web site: www.kirche-shg.de/

Evangelische Kirche der schlesischen Oberlausitz
Promenadenstrasse 57a, 02827 Görlitz
Phone: 011-49-3581741030
Web site: www.eksol.de/

Evangelisch-Lutherische Kirche in Thüringen (Thuringia)
Dr. Moritz-Mitzenheim-Strasse 2a, 99817 Eisenach
Phone: 011-49-369167899. Fax: 011-49-3691678355
E-mail: LandeskirchenamtEisenach@compuserve.com
Web site: ourworld.compuserve.com/homepages/
   LandeskirchenamtEisenach/

Evangelische Kirche von Westfalen (Westphalia)
Altstädter Kirchplatz 5, 33602 Bielefeld
Phone: 011-49-5215940. Fax: 011-49-521594129
E-mail: LKA@ekvw.de
Web site: www.ekvw.de/

Evangelische Landeskirche in Württemberg
Gänsheidestrasse 4, 70184 Stuttgart
Phone: 011-49-71121490. Fax: 011-49-7112149236
Web site: www.elk-wue.de/

As you can see, in the past the Protestant churches in Germany were divided into several sects. If you know your emigrant ancestor from Germany was a member of the Evangelical Church, it will help you in your search if you can discover just which sect he belonged to in the old country.

You will find the various church headquarters staff anxious to be of help to you but you must not ask for the impossible. For example, people have been known to write to the North Elbian Evangelical Lutheran Church to the effect "My great-grandfather was a member of the Evangelical Church and came from somewhere near you. He was born in 1870 or thereabouts. Can you look up the baptism entry in the register?" The North Elbian area covers Schleswig-Holstein, Hamburg, Eutin, and Lübeck. You can imagine how impossible it would be to even start to search.

When you write to a church organization, or a small individual church, please remember to enclose an addressed airmail envelope and at least three International Reply Coupons. I am sorry to have to keep repeating myself on this subject, but if you do not pay the return postage you may not get a reply. In addition, it will not hurt your chances of successful cooperation if you offer, in advance, to pay whatever search fees are required. If the search is an easy one you may not be charged anything.

Finally, if you can, write in German. If you cannot, then at least end your letter with the words "Mit freundlichen Grüssen" ("With friendly greetings").

The headquarters of the branches of the Evangelical Church are as follows:

Evangelical Church in Germany (EKD)
Herrenhauser Strasse 12, 30419 Hannover
Phone: 011-49-511-2796-266
Web site: www.ekd.de

Evangelical Church of the Union (EKU)
Jebensstrasse 3, 10623 Berlin

The United Evangelical-Lutheran Church of Germany (VELKD)
Richard-Wagner-Strasse 26, 30177 Hannover
Phone: 011-49-511-6261-236
Web site: www.velkd.de

German Lutheran Churches in Memel

When Memel was transferred to the USSR in 1945, the records of the Lutheran churches in the area disappeared from view. I have not been able to obtain any definite information about their present whereabouts, but it seems probable that they have been moved elsewhere, since several of the churches are now closed. The most likely present location is in the Lithuanian State Archives in Vilnius (see page 16).

The parishes concerned are Coadjuthen, Dawillan, Crottingen, Heydekrug, Kairinn, Karkelbeck, Kinten, Laugszargen, Nattkischken, Nidden, Paleiten, Paszieszen, Piktopen, Plaschken, Plicken, Prokuls, Ramutten, Rucken, Russ, Saugen, Schwarzort, Szugken, Wannagen, Wieszen, and Wischwill.

Evangelical Churches in East Prussia (Ostpreussen)

Before the invasion of East Prussia by the Red Army, the parish registers and church books (Kirchenbücher) from about 500 parishes were removed to what was then West Berlin. They are in the Central Archives of the Evangelical Church (Evangelisches Zentralarchiv in Berlin, Bethaniendamm 23-29, 10997 Berlin).

There are some missing and many gaps in the ones that survive, but if your ancestors came from East Prussia and were members of the Evangelical Church, these records may be vital to you. There is no listing of the parishes available, but the archives are planning a book about them.

Although 500 parishes are represented, there are in fact over 6,800 books involved, so you can see that the transfer and saving of these records was a major undertaking that reflects great credit on all the people concerned in this enterprise.

THE CATHOLIC CHURCH

The Catholic Church in Germany is organized in ecclesiastical provinces (each under an archbishop), bishoprics (Bistum), and the local parish (Pfarr). There are twenty-seven church archives. These hold the earlier parish registers, as well as confirmation and communion records and, in many cases, the Family Books (Liber de Statu Animarum). There is no countrywide accepted date for the surrender of early records to the various archives.

The Family Books were first introduced in 1614 and include full details of each family in the parish, together with the names of any servants, and the occupation of the head of the family. The books were kept in Latin and German and are more complete in some areas than in others. It was compulsory for the priest to maintain the books up to 1918, but since then it has been quite voluntary. The division of Germany after World War II did not affect the boundaries of the various dioceses, and so the re-unification in 1990 had no effect on ecclesiastical divisions.

The address of the Catholic Church headquarters is as follows:

Sekretariat der Deutschen
Kaiserstrasse 163, 53113 Bonn
Phone: 011-49-2281030. Fax: 011-49-2281013299
E-mail: pressestelle@dbk.de
Web site: www.kath.de

The addresses of the various Catholic Archives are set out below. It should not be difficult for you to decide to which address you should write. If, for example, your ancestors came from Wanzleben, a gazetteer or a good map in your local library will show you it is near Magdeburg, and the list below will give you the address for that diocese. Generally speaking, you will find that the headquarters of each Bistum are located in the largest city of the area:

Klosterplatz 7, 52062 **Aachen**
Phone: 011-49-2414520. Fax: 011-49-241452496

Fronhof 4, 86152 **Augsburg**
Phone: 011-49-82131660. Fax: 011-49-8213166311

Domplatz 3, 96049 **Bamberg**
Phone: 011-49-9515020. Fax: 011-49-951502238

Wundtstrasse 48/50, 14057 **Berlin**
Phone: 011-49-30326840. Fax: 011-49-3032684193

Käthe-Kollwitz-Ufer 84, 01309 **Dresden**
Phone: 011-49-35133646. Fax: 011-49-3513364791

Leonrodplatz 4, 85072 **Eichstätt**
Phone: 011-49-8421500. Fax: 011-49-84218451

Hermannsplatz 9, 99048 **Erfurt**
Phone: 011-49-36165720. Fax: 011-49-3616572444

Zwölfling 16, 45127 **Essen**
Phone: 011-49-20122041. Fax: 011-49-2012204507+570

Herrenstrasse 35, 79098 **Freiburg**
Phone: 011-49-76121881. Fax: 011-49-7612188599

Paulustor 5, 36037 **Fulda**
Phone: 011-49-661870. Fax: 011-49-66187578

Carl-von-Ossietzky-Strasse 41, 02826 **Görlitz**
Phone: 011-49-358147820. Fax: 011-49-3581478212

Danziger Strasse 52 a, **Hamburg**
Phone: 011-49-40248770. Fax: 011-49-4024877233

Domhof 18-21, 31134 **Hildesheim**
Phone: 011-49-51213070. Fax: 011-49-5121307488

Marzellenstrasse 32, 50668 **Köln**
Phone: 011-49-22116420. Fax: 011-49-2211642700

Postfach 13 55, 65533 **Limburg**
Phone: 011-49-64312950. Fax: 011-49-6431295476

Max-Josef-Metzger-Strasse 1, 39104 **Magdeburg**
Phone: 011-49-39159610. Fax: 011-49-3915961100

Bischofsplatz 2, 55116 **Mainz**
Phone: 011-49-61312530. Fax: 011-49-6131253401

Postfach 33 03 60, 80063 **München**
Phone: 011-49-8921370. Fax: 011-49-8921371585

Domplatz 27, 48143 **Münster**
Phone: 011-49-2514950. Fax: 011-49-2514956086

Hasestrasse 40a, 49074 **Osnabrück**
Phone: 011-49-5413180. Fax: 011-49-541318117

Domplatz 3, 33098 **Paderborn**
Phone: 011-49-52511250. Fax: 011-49-5251125470

Residenzplatz 8, 94032 **Passau**
Phone: 011-49-8513930. Fax: 011-49-851393830

Niedermünstergasse 1, 93047 **Regensburg***
Phone: 011-49-94159701. Fax: 011-49-9415971055

Eugen-Bolz-Platz 1, 72108 **Rottenburg**
Phone: 011-49-74721690. Fax: 011-49-7472169561

Kleine Pfaffengasse 16, 67346 **Speyer**
Phone: 011-49-62321020. Fax: 011-49-6232102300

Hinter dem Dom 6, 54290 **Trier**
Phone: 011-49-65171050. Fax: 011-49-6517105498

---

*A number of church registers from West Prussia are now in these archives. Detailed information is not available but if your Catholic ancestors came from a known location in West Prussia you should check whether the registers are here.

Domerschulstrasse 2, 97070 **Würzburg**
Phone: 011-49-9313861. Fax: 011-49-931386334

The church registers are either in the original parish church or in one of the church archives listed above. Unfortunately, there is no hard-and-fast rule which says that registers must be sent to the archives on a certain date. In fact, there is no law at all controlling this matter. Even if a church is closed, it is not possible to say with certainty that the registers were then lodged in the church archives. They may have been transferred to the near-est church remaining in operation.

If you know the exact location of the place from which your ancestor came, you can probably identify the particular archive that may have the registers. If you cannot, then I would write to the Sekretariat and ask them where the registers for that particular church are now.

OTHER RELIGIOUS GROUPS

The two largest of the Protestant free churches, the Methodists and the Evangelical Community (Evangelische-Gemeinschaft), joined in 1968 to form the Evangelical Methodist Church (Evangelisch-Methodistische Kirche). There is also the Alliance of Free Evangelical Congregations—Baptists (Bund Evangelisch-Freikirchlicher—Baptisten), as well as Men-nonites, Quakers, and Jews. By and large, all these organizations leave the registers and other records in the individual churches.

In 1933 there were over half a million Jews living in Germany. Today there are thirty thousand in the former Federal Republic and about seventy Jewish congregations—the largest being in what was West Berlin and in Frankfurt-am-Main with over five thousand members each. Figures are not available for the former D.D.R. The address for the Jewish headquarters is:

Zentralarchiv zur Eforschung der Geschichte der Juden in Deutschland
Bienenstrasse 5
69117 Heidelberg

THE CALENDAR

Before searching German records, you should be aware of changes in the calendar which, over a period of some years, produced either opposing and contradictory systems, or two different systems existing side by side.

Until 1582 the Julian calendar, established by Julius Caesar, was used in Germany and, indeed, in all civilized countries. This calendar divided the year into 365 days, plus an extra day every fourth year. The system was in operation until 1582, but astronomers had discovered that it exceeded the solar year by eleven minutes—or three days every four hundred years. Between the date when the Julian calendar was established in 325 and the year 1582, the difference amounted to eleven days. Since this affected the calculations for Easter, Pope Gregory XIII decreed that ten days be dropped from the calendar in order to bring Easter to the correct date. To prevent a recurrence of the problem, he also ordered that in every four hundred years leap year's extra day be omitted in a centennial year when the first two digits could not be divided by four without a remainder.

Are you still with me? Well, it means that it was omitted in 1700, 1800, and 1900 but will not be omitted in 2000. The Pope also changed the beginning of the New Year from March 25 to January 1, and this new system became known as the Gregorian calendar.

Generally speaking, the new calendar came into force in Germany between 1582 and 1585, depending on the locality. There were some places that started it later and the most important of these are listed below:

Prussia (Preussen)	1612
Pfalz-Neuburg	1615
Osnabrück	1624
Minden	1630
Hildesheim	1631
Friesland	1700

Basically, the Protestant areas were reluctant to make the change, while the Catholic areas started as soon as possible after the papal decree was issued. So you will find places where the Catholic Church accepted the New Year as starting on January 1 and so called September the ninth month, while the Lutheran Church in the same place regarded March 25 as the New Year and regarded September as the seventh month.

When the change did take place, it led to confusing entries of dates in church registers for a brief period. Once the reason is clear to you, you will not be puzzled to find that an ancestress of yours had one child born in one year and a second born a few months later. It was the calendar that changed and not the nine-month gestation period, so all is well!

CHURCH RECORDS

Some church records date back to the fifteenth century, but in fact you should not expect to find many of them before about 1563 for the Catholic Church and a few years later for the Lutherans. Some of the exceptions are to be found in Baden and Württemberg, where there are Lutheran and Catholic registers dating back to the early 1500s.

Although civil registration did not come into force until recent times, very early church registers often contained detailed information about individuals in the parish. Remember, of course, that most church records showed only dates of baptism, marriage, and burial, and you may never find out the dates of birth and death.

Many of the registers have been destroyed as the result of civil wars, rebellions, and invasions over the centuries, but in some cases duplicates were kept in a separate location, so all is not necessarily lost. In Mecklenburg, for example, copies were kept from 1740 onwards.

If you are searching church registers in person, you must be prepared to cope with entries in Latin (until the mid-nineteenth century) and the old German script, plus bad handwriting, and even a style of handwriting that is very different from that of the present day. No one ever said ancestor-hunting was easy!

Illegitimacy was fairly common in some rural areas of Germany. The illegitimate children were always baptized, but often the entry was made upside-down or sideways to emphasize the difference. The entry itself was very specific. The child was a bastard (Hurenkind), the mother a whore (Hure), and the father a fornicator (Hurer) or an adulterer (Ehebrecher).

The entries in the church registers usually include the following information:

BAPTISMS: Name, sex, date, names of parents, father's occupation, place of birth, names and addresses of godparents.

MARRIAGES: Name, age, and address of bride and bridegroom, occupation of groom, names and addresses of parents, occupation of the two fathers.

BURIALS: Name, age, place of death, cause of death, names of parents, name of husband or wife if still alive, date and place of burial.

Usually the above entries were made in three separate registers, but occasionally you will find all three events entered in one register in chronological order as they occurred.

In some parishes, particularly in the eighteenth and nineteenth centuries, you may find Family Books (Familienbücher or Liber de Statu Animarum). These contained complete records of a family and are of great genealogical value. Always check in a particular locality with the Catholic priest or the Lutheran minister as to the existence of a Family Book.

The book showed the name of the head of the household at the time the entry was made, the full names of the various members of the household, their places of birth, their marital status, the dates of death of deceased family members, and the place to which a family member moved if he or she left home (for marriage, work, or emigration). Check also for

Kirchenbuchduplikate, a duplicate of entries in the church register which was sent each year to the nearest headquarters of the particular church.

OTHER CHURCH RECORDS

Grave Registers (Grabregister)

These were maintained in the parish church, and although they were a duplicate of the entry of burial in the church register, they often contained additional information such as the date of death and the exact age (i.e., 38 years, 204 days). As the burial entries usually gave the date of *burial* and the age only in years, the grave registers can be of great help.

Church Receipt Books (Einnahmebücher)

These gave details of payments received from church members for such services as bell-tolling for a funeral (with name of deceased and date), and payment for burial plots and funeral cloths (Leichenhemden).

Confirmation Records (Konfirmationbücher)

Most children were between thirteen and twenty when they were confirmed, in both the Catholic and the Lutheran churches. The list gives the child's name and place and date of birth; the name and occupation of the father; and—quite often—the later marriage of the child. These records are either in the original churches or in the church archives.

There is one problem you should consider in connection with church records. If you know the religion of your ancestor but have problems with the location of his or her birthplace because you discover a number of places in Germany with the same name, you may find some help in knowing which religion was predominant in certain areas.

For example, let us suppose you know your Catholic ancestor came from a place named Schwarzenberg. You find there is one place with that name in Hesse (Hessen), one in Brandenburg, one in Prussia (Preussen), and one in Bavaria (Bayern). The odds are that the place you want is in Bavaria, because Brandenburg and Prussia are mainly Lutheran, and Hesse is Protestant but not necessarily Lutheran. This is not an infallible method, but it may help.

The other problem that may cause you difficulty, particularly in Schleswig-Holstein and Friesland, is different naming practices. Farms carried a name, usually the one given to them by the original owner. The name stayed with the farm even when the ownership changed. The trouble is that when a new owner bought the farm he would take its name as his own or, if a man's wife inherited a farm, he would change his name to her maiden name. This could produce the complication of children bearing different surnames within the same family. If you run into this problem, find out if the confirmation books are available for the particular parish, because these records usually give the original name and the later one.

Another naming problem makes life even more difficult. If you see Wilhelm Brode von Magdeburg, for example, in a list, it does not necessarily mean that Wilhelm was a noble. It could simply be that he was a man named Wilhelm Brode who came from Magdeburg. It could be the case that he had moved from Magdeburg to Hannover and found that Brode was a common name, and so to distinguish himself from all the other Wilhelm Brodes he added the words "von Magdeburg." A generation later it could be shortened by his son to Ernst von Magdeburg.

So the surname may, in fact, be your guide to the actual place of origin of the family. Your next problem will be to discover the original surname, and this you may find if you can trace the baptismal or confirmation record of Ernst, because they are likely to give the true surname.

The final naming problem in this particular area is that of the practice of using patronymics—the naming of a child by giving him a new surname based on the first name of the father. Thus Wilhelm, son of Ernst Borgman, could be christened as Wilhelm Ernst. In instances like this, you must again have recourse to baptismal and confirmation records in order to trace the real surname. If you trace an ancestor back to a particular place and find no one of that name in the place before him, then your most obvious reaction is to assume he must have come there from elsewhere. However, do not make this assumption until you have checked out the possibility of a name change.

PASSENGER LISTS

In most countries these are either nonexistent or so few in relation to the whole that they need not be considered as a source of genealogical information. In Germany, however, the story is very different, and that is why I put them second to church registers as a good source of information. In fact, they are equally vital to people whose ancestors came from many other countries in Europe—Austria, Bulgaria, the former Czechoslovakia, Hungary, Poland, Romania, Serbia, the Scandinavian countries, and the former USSR.

Bremen and Hamburg were the main ports for European emigration from 1832 (Bremen) and 1845 (Hamburg) up to 1934. Unfortunately, the Bremen lists were destroyed, but the Hamburg lists are available and on microfilm.

They contain the names of over five million people who emigrated through the port and the lists are located in the Hamburg State Archives. Microfilm copies of the 1850–1934 Hamburg emigration lists are available from the LDS Family History Library or, upon request, from the Hamburg Historic Emigration Office, Steinstrasse 7, 20095 Hamburg. If you know the exact year of emigration, the cost of a search by the Emigration Office will be at least thirty dollars per name and year searched. For this you will receive an official certificate, which will include the information that appears in the original passenger list: passenger's name, age, occupation, hometown, date of departure, and sometimes his marital status, number of children, and destination.

On the other hand, since the LDS Church has also microfilmed the lists, I think you will find it cheaper to deal with them (35 North West Temple, Salt Lake City, UT 84150).

The State Archives in Hamburg house the original passenger lists of emigrants who sailed overseas directly from Hamburg, or indirectly via Hamburg to other European ports. For example, many emigrants sailed to a British port such as Gravesend or Harwich, crossed the country by train, and then sailed overseas from Liverpool. The period covered by the passenger lists is from 1850 to 1934, with the exception of January to June 1853 and August 1914 to 1919. However, the lists were only compiled for ships with more than twenty-five passengers. They are indexed on a yearly basis in rough alphabetical order. The LDS index is more accurate.

The passenger lists are divided into direct and indirect records. Most emigrants traveled *directly* to a port in their new homeland. For example, the great majority of emigrants to the United States landed in New York; from there they scattered across the country and to Canada and South America.

You will not need to search the lists, of course, if you already know the place of origin of your emigrating ancestor, and the details of his or her family. It will be much easier and less expensive to try other sources first (family stories, diaries, Bibles, naturalization records, or letters).

It is important to realize that not all emigrating Germans used Hamburg or Bremen. Some sailed from Le Havre in France. You must remember, too, that the place of origin shown in the passenger lists is not always the birthplace. However, in that case the odds are that the place of birth was quite near the place of domicile. For example, your ancestor may be shown as coming from Herrenhäusen (a small city), whereas his place of birth may have been Neuburg, a little village a few miles away.

Even if you find no record in the Hamburg lists, all is not lost. Several of the German states kept their own records of emigration from the state, notably Brunswick (Braunschweig), Hesse (Hessen), and Württemberg. Other similar records were kept in many individual cities and towns.

If you are consulting the lists yourself the following glossary may be of help to you:

Alter	Age
Anschrift	Address
Auswanderer	Emigrant
Beruf	Occupation
Bestimmungsort	Destination
Datum	Date
Erwachsen	Adult
Geboren	Born
Geburtsort	Birthplace
Gewerbe	Occupation
Herkunftsort	Place of origin
Kinder	Children
Länder	Provinces or states
Ledig	Single
Namen	Names
Nationalität	Nationality
Ort	Place
Strasse	Street
Verheiratet	Married
Vorname	Given name
Wohin	Destination
Zuname	Surname

Other possible sources of information are the official lists of permits to emigrate. Most of these have been lost, but some have been published for the areas of Brunswick (Braunschweig), Nassau, Sachsen-Weimar, and Waldeck. The German Genealogical Society of America has copies of these.

Another source of information about arrivals in the United States from the Germanic areas of Europe is a series of volumes called *Germans to America: Lists of Passengers Arriving at U.S. Ports 1850–1891,* ed. Ira A. Glazier and P. William Filby. This is an on-going project.

Names

In your search of records remember it was common in the middle 1700s in the Germanic areas to use only the *second* baptismal name in official records in later life. The first name was that of a parent or grandparent and was given as a compliment but never used officially. So Oskar Georg Weber would only appear as Georg Weber.

INTERNAL MIGRATION

We have talked about German emigration to countries overseas, but we must also give attention to internal migration of Germans within Europe, including immigration of Germans *into* Germany. There are many instances of this; the following provide four major examples:

1. Early in the twelfth century the King of Hungary invited German settlement in the easternmost province of his country, Transylvania, which was underpopulated and open to invasion from warlike tribes to the east. Some five thousand settlers accepted the invitation; mostly they came from the Rhineland, although they later became known as Saxons. They were given as much land as they could cultivate and were granted freedom from taxes and military service, and allowed the right to maintain their own language. Since that time they have been able to preserve their traditions and customs within the area of original settlement, known as the King's land or Königsboden. Of course, many of the settlers found the limited area more than a little confining and some moved out to work for the Hungarian landowners in other parts of Transylvania or to the Banat area to the southwest.

During the period of the Reformation, the "Saxons" became Lutheran, the Magyars were divided between Catholic and Calvinist, and the Szeklers (a race related to the Hungarians) became Catholic, Calvinist, and Unitarian.

2. In 1731–38 some 30,000 German Protestants were expelled from the Salzburg area of Austria by the Catholic prince-bishop. These people, generally speaking, were resettled in Prussia (Preussen). For further information, see the chapter on Austria.

3. Catherine the Great of Russia invited Germans to colonize areas of the fertile Ukraine and the basin of the Volga. This mass migration continued between 1763 and 1862. Most of the emigrants to Russia came from Hesse (Hessen) and the Rhineland, with smaller numbers from other parts of the Germanic area. There were also emigrants from Denmark, France, Sweden and Finland, and Switzerland.

When the German armies invaded the USSR in 1941, they were welcomed by the majority of the Germans living in Ukraine. When the Wehrmacht retreated in 1942, many of the German settlers left, too, fearing reprisals from the Red Army, and they were wise. They made their way back to Germany, the fatherland their ancestors had left over a century before, and those left behind were killed or imprisoned, or exiled to Kazakhstan.

4. In 1945 Czechoslovakia regained the Sudetenland. This German-speaking area had been taken from Austria in 1919 and awarded to the new

country of Czechoslovakia. In 1938 it was reunited with Germany. After 1945 the three and a half million German inhabitants were forcibly expelled and their property and possessions seized.

Note: After the Second World War, thirteen million Germans returned to Germany (most to West Germany). Some of these came voluntarily, but the great majority were given no choice by Czechoslovakia, Poland, and the USSR.

Quite apart from the mass movements of population shown above, there was, of course, a continual movement to and fro between the various states before and after unification in 1871. Most of these movements of individuals were recorded. If a man wished to move from Hannover to Brunswick, for example, he would notify the Hannover police of his impending departure and his destination. On arrival in Brunswick he had to report his arrival to the police within three days. They in turn notified the police in Hannover that he had arrived. Although many of these police records were destroyed in the Second World War, the majority survived and are either in city archives, the local police headquarters, or the provincial archives. Here again you will have to check in the place of your interest to find out if the police records still survive.

Civil Registration (Reichspersonenstandsgesetz)

This started in 1875 following the unification of Germany, but only so far as the main Germanic area was concerned. In some areas the system had started earlier. There is a Register Office (Standesamt) for each particular area. All records of births, marriages, and deaths are kept there, but a duplicate of each entry is sent to the state capital. It should be noted that a registration area can be quite large, covering several towns and villages.

In those areas originally under French control, such as Alsace-Lorraine (Elsass-Lothringen) and a few other small areas west of the Rhine, registration started in 1810; in Frankfurt (once a Free City) it began in 1850, in Lübeck and Oldenburg in 1811, in Hannover in 1809, and in most parts of Prussia in about 1870. The death registers are particularly useful because they very often give not only the place and date of death, but also the names of the parents of the deceased and any surviving children.

Wills (Testamente)

The probate system in Germany is a little complicated. Once a lawyer has drawn up a will, a copy is deposited in the district courthouse (Amtsgericht) for the area in which the testator is *living*. The local authorities then notify the Civil Register Office (Standesamt) in the district where the testator was *born*. When he dies, the Standesamt in his place of death notifies the Standesamt in his place of birth, and the latter, in turn, notifies the Court of

Law of the location of the will. The court then executes the will. Original wills are either in the district courthouse or in the state archives (Staatsarchiv) in each province.

Censuses (Volkszählungen)

These have been held on a countrywide basis since 1871, but others were held at irregular intervals in various areas. Germany has traditionally conducted the censuses through the states, or provinces, rather than through the central government:

GERMANY: 1871, 1880, 1885, 1890, 1895, 1900, 1905, 1910, 1919, 1925, 1933, 1939

WEST GERMANY: 1946, 1950, 1961, 1970

EAST GERMANY: 1946, 1964

BADEN: 1852, 1855, 1858, 1861, 1867, 1925, 1933, 1946

BADEN-WÜRTTEMBERG: 1946, 1950, 1961, 1970

BAVARIA (BAYERN): 1846, 1849, 1852, 1855, 1858, 1861, 1867, 1946, 1950, 1961, 1970

BERLIN (WEST): 1945, 1946, 1950, 1961, 1970

BERLIN (EAST): 1945, 1946, 1964

BREMEN: 1900, 1905, 1946, 1950, 1961, 1970

COLOGNE (KÖLN): 1961

DRESDEN: 1871

HAMBURG: 1866, 1867, 1871, 1946, 1950, 1961, 1970

HESSE (HESSEN): 1925, 1946, 1950, 1961, 1970

NORTH-RHINE-WESTPHALIA (NORDRHEIN-WESTFALEN): 1946, 1950, 1961, 1970

PRUSSIA (PREUSSEN): 1895, 1900, 1905, 1910

RHINELAND-PALATINATE (RHEINLAND-PFALZ): 1946, 1950, 1961, 1970

SAARLAND: 1927, 1935, 1961, 1970 (see under France for 1945-57)

SCHLESWIG-HOLSTEIN: 1803, 1835, 1840, 1855, 1860, 1946, 1950, 1961, 1970

WÜRTTEMBERG: 1821, 1832, 1843, 1846, 1849, 1852, 1855, 1858, 1861, 1867, 1946, 1950

DEUTSCHES ZOLLVEREIN: 1855 (This was the area included in a Customs Union of North German States.)

Note: Some of these returns are only head counts, some name only the head of the household, some name only men. Do not assume the early returns (particularly in Prussia) will solve any problems. Many of the above census returns have been copied by the LDS Church.

The federal government receives the results from the states in order to make a "national head-count," but the original returns are kept in the individual states and copies can be obtained from the municipal archives (Stadtarchiv) or the Civil Register Office (Standesamt) in each city or district. East Germany, when it was independent, destroyed its census returns once they were counted and so they are not available for research.

In order to consult the census returns or obtain a copy of the original return, you will, of course, need to have an address in either a city or a village. For the former you will want a street name but for the latter it is not so essential. When writing, you should give the full name of your ancestor, if known, and the names of his or her spouse and children. This will enable the authorities to distinguish between people of the same name. It will be no use asking for a copy of the census return of Wilhelm Müller in Neudorf, Hesse; there might be twenty of them living there at the same time. Wilhelm Erich Müller would narrow it down, and Wilhelm Erich and his wife, Elisabeth, and his sons, Erich and Heinrich, would pinpoint it.

You must also be prepared to find that some census returns were destroyed by bombing in the Second World War. It may be wise for you to contact the central census authority and ask if the census returns exist for a particular location and where they are located. The address is:

Statistisches Bundesamt
Gustav-Stresemann-Ring 11
Postfach 5528, 65189 Wiesbaden
(Postal address: Postfach 5528, 65180 Wiesbaden)
E-mail: info@statistik-bund.de
Web site: www.statistik-bund.de/e_home.htm

In addition to the censuses listed above there were others conducted at irregular intervals over the years by individual cities, for example, Mecklenburg in 1819. You will have to check on these by writing to the state and municipal archives for the area in which you are interested.

Police Registration (Einwohnermelderegister)

This started in most of the states in about 1840 and controlled internal movement. The records included full name, family details, date and place of birth, and occupation. As I mentioned earlier in this chapter, the records are usually held in local archives, police headquarters, or state archives.

Military Records (Kriegslisten)

These are incomplete and not always easily accessible but they are worth working on because every male was liable for military service in the various state armies. If your ancestors came from the Schleswig-Holstein area, you are luckier than most. The system there involved the registration of every male child at birth and the record was kept up to date as far as addresses were concerned until his call-up date. A good sequence of discoveries can follow: if you find your ancestor's addresses from the military records, you can trace the census returns; if you find the census returns you find the place of birth; if you find the place of birth you find the church records, you lucky people from Schleswig-Holstein! The military lists in general date back to the early 1700s and are in the state archives.

Certificate of Birth (Geburtszeugnis or Geburtsbrief)

When a person wanted to establish citizenship in a city or town, or get married, or join a guild (see below), he or she would have to produce this document. The individual had to produce a letter from the priest or pastor in his or her birthplace and the civil authorities would then issue the certificate.

Guild Records (Gilderbücher)

These can provide valuable information for you. The guild (like the trade union of today) was powerful in the work field. It permitted its members to work only at a particular trade, in a particular place. It made sure that a newcomer in town became a citizen before he joined the guild. Remember that being an inhabitant was not the same as being a citizen. Anyone could be an inhabitant, but you had to earn the right to become a citizen. You had to work hard, not be a charge on the community, not be a bastard, be sober, be a churchgoer, and know the right people.

Then, and only then, the good citizen could apply to join a guild, and the guild records show his name, his trade, the names of his wife and children, the date and place of his birth, the date and place of his marriage, and the date of his arrival in the city and his entry into the guild. The guilds exercised so much control over their members that they could dictate the area of the city in which they lived, and even whom they married (preferably the daughter of another guild member).

The guild records are either in local archives or in state archives, and they date back in many cases to the early seventeenth century, and in a few instances even earlier.

Other Available Records

There are three important sources of information in Germany that are often overlooked. They are, in order of value, Ortssippenbücher (Local Family Books), Geschlechterbücher (Lineage Books), and Leichenpredigten (Funeral Sermons).

These records should be used in conjunction with all the other sources I have listed; none of them, on their own, will provide you with all the answers, but they may well fill gaps, solve relationship puzzles, and give you the place of origin, or marriage, or death of a particular ancestor. Unfortunately, the records I mention are not in any one place, nor are the locations listed. You will have to write to the particular place or general area in which you are interested: to the Mayor (Bürgermeister) for a village, town, or city; or to the local Catholic priest or Lutheran minister; or to the director of the city archives (Stadtsarchiv) or the provincial archives (Landesarchiv or Staatsarchiv). You will have to ferret out the locations for yourself, but I never promised you a Rosengarten!

One final word of warning: be sure to send three International Reply Coupons and a self-addressed airmail envelope, and be prepared for a little resistance in some places to producing the Ortssippenbücher for reasons made clear below.

Local Family Books (Ortssippenbücher)

German genealogists and sociologists have been very interested since the early part of this century in studying the various families living in a particular area. This is partly pure research, partly love of history, and partly the German passion for tidiness, for having everything in its proper place. The Ortssippenbuch for a particular area will list all the members of every family (living and dead) and their relationship with each other. The source of the information was, of course, the church register, both Lutheran and Catholic.

As interest in the projects grew, the organization of them was taken over by a branch of the government, and as each district was completed, the results were published in book form. The ultimate aim was to have a genealogical record of the entire German people.

This was a point where the interests of genealogists in tracing family descent coincided with the National Socialist racial policies for a brief period. After 1933 many German citizens, particularly farmers, storeowners, and teachers, were required to provide a certificate proving their Aryan descent—der Ahnennachweis, as it was called—and the existence of a completed Ortssippenbuch for their district simplified their task. The tracing of lineage was required back to the early nineteenth century; only the S.S. demanded lineage back to 1750 for their members.

Publication was suspended in 1940; after the war the task was taken over by the genealogical organizations without regard to any racial purity, and today some 150 books are in print. In addition, very many books were started and never finished, or finished and never printed. You will find the books or manuscripts in local and state archives. The present-day compiling of the books is not being done on a very even basis, since it depends very much on the energy and dedication of the various genealogical organizations. About half of the completed books refer to districts in the Länder of Baden and Hessen-Nassau.

It should be mentioned that some manuscripts are still in the possession of the individuals who worked on them, and if you are referred to a private individual your approach should be a tactful one, since not everyone wishes to be reminded of the original reasons for their genealogical research.

German Lineage Books (Deutsche Geschlechterbücher)

These books date back in some cases to the late eighteenth century when the first known one was published. The contents, of course, go back very much further. They contain the details of descent of bourgeois families, i.e. middle class and lower upper class, not the nobility. Each book contains a number of family trees of various German families. They are on a regional basis in that all the families in the book are from one district.

Some two hundred of the Geschlechterbücher have been published, and more are on the way. Each family section starts with the earliest known member and descends through the years to the date of publication. It also lists occupations and places of baptism, marriage, death, and residence.

Funeral Sermons (Leichenpredigten)

This source of genealogical information is almost unique to Germany but I have found similar records in Hungary. They originated in the sixteenth century for a rather odd reason. When the Reformation reached Germany, it meant the end of a very ornate and impressive funeral mass in the Catholic Church. This was a great occasion in which the deceased was praised at length by a local orator (often a professional, paid for his services), a large choir performed, and a sermon was delivered by the local priest (or by the bishop if the dead man or woman was important enough, or if the remaining spouse was generous to the church).

The end of this kind of ceremony left a gap in the lives of many people, mainly among Lutherans and Calvinists. They had embraced a simple and stark religion, but many of them missed a good funeral mass! So the funeral sermon was born and took the form of a eulogy at the graveside. Some sermons were entirely religious in content, but many were biographical and recounted the whole life of the deceased with details of births, marriages, public or military service, and other events of note.

After the ceremony the sermons were printed and circulated to all the friends of the family. There are well over one hundred thousand of these preserved in various locations and covering the period from about 1550 up to around 1800. Some of them are only a page or two in length, but some, if the deceased was famous, run to a hundred pages or more!

You can usually depend on the information contained in them being accurate; since the sermon was to be circulated among family and friends there was no point in lying or exaggerating the life and accomplishments of the deceased. Obviously, certain events would probably be quietly ignored: a period of insanity, a bastard child, dishonorable discharge from the army, a conviction for theft—that sort of thing would be left unsaid.

You can see that these three sources may well be of great value to you. Remember, though, that two of them are limited in their scope. The Lineage Books are confined to the bourgeois families, the Funeral Sermons to the

wealthier Protestants; only the local Family Books record everybody—
Catholic and Lutheran, rich and poor, in fact all classes of society.

Because the records I have mentioned are scattered in so many municipal
offices, libraries, and archives, the search for one that includes your own
family may be long-drawn-out, but if you are successful you may find your
family lineage for a good many years, even two or three centuries.

There are still more available records of use to you. In some localities you
will find all of them, in others only one or two:

	Approximate starting date
Adressbuch (City Directory)	1750*
Bürgerbuch (Citizenship Record)	1300
Familienregister (Family Registers)	1800
Gerichtsprotokolle (Court Records)	1500*
Grundbücher (Land Records)	1000*
Lehrlingsbücher (Apprentice Records)	1550
Polizeiregister (Police Registers)	1800
Stadtchroniken (City Chronicles)	1600
Steuerbücher (Tax Records)	1400
Zeitungen (Newspapers)	1800*

The dates are approximate because they vary from province to province,
and from city to city. Generally speaking, the records marked with an
asterisk are in the provincial archives (Staats- und Landesarchiv) and the
others in city archives (Stadtarchiv) or district archives (Kreisarchiv), but
there are exceptions to this.

One of the major problems about German records of interest to the ancestor-hunter is that they are scattered among church archives, state archives,
city, town, and village archives, some government departments and offices,
libraries, and museums. To make matters worse, only one attempt has been
made to list the location of all genealogical archives and that effort, though
praiseworthy, is very incomplete. Make no mistake: the material is there; it
is available and informative, and it goes back over the centuries. Even
minor local events were recorded and will be of interest to you.

Central Office for Genealogy (Zentralstelle für Genealogie)

Even though this has now been incorporated into the Sachsen State
Archives (Sächsisches Staatsarchiv Leipzig, Schongauerstrasse 1, 04329
Leipzig; Phone: 011-49-341-2555551; Fax: 011-49-341-2555555), it still
exists as a distinct collection.

The various holdings include the following:

1. A pedigree and ancestor list includes more than 12,000 family trees,
including over two million card-indexes of individual names. If you are

consulting these cards in person (and you may obtain permission to do so), you must know the system. Because of the variation in the spelling of surnames, it was decided to follow a system of phonetic spelling and file under one spelling variation only. So, for example, under the name Maier you will also find Mayer, Meier, and Meyer.

2. A catalogue of personal writings and eulogies covers the sixteenth to eighteenth centuries and consists of some 700 works. It is being added to on a regular basis and is certainly only in its infancy, and it includes many printed funeral orations and sermons (I have referred to this German custom earlier in this chapter).

3. The Zentralstelle für Genealogie (Z.G.) contains photocopies and microfilms of a number of church registers of all denominations. There is no list available, but this is understandable because the additions are being made constantly and any list would soon be out of date.

4. There are more specialized items in the Z.G. records such as:

(a) A list of the population of Leipzig before 1800, including the surrounding area.

(b) Records of the Huguenots who fled from France after the bloody persecution that followed the revocation of the Edict of Nantes in 1685.

5. The library of Z.G. includes 22,000 writings on genealogical subjects, in both published and manuscript form, covering the period from the seventeenth century to the present day.

ARCHIVES

The many divisions of the Germanic area are the cause of the peculiar distribution of archives. From the fourteenth to the nineteenth century, central power over the Germanic lands was exercised by the Hapsburg dynasty, so the central archives of the old Reich are in Vienna. (See the chapter for Austria.)

Since then, the various states have preserved their own archives; as a result, there are archives of all kinds scattered throughout Germany, from major cities down to small villages, and there are no central archives with precious genealogical records.

You will find Staatsarchiv (national), Staatsarchiv (provincial), Landesarchiv (provincial), Stadt (city), Bezirk (district), Dorf (village), Familien (family), Dom (cathedral), Pfarr (parish), Gutsarchiv (property), plus many others for individuals, families, professions, manufacturing plants, religious orders, and youth organizations.

In the following pages you will find details of many of the archives of value to the ancestor-hunter: first, the provincial or state archives; then a list of local archives alphabetically by city, town, and village; and finally a list of church archives at a level lower than those included earlier in this chapter. In addition you will find a list of archives devoted to the papers of noble families.

State/Provincial Archives

Landesarchivdirektion Baden-Württemberg
Eugenstrasse 7
70182 Stuttgart
Phone: 011-49-7112124272. Fax: 011-49-71121242 83
Web site: www.lad-bw.de/fr-lad.htm

Hauptstaatsarchiv Stuttgart
Konrad-Adenauer-Strasse 4
70173 Stuttgart
Phone: 011-49-7112124335. Fax: 011-49-71121243 60
Web site: www.lad-bw.de/hstas.htm

Generealdirektion der Staatlichen
Archive Bayerns
Schönfeldstrasse 5
80539 Munich
Phone: 011-49-8928638482. Fax: 011-49-8928638615

Landesarchiv Berlin
Kackreutnstrasse 1-2
10777 Berlin
Phone: 011-49-30218830. Fax: 011-49-21283177
E-mail: info@landesarchiv-berlin.de
Web site: www.landesarchiv-berlin.de/

Brandenburgisches Landeshauptarchiv
Ander Orangerie 3
Postfach 60049
14404 Potsdam
Phone: 011-49-33156740120. Fax: 011-49-33156741122

Staatsarchiv Bremen
Am Staatsarchiv 1
28203 Bremen
Phone: 011-49-4213616221. Fax: 011-49-42136110247
Web site: www.bremen.de/info/staatsarchiv/bestand/ubersich/starter.htm

Staatsarchiv Hamburg
Kattunbieiche 19
22041 Hamburg
Phone: 011-49-4036813200. Fax: 011-49-4036813201
Web site: www.hamburg.de/Behoerden/Staatsarchiv/

Hessisches Hauptstaatsarchiv
Mosbacher Strasse 55
65187 Wiesbaden
Phone: 011-49-6118810. Fax: 011-49-611881145

Landeshauptarchiv Schwenn
Graf-Scrack-Alee 2
19053 Schwenn
Phone: 011-49-3855929610. Fax: 011-49-3855929612

Niedersächsisches Hauptstaatsarchiv
Am Archiv 1
30169 Hannover
Phone: 011-49-5111206601. Fax: 011-49-5111206699
E-mail: poststelle@staatsarchiv-h.niedersachsen.de
Web site: www.staatsarchive.niedersachsen.de/

Nordrhein-Westfälisches Hauptstaatsarchiv
Mauer Strasse 55
40476 Düsseldorf
Phone: 011-49-2119449902. Fax: 011-49-21194497002

Landeshauptarchiv Rheinland-Pfalz
Karmeliterstrasse 3
56068 Koblenz
Phone: 011-49-26191290. Fax: 011-49-2619129112
E-mail: info@landeshauptarchiv.de
Web site: www.landeshauptarchiv.de/uebersicht.html

Landesarchiv Saarbrücken
Dudweilerstrasse 1
66133 Saarbrücken
Phone: 011-49-681980390. Fax: 011-49-681980039133

Sächsisches Hauptstaatsarchiv Dresden
Archivstrasse 14
01097 Dresden
Phone: 011-49-35180060

Sächsisches Staatsarchiv Leipzig
(see address below)

Landesarchiv Magdeburg Landeshauptarchiv
Hegelstrasse 25
39104 Magdeburg
Phone: 011-49-39156643. Fax: 011-49-3915664440

Landesarchiv Schleswig-Holstein
Prinzenpalais
24837 Schleswig
Phone 011-49-4621861800. Fax: 011-49-4621861801
E-mail: LASH.SL@t-online.de
Web site: www.schleswig-holstein.de/archive/lash/index.html

Thüringisches Hauptstaatsarchiv Weimar
Marstallstrasse 2
(Postfach 726, 99408 Weimar)
99423 Weimar
Phone: 011-49-36438700. Fax 011-49-364870100

City Archives (Stadtarchiv)

The type of record you will find in local archives includes all or some of the following. It is up to you to write and find out what is available for your particular district. Try to write in German, because even though there may be someone there who understands English, he or she may not read it well enough to understand just what you want to know. I once wrote and asked for the correct name of a book about leading families in a particular city. I had a reply in flawless English telling me they had only one copy of the book, and in any case it would be too heavy to send through the mail! They did not mention the name of the book, either, so I had to write again in German, and then all was well. You may also find that when you write in English you will be answered in German. In this case you can try to find someone who speaks German, a friend or a local teacher, or settle down with a good German-English dictionary in the local library.

At this point let me again remind you to enclose a self-addressed airmail envelope and three International Reply Coupons to cover return postage. If you are planning a great deal of correspondence with Germany, it will save money if you buy German stamps. Write to the post office (Postamt) of any German city, enclose a bank draft for a sum of money (five or ten dollars), and ask them to mail you German stamps of the right value for airmail letters to this country.

The type of records you will find are listed below:

Address Books (Adressbücher)
Apprentice Lists (Lehrlingsbücher)
Census Returns (Volkszählungen)
City Chronicles (Stadtchroniken)

City Directories (Adressbücher)
Citizenship Lists (Bürgerbücher)
Court Records (Gerichtsprotokolle)
Emigration Lists (Auswanderungregister)
Family Books (Ortssippenbücher)
Family Registers (Familienregister)
Funeral Sermons (Leichenpredigten)
Grave Registers (Grabregister)
Guild Books (Gilderbücher)
Land Records (Grundbücher)
Lineage Books (Geschlechterbücher)
Newspapers (Zeitungen)
Parish Registers (Kirchenbücher)
Police Registers (Polizeiregister)
Probate Records (Testamente)
Tax Records (Steuerbücher)
Wills (Testamente)

The following abbreviations are used in the list of cities, towns, etc., below to show the provinces or Länder in which the places are located:

B	Bayern
BL	Bremen
BR	Brandenburg
BW	Baden-Württemberg
H	Hessen
HL	Hamburg
MV	Mecklenburg-Vorpommern
NS	Niedersachsen
NW	Nordrhein-Westfalen
RP	Rheinland-Pfalz
S	Saarland
SA	Sachsen
SAA	Sachsen-Anhalt
SH	Schleswig-Holstein
T	Thüringen

Aachen (NW)	Altenburg (SA)	Annaberg-Buckholz
Aalen (BW)	Alt-Wallmoden (NS)	(SA)
Abensberg (B)	Alzey (RP)	Annweiler (RP)
Ahaus (NW)	Amlishagen (BW)	Ansbach (B)
Ahrweiler (RP)	Amöneburg (H)	Apolda (T)
Alsfeld (H)	Amstetten (B)	Arnsberg (NW)
Altdorf (B)	Andernach (RP)	Arnstadt (T)
Altena (NW)	Anklam (MV)	Artern (SAA)

Aschaffenburg (B)
Ascherleben (T)
Aue (SA)
Augsburg (B)
Babenhausen (H)
Bacharach (RP)
Backnang (BW)
Balingen (BW)
Bamberg (B)
Baunatal (H)
Bayreuth (B)
Beeskow (BR)
Bensheim (H)
Bentheim (NS)
Bergisch-Gladbach (NW)
Bad Bergzabern (RP)
Berleburg (NW)
Berlin
Bernburg (SAA)
Besighem (BW)
Bevensen (NS)
Biberach (BW)
Bielefeld (NW)
Bingen (RP)
Bischofswerda (SA)
Bitterfeld (SAA)
Blaubeuren (BW)
Blomberg (NW)
Bocholt (NW)
Bochum (NW)
Bonn (NW)
Borken (NW)
Borna (SA)
Bottrop (NW)
Flecken Bovenden (NS)
Brafkenheim (BW)
Brakel (NW)
Brandenburg an der Havel (BR)
Brandestein bei Elm (H)
Braunschweig (NS)

Breckerfeld (NW)
Breisach (BW)
Bremen (BL)
Bremerhaven (BL)
Brilon (NW)
Brühl (NW)
Bad Buchau (BW)
Bühl (BW)
Büren (NW)
Burg auf Fehmarn (SH)
Burg bei Magdeburg (SAA)
Burgbernheim (B)
Burghausen (B)
Burgkunstadt (B)
Burgsteinfurt (NW)
Burkheim am K (BW)
Butzbach (H)
Buxtehude (NS)
Calbe (SAA)
Calw (BW)
Castrop-Rauxel (NW)
Celle (NS)
Cham (B)
Chemnitz (SA)
Coburg (B)
Coesfeld (NW)
Coswig (SAA)
Cottbus (BR)
Crimmitschau (SA)
Cuxhaven (NS)
Darmstadt (H)
Deggendorf (B)
Deidesheim (RP)
Delitzch (SA)
Demmin (BR)
Dessau (SAA)
Detmold (NW)
Diez (RP)
Dillingen/Donau (B)
Dingolfing (B)
Dinkelsbühl (B)
Dinslaken (NW)

Doberlug-Kirchhain (BR)
Donauwörth (B)
Dornburg/Elbe (SAA)
Dorsten (NW)
Dortmund (NW)
Dreieichenhain (H)
Dresden (SA)
Dubeln (SA)
Duderstadt (NS)
Duisburg (NW)
Dulmen (NW)
Düren (NW)
Bad Durkheim (RP)
Düsseldorf (NW)
Eberbach (BW)
Eberswalde (BR)
Ebingen (BW)
Eckernförde (SH)
Edenkoben (RP)
Eggenfelden (B)
Eichstatt (B)
Eilenburg (SA)
Einbeck (NS)
Eisenach (T)
Eisenberg (RP)
Eisenberg (T)
Eisfeld (T)
Eisleben (SAA)
Ellwangen (BW)
Emden (NS)
Emmerich (NW)
Bad Ems (RP)
Endingen (BW)
Engen (BW)
Erding (B)
Erfurt (T)
Erkelenz (NW)
Erlangen (B)
Eschwege (H)
Esslingen/Neckar (BW)
Eutin (SH)
Feuchtwangen (B)

Flensburg (SH)
Forchheim (B)
Forst/Lausitz (BR)
Bad Frankenhausen
   (SAA)
Frankenthal (RP)
Frankfurt/Main (H)
Frankfurt/Oder (BR)
Frechen (NW)
Freiberg (SA)
Freiburg/Breisgau
   (BW)
Freising (B)
Freudenstadt (BW)
Friedberg/Hessen (H)
Friedrichshafen (BW)
Fritzlar (H)
Fulda (H)
Furstenau (NS)
Furstenwalde (BR)
Fürth (B)
Füssen (B)
Gaildorf (BW)
Gardelegen (SAA)
Garmisch/
   Partenkirchen (B)
Geinhausen (H)
Geislingen (BW)
Gelsenkirchen (NW)
Gengenbach (BW)
Gera (T)
Gernrode (SAA)
Gerolzhofen (B)
Geseke (NW)
Gevelsberg (NW)
Giengen (BW)
Giessen (H)
Glücksburg (SH)
Glückstadt (SH)
Gnandstein (SA)
Göppingen (BW)
Görlitz (SA)
Goslar (NS)
Gotha (T)

Göttingen (NS)
Greifswald (MV)
Greiz (T)
Greussen (T)
Grimma (SA)
Groitzscg (SA)
Grossbottwar (BW)
Gross-Gerau (B)
Grünberg (H)
Grunstadt (RP)
Guben (BR)
Gudensberg (H)
Güstrow (MV)
Hachenburg (RP)
Hagen (NW)
Halberstadt (SAA)
Halle an der Saale
   (SAA)
Hamburg (HL)
Hameln (NS)
Hanau (H)
Hann-Munden (NS)
Hannover (NS)
Haslach (BW)
Hattingen (NW)
Heidelberg (BW)
Heidenheim/Brenz
   (BW)
Heilbad Heiligenstadt
   (T)
Helmstedt (NS)
Herberg/Elster (BR)
Herford (NW)
Herne (NW)
Herrenberg (BW)
Hersbruck (B)
Bad Hersfeld (H)
Herten (NW)
Hildburghausen (T)
Hilden (NW)
Hildesheim (NS)
Hochstadt (B)
Hof (B)
Hofgeismar (B)

Homberg (H)
Bad Homburg (H)
Horb/Neckar (BW)
Hornburg (NS)
Höxter (NW)
Hüfingen (BW)
Husum (SH)
Ilmenau (T)
Ingelheim (RP)
Ingolstadt (B)
Iserlohn (NW)
Isny (BW)
Itzehoe (SH)
Jena (T)
Jever (NS)
Jülich (NW)
Juterbog (BR)
Kaiserlautern (RP)
Kalkar (NW)
Kamenz (SA)
Kandel (RP)
Karlshafen (H)
Karlsruhe (BW)
Karlstadt (B)
Kassel (H)
Kaufbeuren (B)
Kelheim (B)
Kempen (NW)
Kempten/Aligäu (B)
Kenzingen (BW)
Kiel (SH)
Kirchheim/Teck (BW)
Kirn (RP)
Kirtorf (H)
Kitzingen (B)
Kleve (NW)
Koblenz (RP)
Köln (NW)
Königshofen (B)
Konstanz (BW)
Korbach/Edersee (H)
Köthen/Anhalt (SAA)
Kranenburg (NW)
Krefeld (NW)

Bad Kreuznach (RP)
Kronach (B)
Krönberg (H)
Kulmbach (B)
Kusel (RP)
Lage-Lippe (NW)
Lahnstein (RP)
Lahr (BW)
Landau (RP)
Landsberg (B)
Landshut (B)
Bad Langensalza (T)
Laubach (H)
Lauenburg/Elbe (SH)
Lauf (B)
Laufen (B)
Lauingen/Donau (B)
Lauterbach (H)
Lauterecken (RP)
Leipzig (SA)
Lemgo (NW)
Leutkirch (BW)
Leverkusen (NW)
Lich (H)
Lichtenfels (B)
Limburg-Lahn (H)
Lindau (B)
Linz (RP)
Lippstadt (NW)
Löbau (SA)
Lörrach (BW)
Lubben (BR)
Lübeck (SH)
Luckenwalde (BR)
Lüdenscheid (NW)
Ludwigsburg (BW)
Ludwigshafen (RP)
Ludwigslust (MV)
Lügde (NW)
Lüneburg (NS)
Lünen (NW)
Magdeburg (SAA)
Mainz (RP)

Mannheim (BW)
Marburg (H)
Marienberg (SA)
Markdorf (BW)
Markleeberg (SA)
Marktredwitz (B)
Marl (NW)
Maulbronn (BW)
Mayen (RP)
Meckenheim (NW)
Meersburg (BW)
Meiningen (T)
Meisenheim (RP)
Meissen (SA)
Meldorf (SH)
Melle (NS)
Memmingen (B)
Menden (NW)
Mengen (BW)
Meppen (NS)
Bad Mergentheim
   (BW)
Merseburg (SAA)
Messkirch (BW)
Metelen (NW)
Mettmann (NW)
Meuselwitz (SA)
Michelstadt (H)
Mindelheim (B)
Minden (NW)
Mittweida (SA)
Moers (NW)
Möhringen (BW)
Mönchengladbach
   (NW)
Monschau (NW)
Montabour (RP)
Mühldorf (B)
Mühlhausen/Thur (T)
Munich (München)
   (B)
Münnerstadt (B)
Münster (NW)

Bad Münstereifel
   (NW)
Namedy (RP)
Nassau (RP)
Nauheim (H)
Naumburg/Saale
   (SAA)
Neckarsteinach (H)
Neheim/Hüsten (NW)
Neuburg (B)
Neuenburg (BW)
Neuenhaus (NS)
Neumünster (SH)
Neuötting (B)
Neuss (NW)
Neustadt (B)
Neustadt (SH)
Neustadt/Donau (B)
Nidda (H)
Nideggen (NW)
Nordhausen (T)
Nordhorn (NS)
Nordlingen (B)
Northeim (NS)
Nürnberg (B)
Nürtingen (BW)
Oberhausen (NW)
Obernburg/Main (B)
Oberndorf (BW)
Oberursel/Taunas (H)
Oberviechtach (B)
Ochsenfurt (B)
Oelsnitz im Vogtland
   (SA)
Offenbach/Main (H)
Offenburg (BW)
Ohrdruf (T)
Öhringen (BW)
Oldenburg (SH)
Oldenburg (NS)
Bad Oldesloe (SH)
Olpe (NW)
Opladen (NW)

Oppenheim (RP)
Oranienburg (BR)
Oschatz (SA)
Oschersleben (SAA)
Osnabruck (NS)
Osterburg (SAA)
Osterrode/Harz (NS)
Otterberg (RP)
Otterndorf (NS)
Paderborn (NW)
Paschim (MV)
Pegau (SA)
Perleberg (MV)
Pforzheim (BW)
Pfullendorf (BW)
Pfullingen (BW)
Pirna (SA)
Plauen im Vogtland
 (SA)
Porz (NW)
Pössneck (T)
Prenzlau (MV)
Pritzwalk (BR)
Bad Pyrmont (NS)
Quakenbrück (NS)
Quedlinnburg (SAA)
Radolfzell (BW)
Rain (B)
Rastatt (BW)
Ratingen (NW)
Ratzeburg (SH)
Ravensburg (BW)
Rees (NW)
Regensburg (B)
Reichenbach im
 Vogtland (SA)
Reinheim (H)
Remagen (RP)
Remscheid (MW)
Rendsburg (SH)
Reutlingen (BW)
Rheda/Wiedenbrück
 (NW)

Rheinberg (NW)
Rheine (NW)
Rhein Hausen (NW)
Rheydt (NW)
Rhoden (H)
Riedlingen (BW)
Rieneck (B)
Riesa (SA)
Rinteln (NS)
Rochlitz (SA)
Romrod (H)
Rosberg (NW)
Rosenheim (B)
Rostock (MV)
Rotenburg (NS)
Roth (B)
Rothenburg (B)
Rottwell (BW)
Rudolstadt (T)
Ruhla (T)
Rüthen (NW)
Saalfeld (T)
Saarbrücken (S)
Saarlouis (S)
St. Goar (RP)
St. Ingbert (S)
Salzgitter (NS)
Bad Salzuflen (NW)
Bad Salzungen (T)
Salzwedel (SAA)
Sangerhausen (SAA)
Schalkau (SAA)
Schleiz (T)
Schleswig (SH)
Schleusingen (T)
Schlitz (H)
Schmalkalden (T)
Schmölin (SA)
Schneeberg (SA)
Schönebeck (SAA)
Schongau (B)
Schopfheim (BW)
Schorndorf (BW)

Schotten (H)
Schramberg (BW)
Schwabach (B)
Schwäbisch Gmund
 (BW)
Schwäbisch Hall
 (BW)
Schweinfurt (B)
Schwelm (NW)
Schwerin (MV)
Schwetzingen (BW)
Seefeld (B)
Seehausen/Altmark
 (SAA)
Sendenhorst (NW)
Senftenberg (BR)
Siegburg (NW)
Siegen (NW)
Sigmaringen (BW)
Sindelfingen (BW)
Singen (BW)
Sinsheim (BW)
Sondershausen (T)
Sonneberg (T)
Bad Sooden (H)
Speyer (RP)
Sprendlingen (H)
Stade (NS)
Stadthagen (NS)
Stassfurt (SAA)
Stendal (SAA)
Stockach (BW)
Stockum (NW)
Straelen (NW)
Stralsund (MV)
Straubing (B)
Stuttgart (BW)
Suhl (T)
Sulz/Neckar (BW)
Tangermunde (SAA)
Telgte (NW)
Tittmoning (B)
Bad Tolz (B)

Torgau (SA)
Traunstein (B)
Treffurt (T)
Trier (RP)
Tübingen (BW)
Überlingen (BW)
Uelzen (NS)
Ulm (BW)
Ulrichstein (H)
Unna (NW)
Velbert (NW)
Verden/Aller (NS)
Viersen (NW)
Villingen (BW)
Vohburg/Donau (B)
Volklingen (S)
Wachtenheim (RP)
Waiblingen (BW)
Bad Waldsee (BW)
Waldheim (SA)
Waldshut (BW)
Wangen (BW)
Wanne-Eickel (NW)
Warendorf (NW)

Warstein (NW)
Wasserburg am Inn
 (B)
Wattenscheid (NW)
Weisen-Oberpfalz (B)
Weil am Rhein (BW)
Weilburg (H)
Weilheim (B)
Weimar (T)
Weingarten (BW)
Weinheim (BW)
Weismain (B)
Weissenburg (B)
Weissenfels (SAA)
Werl (NW)
Werne an der Lippe
 (NW)
Wernigerode (SAA)
Wertheim (BW)
Wesel (NW)
Wetzlar (H)
Wiesbaden (H)
Wilster (SH)

Bad Wimpfen (BW)
Bad Windsheim (B)
Winsen (S)
Wismar (MV)
Witten (NW)
Wolfach (BW)
Wolfenbüttel (NS)
Wolgast (MV)
Wolmirstedt (SAA)
Wormeln (NW)
Worms (RP)
Wülfrath (MW)
Wünsiedel (B)
Wuppertal (NW)
Würzburg (B)
Xanten (NW)
Zeitz (SAA)
Zelia-Mehlis (T)
Zerbst (SAA)
Zeulenroda (T)
Zittau (SA)
Zweibrücken (RP)
Zwickau (SA)

I do not claim that the above list is complete. It has been put together from a variety of sources, and there will probably be omissions, particularly of smaller places. Correspondence should be sent to the Direktor, Stadtarchiv, followed by the name of the city and the province or Länder.

In addition to the above, there are specialized archives in such places as Jena, for example, where you will find the archives of the Karl Zeiss Company and the Jena Glassworks. If you know your ancestor worked for a large corporation it may be worthwhile to write to the company concerned to ask if it has archival or personnel records available.

There is also the Red Cross Archives in Dresden (Das Zentral Verwaltungsarchiv des Deutschen Roten Kreuzes, Kaitzerstrasse, 01069 Dresden). This may be useful if you are trying to trace someone who was a refugee from the area of Germany in former Soviet territory.

Parish Archives (Pfarrarchiv)

Many of the city archives shown above also have local church records, but given below are separate church archives known to exist and *not* included in the major church archives previously listed. After the province code, a C or L is given in parentheses to indicate whether the archives hold Catholic or Lutheran records, or both:

Amöneburg (H) (C)
Balingen (BW) (L)
Biberach (BW) (L and C)
Bochum (NW) (L)
Bottrop (NW) (C)
Brakel (NW) (C)
Burgensteinfurt (NW) (L and C)
Duderstadt (NS) (L and C)
Duisburg (NW) (L)
Dulmen (NW) (L)
Emden (NS) (L)
Emmerich (NW) (L and C)
Engelskirchen (NW) (C)
Erfurt (T) (L and C)
Essen (H) (C)
Flensburg (SH) (C)
Göttingen (NS) (L and C)
Gudow (SH) (L)
Hagen (NW) (L and C)
Hattingen (NW) (L)
Herford (NW) (L and C)
Herrenberg (BW) (L)
Hof (B) (L)
Höxter (NW) (C)

Isny (BW) (L)
Karlsruhe (BW) (L)
Kassel (H) (L)
Kulmbach (B) (C)
Leer (NS) (L)
Lich (H) (L)
Lübeck (SH) (L)
Methler (NW) (L)
Molzen (NS) (L)
Munstereifel (NW) (L)
Neuss (NW) (L)
Remagen (RP) (L and C)
Rottwell (BW) (C)
St. Goar (RP) (L)
Schwäbisch Hall (BW) (L)
Siegburg (NW) (C)
Stockum (NW) (C)
Überlingen (BW) (C)
Uelzen (NS) (L)
Viersen (NW) (C)
Wattenscheid (NW) (L and C)
Wetzlar (H) (L and C)
Xanten (NW) (C)
Zweibrücken (RP) (L)

Family Archives (Familienarchiv)

Many of the princely, noble, or prominent German families have either donated the family papers and records to the state, or opened their documents to the general public. Searches can be made without charge—according to local decision. These family archives may be located in the original family residence (often a Schloss, or castle) or in archives in the state or nearest city or village. You will have to do some letter-writing about this because the variations are infinite. If your ancestors were employed by these families, or were tenant farmers on the estate, the information can be of very great value to you.

The family archives I have been able to discover are listed below, showing the place, the abbreviation for the province or Länder, and the name of the family. (Note: The abbreviations are the same as those given on page 140.)

Adelebsen (NS), Adelebsen
Ahausen (NW), Spee
Alme (NW), Spee zu Alme
Altenhof (SH), Reventlow
Althausen (BW), Württemberg
Amecke (NW), Wrede-Amecke
Amorbach (B), Leiningen
Anholt (NW), Salm
Antfeld (NW), Papen zu Antfeld
Apelern (NS), Münchhausen
Artelshofen (B), Harlach
Aschhausen (BW), Zeppelin
Assenheim (H), Solms-
  Rödelheim
Assumstadt (BW), Waldburg-
  Wolfegg
Aufsess (B), Aufsess
Augsburg (B), Fugger
Aulendorf (BW), Königsegg-
  Aulendorf
Banteln (NS), Benningsen
Beetzendorf (SAA), Von der
  Schulenberg
Beichlingen (T), Werthern-
  Beichlingen
Bentlage (NW), Wittgenstein-
  Berleburg
Berleburg (NW), Wittgenstein-
  Berleburg
Besselich (RP), Barton-Stedman
Bietigheim (BW), Hornstein
Binningen (BW), Hornstein
Birkenau (H), Unstadt
Birstein (H), Isenburg
Bödigheim (BW), Collenberg
Bodman (BW), Bodman
Boltzenburg (MV), Von Arnim
Haus Borg (NW), Kerkerinck
Braunfels (H), Solms-Braunfels
Breitenburg (SH), Rantzau
Breitenhaupt (NW), Kanne
Haus Brinke (NW), Korff-Bilkau
Buchholz (BW), Ow

Budingen (H), Ysenburg
Buldern (NW), Romberg
Burgsteinfurt (NW), Bentheim
Burkeim (BW), Fahnenberg
Caen (NW), Geyr
Calmsweiler (S), Buseck-Weber
Canstein (NW), Elverfeldt
Cappenberg (NW), Stein
Castell (B), Castell
Celle (NS), Lüneberg
Coesfeld (NW), Salm-Horstmar
Corvey (NW), Ratibor
Crassenstein (NW), Ansembourg
Crollage (NW), Ledebur
Dalwigksthal (H), Dalwigk
Darfeld (NW), Vischering
Derneburg (NS), Münster
Deutsch-Nienhof (SH),
  Hedemann-Heespen
Die Poltsdorf (B), Enderndorf
Diersburg (BW), Roeder
Diersfordt (NW), Wernigerode
Dillingen (B), Fuggers
Donaueschingen (BW),
  Fürstenberg
Donzdorf (BW), Rechberg
Drensteinfurt (NW), Landsberg-
  Velen
Dresden (SA), Wolkenstein
Bad Driburg (NW), Oeynhausen
Dulmen (NW), Croy
Durbach (BW), Windschläg
Dyck (NW), Reifferscheidt
Ebnet (BW), Gayling
Egelborg (NW), Oer
Eglofs (BW), Syrgenstein
Eichtersheim (BW), Venning
Elbenberg (H), Buttlar
Ellingen (B), Wrede
Eltville (H), Eltz
Erbach (H), Erbach
Erpernburg (NW), Wartenberg-
  Brenken

Erzelleben (SAA), Alvensleben
Eschenbach (B), Eschenbach
Essingen (BW), Woellwarth
Eybach (BW), Degenfeld-
    Schonburg
Fachsenfeld (BW), Fachsenfeld
Fischbach (B), Enderndorf
Frankenberg (B), Pöllnitz
Frankisch-Crumbach (H),
    Gemmingen
Furth-Burgfarrnbach (B), Pückler
Gärtringen (BW), Gärtringen
Gemünd (NW), Harff-Dreiborn
Gemünden (RP), Salis-Soglio
Gersfeld (H), Ebersberg-Froberg
Gödens (NS), Wedel
Göppingen (BW), Liebenstein
Gotha (T), Hohenlohe
Greifenberg (B), Perfall
Grevenburg (NW), Oeynhausen
Gross-Brunsrode (NS), Bülow
Grünsberg (B), Reichenbach
Guttenberg (B), Guttenberg
Burg-Guttenberg (BW),
    Gemmingen
Hahnstatten (RP), Bieberstein
Haidenburg (B), Aretin
Haimendorf (B), Rehlingen
Harff (NW), Mirbach
Havixbeck (NW), Twikkel
Heimerzheim (NW), Böselager
Heltorf (NW), Spee
Herbern (NW), Merveldt
Herdringen (NW), Fürstenberg
Heroldsberg (B), Geuder
Herrnstein (NW), Reichenstein
Hinnenburg (NW), Asseburg
Hohenstadt (BW), Adelmann
Höllinghofen (NW), Böselager
Hornberg (BW), Gemmingen
Hugstetten (BW), Mentzingen
Irmelshausen (B), Bibra
Jagsthausen (BW), Berlichingen

Jettingen-Eberstall (B),
    Stauffenberg
Kalbeck (NW), Vittinghoff
Kellenberg (NW), Hoensbroech
Kendenich (NW), Kempis
Kleinbottwar (BW), Schaubek
Königseggwald (BW), Aulendorf
Korschenbroich (NW),
    Wüllenweber
Kronburg (B), Westernach
Laibach (BW), Racknitz
Langenstein (BW), Douglas
Laubach (H), Solms-Laubach
Lauterbach (H), Riedesel
Lenthe (NS), Lenthe
Lich (H), Solms-Lich
Lipporg (NW), Galen
Loburg (NW), Elverfeldt
Marck (NW), Grüter
Marxwalde (BR), Hardenberg
Massenbach (BW), Massenbach
Merkstein (NW), Brauchitsch
Merlsheim (NW), Mühlen
Mespelbrunn (B), Ingelheim
Meuselwitz (SA), Seckendorff
Mitwitz (B), Würtzburg
Moyland (NW), Steengracht
Nassau (RP), Stein
Neuenburg (B), Gagern
Neuenstein (BW), Hohenlohe
Neunhof (B), Welser
Neuwied (RP), Wied
Niedenstein (BW), Venning
Niederstotzingen (BW),
    Maldegem
Oberbalzheim (BW), Balzheim
Obernzenn (B), Seckendorff
Oberstadion (BW), Schönborn
Öhringen (BW), Hohenlohe
Ostwig (NW), Lüninck
Ottingen (B), Ottingen
Pöttmes (B), Gumppenberg
Rammersdorf (B), Eyb

Ratzenried (BW), Trauchberg
Regensburg (B), Thurn-Taxis
Rentweinsdorf (B), Rotenhan
Rheda-Wiedenbrück (NW),
   Tecklenburg
Rösberg (NW), Weichs
Rotha (SA), Friesen
Rugland (B), Crailsheim
Ruhr (NW), Mühlen
Rust (BW), Böcklinsau
Schatthausen (BW), Ravensburg
Schillingsfürst (B), Hohenlohe
Schlatt (BW), Reischach
Schlitz (H), Görtz
Schönstein (RP), Wildenburg
Schopfheim (BW), Roggenbach
Schwarmstedt (NS), Lenthe
Schwarzenberg (B),
   Schwarzenberg
Schwarzenraben (NW), Ketteler
Schweinsberg (H), Schweinsberg
Sigmaringen (BW), Hohenzollern
Simmelsdorf (B), Simmelsdorf
Singen (BW), Enzenberg
Somborn (H), Savigny
Stapel (NW), Raitz-Frentz-Droste
Steisslingen (BW), Stotzingen
Stetten (BW), Stetten
Sulzfeld (BW), Ravensburg
Surenberg (NW), Heereman-
   Zuydtwyck
Syburg (B), Geyern
Tambach (B), Ortenburg

Tannhausen (BW), Thannhausen
Tannheim (BW), Schaesberg
Thurnau (B), Giech
Trier (RP), Kesselstatt
Trockau (B), Trockau
Ullstadt (B), Frankenstein
Volkershausen (B), Stein-
   Ostheim
Vörden (NW), Haxthausen
Vornholz (NW), Nagel-Doornick
Waake (NS), Wangenheim
Waal (B), Leyen
Wachendorf (BW), Ow-
   Wachendorf
Wallerstein (B), Oettingen
Warthausen (BW), Warthausen
Weeze (NW), Loë
Weissenburg (B), Geyern
Welbergen (NW), Welbergen
Wernstein (B), Künsberg
Wertheim (BW), Löwenstein-
   Wertheim
Westerholt (NW), Westerholt
Westerwinkel (NW), Merveldt
Wewer (NW), Brenken
Wiesentheid (B), Wiesentheid
Wittgenstein (NW), Wittgenstein-
   Hohenstein
Wolfegg (BW), Waldburg-
   Wolfegg
Worms (RP), Hernsheim
Zeil (BW), Waldburg-Zeil

Libraries (Bibliotheken)

The public libraries in cities and towns should not be neglected as a source of information. They usually contain directories, local histories, and newspapers—all of which may date back to the middle or early part of the nineteenth century. In many places names have been abstracted from newspapers and placed on index cards.

Other Records

The LDS Church has some miscellaneous material on microfilm from Neubrandenburg, Rostock, and Schwerin. The Landeshauptarchiv in Dresden has eighty-four volumes of parish registers from former Sachsen Garnisonsorte (military posts in Saxony).

German Archives in the Czech Republic and Poland

The archives of the following cities (originally German) are in the Czech Republic and Poland. The authorities are helpful in answering queries if you can write either in the language of the country or in German or English, preferably the first. Of course, you will remember to cover the return postage by sending three International Reply Coupons and also a self-addressed airmail envelope. You should also offer to pay whatever fees are required. For more information about archives in the two countries, see the chapters on them.

The Czech Republic

Correspondence should be sent to Státní Oblastní Archiv, followed by the street address and new city name, i.e. the names in parentheses below (the German name is given first and the present Czech name is shown in parentheses):

Krajská 1, 41274
Leitmeritz (Litoměřice)

Snemovní 1
74622 Troppau (Opava)

Poland

Correspondence should be sent to Archiwum Państwowe, followed by the street address and new city name, i.e. the names in parentheses below (the German name is given first and the present Polish name is shown in parentheses):

ul. Zamkowa 3
Allenstein (10521 Olsztyn)

ul. Pomorska 2
Breslau (50215 Wrocław)

ul. Dworcowa 65
Bromberg (85009 Bydgoszcz)

ul. Waly Piastowskie 5
Danzig (80958 Gdańsk)

Stary Kiselin 31
Grünberg (66002 Zielona Góra)

ul. Jagiellonska 25
Kattowitz (40145 Katowice)

ul. Zywcięstwa 117
Köslin (75950 Koszalin)

ul. Zamkowa 2
Oppeln (45016 Opole)

ul. Brama Wybranców 2
Pless (43200 Pszczyna)

ul. 23 Lutego 41/43
Posen (60967 Poznań)

ul. Kilinskiego 12
Schneidemühl (64920 Piła)

ul. sw. Wojciecha 13
Stettin (70410 Szczecin)

pl. Rapackiego 4
Thorn (87100 Toruń)

German Records in Belgium

Under the terms of the Peace Treaty of Versailles the German areas of
Eupen and Malmedy were transferred to Belgium. Church and civil records
relating to that area are in the Belgian Provincial Archives et Liège (Archives de l'État, rue de Chéra 72, 4000 Liège).

Genealogical Associations

There are a number of genealogical associations in Germany. They are all
loosely associated with a national genealogical association: Deutsche
Arbeitsgemeinschaft Genealogischer Verbände or DAGV, Auf der
Rosenhöhe 34B, 63069 Offenbach am Main (Phone: 011-49-69832433;
Fax: 011-49-698383252; E-mail: g.gramlich@t-online.de). I list the various associations below. It is important that you make contact with the one
operating in your area of Germany because (a) they will probably know if
someone else has already researched your family; (b) many of them have
their own libraries and archives, which may contain items of vital interest to
you; (c) many of them publish magazines at regular intervals and will
publish small ads or queries, either free or for a small charge. Some of them
only accept queries for their own members, so you might consider joining.

The DAGV issues good advice in English to people sending inquiries to
them, or to the individual associations. It is worthwhile giving you a précis
of the advice.

1. There is no connection between the church records of the two major denominations. If you want a search made in a church archive or register, you must know the actual religion.

2. There can be no answer to questions about an ancestor unless you know a place of origin, birth, or marriage. Inquiries based on "Germany," or "Pruessen," or "near Stuttgart" cannot be answered.

3. Do all the research you possibly can in your own country through family papers, wills, obituary notices, and family Bibles.

4. If you are asking questions about several people who came from different locations, write each query on a separate sheet of paper.

5. If you have already done some research, give all the details.

6. Good English is better than bad German. Use a typewriter, or print all names of persons and places.

7. Send _four_ International Reply Coupons to cover postage and expenses. Donations are appreciated.

The list of associations I mentioned is given below. It is as complete as I can make it, but bear in mind addresses can change, and there can always be additions or deletions. If you do not find one that covers your area of interest, write to the DAGV for further information:

I am listing the DAGV branches and their addresses in German and not in English. Many of them are in small towns where there is little knowledge of English, and I am told that delivery is not always certain because of this. Even if you speak no German, you can look at the last word in each address and that will be the name of the city or town. You will surely know the name of the nearest city to your ancestral place of origin and should have no problem. DAGV agrees with this advice.

Arbeitskreis Familienforschung **Ahlen** und Umgebung e. V., Fritz-Winter-Weg 23, 59227 Ahlen

Deutsch-**baltische** genealogische Gesellschaft, Herdweg 79, 64285 Darmstadt

Bayerischer Landesverein für Familienkunde e. V., Ludwigstraße 14/I, 80539 München

Bergischer Verein für Familienkunde e. V., Dr. Michael Knieriem, Engelsstraße 10, 42283 Wuppertal

Herold, Archivstraße 11, 14195 **Berlin**

Die Maus, Gesellschaft für Familienforschung e. V., Am Staatsarchiv 1/Fedelhören, 28203 **Bremen**

Genealogischer Verein **Chemnitz** e. V., Straße Usti nad Labem 23, 09119 Chemnitz

Arbeitskreis **donauschwäbischer** Familienforscher e. V., Goldmühlestraße 30, 71065 Sindelfingen

Roland zu **Dortmund**, Postfach 103326, 44033 Dortmund

Düsseldorfer Verein für Familienkunde e. V., Norbert Degenhard, Krummenweger Straße 26, 440885 Ratingen

Familienkundliche Arbeitsgemeinschaft der "Männer vom Morgenstern" (zwischen **Elb- und Wesermündung**), Müggenburgweg 2, 27607 Langen

Emsländische Landschaft, Arbeitskreis Familienforschung, Ludmillenstraße 8, 49716 Meppen

Gesellschaft für Familienforschung in **Franken** e. V., Archivstraße 17, 90408 Nürnberg

Genealogisch-Heraldische Gesellschaft **Göttingen**, Postfach 2062, 37010 Göttingen

Arbeitskreis für Familienforschung im **Hagen**er Heimatbund e. V., Alper Straße 71-75, 58091 Hagen

Genealogische Gesellschaft **Hamburg**, Postfach 302042, 20307 Hamburg

Hessische familiengeschichtliche Vereinigung e. V., Karolinenplatz 3, 64289 Darmstadt

Mosaik. Familienkundliche Vereinigung für das **Klever** Land e. V., Lindenallee 54, 47533 Kleve

Gesellschaft für Familienkunde in **Kurhessen und Waldeck** e. V., Postfach 101346, 34013 Kassel

Leipziger Genealogische Gesellschaft, Bahnhofstraße 95, 04448 Wiederitsch

Arbeitskreis für Familienforschung e. V., Mühlentorplatz 2, 23552 **Lübeck**

Arbeitsgemeinschaft Genealogie **Magdeburg**, Thiemstraße 7, 39104 Magdeburg

Verein für **Mecklenburgische** Familien- und Personengeschichte e. V. Thünen-Museum, 17168 Warnkerhage

Arbeitsgemeinschaft für **Mitteldeutsche** Familienforschung e. V. Marlene Müller, Waldweg 5, 04416 Markkleeberg

Familienkundliche Gesellschaft für **Nassau und Frankfurt** e. V., Mosbacher Strasse 55, 65187 Wiesbaden

Niedersächsischer Landesverein für Familienkunde, Am Bokemahle 14-16, 30171 Hannover

Gesellschaft für Familienforschung in der **Oberpfalz** e. V. Rachelstraße 12, 93059 Regensburg

Oldenburgische Gesellschaft für Familienkunde, Lerigauweg 14, 26131 Oldenburg

Arbeitskreis Familienforschung **Osnabrück**, Kiwittstraße 1a, 49080 Osnabrück

Upstalsboom-Gesellschaft für historische Personenforschung und Bevölkerungsgeschichte in **Ostfriesland** e. V., Fischteichstraße 16, 26603 Aurich

Verein für Familienforschung in **Ost- und Westpreußen** e. V., An der Leegde 23, 29223 Celle

Pfälzisch-Rheinische Familienkunde e. V. Rottstraße 17, 67061 Ludwigshafen

Arbeitsgemeinschaft für **Saarländische** Familienkunde e. V. Hebbelstraße 3, 66346 Püttlingen

Siegerländer Heimat- und Geschichtsverein e. V. Siegen, Postfach 10 05 41, 57005 Siegen

Sudetendeutsches Genealogisches Archiv, Erikaweg 58, 93053 Regensburg

Arbeitsgemeinschaft Genealogie **Thüringen** e. V. Martin-Andersen-Nexö-Straße 62, 999096 Erfurt

Westdeutsche Gesellschaft für Familienkunde e. V. Unter Gottes Gnaden 34, 50859 Köln

Westfälische Gesellschaft für Genealogie und Familienforschung, Postfach 6125, 48133 Münster

Verein für Familien- und Wappenkunde in **Württemberg und Baden** e. V. Postfach 105441, 70047 Stuttgart

There are also some organizations concerned with more specific subjects:
Mennonitischer Geschichtsverein, Am Hollerbrunnen 7, 67295 Bolanden
Salzburger Verein e. V. Memeler Straße 35, 33605 Bielefeld

The following organizations are sources of information about **Huguenotten (Huguenots)**:
Deutscher Hugenottenverein e. V. Hafenplatz 9 a, 34385 Bad Karlshafen

Hugeunot and Walloon Research Association, Malmaison, Church Street, Great Bedwyn, England SN8 3PE (information about Huguenot refugees from Germany)

Consistorium der Französischen Kirche, Joachim-Friedrichstrasse 4, 10711 Berlin 31

Anglo-German FHS, 14 River Reach, Teddington, London TW11 90L England (information about Huguenot refugees from France)

There are also over 200 historical associations and societies in all the major cities and towns. It is impossible to list them all, but a letter addressed to *Historischer Verein* followed by the name of the place will probably produce results. Historical organizations very often have a great deal of information about local families even if genealogy is not the main object of their existence.

GERMAN SETTLERS IN RUSSIA

Perhaps, even though you are of pure German ancestry, your family is descended from the Germans who emigrated to Russia between the mid-1700s and the mid-1800s. In that case you may have assumed there is no chance of tracing your forebears back to their place of origin in the area that is now Germany. In fact there is a very good chance that records exist which will give you some vital information.

In 1763 the Empress Catherine II of Russia invited all foreigners who possessed skills of some kind to come to her country as settlers and colonists. In cases of financial hardship the cost of transportation was paid. In addition, all settlers received a loan of money toward the costs of building a house and buying livestock and farm or trade equipment, with repayment required in ten years.

The proclamation of the Empress was distributed throughout Europe but did not meet with any great response except in the Germanic area. Most of the colonists came from Hessen and the Rhineland, but many other German-speaking areas were represented to a lesser extent.

Purely as an aside, and with nothing to do with your ancestry, I want to share with you the extraordinary number of titles held by the Empress and included in her proclamation of 1763: "Empress and Autocrat of all the Russians at Moscow, Kiev, Vladimir, Novgorod, Czarina of Kasan, Czarina of Astrachan, Czarina of Siberia, Lady of Plaskow, Grand Duchess of Smolensko, Duchess of Estonia and Livland, Carelia, Twer, Yogoria, Permia, Viatka, and Bulgaria, and others; Lady and Grand Duchess of Novgorod in the Netherland of Chernigov, Resan, Rostov, Yaroslav, Belooseria, Udoria, Obdoria, Condonia, and Ruler of the entire North Region and Lady of the Yurish, of the Cartalinian and Grusinian czars, and the Cabardinian land, of the Cherkessian and Gorisian princes, and the lady of the manor and sovereign of many others."

The areas opened up for settlement by the Empress were underpopulated, and open to frequent attack by the Ottoman Turks. The Germans, for their part, were eager to settle for many different reasons, among them religious persecution, starvation, high taxes, civil disorders and foreign wars, compulsory military service, and a high population density.

Between 1804 and 1842 over 72,000 people emigrated, and total estimates for the entire period range as high as 150,000 from the German area alone. It was one of the great mass movements of history. For a century Germans poured into Russia and established themselves in fairly close areas of settlement in the Volga region, the Black Sea area, and the Caucasus.

The whole story is documented in a remarkable book by Dr. Karl Stumpp entitled *The Emigration from Germany to Russia, 1763-1862* and published in 1978 by the American Historical Society of Germans from Russia, 631 D Street, Lincoln, NE 68502. It lists the names of some 50,000 German settlers, with their places of origin and settlement.

It may be helpful to quote the areas of origin and settlement over the century:

Period of Emigration	Place of Origin	Area of Settlement
1763–68	Hessen, Rheinland, Pfalz, Sachsen, Württemberg, Switzerland	Volga (Evan.[1] and Luth.[2])
1765	Sulzfeld, Württemberg	Reibensdorf (Evan.)
1766	Hessen, Württemberg, Brandenburg	Petersburg, Black Sea
1766	Hessen	Belowesh (Evan. and Cath.[3])
1780	Preussen, Württemberg, Bayern	Josefstal, Fischerdorf, Jamburg, in Dnieper area
1782	Sweden	Schwedendorf (Evan.)
1786	Preussen	Alt-Danzig
1789–90	Danzig, West Preussen	Chortitza (Menn.[4])
1804–6	Alsace, Pfalz, Baden	Franzfeld, Mariental, Josefstal, by Odessa (Cath.)
1804–6	Württemberg, Alsace, Pfalz, Baden, Hungary	Grossliebental, Neuburg, Alexanderhilf
1804–6	Danzig, West Preussen	Halbstadt, Molotschna (Menn.)

---

[1]Evangelical, [2]Lutheran, [3]Catholic, [4]Mennonite.

Period of Emigration	Place of Origin	Area of Settlement
1804–6	Württemberg, Baden, Hessen	Prischib, Molotschna (Evan. and Cath.)
1804–6	Württemberg, Switzerland	Neusatz, Zürichtal, in the Crimea (Evan. and Cath.)
1808–10	Württemberg, Alsace, Pfalz	Bergdorf, Glückstal, Kassel, Neudorf, area of Odessa (Evan.)
1808–10	Alsace, Baden, Poland	Baden, Elsass, Kandel, Selz, Mannheim, Strassburg (Cath.)
1808–10	Alsace, Baden, Pfalz, Württemberg	Beresan and Odessa (Cath.)
1812–27	Württemberg, Baden, Hessen	Prischib, Molotschna (Evan.)
1814–16	Württemberg, Preussen, Bayern, and Poland	Bessarabia, and near Odessa
1817–18	Württemberg	South Caucasus (Evan.)
1821–34	Württemberg, Preussen, Bayern, and Poland	Bessarabia, and near Odessa
1822–31	Württemberg	Swabian colonies near Berdjansk (Evan.)
1823–42	Danzig, West Preussen, Baden, Hessen, Rheinland	Grunau area (Evan. and Cath.)
1853 and 1859–62	Danzig, West Preussen	Samara (Menn.)

This was the last emigration from Germany.

GREECE

After the Roman Empire was divided into eastern and western sections in 395, the history of Greece was tied to that of the eastern section, the Byzantine Empire. There were invasions by Visigoths, Huns, Slavs, and Bulgars, and finally in the fifteenth century by the Turks. A few parts remained unconquered. Genoa ruled Chios until 1566, and Venice controlled Crete until 1669. In addition, a continuing series of wars between Venice and the Turks meant that several islands and even Athens itself were occupied by the Venetians on various occasions. Greece itself became a poor and neglected province of the Ottoman Empire, although many Greeks made their peace with the conquerors and held high administrative positions in the empire.

The long period of darkness ended in the early nineteenth century with a sudden resurgence of Greek nationalism. In 1821 a struggle for independence started and soon involved Great Britain, France, and Russia. Turkey gave Greece local autonomy in 1829, and in 1832 the country declared its complete independence. Crete remained under Turkish control until 1898, then it became independent, but it finally joined Greece in 1913.

Greece became involved in the Balkan Wars in 1912–13, and then in the First World War in 1917. As a result of these wars and the later peace conferences, Greece added to her territory with the inclusion of parts of Macedonia, the whole of Thrace, and the islands of the Dodecanese. In 1921 she invaded Turkey but was defeated in the following year.

In 1923 there was a massive interchange of populations, organized by the League of Nations. One and a half million Greeks left Asia Minor (where there had been Greek settlements for centuries) for Greece, and 800,000 Turks and 80,000 Bulgarians from areas transferred to Greece went back to their homelands. The wounds left by this great exodus of people have never healed.

In 1940 Italy, and later Germany and Bulgaria, invaded Greece and occupied it until the end of the Second World War. There was constant guerrilla warfare, and many churches and local government offices and their records were destroyed.

Archives

The main archives are the State General Archives (Genika Archeia Toù Kratous, Theatrou 6, 10552 Athens. Phone: 011-30-1-321-9601; Fax: 011-30-1-321-9935). Records there are available for research after a period of fifty years; however, the genealogical information in the archives is confined to records brought from Asia Minor after the evacuation of 1922. This collection, which was brought to Athens by Greek officials and refugees, contains church registers, family papers, wills, and many other documents covering the period from 1800 to 1922.

There are also genealogical records of various kinds in the Historical Archives of Crete (Historika Archeia Kritis, Odos I. Sfakianaki 20, Khanea, Kriti; Phone: 011-30-821-92-606). Other small archives are in some of the Ionian Islands—Corfù, Cefalonia, Paxi, Levkas, Zakynthos, Ithaki, and Kythera.

Church Registers

There are no central records of church registers or even information about their whereabouts. Basically, the records are in the individual churches (if they have not been destroyed), but they are fairly recent, since the keeping of records was a very chancy affair before 1800. His Grace Maximos Xydas, the Archimandrite of the Greek Orthodox Church, told me with regret that it is impossible to provide ancestor-hunters of Greek descent with addresses of churches, indexes to records, or even any information as to whether parish records exist or not.

The country is divided into "Metropolis" areas (each under a metropolitan, or bishop) and these include very many individual parishes. If you know the village from which your Greek ancestors came you should write directly to the priest there. Do try to get your letter translated into Greek, because it is most unlikely that a village priest will read any English, or that anyone else in the village will read it. If you receive no reply, you should write to the headquarters of the Orthodox Church (Aghias Filotheis 21, 10556 Athens; Phone: 011-30-1-3352-300), and ask for the address of the metropolitan whose territory includes your particular village. Then write to him for information.

Civil Registration

This started on a local basis in 1831. The records are kept in the municipal offices, but many have been destroyed. In 1925 it was organized on a national basis; registration bureaus were set up in Athens, Piraeus, and Thessaloniki. In other cities, and in villages, the mayor or an official appointed by him acts as registrar. Marriage certificates are also issued by the local priest. If you know the exact place of origin, you can write to the mayor for information about the specific vital event. My advice above about writing in Greek will apply here, too. If you have difficulties you should write to the Department of Registry, Ministry of the Interior, Stadiou 31, 10559 Athens, or Special Registry Office for Greeks living abroad, Mitropoleos 60, 10563 Athens (Phone: 011-30-1-324-0722 or 011-30-1-324-0737; Fax: 011-30-1-322-5664).

Censuses

These started in 1907 and have been held at intervals of about ten years since then. However, most of the earlier ones have been destroyed. Access to recent ones is restricted, but special permission can be given by the Director, National Statistical Service, Evaggelistrias 2, 10563 Athens (Phone: 011-30-1-322-4794), providing that you can prove descent or relationship, and explain that the information is needed for genealogical research into your own family.

Wills

These date back to 1843 and are located in the Notary Offices and Land Registry, Mesogion 96, 11527 Athens (Phone: 011-30-1-771-3631 or 011-30-1771-0566).

Genealogical Research

It is not wise to be optimistic about your genealogical research in Greece. It all depends on whether your ancestral village was destroyed or damaged; on your ability to get your letters written in Greek; on the ability of the local priest to reply; and on your own persistence. You are more likely to succeed if your ancestor came from one of the three big cities, but all the odds are that he or she came from a small village. If your area is the Aegean Sea and its islands, you may be luckier than if it were on the mainland because there was less destruction of records.

HERZEGOVINA

This small Balkan country has been allied with Bosnia since the 1300s and has had very little political or economic independence. You will find details of its archives and genealogical records under Bosnia, on page 58.

It was first linked with Bosnia as a measure of protection against a threatened invasion by forces of the Ottoman Empire. This invasion finally occurred in the period 1463–1465, and both countries were occupied. The association continued from that time on, until and including the present day.

HUNGARY

The Magyars, or Hungarian people, originated in an area of present-day Russia, between the Volga River and the Ural Mountains. There are slight similarities between Hungarian, Finnish, and the dialect in use in the Baskir autonomous area. It is thought that in about 2000 B.C. the Hungarians moved east into the Urals, and the Finns and the Estonians moved west toward the Baltic Sea. By the year 600 the Hungarians, under pressure from Asiatic nomadic peoples, also moved west, and by 896 they had occupied most of present-day Hungary. The Hungarian language is among the purest in Europe in that it resembles most closely its original form of 3000 years ago (apart from a few Bulgarian and German words picked up during the great migration of the seventh century).

The Hungarian alphabet has 38 letters, consisting of 22 of our 26 (Q, W, X, and Y are missing) and 16 additional letters:

á   cs   é   gy   í   ly   ny   ó   ö   ő   sz   ty   ú   ü   ű   zs

By 1000 Hungary had become a unified kingdom, but by 1541 it had collapsed, owing to invasion by the Ottoman Turks from the east and the southeast. The western section of the country fell under Hapsburg control for the next four centuries; the central plains were occupied by the Turks; and the eastern part, or Transylvania, was ruled by Hungarian princes who accepted the suzerainty of the Ottoman Empire and paid an annual tribute. In 1686 Budapest was captured by the Hapsburgs, and in the following year the Turks withdrew from Transylvania. There was an unsuccessful revolt by the Hungarians, which ended in 1711, and another attempt at independence was not made until 1849. This was partially successful in that it led to reforms in the administration of the country.

In 1867, after Austria had been defeated in war by Prussia, it became more amenable, and the Austro-Hungarian Empire was created, with Hungary as an equal partner. At this time Hungary included Transylvania, Croatia-Slavonia, Ruthenia, Slovakia, the Burgenland, and the Banat. If your ancestors came from these areas it is vital for you to understand that the genealogical records you need may still be in Hungary, or they may be in one or more of the so-called "Successor States."

In 1919, after the First World War, Hungary paid the price of being on the losing side (not that it had any choice in the matter), and when the Austro-Hungarian Empire disintegrated Hungary lost two-thirds of its territory under the harsh terms of the peace treaty. The Burgenland was transferred to Austria; Slovakia formed part of the new country of Czechoslovakia; Yugoslavia took Croatia, Slavonia, and part of the Banat; and Romania took the rest of the Banat and the whole of the province, and ancient principality, of Transylvania.

There are twenty counties (Megye), apart from the capital (Budapest), and they each have their own archives. These come under the control of the National Archives (see below for contact information). However, you are quite welcome to correspond directly with the archive for the place in which you are interested.

Archives (Levéltárak)

National Archives of Hungary (Magyar Orzágos Levéltár)
Bécsikapu tér 2-4
1014 Budapest
(Mailing address: Postafiok 3, 1250 Budapest)
Phone: 011-36-1-356-5811. Fax: 011-36-1-212-1619
E-mail: mail@natarch.hu
Web site: www.natarch.hu

The National Archives has on microfilm the entries in every church register in the territory of present-day Hungary. Every archive in Hungary, including the National Archives, has two addresses—the normal street one and a postal box (*Postafiok*), which should be used for mail.

Regional Archives (Megye Levéltárak)

I list the counties and their archives below, together with the city and postal code. I am not listing street addresses, postal boxes, phone and fax numbers, web sites, or e-mail addresses. There are eighteen of these archives, and the details change frequently. This detailed information can be obtained from the National Archives in Budapest.

BÁCS-KISKUN: 6000 Kecakemét
BARANYA: 7621 Pécs
BÉKÉS: 5700 Gyula
BORSOD-ABAÚJ-ZEMPLÉN: 3525 Miskoloj
CSONOGRÁD: 6720 Szeged
FEJÉR: 8000 Szekésfehérvár
GYÓR-MOSON-SOPRON: 9022 Gyór
HADJÚ-BIHAR: 4024 Debrecen

HEVES: 3300 Eger
KOMÁROM-ESZTERGOM: 2500 Esztergom
NÓGRÁD: 3100 Salgótarján
PEST: 1052 Budapest
SOMOGY: 7400 Kaposvár
SZABOLCS-SZATMÁR-BEREG: 4400 Nyiregháza
TOLNA: 7100 Szekszárd
VAS: 9700 Szombathely
VESZPRÉM: 8200 Veszprém
ZALA: 8900 Zalaegerszeg

This is the complete list of regional archives, but there is another archive that should be included here, although it is not technically a regional archive, and that is the Budapest City Archives (Pōváros Levéltára, Városház u. 9-11, 1052 Budapest [Pf 1]; Phone: 011-361-117-2033; Fax: 011-361-118-3319; Web site: www.fph.hu/bphome/leveltar/INDEXE.HTM).

Before we start talking about the various sources of information in Hungary, and there are plenty, let me deal with some of the problems first:

1. Just because your grandfather's immigration or naturalization papers state he came from "Hungary," do not assume that this means within the boundaries of present-day Hungary. The records you need may well be in Austria, Croatia, Czech Republic, Romania, Slovakia, Ukraine, or Yugoslavia, because the place in which he was born may have become part of one of these countries.

2. If your ancestor's nationality appears as "Austrian," this may simply mean he was born within the boundaries of the Austro-Hungarian Empire, and he might have been born in Hungary, or in any one of a dozen other countries.

3. Allow for the fact that he may have changed or simplified his original name, or even that an immigration officer may have anglicized his name out of kindness (or malice).

4. If the present generation of your family no longer speaks Hungarian, try to find someone to translate your letters of inquiry, and the subsequent reply. You will find practically no Hungarians in the smaller towns or villages who speak English.

5. Be patient. Your letters will not be answered quickly. Remember you are not the only ancestor-hunter of Hungarian descent who is writing to the archives or the village priest or pastor!

6. Finally, don't be too demanding; be polite and friendly. No one is required to answer your letter.

Civil Registration (Állami Anyakőnyv)

This started in 1895; before that date the only records of vital events were the entries of baptism, marriage, and burial in the church registers. The original entries of registration since 1895 are kept in registration offices in each municipality, with copies in the county archives (Megyei Levéltár). Access is normally restricted to recent records, but special application can be made, giving the reason the information is required and proving descent from the person named in the entry. The churches still maintain their own registers as they did before 1895, but only civil registration is compulsory and of legal value.

If you have problems obtaining civil registration certificates, you should complain directly to the main administrative office of the Archives.

Church Registers (Egyhazi Anyakőnyv)

Hungary is mainly Catholic, but other religions include the Reformed Church, Lutheran, Greek Orthodox, Greek Catholic, and Jewish. All the church registers up to 1895 are in the original churches, but microfilm copies are in the county archives (Megyei Levéltár). Registers since 1895 (the first year of civil registration) are also in the churches, of course, but are not on microfilm in the various archives. The registers for the churches located in those parts of Hungary "lost" after the First World War are no longer within the boundaries of Hungary, although some of them have been microfilmed and copies are in the county archives. Fuller details about these are given later in this chapter.

Although the keeping of church registers was ordained at the Council of Trent in the middle 1500s, the early Hungarian church registers were nearly all destroyed by the invading Ottoman Turks and not many exist before 1700. To take random examples, you will find earlier ones for Hédervár (1673), Ágfalva (1661), Győr (Győrsziget) (1642), Magyarfalva (1636).

The early registers were in Latin, but by the middle nineteenth century the entries were in Hungarian.

Baptisms (Keresztelő)

These registers for all the denominations (except Jewish) include the full names of the children, address and occupation of parents, and names of godparents or witnesses.

Marriages (Házasság)

These include names, addresses, places of birth, occupations, names and addresses of parents, and names of witnesses.

Burials (Temetés)

These show the name and age of the deceased, place of birth and death, cause of death, and quite often, occupation and names of survivors and/or next of kin.

The Hungarian names of the major denominations are:

Catholic (Katholikus)
Reformed (Református)
Greek Orthodox (Görög Keleti)
Greek Catholic (Görög Katholikus)
Lutheran (Evangelikus)
Jewish (Izraelita)

The number of church registers of all denominations held on microfilm in the National Archives or elsewhere is too great to list by name—there are over 3500 of them. The actual figures are: Catholic, 1679; Reformed, 1033; Greek Orthodox, 84; Greek Catholic, 101; Lutheran, 297; and Jewish, 314. The National Archives of Hungary (Magyar Országos Levéltár) has published a complete list of these microfilmed registers (Egyházi Anyakönyvek Mikrofilm-Másolatai), which you can purchase.

It is possible, however, to list the microfilmed registers available for those areas ceded to Austria, Czechoslovakia, Romania, and Yugoslavia, and they are given below with their present location:

Austria

Microfilms of the Burgenland parishes originally part of Hungary (until 1919) are located in two of the county archives (Megyei Levéltár):

Vas Megyei Levéltár

Catholic. Alsóbeled, Alsóőr, Arokszállas, Badafalva, Baksafalva, Bándol, Barátfalva, Borostyánkő, Burgóhegy, Csém, Egyházasfüzes, Felsőkethely, Felsőőr, Felsőszénégető, Gyanafalva, Incéd, Karácsfa, Kicléd, Királyfalva, Kukmér, Kupfalva, Léka, Lödös, Magashegy, Máriafalva, Nagyfalva, Nagysároslak, Nagyszentmihály, Németcsencs, Németlövő, Németszentgrót, Németújvár, Óbér, Óriszentmárton, Pásztorháza, Pinkafő, Pinkakertes, Pinkamiske, Pörgölény, Posaszentkatalin, Pusztaszentmihály, Rábakeresztúr, Rábaszentmárton, Rohonc, Rótfalva, Sámfalva, Strém, Szentelek, Szentkút, Újhegy, Városszalónak, Várszentmiklós, Vasdobra, Vasfarkasfalva, Vasjobbágyi, Vaskomját, Vasvörösvár, and Vörthegy.

Reformed. Felsőőr.

Lutheran. Alhó, Alsólövő, Borostyánkő, Felsőlövő, Felsőőr, Kukmér, Nagyszentmihály, Némethidegkút, Őrisziget, Pinkafő, Rohonc, Ujkörtvélyes, Vágod, Városszalónak, Vasdobra.

Győr-Sopron Megye 2 sz Levéltár

Catholic. Alsópulya, Alsórámóc, Barátudvar, Boldogasszony, Borbolya, Borsmonostor, Büdöskút, Cinfalva, Császárfalu, Császárkőbánya, Csáva, Darázsfalu, Darufalva, Feketeváros, Felsőkismartonhegy, Felsőlászló, Felsőrámóc, Féltorony, Fertőfehéregyháza, Fertőmeggyes, Fertőszéleskút,

Fraknó, Fraknónádasd, Füles, Gálos, Gyirót, Harácsony, Illmic, Kabold, Kelénpatak, Királyhida, Kisboldogasszony, Kishöflány, Kismarton, Kisostoros, Köpcsény, Középpula, Lajtafalu, Lajtakáta, Lajtakörtvélyes, Lajtapordány, Lajtaszék, Lajtaszentgyörgy, Lajtaszentmiklós, Lajtaújfalu, Lánzsér, Ligvánd, Locsmánd, Lók, Loretto, Malomháza, Márcfalva, Miklóshalma, Mosonbánfalva, Mosonszentandrás, Mosontarcsa, Mosontétény, Mosonújfalu, Nagyhöflány, Nagymarton, Nemesvölgy, Némethidegkút, Németjárfalu, Nezsider, Nyulas, Oka, Oszlop, Pandorfalu, Pátfalu, Pecsenyéd, Pomogy, Récény, Répcebónya, Répcekethely, Répcekőhalom, Répcesarud, Rétfalu, Ruszt, Sásony, Selegszántó, Sérc, Siklósd, Somfalva, Sopronkeresztúr, Sopronkertes, Sopronnyék, Sopronszentmárton, Szabadbáránd, Szárazvám, Szarvkő, Szentmargitbánya, Szikra, Tormafalu, Valla, Vámosderecske, Védeny, Veperd, Vimpac, Völgyfalu, Vulkapordány, Zárány, and Zurány.

Romania

Microfilms exist for a very few of the churches in the Kolozsvár area of Romania (ceded in 1919). There are copies in the Hungarian National Archives, but otherwise they are in the Romanian State Archives at Cluj (originally Kolozsvár):

Catholic. Kolozsvár (Főtér), Kolozsvár (Monostor).

Greek Catholic. Kolozsvár.

Reformed. Beszterce, Kolozsvár.

Lutheran. Kolozsvár.

Greek Orthodox. Kolozsvár.

Unitarian. Kolozsvár.

Slovakia

Microfilms of the parish registers in areas ceded to this country by Hungary in 1919 are in the following archives, which are now located in Slovakia, with copies also in the Hungarian National Archives:

Slovenska Archívní Správa, Bratislava (Pozsonyi Állami Levéltár)

Catholic. Bazin, Modor, Nagyszombat, Pozsony (Szent Márton), Pozsony (Blumenthal), Szentgyörgy.

Lutheran. Bazin, Modor, Nagyszombat, Pozsony (Német), Pozsony (Szlovák-Magyar), Selmecbánya.

Slovenska Archívní Správa, Bánská-Bystrica (Besztercebányai Állami Levéltár)

Catholic. Besztercebánya, Selmecbánya.

Lutheran. Besztercebánya.

Slovenska Archívní Správa, Košice (Kassai Állami Levéltár)

Catholic. Abaújnádasd, Jának, Kassa, Királyhelmec, Nagykázmér, Nagykövesd, Nagytárkány.

Yugoslavia

Microfilms of the registers of the parishes ceded to this country by Hungary in 1919 are located in the following Hungarian Archives, with additional copies in the National Archives in Budapest:

Vas Megyei Levéltár, Szombathely

Catholic. Alsószentbenedek, Csendlak, Felsőlendva, Mártonhely, Muraszombat, Nagydolány, Perestó, Péterhegy, Szentsebestyén, Vashidegkút, Vizlendva.

Zala Megyei Levéltár, Zalaegerszeg

Catholic. Alsólendva, Bagonya, Belatinc, Cserföld, Lendvavásárhely.

Kalocsai Érseki Levéltár (Archdiocese of Kalocsa), Kalocsa

Catholic. Ada, Adorján, Apatin, Bács, Bácsföldvar, Bácsgyulafalva, Bácskertes, Bácskossuthfalva, Bácsordas, BácsSzentiván, Bácstóváros, Bácsújfalu, Bácsújlak, Bajmok, Bajsa, Béreg, Bezdán, Borócz, Csantavér, Csonoplya, Csurop, Dernye, Doroszló, Dunabökény, Dunacséb, Gádor, Gombos, Hódság, Horgos, Kerény, Kishegyes, Körtés, Kucora, Kula, Kullöd, Ludas, Magyarkanizsa, Martonos, Militics, Mohol, Monostorszeg, Nemesmilitics, Óbecse, Okér, Ószivac, Őrszallás, Pacsér, Palánka, Palona, Paripás, Péterréve, Regőce, Sándor, Szabadka, Szabadka (Szent György), Szabadka (Szent Rókus), Szentfülöp, Szenttamás, Szépliget, Szilberek, Szond, Temerin, Tiszakálmánfalva, Titel, Topolya, Újfutak, Újverbász, Újvidék, Vajszka, Veprőd, Zenta, Zenta (Felsőnegy), Zombor, Zzablya.

Hungarian Church headquarters of various religions are given below. Some difficulty was experienced in obtaining such information. In case of any difficulty consult your nearest embassy or consulate, or any Hungarian society in North America:

Catholic Church Archives (Katholikus Levéltár)

Archdioceses (Főegyházmegye)

EGER	Szechenyi ut 1
	3301 Eger
ESZTERGOM	Berényi Zsigmond ut 2
	2500 Esztergom

| KALOCSA | Szabadság tér 1 |
| | 6300 Kalocsa |

Dioceses (Egyházmegye)

CSANAD	Aradi Vértanúk tér 2
	6701 Szeged
GYŐR	Káptalan-domb 1
	9002 Győr
PÉCS	István tér 23
	7624 Pécs
SZÉKESFEHÉRVÁR	Szabadság tér 10
	8000 Székesfehérvár
SZOMBATHELY	Berzsenyi Dániel tér 3
	9701 Szombathely
VÁC:	Vak Bottyán tér 1
	2600 Vác
VESZPRÉM	Tolbuhin ut 16
	8020 Veszprém

Evangelical Lutheran Church (Evangélikus Országos Levéltár)

Ullói ut 24, 1085 Budapest
Phone and Fax: 011-361-313171826
E-mail: eol@lutheran.hu

Most of the records concern administration, pastors, Lutheran secondary schools in Budapest, and details of local churches. Registers are in the churches.

Byzantine Catholic Diocese (Hajdúdorog Püspoki Hivatal)

Bethlen G.u.5, 4400 Nyíregyháza
E-mail: eparchia@hcbc.hu

Reformed Church Archives (Magyar Reformatus Levéltár)

Kálvin tér 8, 1091 Budapest

IMPORTANT: Many church registers have been copied by the LDS Church.

Censuses (Népszámlálások)

Although censuses are held at regular intervals, they are only used for statistical purposes, and the returns are later destroyed. However, a number of local or regional censuses have been held over the centuries and you should check with the appropriate county archives (Megyei Levéltár) about these. Some fragments also remain of national censuses held in 1527, 1715, 1720, and 1828 and these are in the National Archives. If, by any chance, your Hungarian ancestor was living in the old county of Zemplén (now in Slovakia), you are lucky. The 1869 census for that county is practically complete and gives names, birthplaces, relationships, ages, occupations, and an exact address. It is in the National Archives in Budapest.

Wills (Végrendeletek)

These date back to the mid-1600s and give much detail about family relationships, apart from details of property involved. In the main they are in the National Archives, but more recent ones are in local municipal offices or archives (Tanacsi Levéltár).

Land Records and Deeds (Telekkönyvek-Telekkönyvezés)

These started in the early 1700s, with the departure of the Turks from various areas, but basically only refer to large estates of the old noble families. They are in the National Archives, as well as county archives. There are also Land Registration records in the county archives and in local courthouses. You will often find details of family relationships spelled out in these records.

Nobility Records (Nemesi Jegyzék)

These records are of use if your ancestors were members of the nobility from the fifteenth century up to the late 1800s. They are in the National Archives and local archives and refer in the main to court or political appointments of members of noble families.

Muster-Rolls (Katonai Anyakönyv or Létszámellenőrzö Ivek)

These are in the National Archives and include personal records of men serving in both regular and local militia units. However, there are many gaps, there is rather inadequate indexing, and in most cases the muster-rolls are only usable if you can specify the particular regiment and the approximate date of your ancestor's service.

So much for the genealogical records of Hungary. You can be very successful in your hunt but you will need patience. It may be of some guidance to note that between 1870 and 1910 over two million Hungarians emigrated, most of them from the northern areas of the country, and mostly through the port of Hamburg, in Germany. I have mentioned the detailed Hamburg Passenger Lists in the chapter on Germany, and if you do not know the exact place from which your family came, a search of the lists may give you that information.

ICELAND

Iceland was settled by Norsemen in the ninth century, and in 930 a Parliament, or Althing, was established. In 1380 the country, with Norway, became part of Denmark. This association continued until 1874. In that year the King of Denmark granted a form of limited self-rule to Iceland. In 1904 home rule was established and continued until 1918, when the country became an independent state nominally ruled by the King of Denmark. After World War II Iceland was declared a republic—free of the last vestige of foreign control.

The country, like other democracies, had both national and local governments together with the religious bodies. In searching for your Icelandic ancestors, you will be mainly concerned with the National Archives (Laugavegur 162, 105 Reykjavik; Phone: 011-354-562-3393; Fax: 011-354-552-5720; E-mail: isarchiv@ismennt.is; Web site: www.archives.is) and the local churches—90 percent of the population is Lutheran.

Originally, there were more than 200 separate municipalities grouped together in regions (hreppur and sýsla). The sixteen major towns and municipalities were excluded from this system, and each formed a separate unit. More recently the country has been divided into administrative units. From December 1997 the municipalities have numbered 163, including 31 towns and 127 districts (sýsla). All these figures are not of major importance to you, but they indicate that Iceland, like other European countries, is facing the problems of population growth and mobility. Forty percent of the population now lives in Reykjavik.

Civil Registration (Skráning)

In 1737 Lutheran pastors were ordered to report births and deaths (but not marriages) to their bishop. In 1746 they were instructed to maintain separate registers for births, marriages, and deaths, and also for confirmations. These records were not kept on a regular basis in some churches until 1784, when the bishops issued strict orders for the registrations, and precise details for their entry into the parish registers. The collection of documental information of BMD did not start until the Statistical Bureau was established in 1913.

Censuses (Mannial)

Many of these have been indexed and published. The first one took place in 1703 as part of a Danish government survey of economic conditions in Iceland. The returns are complete for the year and are in the National Archives. Names and ages were recorded, as were the relationship to the head of household, occupations, and full addresses. There was another census in 1729, but most of those returns were lost. Only three have survived—Arnessýsla, Hnappadalssýsla, and Rangárvallasýsla. Other censuses were taken in 1762, 1801, 1816, 1835, 1840, 1845, 1855, 1860, and then every ten years to 1901, and then every ten years from 1910 to 1960. The information requested varies considerably. Other censuses were taken at various times and in various places over the centuries, and all of them are in the National Archives. The censuses of 1950 and the special one in 1952 were the basis for the original roster of the National Register. This has replaced the holding of regular censuses. (The 1952 census remains in the Statistical Bureau and has not been transferred.)

National Register (ñjódskra)

This was started in 1953, with the object of providing a central registration of the population for administrative and statistical purposes. It meant that civil registration and regular censuses were no longer necessary. The National Register is updated daily or when reports arrive—these come from the district commissioners. Changes of address are reported by the individual to the municipality to which he or she moves, and this event is then recorded and passed on to the National Register office.

Lutheran pastors must report all births and marriages. Deaths are reported by the district commissioner. The Ministry of Justice reports naturalization, adoption, and divorce. Local magistrates report details of separation orders granted to husbands and wives.

The information contained in the National Register is the name, address, nationality, place of birth, date of birth, and personal eight-digit number. Every individual over the age of thirteen receives an identity card. The records are kept in the Statistical Bureau (Skuggasund 3, 150 Reykjavik; Phone: 011-354-560-9880; Fax: 011-354-562-8865; E-mail: statice@ statice.is; Web site: www.statice.is).

Church Registers (Kirkjubaekur)

These are kept in the National Archives but most recent ones are still in the churches. Officially the registers date from 1664 but generally do not start until about 1711, and in fact, a more reliable date for the start of complete coverage would be 1784. The information is of the usual nature—births, marriages, deaths, and confirmations, plus names in full, ages, and addresses.

Confirmation reports are not parish records but form a part of the archives of the Lutheran Church. The pastors collect them from the records and send them to the bishop annually. Records up to and including 1993 are now in the National Archives.

The address of the headquarters of the Evangelical Lutheran Church is Biskup Islands, 101 Reykjavik. In actual fact, the president of Iceland is also the head of the church, but he delegates his authority to the bishop and the Church Assembly.

There were also church censuses, which were started in 1748 (later in some places) and discontinued after 1952, when the National Register took over. They can be very valuable to the genealogist since, apart from the usual census information, they give details of people leaving the parish and their destinations in Iceland or overseas. There is a double-check on emigration details—there are also emigration lists in the offices of the regional municipalities (sýslur).

The National Archives also possess many biographies of pastors dating back to 1000. Since the Lutheran Church has been, and is, so prominent in the history and development of the country, it is always possible that one or more of your ancestors are included in these records.

Surnames

One major problem in researching your ancestry in Iceland is the continued use of patronymics. For example, according to the Personal Names Act of 1925, every Icelandic citizen is entitled to "one or two" Icelandic names. Icelanders with a surname, as we understand the meaning of the word, are in a small minority in the telephone directory of Reykjavik; for example, all people are listed under the first letter of their Christian name, and people with a family or surname may be listed under the first letter, too (so Tryggvi Thoroddsen could be listed under T or Th). However, a new name law came into force in 1996, with a more liberal approach to allowable names and the number of Christian or given names than before.

Intestate Registers

The National Archives hold these from about 1717 up to about 1965. Later registers are in the custody of local courts. It should be noted that under Icelandic law the disposal of property is controlled by automatic succession, and so wills are not needed.

Other Records

In addition to these records in the National Archives, there are other large sources available for ancestor-hunters in the Manuscript Collection of the

National and University Library in Reykjavik (Landsbókasafn Íslands-Háskólabókasafn, Arngrímsgata 3, 107 Reykjavik; Phone 011-354-525-5600; Fax: 011-354-525-5615; E-mail: lbs@bok.hi.is; Web site: www.bok.hi.is).

There are many people of Icelandic descent scattered around the world. Those of them trying to trace their families have many things in their favor—they are descended from close-knitted communities in a country with no experience of wars or violent risings and revolutions, and one that has superb archival collections that have been cared for and expanded over the centuries.

The manuscript treasures in the archives, and in the library at the university, together with records in regional municipalities, are a priceless treasure—only surpassed, in my opinion, by the United Kingdom, France, Italy, and Spain (with its records of the great Armada). Now, if only someone could discover a copy of Leif Ericsson's diary!

ITALY

Italy was, of course, the core of the Roman Empire until its end in 476. Then waves of invasion by Goths, Byzantines, Lombards, Franks, Magyars, Arabs, Carthaginians, and Germans followed in the area that we now know as Italy. These invasions were followed by a union of Italy and Germany and the beginning of the Holy Roman Empire.

By 1250 the Papacy had become the predominant power in the Italian peninsula, but it existed side by side with the great princely and ducal families of Visconti, Sforza, Gonzaga, and Este, and the powerful republics of Venice, Florence, and Genoa. At the end of the fifteenth century the Kingdom of Naples and Sicily was established in the south, the Papal States controlled the central part, and in the north power was possessed by the great duchies of Ferrara, Mantua, Milan, Modena, and Savoy, and by the republics of Venice and Genoa.

At the end of the century the invasions began again, this time by France, Spain, and Austria. By 1748 Naples, Sicily, Parma, and Piacenza were under Spanish control, and the Austrians then occupied Milan, Mantua, Modena, and Tuscany. The only independent areas left were the Papal States, and Venice, Genoa, Lucca, and Sardinia.

When Napoleon defeated the Austrians in 1796 he redrew the map of the peninsula. A puppet kingdom was set up under his brother Joseph as king, and other areas were included in France. These were Savoy, Piedmont, Parma, Liguria, Tuscany, and the Papal States. The Congress of Vienna in 1814–15 restored the status quo, except that Venetia and Lombardy became Austrian, and Naples and Sicily were united in a separate kingdom.

In 1848 rebellions broke out, ending in 1861 when the kingdom of Italy was established. In 1866 Venetia was included, and in 1870 Rome was annexed. Austria retained the South Tirol and Trieste until 1919. After the Second World War, Italy lost several small Alpine districts to France (mainly Brigue and Tende) and several islands and part of Venezia Giulia to Yugoslavia. In 1954 Trieste, and the surrounding area which had been under United Nations supervision, were returned to Italy.

It is important to understand Italy's unfortunate history over the centuries. Before 1861 it was a most extraordinary collection of kingdoms, principalities, dukedoms, Papal States, republics, city-states, personal fiefdoms. You name it; Italy had it! The result is that there is very little centralization of genealogical records. Oh, the records are there, but the problem is finding them, and then fighting your way through the almost impenetrable bureaucratic jungle that surrounds them! With all due respect to my archivist friends in Italy, the staff of the state archives are not renowned for their speed in answering questions, and their answers (when you eventually receive them) will probably be long on charm and politeness and loquacity and short on hard information. In fact, you may find you have to start all over and repeat your original letter but use different words.

One major problem, of course, is that Italians are not fluent in English, and you must really try to find someone locally who can translate your letter into Italian, and then interpret the answer for you when it arrives. A letter written in English will produce any one of three results: (a) you will receive a reply in Italian; (b) you will receive a reply in a form of English that will be difficult to understand (but at least they were kind enough to try); (c) you will receive no answer at all (even though you have sent three International Reply Coupons and a self-addressed airmail envelope). So far as (a) is concerned, you may find that the letter is friendly and polite but does not answer a single question!

A letter written in Italian is ninety percent certain to produce a reply, and this applies particularly when writing to a local priest. As far as the latter is concerned, gamble by enclosing a ten dollar (U.S.) bill. The average priest is underpaid and overworked. The donation will ensure an answer as he is very likely to have been caught before by overseas inquirers who obtain information and send no payment. The same remarks apply to local municipal officials. You can't pour out money without results but I think this advice will work for you!

You may find all he can tell you is the location of the parish registers, because they may now be in the custody of the diocesan archives (archivio diocesano). These archives seem a little reluctant to reply to inquiries and here, again, an advance donation should help. Unfortunately, there is no central source of information that gives you the location of church registers, nor is there any particular law setting down when registers should be deposited in the archives, either civil or ecclesiastical. In many places the registers are kept in the church under appalling conditions and are subject to flooding, benign neglect, dampness, carelessness, and theft. When the Arno overflowed its banks in Florence a few years ago, a number of church registers were last seen floating down the river.

There are 103 state archives in Italy. The country is divided into 19 regions (Regioni) and within these regions are 102 provinces, each with a state archive. The 103rd archive is in Rome (Roma) and is the Central State Archives (Archivio Centrale dello Stato, Piazzale degli Archivi 27, 00144 Rome; Phone: 011-39-6-545481; Fax: 011-39-6-5413620; E-mail: acs@archivi.beniculturali.it; Web site: www.archivi.beniculturali.it). This should not be confused with the State Archives of the Province of Roma (Archivio di Stato, Corso del Rinascimento 40, 00186 Rome; Phone: 011-39-6-6819081; Fax: 011-39-6-6864123; Web site: www.archivi.beniculturali.it/ASRM/istituto.html).

Because of Italy's piecemeal development it is impossible to generalize and say that parish registers began in 1545 or that notarial records started in 1456. Nearly every region is based on an ancient independent state with its own laws and records and systems of record-keeping.

The regions and the provinces within them are set out below. Each province is named after the chief city in that province, so when writing to the state archives, all you need to do is to address the envelope to Direttore, Archivio di Stato, and then the name of the city and that of the region:

ABRUZZO: Chieti, L'Aquila, Pescara, Teramo.

BASILICATA: Matera and Potenza (Basilicata was formerly Lucania).

CALABRIA: Catanzaro, Cosenza, Crotone, Reggio di Calabria, Vibo Valentia.

CAMPANIA: Avellino, Benevento, Caserta, Napoli, Salerno.

EMILIA-ROMAGNA: Bologna, Ferrara, Forli-Cesena, Modena, Parma, Piacenza, Ravenna, Reggio Emilia, Rimini.

FRIULI-VENEZIA GIULIA: Gorizia, Pordenone, Trieste, Udine.

LAZIO: Frosinone, Latina (Littoria), Rieti, Roma, Viterbo.

LIGURIA: Genova, Imperia, La Spezia, Savona.

LOMBARDY (LOMBARDIA): Bergamo, Brescia, Como, Cremona, Lecco, Lodi, Mantova, Milano, Pavia, Sondrio, Varese.

MARCHE: Ancona, Ascoli-Piceno, Macerata, Pesaro-Urbino.

PIEDMONT (PIEMONTE): Alessandria, Asti, Biella, Cuneo, Novara, Torino, Vercelli.

PUGLIA: Bari, Brindisi, Foggia, Lecce, Taranto (Ionio).

SARDINIA (SARDEGNA): Cagliari, Nuoro, Oristano, Sassari.

SICILY (SICILIA): Agrigento, Caltanisetta, Catania, Enna, Messina, Palermo, Ragusa, Siracusa, Trapani.

TRENTINO-ALTO ADIGE: Bolzano and Trento.

TUSCANY (TOSCANA): Arezzo, Firenze, Grosseto, Livorno, Lucca, Massa Carrara, Pisa, Pistoia, Prato, Siena.

UMBRIA: Perugia and Terni.

VALLE D'AOSTA: Aosta.

VENETO: Belluno, Padova, Rovigo, Treviso, Venezia, Verona, Vicenza.

There are also sub-archives at Anagni Guarcino, Barletta, Caltagirone, Camerino, Castrovillari, Este, Fabriano, Faenza, Fano, Fermo, Foligno, Gubbio, Imola, Lamezia Terme, Lanciano, Locri, Lucera, Modica, Noto,

Orvieto, Palmi, Pescia, Pontremoli, Sanremo, Sciacca, Spoleto, Sulmona, Termini Imerese, Trani, Urbino, Varallo, Ventimiglia, and Verbania.

Civil Registration (Stato Civile)

This began in 1869 for the whole country but the system was not centralized. So, to obtain details from these records, you need to know where your ancestor was born, was married, or died. In some parts of Italy a form of registration came into force much earlier, a beneficial result of so many different states and laws. In the state archives in Florence (Firenze) there is a complete collection of civil registration records for the whole of Tuscany (Toscana) for 1808–66; in the state archives in Napoli there are records for Napoli and Sicily (Sicilia) for 1806–70; in parts of northern Italy civil registration started in 1803–15; in the south, in Abruzzo, Campania, Puglia, Basilicata, and Calabria, it started in 1820. You must check with the nearest archive for more information. In Trentino (South Tirol) civil registration started in the sixteenth century, but there are gaps.

Details contained in the records for births, marriages, and deaths are as follows:

Births

Birth records contain name, date and place of birth, names of parents with mother's maiden name, and father's occupation. From 1900 on you will also find a marginal entry (similar to those in France) containing later information about eventual marriage with date, place, and name, and finally, date and place of death.

Marriages

Marriage records include name and age of bride and groom; marriage date and place; marital status; place of birth of each; names of parents and maiden name of mother; names of witnesses; occupation and addresses of all concerned (bride and groom, their parents, and witnesses); and date of consent of parents or guardians.

Deaths

Death records contain name of the deceased and date and place of death, date and place of birth, names of parents and address if they are still alive, name of the spouse of the deceased, occupation and address of the deceased.

The above records are in the Civil Registry Office (Ufficio di Stato Civile) in the city, town, village, or commune where the event took place. Be sure you request a full certificate. This way you will get all the details on the original entry, for otherwise the information will be just the bare essentials. You will certainly want the names of parents, both as a check and also to take you further back, and the magic sentence is "Favorisca inviare estratti con nomi dei genitori" or "Please send extracts with names of parents." If you run into any difficulties over civil registration (you cannot trace the location of a place, or the local office does not reply) write, explaining your difficulties, to the Central Statistical Institute (Istituto Centrale di Statistica, Via Cesare Balbo 16, 00100 Rome).

Certificate of Family Genealogy (Certificato dello Stato di Famiglia)

This kind of record is unique to Italy. It started in about 1869 and although there are gaps, and even places that did not begin recording information until this century, it can be of great value. Basically, it is an attempt by the authorities to have a complete record of each family in each locality. It contains names, relationships, birth dates, and birthplaces of all living family members at the time it was put on record. The office that undertakes the task and preserves the information in each municipality is the Ufficio Anagrafe.

Emigration Records (Registri dell' Emigrazione)

These records are in the various state archives, and also in the Ministry of the Interior (Ministero dell' Interno, Rome). They are not open for inspection, even though they date back as far as 1869, but the authorities have been known to give some details to overseas inquirers, provided that the relationship is proved, and the reason for the research given.

Conscription Records (Ufficio Matricola e Centro Documentale)

These started in 1869 and continue to the present day. They include name, birth date, town of residence, and whether the draftee served, was refused, was exempted, died, or emigrated before the call-up age of eighteen. The records are in the custody of the local Military District (Distretto Militare). The address for the area in which you are interested can be obtained from your nearest Italian Embassy or Consulate. The state archives can supply records from 1870–1920.

Clerical Survey (Status Animarum)

These records were kept from the early 1700s until about 1860 and list all persons under the jurisdiction of the parish church. Many have disappeared or been damaged, and not all parishes bothered to maintain them. Certainly it is worth checking to see if they exist if you are writing to the local priest, because they might just solve a problem, but it is very unlikely.

Notarial Records (Atti Notarili)

Never omit a check on these frequently ignored records. They can date back to as early as 1340 and they come right up to the present day. Generally speaking, any record older than one hundred years is in the state archives, and since then is either in the notarial offices or in the local notarial archives. The information recorded can cover an endless list of items, but the main ones are marriage contracts and settlements, dowries, contracts of sale and purchase of land or houses, wills, lawsuits, inheritance, and property inventory and division. However, if your ancestors did not own land or property, it is unlikely their names will appear in such records. A poor Italian scratching a precarious living on his fazzoletto (handkerchief) of soil was not likely to have any reason or money to consult a notary. The entries were in Latin until 1725 and since then have been in Italian.

Passports (Passaporti)

These were issued by the various state governments between 1800 and 1869, and then the issuance was taken over by the local police headquarters (Questura). Passports up to 1920–30 (depending on the region) are in the state archives; later passports are in the local Questura.

Wills (Testamenti)

These can date back to the 1300s in certain areas and are either in the state archives or in the local notarial archives (depending on the date), or in the local registry office (Ufficio del Registro) in the particular town.

If you have any problem tracing the location of a notarial archive, or obtaining an answer, you should get in touch with the head of the notarial archives (Ispettore Generale, Archivio Notarile, Via Flaminia 160, Rome).

University Records (Registri delle Università)

If your ancestor attended one of the very ancient universities in Italy, you will find the registers of students dating back to 1267, giving not only age and address and graduation date, but also much more detailed biographical information. The records are either in the state archives or in the actual university, sometimes half in one and half in the other.

Genealogical Collections (Archivi Genealogici)

These can be found in both published and manuscript form in the various state and municipal archives, and also in many university libraries. However, in the main they are about noble families or leading members of the clergy.

Censuses (Censimenti)

These have been held every ten years from 1861 to 1931, then in 1936, and again every ten years from 1951 to 1991. Not all the census returns are open for public search, and since some changes are being contemplated in the law governing this, I suggest you write for information about availability to the Direzione Generale dei Servizi Tecnici, Istituto Centrale di Statistica, Via Cesare Balbo 16, 00100 Rome.

Tax Assessments (Catasti)

As you may imagine, there are a variety of tax records: taxes on land, taxes on houses, taxes on land sales, taxes on heads, special taxes and imposts. It is no wonder that Italians are famed for tax-avoidance—they have been doing it successfully for many centuries. I am not going to even try to list the various tax records, but basically you will find records of taxes paid to the national or provincial governments in the state archives and those of municipal taxes in the town or village offices. They are generally not indexed and are certainly not easy to consult. Keep your knowledge of them in the back of your mind and do not use them unless you really need them.

Church Registers (Registri Parrocchiali)

So far as the Catholic Church is concerned, the parish registers started in 1545, but very few exist before the beginning of the seventeenth century. The earliest known ones are those of Guardiagrele (Chieti), 1325; Cava dei Tirreni (Salerno), 1350 (for baptisms only); Lucca, Pisa, Siena, baptisms and deaths from 1360, and Florence (Firenze) from 1423. Registers of baptism were called Liber Baptizatorum, those of marriages Liber Matrimoniorum, and those of burials Liber Defunctorum. They were kept with great care by the priests, as until the introduction of civil registration in 1869 they were the only records of the vital events of a family.

Many parishes have been abolished or merged with a neighboring one, and in these cases, where a church no longer stands or is closed, you will usually find the church registers lodged in the Diocesan Curia, or office of the Bishop of the Diocese in which the church is located.

The parish church may have other records as well as the usual baptisms, marriages, and burials. These may include land records of the parish (cadastral), confirmations, and church accounts including records of donations, payments for masses for the dead, payments for bell-tolling, and payments for the purchase or rental of burial vaults. All of these records are likely to be of value to you. You may find that they have been transferred to the Diocesan Archives (Archivio Vescovile della Diocesi). If the local priest replies to your letter, he will certainly give you the address of this archive if his records have been transferred there.

This whole question of transfer of registers to other archives creates problems for an ancestor-hunter in Italy. For example, in Umbria all the parish registers, except for the most recent years, are in the Diocesan Archives; in Rome itself eighty percent of the registers are deposited in the Sacred Archives of the Vatican (Archivio Segreto del Vaticano) and, very unfortunately, it seems impossible to obtain any reply even with the inclusion of the usual three International Reply Coupons and self-addressed envelope. I have reported this on several occasions, and even my complaints have been unanswered. You may, perhaps, be able to obtain some help from your own parish priest.

The information you will find entered in the average parish register is as follows:

Baptismal Records (Atti di Battesimo)

These include date and place of birth and/or baptism; sex; name; name of father; maiden name of mother; often, names and addresses of godparents, their fathers' names, and their relationship to the child; names of proxies standing in for the godparents if they were absent.

Marriage Records (Atti di Matrimonio)

These contain name and address of the bride and groom; age and place of birth; names of the fathers of the bride and the groom; names (and maiden names) of the mothers of the bride and the groom; names of other parishes where the banns were also published (since a marriage usually took place in the commune where the bride lived, this will give you the place of origin of the groom); marital status; and letters of consent of parents or guardian.

Burial Records (Atti di Sepoltura)

Burial records contain date and place of death; name and age of deceased; often, the cause of death; address at the time of death; names of parents and surviving spouse, or next of kin; and place and date of burial.

Confirmation (Cresima)

These also date back to 1545 and include the personal details of the child and witnesses' names and addresses. They are usually in the Diocesan Archives, together with records of Excommunication (Scomunica), special dispensations (dispensa), and details of tenants of church property and land.

In addition, the Secret Archives of the Vatican have the tax and census records of the Papal States from the mid-1300s. These states included the modern provinces of Ancona, Ascoli Piceno, Macerata, Pesaro-Urbino, Perugia, Terni, Frosinone, Latina, Rieti, Roma, and Viterbo.

Waldensian Registers

This small Protestant sect is confined to a few remote valleys in the Piedmont area on the border with France. Its history began in Lyons, France, in 1179, when Pierre Valdes started to preach a gospel of extreme simplicity within the Catholic Church. His followers were called "the poor men of Christ." After much persecution (12,000 of them were in prison in 1686) they became Protestants and established relations with Calvinists and Lutherans in Switzerland and Germany. On at least two occasions there were mass flights to safety into Switzerland and Germany, and even as far away as the Netherlands, England, and Ireland. Most of the refugees eventually returned and were granted complete freedom of religion by Napoleon.

A few final words about ancestor-hunting in Italy. The records are there—the problems are to discover where they are and then to obtain access to them. This applies particularly to church records. As I mentioned earlier, these are either in the Papal Archives, the bishopric office of the area in which you are interested, or the original parish, or are lost in some ancient transfer from one location to another. There are some possible alternatives.

The LDS Church has persuaded a few bishops to allow the registers of their diocese to be copied—however, there are over 300 bishoprics in Italy, and each one may contain a similar number of parishes. A parish may consist of a few houses clustered on the top of a mountain or 300 houses down in the valley.

You can spend your money visiting Italy to do your own research, but DON'T. Elsewhere in this book I have referred to the handful of archivists who regard their archives as their personal property and resent being bothered by genealogists. They must have been trained in Italy. This is not intentional resistance or lack of goodwill. It is an attitude of mind that cannot be changed. So what are you left with? A genealogical society. Fortunately, there are two of these in Italy and several in North America:

Instituto Genealogico Italiano
Via Santo Spirito 27, 50125 Firenze
Phone: 011-39-55213090. Fax: 011-39-55289643
E-mail: info@genealogia.it
Web site: www.fol.it/igi/index.html, and www.genealogia.it

Instituto didi Genealogica et Araldica
Antonio Cerasi 5a, 10100 Rome

Italian Genealogy and Heraldry Society of Canada
Eugenie Street West
Windsor, ON NSX 4Y6 Canada

POINT (Pursuing Our Italian Names Together)
PO Box 2977, Palos Verdes Peninsula, CA 90274

The first three are typical genealogical societies with helpful members but requiring a fee to cover expenses. The fourth is a commercial organization with a database of many thousands of surnames and good connections with local archives in various parts of Italy.

There is also the LDS Church, ready and willing to help non-members of the Church.

LATVIA

Latvia was formed from four historic areas—Latgale and Vidzeme, which were part of Livonia, and Kurzeme and Zemgale which belonged to the Duchy of Courland. Its population is Lett, but there are Lithuanian, Russian, Belarussian, Polish, German, and Jewish minorities.

The Letts were conquered and Christianized by the Livonian Knights in the thirteenth century. Latvia was part of Livonia until 1561. It then passed to Poland, to Sweden in 1629, and to Russia in 1721. During this whole period, German remained the official language until it was supplanted by Russian in 1885. There were many uprisings over the years until Latvia became independent in 1918 after World War I. Its freedom only lasted until 1940. In that year the German-Soviet Pact transferred it to the USSR, while nearly all the German inhabitants were returned to Germany. It declared its independence again in 1991, and this fact was recognized by the former Soviet Union and the United Nations.

There are three state archives—all located in the capital city (Riga), and three church archives in the same city. Most of the records you need are in the state archives, but you will also find genealogical information in the archives of the three main religious organizations. The state archives are in the following locations:

State Archives

The Historical Archives of Latvia (Valsta Vestures archīvs)
Slokas iela 16, Riga 1050
Phone: 011-371-7612406. Fax: 011-371-7612406
E-mail: histarch@com.latnet.lv
Web site: www.arhivi.lv

The State Archives of Latvia (Valsts archīvs)
Bezdeligu 1, Riga 1007
E-mail: lva@archiv.org.lv
Web site: www.archiv.org.lv/index.html

The State Audiovisual Documents Archives (Valts Kinofotofono Dokumentu archīvs)
Šmerļa iela 5, Riga 1006
Phone: 011-371-7529822. Fax: 011-371-7529954
Web site: www.arhivi.lv

The Historical Archives contain records of the pre-Russian period, and the State Archives for the period since then. They contain records of civil registration, censuses, church registers (recent ones are still in the churches), wills, and land records. You are free to visit the archives to do your own research, or—for a fee—the staff will search records for you.

Church Archives

The three church archives are:

Consistory of the Evangelical Lutheran Church (evangëliski luteriskās Baznīcas)
M. Pils iela 4, Riga 1050

Synod of the Orthodox Church (Pareizticigas Baznīcas Sinode)
Pils iela 14, Riga 1050

Curia of the Riga Metropolos Roman Catholic Church (Romas katolu Baznīcas Rīgas metropoliias Kūrija)
M. Pils iela 2, Riga 1050

The various religions have always played a vital part in the life and politics of the country, and it will, I think, be helpful if I made the differences of the three major positions clear and, at the same time, mention the various other minor religions that are in existence. Many of these exist because they represent various ethnic differences among the population, and I will explain these as well.

Population by ethnic origin
Latvian	55.3%
Russian	32.5%
Byelorussian	4.0%
Ukrainian	2.9%
Polish	2.2%
Lithuanian	1.3%
Jews	0.4%

Religions
The number of congregations:
Lutheran	301
Catholic	235

Orthodox	116
Old Believer	65
Baptist	81
Adventist	44

If your ancestors were Lutherans, you will find a visit to the church headquarters very worthwhile since the doctrines of Martin Luther were well established in Latvia in the sixteenth century.

Because of the conquest of the country over the centuries, various religions became paramount in Latvia from time to time. The country was basically Catholic until the Reformation and Protestant since then, but the Evangelical Lutheran Church was not officially established until 1922 (see above for the address of the church archives).

LIECHTENSTEIN

The Principality of Liechtenstein was formed in 1719 by uniting the county of Vaduz and the barony of Schellenberg. The area was owned by the family of the same name, which also owned vast estates in Austria. It became a sovereign state in 1806, after the German Empire had been overthrown by Napoleon. It was a member of the German confederation from 1815 to 1866, at which time it became independent. Liechtenstein is a member of several international organizations, including the United Nations and the Council of Europe. In most countries it is represented diplomatically and politically by Switzerland.

The National Archives are the central archives for all records from government offices. Some of the material in the Archives dates from the late Middle Ages. Government and court files are mostly complete from the early nineteenth century to the present.

National Archives of Liechtenstein
Liechtensteinisches Landesarchiv
Städtle 51
9490 Vaduz
Phone: 011-423-236-63-40. Fax: 011-423-236-63-59
E-mail: Landesarchiv@llv.li
Web site: www.firstlink.li/la/

Civil Registration

This started in 1878, and the registers were kept by the local Catholic priest acting on behalf of the government. Before that year the records were part of the parish registers; they are still located in the local churches or the church archives, and some are kept in the National Archives. Since 1974 they have been in the custody of the National Register Bureau in the capital—Vaduz. Copies of birth, marriage, and death records can be obtained from the National Archives for a small fee or without charge, depending on the time it takes and the staff available for the search.

All inquiries for documents should be sent to the Zivilstandsamt Vaduz 9490, Liechtenstein; Phone: 011-423-236-61-11; Fax: 011-423-336-63-59; E-mail: Landesarchiv@lv.li

Church Registers

These date back to the seventeenth century or early eighteenth century. The oldest one started in 1638.

Wills

These date back to 1690 and are in the National Archives.

Other Archives

There are village and church archives in the following places: Balzers, Eschen, Gamprin, Mauren, Planken, Ruggell, Schaan, Schellenberg, Triesen, Triesenberg, and Vaduz (here are also the archives of the ruling family).

LITHUANIA

The Liths are thought to have settled in the area as far back as 1500 B.C., although there is some dispute about this. In the thirteenth century the German military order—the Livonian Brothers of the Sword (also known as the Livonian Knights) occupied part of the country. Later an independent state under a Grand Duke was established; Lithuania became a great and powerful nation in the fourteenth century, including all of Belarus, a large part of Ukraine, and part of Russia itself.

In 1386 a dynastic marriage joined the country with Poland. In 1410 the joint forces of the two countries defeated the Livonian Knights at Tannenberg. In 1569 there was a complete merger with Poland, but during the two partitions of Poland Lithuania disappeared from the map as an independent state and became part of Russia.

After World War I Lithuania proclaimed its independence. In 1920 the capital, Vilnius, was seized by Poland, and in 1923 the Lithuanians took Memel from Germany. In 1939 Vilnius was returned by Poland and Memel returned to Germany. In 1940 the Red Army occupied the country and Lithuania became part of the Soviet Union.

In 1991 Lithuania declared its independence once again and this was recognized by the former Soviet Union and the United Nations.

There are three state archives in Vilnius:

Historical State Archives (Lietuvos valstybinis istorijos archyvas)
Gerosios Vilties 10, 2015 Vilnius
Phone: 011-370-2652-254. Fax: 011-370-2652-314
E-mail: arch.dep@post.omnitel.net

State Parish Register Archives (Centrinis metrika archyvas)
21 Kalinausko 21, 2009 Vilnius
Phone: 011-370-2637-846

Lithuania State Archives (Lietuvos valstybinis metrikuarchyvis)
Mindaogo 8, 2009 Vilnius
Phone: 370-2-652-254. Fax: 370-2-652-314
E-mail: arch.dep@post.omnitel.net

The latter archives contain birth, marriage, and death registers, wills, land records, and all other records of genealogical interest (except for the parish registers, which are in the State Parish Register Archives mentioned above).

During the brief period of independence between 1918 and 1940 the church registers were in the churches, but were later transferred to the archives. Original present-day registers are still in the churches, but copies are sent to the State Parish Register Archives.

You may search in the archives yourself, but must pay for any photocopies you require. At present there is no charge made for personal searches. If you do plan a visit it would be wise to write beforehand to make sure the registers or records you need do, in fact, exist.

The State Archives will also search the records for people unable to visit the country. There is an initial, non-returnable fee ($50 at the time of this writing), as you are paying for the search and not for the results. How soon they learn of the benefits of capitalism! The amount deposited may not be enough to cover the costs of a prolonged search, and in such a case you will be told of the additional sum required. Your payment may be made to the archives by personal certified check, or to the Vneshekonombank in Vilnius (Account No. 676305137).

So far as the records of the Catholic Church are concerned, these may be retained in churches using the Polish language. The addresses of the headquarters of the three main religions in the country are:

CATHOLIC
Valanciaus, Kaunas

ORTHODOX
Ausros Vartu, Vilnius

LUTHERAN
68 Laisves, Tauragė

The Belzekas Museum of Lithuanian Culture (6500 S. Pulaski Road, Chicago, IL 60629; Phone: 773-582-6500; Fax: 773-582-5133; E-mail: Balzekas@aol.com) and the Chicago Public Library (400 S. State Street, Chicago, IL 60605; Web site: www.chipublib.org).

LUXEMBOURG

Luxembourg was originally a county that included the present Belgian province of Luxembourg. It first came to prominence in 1308 when its count was elected Holy Roman Emperor. His grandson, the emperor Charles IV, made Luxembourg a duchy in 1354. In 1445 it became part of the Duchy of Burgundy, and in 1482 it became part of the vast Hapsburg domains. For the next three centuries its history was that of the south Netherlands as it passed from Spain to Austria to France, and back again to Spain and France, the inevitable fate of a small country in that part of Europe.

The Congress of Vienna (1814–15) made Luxembourg a grand duchy in personal union with the King of the Netherlands. At the same time it joined the German Confederation, and the capital (which is also named Luxembourg) was garrisoned by Prussian troops. When Belgium rebelled against the Netherlands in 1830, Luxembourg joined in on the Belgian side. As soon as Belgium gained its independence it rewarded Luxembourg by claiming the whole country. In 1839 Luxembourg was forced to cede the territory that is now the Belgian province of the same name. The remainder became autonomous, though still a member of the German Confederation and in personal union with the King of the Netherlands.

In 1866 the King decided to sell the country to France and nearly brought about a war between France and Prussia. In 1867 the European powers declared Luxembourg a neutral country. It was occupied by Germany during the First and Second World Wars. Now Luxembourg is a member of Benelux, the economic union of Belgium, the Netherlands, and Luxembourg. The official language is French but German is widely spoken, as is Letzeburgesch (a Low German dialect). The country is divided into two administrative regions, Luxembourg and Diekirch, basically the north and south areas of the country.

The National Archives (Archives Nationales du Grand-Duché de Luxembourg) are on the Plateau du Saint Esprit, BP 6, 2010 Luxembourg

(Phone: 011-352-478-6661; Fax: 011-352-47-46-92; E-mail: archives. nationales@mc.etat.lu; Web site: www.etat.lu/AN). There are also municipal archives in the Hôtel de Ville, Place Guillaume, Luxembourg. The Catholic Church archives are in the office of the bishop (Évêché de Luxembourg, BP 419, 2010 Luxembourg).

Civil Registration (Enregistrement Civil)

This started in 1796 and the records are in the local municipal offices throughout the country. A copy remains there and a duplicate is lodged in the Courts of Justice in Luxembourg and Diekirch. Every ten years all entries are indexed, and the indexes placed in the National Archives.

Censuses (Recensements)

These have been held every ten years since 1793 and the returns are in the National Archives.

Church Registers (Registres Paroissiaux)

These are still in the original churches, but microfilm copies of them all are in the same archives. The earliest registers for the city of Luxembourg date back to 1601, but there are many gaps. There were about 150 parishes in the country in the eighteenth century, but it is probable that the number has been reduced since then.

Notarial Records (Les Protocoles Notariaux)

These are details of court cases over property rights, executors' disputes, and the drawing up of marriage settlements, dating from 1612. More recent records are in the offices of local notaries, but any documents more than sixty years old must be lodged in the National Archives.

Scholarships (Bourses d'Études)

This is a record that I have not found in any other country. The scholarships started in 1882 and there is a great deal of information about the family background of successful entrants. The records are indexed in a very useful book entitled *Fondations de Bourses d'Études Instituées en Faveur des Luxembourgeois, 1882–1907*.

I am fairly sure there is a wealth of genealogical information in the National Archives. Unfortunately, they do not have enough help to attend to written requests about Luxembourg ancestry. If you have a query or need more detailed information, I suggest you write directly to Le Directeur des Archives Nationales, Archives Nationales du Grand-Duché de Luxembourg, at the address above.

MACEDONIA

Macedonia was a republic in the Yugoslav Federation until it declared its independence in 1991. It has since been recognized by the United Nations and the European Community. In researching your ancestry in Macedonia you will probably find it necessary to deal with Yugoslav records as well, since there are many documents that could not easily be separated when the Macedonian Archives were established after the country became independent.

Macedonia's ancient territories included areas of Bulgaria and Greece. It has always been the victim of warring nations, and land-hungry neighbors. At various times in its long history, Macedonia has been under the control of Romans, Byzantines, Goths, Huns, Slavs, Bulgarians, Greeks, and Turks. In modern times covetous neighbors such as Bulgaria, Greece, and Serbia have made claims to the Macedonian areas.

After the two Balkan Wars of 1912 and 1913, the Treaty of Bucharest awarded a small portion of Macedonia to Bulgaria and divided the rest between Greece and Yugoslavia. During World War II the territory of Macedonia was occupied by Bulgaria and Italy. The Republic was established in 1944, with Skopje as its capital.

Macedonia is predominantly Orthodox, but there are Muslims and Catholics as well. According to the 1991 census there are 230,000 Albanians living in the country. However, this number will probably have increased because many refugees from Kosovo crossed the border in their flight from attacks by Yugoslavia. Many thousands were given refuge in Macedonia in 1999, and some may remain there.

Archives

There are central archives in the capital, and others in major centers throughout the country. They contain records of civil registers, church and census records, and historical documents.

State Archives of Macedonia (Dr'aven arhiv na Republika Makedonija)
Grigor Prlichev 3, Skopje 91000
Phone: 011-389-91-115-783. Fax: 011-389-91-115-827
Web site: www.arhiv.gov.mk

Archives of Skopje
Moskovska 1, Skopje 91000
Phone: 011-389-91-376-461
Web site: www.arhiv.gov.mk/atekst236.htm

Archives of Kumanovo
Goce Delchev 25, Kumanovo 97000
Phone: 011-389-97-901-20-464
Web site: www.arhiv.gov.mk/atekst233.htm

Archives of Bitola
Prvi maj Boul 55, Bitola 97000
Phone: 011-389-97-32-496
Web site: www.arhiv.gov.mk/atekst232.htm

Archives of Ohrid
Nikola Karev 6, Ohrid 96000
Phone: 011-389-96-32-104
Web site: www.arhiv.gov.mk/atekst234.htm

Archives of Prilep
Aleksandar Makedonski 134, Prilep 97500
Phone: 011-389-98-24-192
Web site: www.arhiv.gov.mk/atekst235.htm

Archives of Strumica
27 Mart 2, Strumica 92400
Phone: 011-389-902-28-709
Web site: www.arhiv.gov.mk/atekst237.htm

Archives of Tetovo
Cvetan Dimov 2, Tetovo 91220
Phone: 011-389-94-21-646
Web site: www.arhiv.gov.mk/atekst238.htm

Archives of Veles
Marshal Tito 53, Veles 91400
Phone: 011-389-93-34-784
Web site: www.arhiv.gov.mk/atekst2310.htm

Archives of Ship
Sane Georgiev 35, Ship 92000
Phone: 011-389-94-21-646
Web site: www.arhiv.gov.mk/atekst239.htm

MALTA

Malta, like many other places in the world located on trade routes or in key strategic areas, has had more than its share of foreign occupation. Over the centuries it has been occupied by Phoenicians, Greeks, Carthaginians, Romans, Saracens, Byzantines, Arabs, Normans, Franks, Knights of Malta (the Knights Hospitallers), French, and British. Malta became independent in 1964, and a republic in 1974.

Great damage was done to government offices and churches and their records by Italian and German bombing during the Second World War. Malta consists of three islands: Malta, Gozo, and Comino, plus a few uninhabited rocklets. The capital is Valletta, on the main island of Malta.

Civil Registration
This started in 1863 and the records are in the Public Registry Office (L'Insinua), 197 Merchants Street, Valletta, for the island of Malta, and in the Public Registry Office, Victoria, Gozo, for the island of that name. A small charge is made for a photocopy of a certificate.

Church Registers
Church registers date back to 1537 for the cathedral in Valletta, and to about 1550 in the various parishes. Some, of course, are partially or wholly missing as the result of the bombing in the last war. Generally speaking, the parish churches hold recent registers and the early ones are in the Cathedral Museum, Archbishop Square, Mdina, or in the Archbishop's Curia, St. Calcedonious Square, Floriana. However, there are still many parish churches that have retained their early registers in their own possession. Each parish has its own Archivium, which may contain useful information for you about tombstones, confirmation records, and so on.

Censuses

These were first held on the islands in 1842, and then in 1851 and every ten years until 1931, and then again in 1948, 1957, 1967, 1977, and 1987. The returns are open for inspection in the Public Library in Valletta, and also in Victoria, Gozo, for that island. The staff will probably look up a specific entry without charge provided that you can give an exact address on the island, and also send them three International Reply Coupons and a self-addressed airmail envelope.

Wills

Wills dating back to the fourteenth century are in the Public Registry Offices in Valletta, Malta, and Victoria, Gozo. However, it was not essential to deposit a will before 1863. Wills since then are either in the Registry of the Civil Courts in Valletta for the island of Malta, or in the similar office in Victoria, Gozo, for that island. Wills may also be found in the Public Registry Offices in Valletta and Victoria. Photocopies may be ordered by mail for a small fee. You must also send a photocopy of the death certificate of the person concerned if he or she died within the past hundred years. For wills before then, no death certificate is needed.

Notarial Archives

These are located at 3 M.A. Vassalli Street, Valletta, and may contain information about wills, probate, and disputes over property. The records date back to 1465. The archives for the island of Gozo are located on Republic Street in Victoria.

There is no genealogical information in the State Library or in the National Library, except that the latter does hold the archives of the Knights of Malta, and these contain information about some of the knights and their families.

There is no genealogical organization in Malta, but there are at least two genealogical researchers, and their names and addresses can be obtained from the National Library or the Archbishop's Curia.

MOLDOVA

This country has had a very checkered history and its future is still being resolved. It was originally an independent principality back in the Middle Ages but came under Ottoman Empire rule in the sixteenth century. Part of it passed to Russia in piecemeal fashion between 1791 and 1812, while the remainder stayed under Turkish control until 1918. It then passed to Romania—with which it has strong ethnic ties—and finally to the Soviet Union in 1940. It was retaken by Romania in 1941 but became a Soviet republic in 1944. When it announced its independence in 1990, it began to consider reunion with Romania. The large Russian minority declared an independent republic in the eastern part of the country, and appealed to Russia for protection. The dispute is not yet resolved, and the state may yet be divided between the two neighboring countries. The capital of Moldova is Kishinev (Chisinau) and the Central State Archives are located in that city (Serviciul de Stat de Arhiva, str. Gh. Asachi 67, Kishinev).

To sum up, the situation politically in the former Soviet Union is still in a state of flux, and no one can foresee the future. Genealogically, there is great improvement and some hope for an eventual wide-open door for research. Every ancestor-hunter can help by ignoring silence or discouragement, and continuing to write, write, write to national and local archives. The more genealogical inquiries are received, the more likely the archive is to appreciate the worldwide demand for information, and the potential income in hard currency.

If you can write in the language of the country it will certainly help. Of course, you will probably receive your reply in the same language, and that will have to be translated. A local ethnic organization can probably help, or even a nearby consulate. If you are willing to gamble you might try sending a five dollar bill with your letter as a donation to archival funds. Maybe you will say "Goodbye!" to your money, or maybe it will be the key that opens the door.

Note: There appears to be an improvement in conditions in the country but no improvement in aid to ancestor-hunters since the above was written for the last edition of this book.

MONACO

This tiny independent principality of 150 hectares consists of the districts of La Condamine, Monte Carlo, and Monaco-Ville (the capital). It has been successively part of the kingdom of the Lombards, part of the kingdom of Arles, under Turkish rule for five centuries, and ruled by the Grimaldi dynasty since the thirteenth century. It was under Spanish protection from 1542 to 1641; under French control from 1641 to 1793; included in France from 1793 to 1815; and under Sardinian protection from 1815 to 1861. Since 1861 it has been under French protection again.

Civil Registration (Enregistrement Civil)
This commenced in 1792 and the records are in the Mayor's Office (Bureau de l'État-Civil), Mairie de Monaco. From 1546 to 1792 the recording of vital events was done by the Catholic Church. The civil registers are not open to public inspection, but information can be given if a relationship can be proved and the object of the inquiry is acceptable.

Church Registers (Registres Paroissiaux)
As mentioned, these started in 1546 and all of them up to the end of the last century are located in the Chancellery of the Bishop's Palace (l'Évêché).

There are five parishes in Monaco: Immaculée-Conception (Cathédrale de Monaco), St. Jean-Baptiste, Ste. Dévote, St. Charles, St. Martin. They have the registers going back to approximately 1900.

Censuses (Recensements)
These started in 1757 and have been held at intervals of between three and seven years ever since. Those held before 1873 are open to public search, and information can be divulged from later ones under the conditions men-

tioned above under Civil Registration. The census returns are also in the custody of the mayor.

Wills (Testaments)

These date back some three hundred years and are in the custody of l'État-Civil.

There are no genealogical organizations in Monaco and it is suggested that initial inquiries by ancestor-hunters of Monégasque descent be sent to the Bureau de l'État-Civil.

THE NETHERLANDS (HOLLAND)

The Low Countries (what is now the Netherlands and Belgium) have had a very checkered history. Because of their strategic position they were almost constantly in a state of war for many centuries. Originally they belonged to the empire of Charlemagne, and later the major part of them came under the control of one of the minor German kings. After 1384 the various provinces were ruled by the Dukes of Burgundy, who acquired them by purchase, blackmail, cession, theft, and marriage (just normal real estate transactions in the Middles Ages)! In 1548 they passed by marriage into the ownership of Spain.

From 1568 to 1648 there was a succession of rebellions in the northern provinces (what is now called the Netherlands), and these were followed by similar revolts in the southern provinces (now Belgium). In 1581 the northern provinces proclaimed their independence and William of Orange became the Statthalter. Spain did not recognize this independence until the Treaty of Westphalia in 1648. From 1810 to 1814 the Netherlands were incorporated into France by Napoleon. In 1815, at the Congress of Vienna, the Netherlands and Belgium (now known as the Austrian Netherlands) were united in one country. In 1831 Belgium seceded and became an independent country.

In view of the constant turbulence in the area over the centuries, it is surprising that genealogical records exist at all. However, they do, and they are well organized and easily accessible. The major drawback to ancestor-hunting in the Netherlands is that there is no central registration of births, marriages, and deaths. Civil registration was started by the French in 1811 and each of the approximately one thousand municipalities kept its own records. From 1811 to 1892 duplicate records were kept in the various provincial archives, but these are not indexed, and so, without knowledge of the city, town, or village from which your ancestor came, it is almost impossible to trace him or her. To make matters worse, before the nineteenth century, births, marriages, and deaths were registered according to religion. So even if you know the exact place, you will still have to check the records of each church unless you are sure about the original religion of your family.

Fifty percent of the inhabitants were Catholic; the remainder were Protestant, divided among Evangelical Lutheran, Restored Evangelical Lutheran, and Netherlands Dutch Reformed (Nederlandse Hervormde Kerk).

Other sects (Mennonite, Huguenot, Walloon) will be considered later in this chapter. Regardless of your family religion, you will be searching the registers of the Dutch Reformed Church, because from 1588 to 1795 it was the official state church, and non-members had to marry in that church, or before a magistrate, as well as in their own churches. So the marriages of Catholics, Jews, and all other religions and sects will be found in the Reformed Church registers.

Archives

The State Archives' Service comprises the General State Archives in The Hague and the eleven archives in the capitals of the state provinces.

General State Archives

General State Archives (Algemeen Rijksarchief)
Prins Willem-Alexanderhof 20
2595 BE The Hague
Phone: 011-31-70-331-5400. Fax: 011-31-70-331-5419
E-mail: ara@rad.archief.nl
Web site: www.archief.nl

Provincial Archives

Rijksarchief in Drenthe
Brink 4
9401 HS Assen
(Postbus 595, 9400 AN, Assen)
Phone: 011-31-592-313-3523. Fax: 011-31-592-314-697
E-mail: info@drentsarchief.org
Web site: www.drentsarchief.org

Rijksarchief in Overijssel
Eikenstraat 20
8021 WX Zwolle
Phone: 011-31-38-454-0722. Fax: 011-31-38-454-4506
E-mail: rao@euronet.nl
Web site: www.obd.nl/instel/arch/rkarch.htm

Rijksarchief in Gelderland
Markt 1
6811 CG Arnhem
Phone: 011-31-26-442-0148. Fax: 011-31-26-445-9792
E-mail: gelderland@rad.archief.nl
Web site: www.archief.nl/rad/gelderland

Rijksarchief in Flevoland
Visarenddreef 1
8232 PH Lelystad
(Postbus 55, 8200 AB Lelystad)
Phone: 011-31-320-265-750. Fax: 011-31-320-265-752
E-mail: rijksarchief@flevoland.nl
Web site: www.archief.nl/rad/flevoland/index.htm

Het Utrechts Archief
Alexander Numankade 199/201
3572 KW Utrecht
Phone: 011-31-30-286-6611. Fax: 011-31-30-273-5791
E-mail: utrecht@ad.archief.nl
Web site: www.hetutrechsarchief.nl/index.htm

Rijksarchief in Noord-Holland
Kleine Houtweg 18
2012 CH Haarlem
Phone: 011-31-23-517-2700. Fax: 011-31-23-517-2720
E-mail: noord-holland@rad.archief.nl
Web site: www.archief.nl/rad/n-holland/index.htm

Zeeuws Archief
Hofplein 16
Postbus 70
4330 AB Middelburg
Phone: 011-31-118-678-800. Fax: 011-31-118-62-80-94
E-mail: info@zeeuwsarchief.nl

Rijksarchief in Noord-Brabant
Zuid-Willemsvaart 2
5211 NW 's-Hertogenbosch
Phone: 011-31-73-681-8500. Fax: 011-31-73-614-6439
E-mail: citadel@euronet.nl
Web site: www.tref.nl/s-hertogenbosch/rijksarchief/default.htm

Rijksarchief in Limburg
St. Pieterstraat 7
6211 JM Maastricht
Phone: 011-31-43-321-7051. Fax: 011-31-43-325-5640
E-mail: rijksarchief_limburg@wxs.nl
Web site: www.rijksarchieflimburg.nl

Groninger Achieven
Cascadeplein 4
9726 AD Groningen
(Postbus 30040, 9700 RM Groningen)
Phone: 011-31-50-599-2000. Fax: 011-31-50-599-2050
E-mail: gronarch@castel.nl
Web site: www.groningerarchieven.nl/

Rijksarchief in Friesland
Boterhoek 3
8911 DH Leeuwarden
(Postbus 2637, 8901 AC Leeuwarden)
Phone: 011-31-58-212-7103. Fax: 011-31-58-213-6854
E-mail: info@ryksargyf.org
Web site: www.ryksargyf.org/nl/ryksargyf.asp

Note: Groningden, Utrecht, and Zeeland (Zeeuws) are being merged with municipal archives in one system. Similar changes are planned for other provinces in the future.

In addition to the above archives there is also the Central Bureau for Genealogy (Centraal Bureau voor Genealogie). This is not exactly an archive, nor is it exactly a genealogical organization. It is a superb combination of both. There will be more about this helpful organization later.

Generally speaking, the General State Archives contain records from the whole country, while the other state archives contain the records of a particular province, plus many records deposited by local municipalities because of lack of local storage space.

The city or municipal archives (Stadsarchief or Gemeentearchief) hold local records from either a city or a municipality. Bear in mind that the latter (Gemeente) can be a city, or it can be a district covering a city and its surrounding villages, or it can be a large district that may include twenty or thirty villages. There are also regional archives (Streekarchieven), which have been established by a group of several municipalities working together to save costs. In addition to the archives there are, of course, city or municipal registry offices (Stads- or Gemeentesecretarie) and city and town halls (Stadhuis and Gemeentehuis) which may contain civil registration. After all this, I must also tell you that there are church archives, which may contain church registers that have not been lodged with the various provincial archives.

Unfortunately, there is no infallible central listing of all archives, and I can only advise you to tread with care through this Low Country morass. If you inquire about a particular record in one archive and are told it does not exist, don't take that as the final answer. Check with another archive—municipal, regional, provincial, or national. Of course, you should also seek guidance from one of the genealogical organizations, or the Central Bureau (see below), or your nearest LDS Family History Center.

The Central Bureau for Genealogy

Prins Willem Alexanderhof 22, The Hague (visiting address)
Postbus 11755, NL-2502 AT The Hague (postal address)
Phone: 011-31-70-315-0500 (general); 011-31-70-315-0570 (genealogical)
Fax: 011-31-70-347-8394
Web site: www.cbg.nl

The Central Bureau for Genealogy was established in 1945 under government supervision. The original collections included many documents acquired by the government, including a collection of 66,000 surnames from 1795 to 1932 of the Fund for Biographical Documentation (Fonds voor Biografische Documentatie); the genealogical manuscripts of the Association for Genealogy (Verbond voor Sibbekunde); and the collection of identity cards of the Office of National Security (Bureau voor Nationale Veiligheid).

After 1945 the Bureau acquired a number of private genealogical collections, and the government donated the identity cards of people dying after 1938. The Bureau also acquired many microfilms of church registers.

The Bureau now has all the genealogical collections in the Netherlands *except* those of the Royal Dutch Society for Genealogy and Heraldry (Koninklijk Nederlandsch Genootschap voor Geslacht-en Wapenkunde), and the Dutch Genealogical Society (Nederlandse Genealogische Vereniging). However, the directorate of the Bureau does include repre-sent-atives of the two societies just mentioned, and it is probable that a full merger will eventually take place. The Bureau is eighty percent state-financed, the remainder being made up by donations and membership fees. It deals with over 7,500 queries a year, so if you write, please don't expect a quick answer! They are very efficient and helpful, but the staff is limited and you must have patience. Briefly, here is a rundown of the holdings of the Bureau:

Library

This contains nearly everything written in Dutch or in other languages about Dutch families—personal papers, obituaries, military lists, telephone books, local and family histories, and inventories of government archives.

Heraldry

There is an index of families entitled to a coat of arms, and if you wish to register a new one for your family it can be arranged for a fee.

Publications

The bureau has a number of publications, mostly in Dutch, of course, but some in English.

The Gelderland Marriages

This is a list of all marriages entered in the registers of the Calvinist churches in this province. It is indexed under the names of both bride and groom.

Military Marriages

These contain details of marriages of military men in the garrison towns of most of the provinces.

Walloon Card Index

This contains over a million cards reproduced on microfiche giving abstracts from baptism, marriage, and burial registers of Walloon churches in the Netherlands, plus a number from Belgium, France, and Germany.

Manuscript Collections

These are donated or acquired by purchase and list 60,000 surnames, including many family trees. They are indexed.

Advertisements

This collection includes several million announcements of births, marriages, and deaths from newspapers dating back to 1795.

Church Registers

Nearly all of these are on microfilm in the bureau.

Civil Registration

This started in most of the Netherlands in 1811 and some of the records are open for public inspection in the bureau.

Red Cross Collections

A card index file is here with the names of people who died and were buried in Germany and other countries during the Second World War, including those in slave labor and concentration camps.

Emigrants Lists

There are some records on cards and computer printouts but, of course, only a fraction of the total number.

Identity Cards

In 1938 a new system was introduced for the Netherlands. Every inhabitant was issued with a card that has the first and family names, date and place of birth, religion, occupation, names of parents and their dates and places of birth, date and place of the card-holder's marriage (when it occurs), name of the husband or wife with date and place of birth, and in the event of divorce, date, place, and reason. It also gives the names, addresses, and dates and places of birth of the children of the card-holder. If a person leaves the Netherlands permanently, the card must be sent to the Central Population Register and it is kept there. If the card-holder moves within the country, his or her card is sent to the new municipality to be recorded and returned to the holder. A copy is kept in the original municipality.

If a person dies, his or her card is sent to the Central Bureau of Statistics. Once a year all the cards of deceased persons are sent to the Central Bureau for Genealogy, where they are retained and indexed. This means that the bureau has a complete card index of all persons who have died in the Netherlands since 1939. The cards are arranged alphabetically for the whole country and the information on a card can cover quite a period of time. For example, if a man died in 1940, aged 80, his card would give the birth dates of his parents, and this could mean information for the period from 1820 to 1940.

The cards are not available for public inspection but a copy will be issued for a fee. Here is one way in which these records can be useful. Let us suppose you know that your father came from the Netherlands but you don't know the place. However, you know he left a brother behind who died in 1940 in Haarlem and you know his name. By obtaining a copy of his card you will know where he was born (and probably where your father was born, too) and, even more important, you will have the names of his parents and details of their marriage!

Now let us talk about genealogical records in the Netherlands in more detail, leaving the most important ones, the church registers, to the end; they are a little complicated, and I would like to talk to you about them after we have solved some other record problems.

Emigration Records

The story of passenger lists is the same in the Netherlands as in almost all countries: the records were destroyed. Some more recent emigrants from Rotterdam are recorded in the existing lists of various shipping companies in that port city but only from about 1914. If you can find details among your family papers of the name of the ship on which your emigrant ancestor sailed, or at least the name of the company, you may find information about him.

The government kept Emigration Registers (Emigratieregisters) from 1847 to 1878 and these are in the central and provincial archives. For these, of course, you need to know the province of residence of your ancestor. The lists give names, ages, occupations, religion, financial state, number of children, name of ship, destination, and date of departure.

From 1875 to 1934 there were similar lists kept and these are in the city archives (Stadsarchief) of Amsterdam and Harlingen.

Population Registers (Bevolkingsregisters)

These started in 1810 and are still maintained. Up until 1850 these records were kept in some localities and not in others. Check with the appropriate provincial archive as to the existence of registers for the 1810–50 period in your area of interest. The registers, like a census, are rechecked at ten-year intervals. You will find the names, ages, religion, relationship, occupation, former residences, and date of arrival in the locality, plus name of previous town or village. You will find copies for a particular area in the local archives as well as in the provincial ones.

Civil Registration (Burgerlijke Stand)

This started in a few places in 1795 but became nationwide only in 1811. Up until about 1900 you will find the registers in the provincial archives, and since then in local registry offices or district courthouses. The registers include rather more items than you will find in similar records in this country.

Because the French introduced the system, the early entries, up to about 1815, are in French. The original system of recording vital events has hardly changed over the years. The entries are in duplicate, both signed by the registrar, the informant, and two witnesses. One copy is kept by the registrar of the city or other municipality and the duplicate is sent to the county court. These duplicates, bound in a volume for each year, are then deposited in the provincial archives. Up to 1892 they are public property and information from them is given quite easily. Every register has an alphabetical index, and for every ten-year period there is an alphabetical index for each municipality.

In the same department of the archives are all the original documents submitted when a marriage was recorded: copies of birth or baptism records, death records of parents, death record of any earlier husband or wife, and details of the groom's army service.

For the period after 1892 the records may not be inspected, but a copy can be obtained by written application and payment of a fee to the local registrar in each municipality (Ambtenaar van de Burgerlijke Stand). Be sure you ask for a full copy and then you will get all the information on the original registration documents. Otherwise an abridged version will be sent to you.

If you want information about a living person, you will have difficulty in obtaining it. This restriction, of course, is a justifiable one designed to protect the privacy of the individual. Imagine if you had quietly shed a few years off your admitted age and then a friend (or enemy) could get a copy of your birth certificate and confront you with it! On the other hand, if the information was needed to prove your right to an inheritance, or to enable an elderly person to be given a pension, a letter of application from a lawyer will either produce a copy of the original certificate or an official letter providing the equivalent information.

Quite apart from the usual records of births, marriages, and deaths, plus names and addresses of parents, witnesses, and so on, you will also find more arcane records in connection with the custom of marriage. For example:

Marriage Intentions and Proclamations (Aankondigiging and Huwelijksaf)

These were in use from 1811–1935 and give personal details about the bride and groom.

Marriage Consents (Huwelijkstoestemming)

These include the above details but also the details of the parents or guardians on both sides and the date of their consent to the marriage. The records started in 1913 and are still in use today.

Marriage Supplements (Huwelijksbijlagen)

These records (dating from 1811) are important if you know the marriage date and place but nothing about birth date or parents. They include birth records of both spouses, and in some cases names of grandparents and great-grandparents. They may also include death dates of parents. These records are not indexed but are in chronological order.

Divorces (Echtscheidingen)

These started in 1811 and are only recorded in the municipality where the marriage took place.

Indexes

There are indexes to the registers of births, marriages, divorces, and deaths. In the early years after 1811 various methods of indexing were tried, both alphabetical and chronological. Sometimes the indexing was exact to the second letter of the family name, sometimes only within each letter and in no other order, so that the B names, for example, could be Br, Ba, Bl, Bo, Be. In the northern provinces, where patronymics (naming after the father's first name) were used, the births and deaths are entered in sequence of first names, followed by patronymics in alphabetical order, then the first and family names of the parents.

Census Records (Volkstellingen)

Some of the earliest censuses date back to 1580, and from then to 1829 they were taken in various parts of the country at various times in various ways. All these early local censuses can be found in local archives, with some duplicates in the provincial archives. After 1829 they were national in scope but only until 1850, when the population registers commenced. Since then a number of the bigger towns have held local censuses at irregular intervals and these are in local archives.

Military Records (Militaire Registers)

These can also be found in all the different levels of archives—except, of course, that those in local archives only refer to that particular area. In 1795 a national militia was established and service in it is still required. Full personal details, including next of kin, are included.

Other military records commence in about 1700 and include length of service, personal descriptions, wounds, location of service, character references, and date of discharge.

Civil Marriages and Divorces (Burgerlijke Huwelijken-Echtscheidingen)

These registers date from 1575 to 1811 and are located in all the different levels of archives. They contain details of the marriages of people who were not members of the Netherlands or French Reformed Churches, and include dates of intention, publication of banns, names of former husband or wife, and names, dates of birth, and addresses. Before 1795 civil marriages were not permitted in the provinces of Groningen, Drenthe, and Friesland; in the latter province, the district court was required to grant permission before the marriage could be performed in a Reformed Church, if one or both parties were not church members.

The College of Law (College van de Wet) had the authority to dissolve civil and church marriages and the decisions are recorded in the Keur Boeken (church books), along with details of the names and ages of any children, and the causes of the divorce. These records are in the various archives and in the Central Bureau for Genealogy.

Notarial Records (Notariële Protocollen)

These date from as far back as 1530. They include wills and codicils, marriage contracts and settlements, divisions of estates, deeds, contracts, mortgages, appointments of guardians, letters of apprenticeship, and civil-court notes and documents. They are partially indexed from 1803 and are in all archives and municipal registry offices.

Tax Rolls and Registers (Belasting Registers)

As you can imagine, these records date back into the mists of time, tax collecting being the second-oldest profession! The registers start, in fact, in 1240 and continue without a break until the present. They are located in all types of archives and cover all kinds of taxes: national and local taxes, head taxes, poll taxes, land taxes, water taxes, trade taxes, and so on. They generally give individual names and addresses, occupations, valuations, and tax assessments. Where inheritance or transfer of property is involved, they may be of great genealogical value.

Guild Records (Gilde Registers)

These date back to 1578 and can be a great source of information. If any of your ancestors were craftsmen in one of the cities, they would have to join a guild in order to set up in business. For example, if your ancestor had served his apprenticeship as a diamond-cutter in Amsterdam, he could not start his own business without applying to join the guild. He would have to produce evidence of his successful apprenticeship, a letter of reference from the master cutter to whom he had been apprenticed, a letter of reference from the priest or minister of his church, other character references from well-known people, evidence of his financial stability, details of his parentage and of his wife and children (if any), and possibly, an offer of employment from a craftsman aware of his ability. All such items are in the guild records in the provincial or city archives.

The guild was all-powerful, and unless the craftsman was accepted for membership he could never be in business for himself. The organization was the closed-shop trade union of the Middle Ages, and its power lasted until the early part of the nineteenth century.

Citizen Books (Burgerboeken)

It was not sufficient to be an inhabitant of a city if you wished to succeed in life, or even to join a guild. You had to be accepted as a citizen, and for this you needed the highest references, both civil and ecclesiastical, and to be financially secure. The records of those granted citizenship in the cities cover the period from 1240 to 1811. The records are in the provincial and municipal archives.

Land Registers (Land Registers)

These are in the archives at all levels and cover the period from 1200 to the present. They give full details of transactions involving land: the buyers and sellers, the lessors and lessees, together with names, addresses, and payments made.

Many of the records I have mentioned in this chapter as being in the various archives are indexed, or are in the process of being indexed. Any information I gave you on this score would be out-of-date by publication day.

So much for all the miscellaneous records in the Netherlands. Now for the church registers. There are a large number of different sects and religions that have developed and faded away over the years, but since many of them were either short-lived or of very minor importance, we will concentrate on the three major denominations: Catholic, Dutch Reformed, and Evangelical Lutheran. The Dutch Reformed Church records are the most valuable because for a period they also included the vital events of other religions not recognized by the state.

Catholic Church (Katholiek Kerk)

As in other European countries, the Catholic Church was the only recognized religion until the Reformation started in 1517. The Netherlands came under its influence and Protestantism developed, particularly in the northern provinces. In 1548 the country came under the rule of Spain and the King attempted to eradicate Protestantism. In 1568 a rebellion against Spanish rule broke out, but Spain quickly subdued the southern provinces, which were, generally speaking, Catholic. The northern provinces continued their resistance, uniting in 1579. Two years later they formed the Republic of the United Netherlands.

A few years earlier the cities of the Netherlands had closed their gates against Spanish troops and confiscated the properties of the Catholic Church, which were then given to the Calvinists (later named the Dutch Reformed Church). Mass was not celebrated in public for twenty years, nor were baptisms or marriages performed by Catholic priests. In 1648 the independence of the northern provinces was accepted by Spain and the Dutch Reformed Church became the state religion. The Reformed Church was quite tolerant toward the Catholics; the civil laws against them were abolished and the mass could again be read. Catholic church registers and records in the north date from this year. In the south, still controlled by Spain, the Catholic records are nearly complete from about 1580.

In the early eighteenth century a split occurred in the Catholic Church and by 1724 the Old Catholic Church was well established in fifty-one parishes in the provinces of Utrecht and Holland. If you are interested in that area and your ancestors were Catholic, remember this split, because it means that the fifty-one parishes still hold all records of the Catholic Church before the division of the church.

In 1853 the Catholic Church was officially re-established in the Netherlands with all its original rights and privileges. At the present time the Netherlands are about equally divided between Catholics and Protestants.

The earliest Catholic records (the documents of the Bishop of Utrecht) date back to 723. Apart from the registers, the churches have confirmation and communion records, and records of graves, of payments for bell-tolling, of donations to priests, and of the provision of mort-cloths for burial.

It was the Council of Trent (1545–63) that ordered the Catholic priests throughout the world to record baptisms, marriages, and burials, but very few registers in the Netherlands date back to that time. Deventer has some dated 1542, Utrecht 1559, and Amsterdam 1564, to name a few.

The entries in the registers were mostly in Latin. Before 1775 it was only the date of baptism and not of birth that was recorded. The children-naming pattern in common usage up until the latter part of the last century was that the first two boys were named after the grandfathers, the first two girls after the grandmothers, and the next boy and girl after the father and mother.

Confirmations

These usually took place between the ages of seven and nineteen and the lists date back in some places to 1542. The names of the child and parents, the places of birth and residence, and the names of witnesses were included.

First Communion Lists (Neocommunicaites)

This event took place between the ages of seven and eight and these lists contain the same personal details as for confirmations.

Marriage Records (Huwelijksregisters)

The laws of 1571–78 allowed marriages to be performed in the Dutch Reformed Church, and in 1584 a law gave non-Catholics a choice of either the Dutch Reformed Church or a civil marriage before an alderman or a sheriff. In 1795 it was ordained that only civil marriages could be performed, but the marriage could be blessed afterwards in a church. All these changes and variations are important for you to understand if your ancestors were Catholic, because you may find the record of their marriage in a Dutch Reformed Church or in the local municipal office.

Since 1811 civil registration of marriage has been compulsory, but the Catholic Church continues to record vital events. These records often give you an extra check on accuracy of the civil records. The early Catholic registers are nearly all in the provincial archives, but some originals and many duplicates are in the individual churches, or in various Catholic Archives:

ARCHBISHOP OF UTRECHT: Veemarktstraat 48
Postbus 90189
3508 RN Breda

BISHOP OF BREDA: Veemarktstraat 48
4811 ZH Breda

BISHOP OF GRONINGEN: Marktstraat 19
9712 BP Groningen

BISHOP OF HAARLEM: Nieuwe Gracht 80
Postbus 1053
2001 BB Haarlem

BISHOP OF 'S-HERTOGENBOSCH: Parade 11
Postbus 1070
5200 BC 's-Hertogenbosch

BISHOP OF ROERMOND: Paredisstraat 10
Postbus 980
6040 AZ Roermond

BISHOP OF ROTTERDAM: Koningin Emmaplein 3–4
                                        3016 AA Rotterdam

The Archives of the Dutch Reformed Church (Overgoo 11, Postbus 405, 2260 AK Leidschendam) also has some details of Catholic records.

It should also be noted that various laws against the Catholic Church resulted in variations in record-keeping in two provinces:

Overijssel. Anti-Catholic laws did not apply in the town of Twenthe (under Spanish control) from 1580 to 1630. Also, in the years 1625–48 all baptisms had to take place in a Dutch Reformed church.

Noord-Brabant. Because of several wars in the province in the sixteenth and seventeenth centuries, many people in Brabant had their children baptized in 's-Hertogenbosch. In addition, from 1609 to 1621, for the same reason, many children were taken to Antwerp, in Belgium, for baptism. From 1625 to 1648 Catholics were banned, and although baptisms and marriages were often performed in secret by a priest, no records exist.

Early records in Catholic churches were in Latin. I give below some words you will come across in the registers in Latin, English, and Dutch:

Latin	*English*	*Dutch*
Acatholicus	Non-Catholic	Niet-Katholiek
Aetas	Age	Ouderdom
Amita	Aunt on father's side	Tante van vader's zijde
An, anno	Year	Jaar
Arbiter	Witness	Getuige
Avia	Grandmother	Grootmoeder
Avunculus	Uncle on mother's side	Oom van moeder's zijde
Baptisatus	Baptism	Gedoopt
Caelebs	Bachelor	Vrijgezel
Cippus	Gravestone	Grafsteen
Coelebs	Single	Vrijgezel
Compater	Godfather	Peetoom
Conjux	Spouse	Echtgenoot, echtgenote
Copulatio	Marriage	Trouwen
Cuis suspectories	Godparents	Peetouders
Defunctus	Dead	Gestorven
Dununciatio	Banns	Huwelijks- afkondigingen
Domus	House	Huis
Filia	Daughter	Dochter

Latin	English	Dutch
Filius	Son	Zoon
Frater	Brother	Broeder
Genitores	Parents	Ouders
Germana	Sister	Zuster
Germanus	Brother	Broeder
Illegitimus	Illegitimate	Buitenechtelijk
Levans	Godfather	Peetvader
Ligatus	Husband	Echtgenoot
Marita	Wife	Echtgenote
Mater	Mother	Moeder
Matrina	Godmother	Peetmoeder
Mors	Death	Dood
Novercus	Stepfather	Stiefvader
Noverca	Stepmother	Stiefmoeder
Orbus	Orphan	Weeskind
Pater	Father	Vader
Patruus	Uncle on father's side	Oom van vader's zijde
Pontificius	Catholic	Katholiek
Puer	Son	Zoon
Puera	Daughter	Dochter
Relicta	Widow	Weduwe
Renatus	Baptized	Gedoopt
Sepultus	Buried	Begraven
Sexus	Sex	Geslacht
Soror	Sister	Zuster
Testes	Witnesses	Getuigen
Vedovus	Widower	Weduwnaar
Vidua	Widow	Weduwe
Virgo	Maiden	Meisje
Xped	Baptized	Gedoopt

The Dutch Reformed Church (Nederlandse Hervormde Kerk)

As mentioned above, the records and registers of this church are important to members of other churches too, because over various periods Catholics, Jews, Mennonites, and so on, were compelled to have their children baptized and married in a Dutch Reformed Church. These mainly anti-Catholic laws affected periods in the sixteenth and early seventeenth centuries.

The registers of the Dutch Reformed Church began at different times in the various provinces. You will recall that the Protestant provinces were the seven northern ones and the approximate starting date for records was:

Holland (1573), Zeeland (1578), Groningen (1580), Utrecht (1583), Gelderland (1587), Friesland (1590), Overijssel (1638).

However, having given you these dates, I must also tell you that in very many places the starting date was much later, even a century later. Once the registers did start, the baptism and marriage entries are accurate and quite comprehensive in their information, with two exceptions: first, in the baptismal registers the name of the mother is not always given, and, second, in the big cities there are many gaps in the burial records. These were caused by the frequent epidemics of the plague and the heavy death toll. The ministers of the church were just too busy with burials to spend time making entries in the registers.

If your ancestors came from Zeeland you may run into some additional difficulties because the provincial archives were destroyed during the Second World War and many church registers were lost. Fortunately, some duplicates did exist, and you should check with the Rijksarchief in Zeeland for more detailed information.

Baptisms

As mentioned, the early entries (before 1792) did not always give the date of birth. You will find great variation in the spelling of surnames and even first names owing to the changes in ministers and their inability to spell. If you are in doubt as to whether, for example, Klaas van der Kist who had a son Henrick is the same man as the Claes van Derkes who had a son Cornelis two years later, you should check the names of the witnesses or sponsors at both baptisms. They were nearly always close relatives, and if the same names appear in both entries you may be certain that the same father is concerned in the two baptisms. Of course, you will also get variations in the spelling of the witnesses' names, but let's not get into that as well!

Marriages

Remember that civil marriages have been permitted since 1584, and if your ancestor was marrying a member of another denomination, or of no denomination at all, the marriage may well have been a civil one in the local town hall. It may, or may not, have been blessed in the Dutch Reformed Church after the civil ceremony. The only exception to this permission to hold civil marriages appears to have been in the small town of Bommenede, in Zeeland. The marriage records also include the Intentions to Marry, and these announcements were usually made from the pulpit for three successive Sundays before the ceremony, and afterward a note was made in the registers.

Burials

These records gave date and, often, the cause of death. They also show whether the burial took place in a family vault within the church, or in the churchyard outside.

Although civil registration has existed since 1811, the Dutch Reformed Church has continued to enter vital events in its registers. (The headquarters of the church is Overgoo 11, Postbus 405, 2260 AK Leidschendam; Phone: 011-70-313-1131; Fax: 011-70-313-1202.)

Evangelical Lutheran and Restored Evangelical Lutheran

These two churches, which split in 1791 and became whole again in 1952, form only a small part of the religions of the Netherlands. However, the Lutheran movement was powerful and influential far beyond its small membership. Many of the Dutch Reformed Church members showed interest in the doctrines and eventually transferred their allegiance. For that reason, if you are of Dutch Protestant stock you should know about the Lutheran movement and its records.

The Lutherans, then mostly of German and Scandinavian origin, established their first church in Amsterdam in 1633 and the faith spread quickly into the other main cities and towns. By the end of the century there were thirty-four churches in the Netherlands, all in urban areas.

As in nearly all Protestant religions that came into being after the Reformation, there were disputes over doctrine and many splits and schisms. Probably the very strong characters of the early Protestant dissenters led to the fierce arguments that spawned the many different sects. In 1791 a breakaway group founded the Restored Evangelical Lutheran Church Society, and congregations in Enkhuizen, Gorinchem, Harlingen, Hoorn, Medemblik, and Zwolle joined the new church. The schism continued, as I mentioned above, to as recently as 1952.

Lutheran ministers were allowed to perform marriages in the province of Holland, but in Zeeland Lutheran marriages had to be solemnized in the Dutch Reformed churches. In Gelderland and Utrecht they could have civil marriages. In Overijssel the Lutherans were totally banned until 1653. After that date they were tolerated and could either have civil marriages or be wed in the Dutch Reformed Church. Lutherans in Groningen province also had this choice until 1735, but after that they could be married in their own church.

Generally speaking, the Lutherans were treated by the Dutch Reformed Church as misguided friends, whereas the Catholics were the enemy. Certainly they did not operate under major restrictions or difficulties for very long, and by the early eighteenth century their ministers were officiating at Lutheran baptisms, marriages, and burials.

The Lutheran records are basically the same as those of the other two religions we talked about. The entries in the early dates were usually in German and in either the German or the Dutch script, neither of which is easy to read.

Registers for the following Lutheran parishes are in the various archives (provincial, regional, and municipal). Some are for baptisms, marriages, and burials, while others are for only one or two of these three categories. The starting dates vary considerably. For example, Amsterdam 1590, Delft 1617, Groningen 1695, Leerdam 1737, Vlissingen 1809:

FRIESLAND: Harlingen, Leeuwarden.

GELDERLAND: Arnhem, Culemborg, Doesburg, Doetinchem, Nijmegen, Zutphen.

GRONINGEN: Groningen, Nieuwe Pekela, Sappemeer (Hoogezand-Sappemeer), Wildervank, Winschoten, Winschoterzijl.

LIMBURG: Maastricht, Vaals.

NOORD-BRABANT: Bergen op Zoom, Breda, 's-Hertogenbosch.

NOORD-HOLLAND: Alkmaar, Amsterdam, Beverwijk, Edam, Enkhuizen, Haarlem, Hoorn, Medemblik, Monnikendam, Naarden, Purmerend, De Rijp, Weesp, West-Zaandam, Zaandijk.

OVERIJSSEL: Deventer, Kampen, Zwolle.

UTRECHT: Amersfoort, Utrecht.

ZEELAND: Middelburg (destroyed 1940), Vlissingen, Zierikzee. The latter two are in the National Archives (Rijksarchief).

ZUID-HOLLAND: Bodegraven, Delft, Dordrecht, Gorinchem, Gouda, 's-Gravenhage, Hellevoetsluis, Leerdam, Leiden, Rotterdam, Schiedam, Woerden.

Finally, the headquarters of the Evangelical Lutheran Church is Jan de Bakkerstraat 13–15, 3411 ED Woerden.

Genealogical Organizations

By far the most important and valuable after the Central Bureau described earlier is the following:

Nederlandse Genealogische Vereniging
Postbus 976
1000 AZ, Amsterdam
E-mail: info@ngv.n/
Web site: www.ngv.n/

It has over 11,000 members and is the second-largest genealogical organization in Europe. Staffed entirely by volunteers, it does not undertake research but will send you a list of members willing to do work for you for an agreed fee. If you become a member yourself, you will receive a monthly magazine (in Dutch) and will be able, when you visit the Netherlands, to use the facilities of the Genealogical Center. This is located at Papelaan 6, 1382 RM Weesp. It contains (1) a large library, (2) a collection of press clippings, (3) a central card-index, and (4) a collection of manuscripts.

Other organizations are listed below:

Koninklijk Nederlandsche Genootschap voor Geslacht-en Wapenkunde
Postbus 85630, 2508 CH 's-Gravenhage

Sectie voor Geslacht-naam-en wapenkunde van het Prov. Genootschap van
Kunsten en Wetenschappen
Maasbandijk 30, Kerkdriel
(Area of interest: North Brabant)

Zuidhollandse Vereniging voor Genealogie
Postbus 404, AK 3000 Rotterdam
(Area of interest: South Holland)

Kommissie voor Westfries Genealogie
Hemmerbuurt 135, Hem
(Area of interest: Friesland)

Gruoninga
Postbus 1127, Groningen
(Area of interest: Province of Groningen)

Genealogysk Wurkforbân de Fryske Akademy
Doelestraat 8, Leeuwarden
(Area of interest: Friesland)

It is possible there are other smaller local organizations, and you should
check with either the provincial archives or the local city or town hall.

Jewish Records

The Amsterdam Municipal Archives keep Netherlands Jewish archives:

Nederlands Joods Familienarchief
Postbus 51140, 1007 EC Amsterdam
Phone: 011-31-20-572-0202. Fax: 011-31-20-675-0596
E-mail: GAASECR@xs4ALL.nl

While the records in the Netherlands are not as good as those in the
Scandinavian countries, they are still among the best in Europe. Because of
the decentralization of records among the various archives (not only the
twelve main ones, but the seventy-five local ones), it will take you longer to
track down sources of information. However, the records are there, and you
must have the dogged determination of your Netherlands ancestors!

NORWAY

If you have already read the chapters on Denmark and Sweden, you will know most of Norway's history, since the three Scandinavian countries were linked, willingly or unwillingly, over the centuries. If you have not read those chapters, I suggest you do so, because as you get further back in your ancestor-hunting you may well find useful genealogical information in their records as well as in those of Norway itself.

Up until the ninth century the country was divided into a number of petty kingdoms. Then there was a brief period of unity under Harold I, followed by two centuries of Norse raids on the coasts of western Europe and Britain, the establishment of the Norse Duchy of Normandy, and then a long period of civil war. In 1397 the three Scandinavian countries were united under the queen of Denmark. Although Sweden soon withdrew from the union, Norway remained as a part of Denmark until 1814, when it was ceded to Sweden. However, Norway was soon recognized by Sweden as a separate country in personal union with Sweden, and given its own Parliament and constitution. In 1905 Norway declared its complete independence, and this was accepted by Sweden after a plebiscite showed the Norwegians to be overwhelmingly in favor of separation. A son of the king of Denmark was elected king of Norway.

There are two forms of language in use in Norway, both Norwegian, but Bokmål is the book language and Nynorsk the so-called country language. Recent grammar reforms have brought the two languages nearer and there is hope that one language (Samnorsk, or common Norwegian) will eventually emerge. Meanwhile, though you will only encounter Bokmål in books, records, and correspondence, you will undoubtedly encounter Nynorsk if you visit the country. The alphabet of both languages is the same as that used for English, with the addition of three extra letters: æ, ø, and å. The country is divided into eighteen counties (fylker), plus the capital district of Oslo. There are, of course, smaller administrative areas, such as kommuner (townships) and prestegjeld and sokn (parishes).

Before 1919 the counties (fylker) were named "amt." The singular of fylker is fylke. This change of name is important for you as you trace back. Quite apart from this change of description for a county, you must also know that a number of counties have changed their names. I give below the name of each of the fylker and in parentheses the old name. Where no name appears in parentheses, it means that the county name has not changed:

Akershus
Aust-Agder (Nedenes)
Buskerud
Finnmark
Hedemark
Hordaland (Søndre Bergenhus, including Bergen)
Møre og Romsdal (part of Søndre Trondheim)
Nordland
Nord-Trøndelag (Nordre Trondheim)
Oppland (Christian)
Oslo (Christiania)
Østfold (Smaalenene)
Rogaland (Ryfylke, also Stavanger)
Sogn og Fjordane (Nordre Bergenhus)
Sør-Trøndelag (part of Søndre Trondheim)
Telemark (Bratsberg)
Troms (Tromsø)
Vest-Agder (Lister og Mandal)
Vestfold (Jarlsberg og Larvik)

Archives

The National Archives (Riksarkivet) of Norway are located at the following address:

Folke Bernadottes vei 21, 0806 Oslo
(postal address: Postboks 4013 Ullevål stadion, 0806 Oslo)
Phone: 011-47-22-02-26-00. Fax: 011-47-22-23-74-89
E-mail: riksarkivet.riksarkivaren.dep.no
Web site: www.riksarkivet.no

Regional Archives (Statsarkivet)

Please note that a new statsarkivet, Kongsberg, was established in 1999. Kongsberg covers Vetsfold, Telemark, and Buskerod—all previously covered by the Oslo Statsarkivet. There are now eight statsarkivet and one sub-archives (Statsarkivet Kontor-Tromsø).

OSLO: Statsarkivet i Oslo (records from Østfold, Akershus, Oslo), Folke Bernadottes 21, Postboks 4015,Ullevål stadion, 0806 Oslo. Phone: 011-47-22-02-26-00. Fax: 011-47-22-23-74-89.

HAMAR: Statsarkivet i Hamar (records from Hedmark, Oppland), Lille Strandgate 3, Postboks 533, 2304 Hamar. Phone: 011-47-62-52-36-42. Fax: 011-47-62-52-94-48.

KONGSBERG: Statsarkivet i Kongsberg (records from Buskerud, Vestfold, Telemark), Frogsvei 44, 3611 Kongsberg. Phone: 011-47-32-86-9-900. Fax: 011-47-32-86-99-10.

KRISTIANSAND: Statsarkivet i Kristiansand (records from Aust-Agder, Vest-Agder), Märthas vei 1, Serviceboks 402, 4604 Kristiansand. Phone: 011-47-38-14-55-00. Fax: 011-47-38-14-55-01.

STAVANGER: Statsarkivet i Stavanger (records from Rogaland), Bergjelandsgt. 30, 4012 Stavanger. Phone: 011-47-51-50-12-60. Fax: 011-47-51-50-12-90.

BERGEN: Statsarkivet i Bergen (records from Hordaland, Sogn og Fjordane), Årstadveien 22, 5009 Bergen. Phone: 011-47-55-31-50-70. Fax: 011-47-55-32-12-65.

TRONDHEIM: Statsarkivet i Trondheim (records from Møre og Romsdal, Sør-Trøndelag, Nord-Trøndelag, Nordland), Høgskoleveien 12, Postboks 2825 Elgesaeter, 7432 Trondheim. Phone: 011-47-73-88-45-00; Fax: 011-47-73-88-45-40.

TROMSØ: Statsarkivet i Tromsø (records from Troms, Finnmark, Spitsbergen), 9293 Tromsø. Phone: 011-47-77-67-66-11. Fax: 011-47-77-67-65-20.

(Although the principal records of the Troms and Finnmark fylker come under the control of the Statsarkivet i Trondheim, they are, in fact, kept in Tromsø.)

In Norway, even more than in many countries, it is vital that you do your homework before you start your search. Try to find out what your emigrant ancestor did for a living in the old country, whether he was a farmer or a farmhand, a clerk or a merchant, a watchmaker or a wheelwright. This could affect the type of records you may be searching. Find out his religion and be sure he did not change it after his arrival in his new country. Find out the correct family name; check to see if the spelling was changed in any way. Bear in mind that surnames could come from three different sources: the family, the father, or the farm. When a farmer sold one farm and bought another, he often changed his name from the name of the old farm to that of the new. If he took a farm laborer with him, the latter might change his name too. Family names, as we know them today, only developed four or five generations ago. This did not apply to the nobility or people of prominent families.

You will be helped in overcoming these difficulties in various ways. Church records often joined the name of a family and a farm together with a hyphen; children baptized or confirmed were often described in the same way. Until the early years of this century there was a pattern of naming children that was widely observed, i.e., oldest son after father's father, second son after mother's father, third son after father, and the same with daughters on the female side. After the first three names were used up in this way, the pattern followed the next generation back, that of the great-grand-parents.

There is a complication to this naming pattern. Nowadays, if we have a child who dies in infancy, we do not usually use the same first name again for a later child. In earlier days this did not apply. The naming pattern was too rigid to disregard and so you may find, in days of high infant mortality, that a first name would be repeated and repeated until eventually a child survived. So, in a birth register you may find three successive sons named Olav, but if you turn to the death entries you will find out what happened to the first two.

Finally, while we are on the subject of names, remember that a name may have been simplified by your emigrant ancestor to make it more easily understood and spelled in his or her new country.

So far as the place of origin is concerned, it is almost essential you produce this from within your own family records. There are a limited number of Norwegian surnames and no one is going to be able, for example, to tell you the birthplace of Olav Andersen who left Norway for overseas in 1855 except someone within your own family. Even then, make sure it is the name of a place and not a farm. There are a limited number of immigration and emigration records, and also passenger lists, but they are a small per-centage of the whole and you should not expect too much of them. Once you know the place, a great many records are open to you.

On this side of the Atlantic there are a number of sources that may either help you to pin down a place of origin or let you know if a history of your family has already been written:

The Norwegian-American Historical Association (1510 St. Olaf Avenue, Northfield, Minnesota 55057; Fax: 507-646-3734; E-mail: naha@stolaf.edu; Web site: www.naha.stolaf.edu/genealogy.htm) has published a number of books about Norwegian ancestry. If you get a list from the association (or check the publications list on their web site), you will be able to borrow them through your local library.

The Supreme Lodge of the Sons of Norway (1455 West Lake Street, Minneapolis, Minnesota 55408; Phone: 612-827-3611; Fax: 612-827-0658; Web site: www.sofn.com/main.html) also has various publications.

Other sources worth checking are the following:

The University of Minnesota Library, Minneapolis
The Memorial Library of the University of Wisconsin, Madison
The Preus Library, Luther College, Decorah, Iowa
The Library of the Lutheran Theological Seminary, St. Paul, Minnesota

In Norway there are a number of places where you may find local histories for the area in which you are interested, or family histories either already published or in manuscript form about many Norwegian families (and not only the prominent ones):

Universitets Bibliotek i Bergen, Haakon Sheteligs plass 7, 15007 Bergen; Phone: 011-47-55-58-25-00
Bibliotek i Trondheim, Erling Skakkes gate 47b, 7013 Trondheim; Web site: www.ub.ntnu.no
Deishmanske Bibliotek, Henrik Ibsens gate 1, 0179 Oslo.
Norsk Slektshistorisk Forening, Akersgaten 7, 0101 Oslo.
Aust-Agder-arkivet, Parkveien, 4800 Arendal.

Parish Records

Many localities in Norway have village books (Bygdebøker) that give very detailed information about farms and families in the parish. The Statsarkiv will be able to tell you what is available for your particular area of interest. The genealogical society mentioned above can also put you in touch with any local genealogical organization that may be operating in a particular fylke that is of interest to you.

Church Records

There is no civil registration of births, marriages, and deaths as we know it in this country. The Lutheran Church is charged with the responsibility of recording vital events and it is with the church that you must deal. Since 1903 the Central Bureau of Statistics (Statistisk Sentralbyrå) has kept copies of the entries in the church registers (Kirkebøker), but these are kept for statistical purposes only and are not available for public search.

The church records are transferred to the regional archives (Statsarkivet) eighty years after the recorded event, so that only the last eighty years are in the individual churches. However, in rural districts a duplicate register is maintained by the deacons of the church and sent to the archives as soon as it is completed.

Registers less than sixty years old are not available for public search without special permission from the regional archivist. However, a copy of a specific entry is supplied on application. It may save delay if, when writing, you enclose your proof of descent from the person for whose certificate of baptism, marriage, or burial you are applying. This is unlikely to cause you any problem because you will probably only be interested in register entries older than sixty years, anyway.

The church registers (Kirkebøker) may contain information about confirmations, vaccinations, engagements, maternal introductions (see p. 208), and movements in and out of the parish, depending on the date. The records start about 1700, but some are much earlier and some much later. Andebu, in Vestfold, for example, started in 1623, while Kvam, in Hordaland, began in 1843.

The vast majority of Norwegians are members of the Lutheran Church, which is the state religion, and it was not until 1891 that any recognition was given to any other denomination. Consequently, *all* vital events had to be recorded in the Lutheran registers, even though the parties concerned were nonconformists. In 1891 the latter were allowed to perform marriages in their churches, and in 1896 Unitarians and Jews were included in these provisions. Even so, the events had still to be recorded in the Lutheran registers by the local Lutheran minister. Those with no religion at all had to report the event to a local magistrate, bailiff, or the chief of police, and the official concerned then passed on the information to the Lutheran minister.

Early entries are in Danish (since, as you know, Norway was originally part of Denmark), and written in the Germanic script. This does not make personal searching very easy. The contents of the registers vary over the years according to the church laws. From 1623 to 1735 they included only details of baptisms, marriages, and burials. From 1736 to 1814 they also included intentions to marry (to 1799 only), introductions, and confirmations (these latter took place when the child was at least fourteen). From 1814 to 1876, possibly key years for you, the registers listed arrivals in the parish and departures. They also included all vaccinations. Details of these various records are as follows:

Births

The information in the registers varies; some give the date of birth, some the date of baptism, and some give both dates. Sometimes, too, only the name of the father is given (no one having told the minister the facts of life!). However, if you are lucky you will find the full name of the child, names of both parents, ages, occupations, addresses, and witnesses and their relationship to the child. Sometimes, if a child was sickly at birth and his or her survival was in doubt, the baptism would take place in the home as soon as possible after birth, and the entry was then made in the church register. Usually, the baptism took place on the first or second Sunday following the birth.

Marriages

The records show the names of both parties, their status (if previously married), occupations, addresses, and since 1830, their places of birth and the names of the two fathers, and whether they were alive at the time of the marriage. The engagement or betrothal of the couple was also entered in the church records and an announcement made from the pulpit. This was the equivalent of publishing the banns.

Deaths

The date, place, and cause of death are given, as well as the address, occupation, and full name. Since about 1890 the place of birth is also shown. Often, the name of the survivor (wife or husband) is given, and also that of the person reporting the death.

Confirmations

This record gives name, age, address, names of parents, and since 1814, date of baptism.

Introductions

This referred to the practice of the mother of a child being "introduced" to the congregation at her first appearance in church after the birth, and being formally "cleansed." Her name and that of her husband are given, together with the date of the birth and the date of the introduction.

Arrivals and Removals (Tilgangslister and Avgangslister)

These records can be of tremendous help to you if the minister of the day was conscientious in keeping these records. The period covered was from 1814 to 1876 and listed people arriving in and leaving the parish. The place from which they came and, in the case of departures, their intended destination are shown. Full names, ages, and parish address are also given.

Vaccinations

During the last century great encouragement was given to the vaccination of children, and the ministers were handed the job of urging that it be done, and of recording the event afterward. The name and address of the child is given, and usually the ages and the names of the parents. The period covered is from 1814 to 1876.

The year 1814 is important for church records because from then on greater care was taken in keeping the records, and much more detail appeared.

The nonconformist churches continue to maintain their own registers in the individual churches; a few have been transferred to the regional archives, but only a few. I suppose that because it took so long to get permission to keep their own records they are reluctant to surrender them to anyone else!

Remember that in rural areas the farm where people lived (as either owners or tenants) was nearly always included in the entry in the registers. Be sure you note this, because the information may help you in other areas. For instance, many land, mortgage, and probate records are indexed by farm name and not by a personal name.

Census Returns (Folketellinger)

We are luckier with census records in Norway than in most other countries. Norway started the censuses earlier, they were more widespread, and in many cases there are records that, while not technically census returns, are similar and predate church registers in many instances. Before the official censuses were started, a head-tax list (Manntall) was started in 1664–66. This covered the rural areas and listed men and boys over the age of twelve. Names and ages were recorded. Copies are in the National Archives, as well as regional archives. In 1701 a similar list was compiled and this, too, is in the same archives. Unfortunately the list is missing for the eastern part of the country, except for Rygge, Odal, part of the Larvik district, and six areas of Romerike.

Another early source of "census-like" information is the county and bailiwick accounts (lens og fogedregnskaper) now in the National Archives. These started in the sixteenth century and include tax lists and real estate registers, and may make it easy for you to trace ownership of a particular farm or estate. There are also similar records for the towns called byregnskaper, and these, too, are in the National Archives.

The first census to list complete families was that of 1769, but it did not apply to the whole country. Check with the regional archives to find out if they have one for your area of Norway. The 1801 census is very good genealogically as it is complete, in both the National Archives and regional archives, and lists farm names, and name, age, occupation, and marital status of everyone in the house. From 1815 a census was taken every tenth year to 1875, but again was not complete for the whole country. The records are in the National Archives (1865 and 1875 are almost complete), and since the returns listed farm names, personal names, places of birth, occupations, religion, marital status, and in the cities, street names and house numbers, they are well worth checking. Copies for 1865 are in the National Archives and for 1875 in the regional archives. The 1870 and 1885 censuses were for towns only and are in both.

From 1890 a census for the whole country has been taken every ten years. They are in the National Archives and regional archives. Only those before 1900 are open to public inspection, but under special circumstances (e.g., inheritance), information from a later census may be divulged by the National Archivist to a notary.

Probate Registers (Skifteprotokoller)

These show the registration, valuation, and division of real estate and property left by the deceased person, and also give the names and addresses of heirs. The registers started in 1660 and were kept by the probate court in the country districts and by magistrates in the towns. They are now in the regional archives. A program of indexing the registers has been started but it will be many a long year before it is completed. Quite often the information from the register is clearer and more accurate than that in a church register or a census.

Registers of Conveyances and Mortgages (Skjøte og pantebøker)

These registers list real estate transactions, mortgages, liens on property, bills of sale, and contracts. They date from about 1700 or later and are either in the regional archives or in the custody of the local town clerk.

Real Estate Books (Matrikler)

These date from 1665 and are in the National Archives. Many have been printed and indexed. They list the names of owners and tenants of farmland.

Court Records (Justisprotokoller)

Don't be afraid to use these records. It is unlikely that you will find great-great-grandfather was a criminal! The courts are more concerned with civil actions than with criminal cases and you will find references to property, probate, marriage contracts, real estate, and sometimes, very detailed information about a family and its land holdings.

Tax Lists (Skattelister)

As you may imagine, there are a variety of these dating from about 1645. They are in the National Archives and regional archives.

Lists of Emigrants

Your first source of information, as mentioned above, is in the parish records. In addition, since about 1858 the police in many districts have kept lists of emigrants with name, home address, date of sailing, destination, and name of ship. You should not assume that your ancestor sailed from a Norwegian port. He or she may well have sailed from Hamburg, in Germany, and the Hamburg Passenger Lists may be of use to you (see the chapter on Germany). The police lists are in the local police station, but the earliest ones for Oslo, Kristiansund, Bergen, Ålesund, Molde, and Trondheim are in the various regional archives. The regional archives in Oslo have the White Star Line's emigrant lists for 1883–1923. The Stavanger emigrant lists were destroyed in a fire.

Other things to bear in mind about the emigrant lists: the address given by the emigrant may be the place in which he is living temporarily while waiting passage, and not his actual place of birth or domicile. Not many of the lists have been indexed, and you will probably need the help of a professional researcher suggested by the archives to check them for you.

Military Records (Militaerprotokoller)

These date from 1643 up to the present. The muster-rolls, as they are called, are not very reliable for the first fifty years or so, but are very detailed since then. Recent ones are in the various military headquarters, but the earlier ones in which you may be interested are in the National Archives and regional archives. Useful genealogical information can be found, as the records show next of kin, wife and family, and home address. Military service in Norway has been compulsory on various occasions over the years, and so the great majority of males will be listed in these records. Unfortunately there are gaps. Oddly enough, you may be told by the regional archives that the muster-roll for a particular district is missing and later you will find it in the local fylke records, or in a town hall.

Guild Records

If your ancestor was a craftsman belonging to a guild in one of the big cities, you may find out a great deal about him and his family in the local city archives, particularly in Oslo. The trade guilds were the ancient version of the trade unions, except that they were more powerful and, because they represented a skilled craft, more exclusive. The guild records give full details of applicants for membership, their qualifications, where they served an apprenticeship, and their address, children, and marital status. Once a man was accepted into a guild, his success in life was assured, he was protected against competition, and he was looked up to by his friends and neighbors. In short, he had arrived!

Other Records

These include citizenship records, school lists, newspapers, card-index biographies in local libraries, trade indexes, land commissions, and deeds.

As you will now have seen, the records in Norway are exceptionally good, but your success in your search is very dependent on knowing your ancestor's place of origin. When you do know it, write a short letter to the local newspaper (a Norwegian embassy or consulate will give you its name) and ask if there are any relatives of your emigrant ancestor still in the neighborhood. You never know how many distant cousins you will discover and what stories they will be able to tell you about your family history.

There is one fairly new source of information. The Norwegian Historical Date Archives were started by the University of Tromsø in 1981 to computerize eighteenth- and nineteenth-century genealogical material. They can offer information to overseas inquirers who are tracing their Norwegian ancestors. You should write to the Data Arkivet, Universitet i Tromsø, 9001 Tromsø.

POLAND

The country is divided into sixteen voiods (the equivalent of our counties). The capital of the country is Warsaw (Warszawa). The present boundaries were established in 1945 after the end of the Second World War and are now recognized by all her neighbors.

It is doubtful that any country in Europe has had such an unfortunate and tragic history as Poland. The combination of geography, the rapacity of its neighbors, and the lack of realism of the Poles themselves has been almost fatal. The area called Poland has varied in size and shape over the centuries. The initial expansion of the country started in the tenth century, and from then on, the Poles fought wars with the Holy Roman Empire, Bohemia, Pomerania, Kiev, Denmark, Hungary, Moldavia, the Ottoman Turks, the Tatars, the Russians, the Austrians, and the Prussians. In addition, there were internal disputes between the Catholic and Greek Orthodox churches, troubles between the kings and the nobles, dynastic changes, and peasant revolts.

The astounding thing is that Poland survived. Poland disappeared from the map of Europe in 1795 and did not reappear until 1918. In 1772, 1793, and 1795 the country was partitioned among Austria, Prussia, and Russia. Rebellions followed (1830–63) in the Russian-held territory where the treatment of the Poles was particularly severe. Only in the Austrian-held area of Galicia were the Poles allowed any kind of autonomy.

In 1919 Poland was reconstituted, but even then some of her eastern areas were lost to the USSR as the result of a short war in 1921. There were also disputes and minor adjustments of some territories with Czechoslovakia and Lithuania. In 1939 a fourth partition took place, the country being divided between Germany and the USSR. In 1945 the areas held by Germany became Polish again but the eastern territories remained in the hands of the USSR. These lands are now divided among Russia, Belarus, Ukraine, and Lithuania.

The destruction of records during the centuries was on an immense scale, and for this reason any genealogical research in Poland is complicated and, in some instances, impossible.

A major complication in ancestor-hunting in Poland is the question of names—both names of families and names of places. Names of families were changed because, after emigration, many people found that their Polish names were virtually unpronounceable to non-Poles, and so Przybyslawski became Price, and Szawlowski became Shaw. Names of places were altered because during the partition period Polish place-names were changed from Polish to German or Russian and then back again. Thus Olsztyn became Allenstein, and Zielona Gorá became Grünberg. In a further complication when Polish territory was ceded to Czechoslovakia, Troppau became Opava and Leitmeritz became Litoměřice. There is also considerable duplication of place-names in Poland. So, tread carefully, and check and double-check both family names and place-names.

There is also the further complication that the Polish alphabet contains nine more letters than ours and, believe me, full use is made of these extra letters! They are as follows:

$$ą, \quad ć \quad ę \quad ł, \quad ń, \quad ó, \quad ś, \quad ź, \quad ż$$

Anyway, try it by yourself and see how it goes. You may find eventually that you need some help from an expert in Polish genealogy.

Archives (Archiwa)

The National Archives are located in Warsaw at the following address:

Head Office of State Archives
ul. Długa 6, skrytka pocztowa 1005
00950 Warsaw
Phone: 011-48-22-31-32-06
Fax: 011-48-22-31-75-63

There are also other archives of genealogical importance:

Central Archive of Historical Records
ul. Długa 7, 00263 Warsaw
Older historical records are housed here.

Archives of New Records
Hankiewicza 1, 02103 Warsaw
This is the Polish national center for newer historical records.

Central Military Archive
(Centralne Archiwum Wojskowe)
00910 Warsaw 72

The country is divided into voivods, the equivalent of our counties. They each have archives (some have branches) and a good amount of genealogical research material, but allow for many gaps because of war damage.

These archives are called Archiwa Panstwówe and mail should be addressed to Archiwum Państwówe, followed by the postal code and city or town names show below. The cities marked with an asterisk (*) also have subsidiary archives in neighboring locations.

15950 Białystok*	97300 Piotrków-Trybunalska*
85009 Bydgoszcz*	09407 Płock*
42200 Częstochowa	60967 Poznań*
80958 Gdańsk*	37700 Przemyśl
62800 Kalisz*	26600 Radom
40145 Katowice*	35959 Rzeszów*
25953 Kielce*	08100 Siedice
75950 Koszalin*	16400 Suwałki*
30360 Kraków*	70410 Szczecln*
64100 Leszno	87100 Torun*
90950 Łodź*	00270 Warsaw
20950 Lublin*	50215 Wrocław*
10521 Olsztyn*	22400 Zamość
45016 Opole	66002 Zielona Góra (Stary Kisielin)*

The archives of the following cities (originally German) are now in Polish archives in the various voivods. The German name is given first and the present Polish name is shown in parentheses. Except for the two cities marked with an asterisk—Pless and Schneidemühl—the Polish name can be found listed in the archives above. The records of Pless (Pszczyna) are in a department (Oddzialy) of the Katowice Archives, and the records of Schneidemühl (Piła) are in a department of the Poznań Archives.

Allenstein (Olsztyn)	Grünberg (Zielona Góra)
Breslau (Wrocław)	Kattowitz (Katowice)
Bromberg (Bydgoszcz)	Köslin (Koszalin)
Danzig (Gdańsk)	Oppeln (Opole)
Pless (Pszczyna)*	Stettin (Szcezcin)
Schneidemühl (Piła)*	Thorn (Toruń)

Note: Two other cities from the German-held area of Poland are now in the Czech Republic: Leitmeritz (Litoměřice) and Troppau (Opava). In these two cases the German name is shown first and the Czechoslovak name is in parentheses. Mail should be sent to Státní Oblastní Archiv, followed by the street address, and the Czechoslovak place-name:

Státní Oblastí Archiv
Dominikánsky Kláster, Litoměřice

Státní Oblastí Archiv
Semovní ulice 1, Opava

The Polish government is not exactly enthusiastic about giving non-Poles permission to search records in the various archives. They prefer you deal by correspondence with the Head Office of the State Archives or with overseas Polish embassies. However, various archivists have told me that an application to do personal research will be considered if you prove your descent from a particular Polish ancestor and give the names of the archives you wish to visit, together with at least three months' advance notice. I have also been told that the result of your application often depends on whether your ancestor left Poland before or after 1945 (the earlier the better)!

Civil Registration (Akta Stanu Cywilnego)

These records commenced in 1809 and were organized originally by priests or ministers of the various churches. It was officially organized by the state in 1946. Generally speaking, you are likely to find that the pre-1919 records are in municipal offices in the German-held areas, the part originally included in Prussia (Preussen). In the areas occupied by the Austrians and the Russians, the churches maintained the records and in some areas still retain them.

So far as modern records are concerned, a copy of a certificate of birth, marriage, or death may be obtained for a small fee from the local Vital Statistics Office (Urząd Stanu Cywilnego) for the town or village. As for Warsaw (Warszawa), there are two different offices serving two halves of the city. Your application should be made to the above office in either Warszawa-Praga or Warszawa-Śródmieście, depending on the particular area in the city in which your ancestor lived. If you don't know, write to either one, giving the address of the individual and the date of the event. There are also copies in state archives and district courts.

Church Records

Many church records and registers of all denominations have been destroyed over the centuries in wars and revolutions. You may also find the register or record but there will be many pages missing. You may be lucky or you may be completely frustrated—be prepared!

It is impossible to be precise about the location of the registers of the various churches in Poland. Some are in the Central Archive of Historical Records, some in the provincial archives, some in church archives, and some still in the original churches. The National Archives cannot always give you the location of a church register. Your best plan is to start at the level of the local church and work up the archival scale from there.

For those registers from what was East Prussia (Ostpreussen), see the chapter on Germany. Most of them were saved.

Bear in mind, too, that after 1808 the various clergymen kept civil registers as well as church registers. They were in Polish and one copy stayed in the town or village and the other went to the nearest civil court, which subsequently passed them on to the Vital Statistics Office. If you find the church registers are missing, these civil records may fill the gap.

Catholic Registers

These start in about 1670 and are scattered in several locations: provincial archives, church archives, parish churches, and in the Vital Statistics Office (since 1850). Generally speaking, Catholic records were kept in Latin until the middle of the last century.

Some of the registers from the eastern territories are in the Central Archive of Historical Records (Archiwum Główne Akt Dawnych, ul. Długa 7, 00263 Warsaw) and others (since 1850) in Archiwum Zabuzańskie, Nowy Świat 18/20, Warsaw.

Information about the location of a particular register can be obtained from the headquarters of the Catholic Church:

Kuria Metropolitalna Warszawa
ul. Miodowa 17/19 00246 Warsaw
Phone: 011-22-31-52-31/32. Fax: 011-22-635-43-24

Many of the registers of all denominations have been microfilmed by the LDS Church.

Birth Registers (Liber Natorum or Księga Urodzin)

These give names of child, parents, and grandparents, as well as addresses and occupations.

Marriage Registers (Liber Matrimonium or Księga Małzeństw)

These give names, ages, and addresses of bride and groom, names and addresses of parents on both sides, names and addresses of witnesses, and ages and occupations.

Death Registers (Liber Mortuorum or Księga Zmarłych)

These give name, address, and parents; surviving spouse or next of kin; date, place, and cause of death; and all surviving children by name.

Evangelical and Evangelical Reformed Registers (Parafie Ewangelicke)

These started in 1595 and contain the same general information you will find in the Catholic registers. These records are in German.

Eastern Orthodox Registers (Parafie Prawosławne)

These started at the same time and have the same information. These records are usually in Russian.

Tombstone Inscriptions (Nagrobki i Tablice)

These lists or extracts are in churches, public cemeteries, and cemetery administration offices in the larger cities. They started in 1380, and because of the widespread destruction of church registers they may be the most valuable source of information you will have available.

Printed Funeral Sermons (Druki)

For some two and a half centuries from 1650 it was the custom for very effusive funeral orations to be made at the graveside or in the church. Sometimes these were given by the priest or pastor, and often by a close relative or family friend or business associate. Afterwards they were printed and distributed among all the relatives, friends, and associates of the dead. Allowing the fulsomeness of the language and the archaic principle of never speaking ill of the dead, they were surprisingly accurate. After all, everyone knew the dead man or woman, and there was no way the family could get away with gross exaggerations or downright lies. If the man was known to beat his wife, it could be said he was active in the affairs of his family. If he had fathered several bastard children in the village, this might be overlooked, and emphasis placed on his close and happy relationship with his legitimate children, and the interest he always took in the youth of the area.

Many of these have been collected and indexed and are in local libraries.

Marriage Records (Allegata do Akt Ślubu)

These are now mainly in provincial archives and give details of the family background of the bride and groom, and their financial status. The records started in about 1790 and had been discontinued by 1900.

Notarial Records (Akta Notarialne)

These date from about 1800 and include such items as wills, estate inventories, marriage contracts and settlements, wills being contested by relatives (often with details of out-of-court settlements), and land transfers and disposals of property. They are in the various provincial archives.

Wills (Testamenty)

There are also details of wills and probate records outside of notarial records. They go back to the fifteenth century and are in provincial or municipal archives.

County Court Documents (Akta Wiejskie)

These cover the period from the late 1400s to the early days of the present century, and are in the provincial archives. Not many have survived, but those that have cover reports of county court decisions in local litigation, often over land boundaries, and may include useful genealogical information, provided that you know, or can discover, the actual village from which your ancestor came. In that case, by all means try a letter to the appropriate provincial archives.

City Documents (Akta Miejskie)

These will be of value if your ancestor came from a city, although there are documents that have survived in a few other municipal areas. They date from the fourteenth century and contain names and addresses of citizens, property transactions, taxes paid, assessments, wills, estate inventories, and details of family relationships. They are in the provincial archives and some of the earlier ones have been published and indexed.

Guild Records (Akta Cechowe)

These cover the period from the early 1600s to the late 1800s; some are earlier and some are later. If your ancestor was a skilled craftsman working in jewelry, leather, clocks and watches, decorative iron, or a dozen other skilled crafts, he would have belonged to a guild. After his long apprenticeship he would not be able to practice his craft without joining the guild. Their records are reasonably complete and include very full personal details, information about his apprenticeship, and reports about his competence, plus his address, place of origin, and marital status. If he was accepted, he was established for life, because he could be assured of controlled competition, stable prices, generous support in times of illness, and a great deal of social status in his community.

Passports (Akta Paszportowe)

These records started in 1851 and continue to the present. The early records are in the Central Archive of Historical Records and those after 1945 are in the Department of Internal Affairs. They give the usual personal information you would expect to find.

Concentration Camp Records (Akta Obozów Koncentracyjnych)

These cover the period 1940–45 and refer particularly to the camps at Auschwitz and Majdanek. The lists include names of prisoners, date and place of birth, name and address of parents, physical appearance, date of entry into the camp, and date of death. The records are in the museums in the two locations (see Jewish Records, page 27), as well as in the Jewish Historical Institute in Warsaw (Żydowski Instytut Historyczny, ul. Gen. Świerczewskiego 79, Warsaw) and in the custody of the Department of Justice.

Emigration Records

These do not exist in Poland itself, but until 1918 your emigrant ancestor would have been either Austrian, German (Prussian), or Russian so far as jurisdiction was concerned. You should, therefore, read the Austrian and German chapters of this book for information about the emigration records of those countries. It is regretted that specific information is not at present available from Russia, Ukraine, and Belarus.

However, the majority of emigrants from what is now Poland left Europe through the port of Hamburg and good records exist there. Here again, please read the German chapter for detailed information.

University and School Records (Akta Instytucji Oświatowych)

These are located in various places and should certainly be consulted. So far as university lists are concerned these are in the archives of Jagiellonski University at Kraków and date from the early 1400s to the present. They include details of students attending foreign universities as well, and give very complete personal details. Similar information is available about students at secondary schools dating back to the nineteenth century; these records are in the various provincial archives up to 1950, and in the schools since then.

Military Records (Akta Wojskowe)

These date from the fifteenth century and include muster-rolls of regular regiments, local militia, and conscription lists. They are in the Central Archive of Historical Records; military records after 1918 are in the Central Military Archive. So far as Austrian-occupied Poland is concerned the Kriegsarchiv in Vienna handed over all its records under the terms of the Peace Treaty of 1919.

Court Records (Akta Instytucji Wymiaru Sprawiedliwości)

Many events were within the jurisdiction of a court of justice besides the usual criminal cases. The courts dealt with wills, estates, marriage contracts and settlements, inheritance, and transfer of property. The early records are fragmented and of doubtful value; the period covered is 1480–1795 and they are in the Central Archive of Historical Records.

If your family is descended from the Polish nobility, there are many records of value to you. It is estimated that a century ago ten percent of the Polish population claimed to be of noble birth and that the other ninety percent lived in abject poverty, semi-serfdom, and downright slavery. Since the great majority of people of Polish descent are not connected with the favored few, I will not list every available noble record but only the main ones.

Royal Court Records (Księgi Kancelarii Królewskiej)

If your noble ancestors held some kind of office in the Royal Court, you may find out something about them from these records; they are in the Central Archive of Historical Records and cover the period from the mid-1400s up to 1794. They list names, estates, social status, and family relationships.

Estate Employees (Akta Personalne Pracowników)

If your ancestors worked on one of the great estates of the Polish nobility, you will probably find quite a bit of information in these records. They are in the provincial archives, but before writing you must know the correct name of the owner of the estate, its location, the period of employment, and the full name of the ancestor. If you cannot supply this information, don't bother to write.

Genealogical Collection (Kolekcje Genealogiczne)

There has always been an interest in genealogy among people of political and social importance. In the Central Archive of Historical Records there is a very large genealogical collection of family trees and family histories, but it is almost entirely concentrated within the narrow ten percent limit mentioned above.

Genealogical Organizations

The Towarzystwo Genealogiczno-Heraldyczne was founded in 1987. It is involved in several research projects, including indexing vital records and compiling bibliographies and inventories of archival sources. Although they do not do research for the public, ancestor-hunters from outside Poland may join the society and receive copies of their quarterly magazine as well as the Genealogical Data Bank, which lists surnames being researched by society members. For more information write to Towaryzstwo Genealogiczno-Heraldyczne, Wodna 27 Pałac Górków, 61781 Poznań.

Land Records (Dokumenty Gruntowe)

These records, many of which are missing or fragmented, are mostly from the areas occupied by Austria and Prussia. Those from the Russian area are not available. They are in the provincial archives and date from 1795 to 1920.

Mortgage Registers (Akta Hipoteczne)

Unusually for European countries, these listings are separate from land records and property transfers. They started in 1808 and ended in 1945 and are located in the provincial archives or district courts. Details are given of all land and property transactions involving a mortgage or a promissory note, and include names, parentage, amount of mortgage and length of term, location of property and addresses of the parties concerned, and actual survey details.

Heraldry

The Poles do have an heraldic organization even if they lack genealogical research into ordinary families. It is the Heraldic Section of the Historical Society of Poland, Rynek Starego Miasta 29/31, Warsaw.

Jewish Records

Many records of Jews in the National Archives of Poland have been copied on microfilm by the LDS Church—more than 2,000 reels now exist. This is an on-going project, and if you are of Jewish descent, you should make contact with the nearest LDS Church Family History Center for up-to-date information.

As I mentioned earlier, and as you will now have realized yourself, there are many problems in doing your own research in Poland: the need to understand one, two, or even three languages; the immense destruction of records; the great lack of centralization; the problems with names, name changes, and name duplication; and the general attitude of the authorities. So far as the latter is concerned, you will find that there is no common pattern. Some archivists are as kindly and helpful as you could find anywhere in the world, while others are most reluctant to provide anything beyond one-word answers.

Finally, remember to do your best to have any letters of inquiry translated into Polish (this will increase your chances of success), and be sure to be polite and express your gratitude in advance. The Poles have very good manners and react favorably to the same good manners on your part.

PORTUGAL

The area that is now Portugal was first occupied by a tribe called the Lusitanians in about 1000 B.C. They were followed by other tribes, and eventually by the Romans, who conquered the region in about 200 B.C. Then came the Visigoths and the Moors. In 1140 Portugal declared its independence after a series of successful battles with the Moors. Spain recognized the new country in 1143 and the Pope did the same in 1179. The southern part of the country, the Algarve, remained under the control of the Moors until 1249, when it was retaken by the Portuguese. Portugal has retained its independence from 1140 until the present except for a brief period under Spanish rule from 1580 to 1640. It has the oldest fixed frontiers of any European country.

Portugal, in alliance with Great Britain, fought against Napoleon from 1807 to 1814 and the country was fought over by both sides (so much better than fighting in your own country)! In 1910 the monarchy was abolished and a republic established. In the First World War the country was neutral at first but joined the Allies in 1916. Portugal was again neutral in the Second World War but did provide air and naval bases for the United States and Great Britain.

At one time Portugal had vast colonial possessions in South America (Brazil), Africa (Angola, Mozambique, Guinea, St. Thomas), India (Goa, Daman, and Diu), and Asia (Timor and Macao). Of these, only Macao remains under Portuguese administration. The Atlantic islands of the Azores (Açores) and Madeira have always been regarded as an integral part of Portugal. The great majority of Portuguese emigrants to North America came from these islands.

The country is divided into eighteen administrative districts on the mainland, three in the Azores, and one in Madeira. The districts, which are listed below, are named after the chief town in each district. Each district has its own archives (Arquivos Distritais), which are located in the administrative center. Most of them have their own separate headquarters but some are part of other organizations, and details are given in the following list:

National Archives

These are located in the capital city, Lisboa or Lisbon, of course.

Instituto dos Arquivos Nacionais-Torre do Tombo
Alameda da Universidade, 1649-010 Lisbon
Phone: 011-351-1-781-15-00. Fax: 011-351-1-793-72-30

The National Archives have been modernized in recent years and more changes are expected. Many records in Portugal are in several different places, and these are likely to change in the future.

The National Archives contain information about wills for the seventeenth century to the present. Passports are available from the early eighteenth century. There are also—believe it or not—the records of the infamous Inquisition of the Catholic Church!

There are also some church registers in the National Archives for the twentieth century for Lisbon, but the great majority of them are still in the original parish churches in various states of disrepair. It is still the policy of the Catholic Church in Portugal to retain custody of its registers. Hopefully this will change before any more damage and neglect occurs.

District Archives

These are located in the following administrative districts—Aviero, Beja, Braga, Braganç, Castelo Branco, Coimbra, Evora, Faro, Guarda, Leira, Lisboa, Portalegre, Porto, Santarém, Setubal, Viana do Castelo, Vila Real, and Viseu.

Note: The district archives in Lisboa are part of the National Archives. Those at Coimbra and Braga are part of the university museum and library, and those at Braga and Ivora are in the local public libraries. There are also district archives in the Azores and Madeira, and details of these will come later.

All of the district archives are located in the chief town in each district and are in the administrative center, but some are part of other organizations, as mentioned above.

Civil Registration

This began officially in 1878. The records are on file in each district archive and also in the Civil Registration Archives (Conservatorias do Registo Civil) in Lisbon. It had also been in operation in many areas on an optional basis since 1832. You will need to find out if these exist in the area in which you are interested by contacting the particular one.

Before the official registrations began vital events (BMD) were the responsibility of the local priest, and we all know what that means! Up until 1911 the priest kept the actual registers, but after that date they were the responsibility of district registrars and the records were kept in the district archives with a copy sent to the National Archives.

Church Registers (Registos Paroquiais)

These are still in the original churches, but when churches have been closed or destroyed by fire the registers are sent either to the district archives or to the National Archives (if they are among the very earliest known records).

In the church registers you will not find, as you will in many countries, marriage contracts, engagements, communion lists, and confirmations, but you will find frequent notes about local events, and personal comments by the local priest about members of his flock. Who knows what you may discover about your ancestors? Judging by the entries in one of the Coimbra parishes you may find "a worthy man and a good Catholic, but I cannot say the same about his wife" or "Baptized his fourth child today—the first one born in wedlock."

The oldest parish register in existence is that of Nabainhos, near Gouveia, which started with a baptism in 1529. Other early ones are Sameice (Seia), Cheleiros (Mafra), Santiago (Torres Novas), Várzea (Alenquer), and Santa Eulália (Seia). The name in parentheses is that of the commune or municipality. There is reference to the registration of marriages as early as 1390 in a letter sent to King Alfonso IV. All these very early records are in the National Archives.

The entries for baptism include the names of parents, grandparents, and witnesses or godparents (and their relationship to the child). The marriage entries also contain full details of parents, grandparents, and witnesses. Burials include the next of kin and all surviving family members.

If you are writing to the parish priest you should also ask if he has a list of the names appearing on the tombstones (Pedras Tumulares). You may well find a great deal of new information from this source.

Although the majority of the church registers have survived the centuries, there were three events that caused great destruction of registers in particular areas:

1. The 1755 earthquake in the area of Lisbon.
2. The French invasions that devastated the provinces of Beira Baixa and Ribatejo.
3. The invasion of Alentejo by the Spanish.

In most cases, after these disasters the parish priest persuaded his church members to give him dates of family events so that to a degree he could reconstruct the most recent entries. This helped, but it did not, of course, replace the irreplaceable.

It should be mentioned that because of the close ties between Great Britain and Portugal and the number of British businessmen resident in the country, there were Church of England churches in Lisbon and Madeira. Registers for the period 1721–1890 are in the custody of the Bishop of London, in England.

Wills (Testamentos)

These date back to the early fifteenth century but of course are only of value to you if your Portuguese ancestors owned land or property of some kind. Wills are kept in the local notarial registry (Cartórios Notarais) and are transferred every thirty years to the district archives.

Passports (Passaportes)

These were first issued in 1757 and continue up to the present. They are in the district archives and list name, date, place of birth, date of the voyage, and destination.

University Records

If your ancestor attended a university, his personal records will be on file. The information dates right back to the fourteenth century and gives names and places of birth up to the early eighteenth century; since then it also includes the names of the parents and grandparents.

Inquisition Records

During the days of the notorious Catholic Inquisition (fifteenth to eighteenth centuries) there were many trials in Lisbon, Coimbra, and Évora. The reports often include very detailed personal biographies of the accused people and they are all in the National Archives.

MADEIRA

The Regional Archives of Madeira (Arquivo Regional da Madeira) are located in the Palácio de S. Pedro, 9000 Funchal, Madeira. However, this archive does not do any genealogical research and only issues certificates of vital events to inquirers providing an exact parish and date. If research is required, you should write to the Bureau of Genealogical Research, Rua da Ponte Nova 42, 9000 Funchal, Madeira.

The archive has no census records, and any inquiries about them should be sent to the Instituto Nacional de Estatistica in Lisbon. Madeira wills date back to the fourteenth century and are all in the archive. All vital records prior to 1860 are located there too, and the registers from 1860 are in the different county Conservatórias do Registo Civil, which are listed later.

Church Registers

The registers of the undermentioned parishes are in the custody of the archives and date from as early as 1539:

Achadas da Cruz, Agua de Pena, Arco da Calheta, Arco de São Jorge, Boaventura, Calheta, Camacha, Câmara de Lobos, Campanário, Canhas, Caniçal, Caniço, Estreito da Calheta, Estreito de Câmara de Lobos, Faial, Fajã da Ovelha, Gaula, Jardim do Mar, Machico, Maria Madalena do Mar, Monte, Paul do Mar, Ponta Delgada, Ponta do Pargo, Ponta do Sol, Porto da Cruz, Porto Santo, Ribeira da Janela, Santa Cruz, Santa Luzia, Santa Maria Maior, Santana, Santo António, Santo António da Serra, São Gonçalo, São Jorge, São Martinho, São Pedro, São Roque, São Vicente, Sé, Seixal, Serra d'Agua, Tábua.

Civil Registers

As mentioned above, registers up to 1860 are in the Conservatórias do Registo Civil and are located in eleven counties; the parishes concerned are listed after the names of the counties:

CALHETA: Arco da Calheta, Calheta, Estreito da Calheta, Fajã da Ovelha, Jardim do Mar, Paul do Mar, Ponta do Pargo, Prazeres.

CAMARA DE LOBOS: Câmara de Lobos, Curral das Freiras, Estreito de Câmara de Lobos.

FUNCHAL: Monte, Santa Luzia, Santa Maria Maior, Santo Antonio, São Gonçalo, São Martinho, São Pedro, São Roque, Sé.

MACHICO: Agua de Pena (part), Caniçal, Machico, Porto da Cruz, Santo António da Serra (part).

PONTA DO SOL: Canhas, Madalena do Mar, Ponta do Sol.

PORTO DO MONIZ: Achadas da Cruz, Porto do Moniz, Ribeira da Janela, Seixal.

PORTO SANTO: Porto Santo.

RIBEIRA BRAVA: Companário, Ribeira Brava, Serra d'Agua, Tábua.

SANTA CRUZ: Agua de Pena (part), Camacha, Caniço, Gaula, Santa Cruz, Santo Antonio da Serra (part).

SANTANA: Arco de São Jorge, Faial, Santana, São Jorge, São Roque.

SÃO VINCENTE: Boaventura, Ponta Delgada, São Vicente.

AZORES (AÇORES)

The Regional Archives of the Azores (Arquivo Regional da Açores) are located in the Palácio Betancourt, Rua Conseilheiro, Angra do Heroismo, Azores.

In view of the large numbers of Portuguese emigrants to North America from the Azores, the records there are of major importance, and it is unfortunate that it is so difficult to obtain information from the archives. You will need patience and a willingness to write several times in order to get an answer to your queries. The LDS Church and the American-Portuguese Genealogical Society have some information, and if you know the name of the particular place in the Azores from which your ancestor came, it will be worthwhile getting in touch with these two organizations.

There are three district archives in Azores:

Ponta Delgada (Ilha de S. Miguel)
District Archives and Public Library
Rua Ernesto do Canto
9500 Ponte Delgada
Phone: 011-351-96-25-766

Angra do Heroismo (Ilha da Terceira)
District Archives and Public Library
Rua da Rosa 49
9700 Angra do Heroismo (Ilha da Terceira-Açores)

Horta
District Archives and Public Library
Rua D. Pedro IV 25
9900 Horta (Ilha do Faial-Açores)

(Please note the archives in the Azores are not under the control of the National Archives in Lisbon.)

Passport Records

Angra do Heroismo: 1775–1818, 1844–45, 1857–1924.
Horta: 1836–39, 1856 to date.
Ponta Delgada: 1836–39, 1856 to date.

Passenger Lists

These are available from 1841 to 1929 and are in the regional archives in Angra do Heroismo.

Parish Registers

These date back to the seventeenth century and in some cases to the sixteenth. They are located in the three district archives and certified copies can be obtained for a small fee. You must supply an approximate date and place, as the archival staff will not undertake protracted searches. In such cases you will be referred to a local researcher.

It has not been possible to obtain detailed information about the parish registers of Angra do Heroismo and Ponta Delgada, but the starting dates of the Horta registers are listed below:

FAIAL: Angústias, 1666; Capelo, 1680; Castelo Branco, 1706; Cedros, 1629; Conceição, 1705; Feteira, 1752; Flamengos, 1661; Matriz, 1655; Pedro Miguel, 1657; Praia do Almoxarife, 1703; Praia do Norte, 1840; Ribeirinha, 1643; Salão, 1728.

PICO: Bandeiras, 1850; Calheta do Nesquim, 1746; Candelária, 1636; Criacao Velha, 1801; Lajes do Pico, 1733; Madalena, 1664; Piedade, 1699; Praínha, 1664; Ribeiras, 1697; Santa Luzia, 1666; Santo Amaro, 1673; Santo António, 1815; São Caetano (missing); São João, 1711; São Mateus, 1673; São Roque, 1582.

FLORES: Caveira, 1860; Cedros, 1860; Fajã Grande, 1861*; Fajãzinha, 1860*; Fazenda (missing); Lajedo, 1860*; Lajes das Flores, 1860*; Lomba, 1862; Mosteiro, 1861*: Ponta Delgada, 1860; Santa Cruz, 1860.

CORVO: Corvo, 1860.

Please note that the starting dates given are those for baptisms. The dates for marriages and deaths may be earlier or later. Those parishes in Flores marked with an asterisk have their baptismal records missing and the dates given refer to marriages and deaths.

One final word if you are going to do your own research in Portugal. The archives are very fussy about identification. Be sure you bring with you a letter of introduction from your parish priest (if you are a Catholic) or from an official of some kind, or from a doctor or lawyer, written on letterhead paper. Then, when you get to Lisbon, visit the United States Embassy there and ask them if they will be kind enough to make a translation of the letter of introduction so that you can present it at the same time. Also, take with you half a dozen passport-sized photographs so that you can make one available to any archive that issues an identity card to you for that particular archive.

Unless your ancestors came from a district hit by one of the three calamities I mentioned, you should have great success in your ancestor-hunting in Portugal. The records are good, they go back a long way, and most of the archivists you meet will be very helpful.

One organization that you should join because you will find it most useful is the American-Portuguese Genealogical and Historical Society (P.O. Box 644, Taunton, MA 02780; Web site: www.apghs.org). The society has a growing Portuguese section in the Taunton Public Library, which includes much information about sources in Portugal as well as in other countries in the world to which the Portuguese emigrated.

ROMANIA

Romania covers the approximate area of the Roman province of Dacia which existed in the second and third centuries, after the conquest of the ancient tribe of the Daci by the Roman emperor Trajan. After the Romans left, successive invasions brought in the Goths, Huns, Avars, Bulgars, and Magyars. The two principalities of Moldavia and Wallachia were the base on which the state of Romania was built; they were vassals of the Ottoman Empire but were semi-autonomous. By 1601 Michael the Brave, of Wallachia, controlled the two states. In 1711 the Turks asserted their control once more, but Russian influence increased briefly in 1828.

In 1856 the Congress of Paris recognized Moldavia and Wallachia as being under Turkish control and also awarded Bessarabia to Moldavia. The two countries united in 1861 under the name of Romania.

In 1878 Romania became completely independent. There followed a period during which two Balkan wars, an invasion of Bulgaria by Romania, and the First and Second World Wars took place. I am not going into any details because if you are descended from a family living in that general area, you will be familiar with all these events. It is quite sufficient, I think, to warn you that the areas affected are Bukovina, Bessarabia, Transylvania, the Banat, Moldova, Russia, and Dobrudja, and Yugoslavia, Bulgaria, and Hungary. The various wars—both great and small—involved transfers of territory from one country to another.

In areas where the vital events of birth, marriage, death, and burial were the responsibility of a church (both Catholic and Orthodox), synagogues, and mosques, you will not be too likely to find destruction. Boundaries could change but the church remained as a solid rock. Other records—such as census returns, legal matters, and civil registration of vital events—were more likely not to be transferred, and locating them could involve you visiting or writing to several different countries.

Civil Registration

This began in 1831 in Wallachia and in 1832 in Moldavia, but in actual fact the priests of the Romanian Orthodox Church, who were responsible for the records of registration, had started earlier in many areas. Registration began in Transylvania in 1895, when it was part of Hungary. In 1865 the recording of vital events was taken over by the state.

Copies of certificates can be obtained from the Office of Vital Statistics (Oficiul Starii Civile) of the city or town in which you are interested. In the case of small villages, the office will be in the nearest large town. The records are kept locally for seventy-five years and then transferred to the National Archives.

Archives

The National Archives (Archivelor Statului) are located at Bulevardul M. Kogălniceanu 29, 70602 Bucharest (Bucureşti); Phone: 011-401-615-4160; Fax: 011-401-312-5848. There are also archives in each administrative district (Judet) and details are given below.

Church Registers

Church registers up to one hundred years ago are still in the original churches, those before that date are in the local archives listed.

Administrative Districts (Judets)

The forty-one districts are listed below, followed by the postal code, name of the district capital, and street address. If you are trying to find family records in these areas you should write to the Director, Archivelor Statului, followed by the address and name of the city. Please enclose a self-addressed airmail envelope and three International Reply Coupons. Write a nice, friendly letter and keep away from politics!

BUCHAREST: 75176 Calea Vacareşti 470
ALBA: 2500 Alba Iulia, Str. Mihai Viteazul 29
ARAD: 2900 Arad, Str. Ceaikovski 2-6
ARGEŞ : 0300 Piteşti, Str. Exercitiului 208
BACĂU: 5500 Bacău, Str. V. Alecsandri 5
BIHOR: 3700 Oradea, Piata Independenţei 1
BISTRITA-NĂSĂUD: 4400 Bistriţa, Str. Gării 1
BOTOŞANI: 6800 Botoşani, Str. Col. Tomoroveanu 7
BRAŞOV: 2200 Braşov, Str. G. Bariţiu 34
BRĂILA: 6100 Brăila, Calea Călăraşi 16
BUZĂU: 5100 Buzău, Str. N. Bălcescu 42
CĂLĂRAŞI: 8500 Călăraşi, Str. Pompierilor 1

CARAŞ-SEVERIN: 1650 Caransebeş, Str. Gen. I. Dragalina 2

CLUJ: 3400 Cluj-Napoca, Str. M. Kogălniceanu 10

CONSTANTA: 8700 Consţanta, Str. Ştefan cel Mare

COVASNA: 4000 Sfântu Gheorghe, Piata Libertătii 7

DÂMBOVITA: 0200 Târgovişte, Str. Diţescu Stan 6

DOLJ: 1100 Craiova, Str. Libertătii 34

GALATI: 6200 Galati, Str. Constructorilor 1

GORJ: 1400 Târgu Jiu, Str. Traian 34

GIURGIU: 8375 Giurgiu, Calea Bucureşti 49

HARGHITA: 4100 Miercurea-Ciue, Bd. Frătiei 6

HUNEDOARA: 2700 Deva, Str. Aurel Vlaicu 2

IALOMIŢA: 8400 Slobozia, Str. Al. Odobescu 4

IAŞI: 6600 Iaşi, Bd. Copou 26

MARAMUREŞ: 4800 Baia Mare, Bd. Bucureşti 26

MEHEDINŢI: 1500 Drobeta-Turnu Severin, Str. Republicii 75

MUREŞ: 4300 Târgu Mureş, Str. Crizantemelor 8

NEAMŢ: 5600 Piatra Neamţ, Str. V. A. Urechea 46

OLT: 0500 Slatina, Str. Primăverii 15

PRAHOVA: 2000 Ploieşti, Str. Logofăt Tăutu 3

SATU MARE: 3900 Satu Mare, Str. 1 Decembrie 1918 No. 11-13

SĂLAJ: 4700 Zalău, Str. T. Vladimirescu 34 A

SIBIU: 2400 Sibiu, Str. Arhivelor 3

SUCEAVA: 5800 Suceava, Str. Ştefan cel Mare 35

TELEORMAN: 0700 Alexandria, Str. Turnu Măgurele 3

TIMIŞ: 1900 Timişoara, Str. Andrei Mocioni 8

TULCEA, 8800 Tulcea, Str. Spitalului 4

VASLUI: 6500 Vaslui, Str. M. Kogălniceanu 2

VÂLCEA: 1000 Râmnicu Vâlcea, Str. Gen. Praporgescu 32 bis

VRANCEA: 5300 Focşani, Bd. D. Cantemir 19

These district archives contain church registers (of all religions) up to one hundred years ago. Since that day they are in the local churches. The archives also hold wills, land records, and other legal documents up to thirty years ago.

The State makes no charge for a short search and visitors are welcome to do their own research in the various archives, provided that prior arrangements are made with the local archivist.

Religions

The majority belong to the Romanian Orthodox Church, with 11,000 parishes. The Catholic Church has two archbishoprics, at Bucharest and Iaşi; the Reformed Church two dioceses, at Cluj-Napoca and Oradea; the Evangelical Church of the Augustan Confession a bishopric at Sibiu; the Evangelical Church of Synodo-Presbyterian Confession a bishopric in Cluj-Napoca; and the Unitarians a bishopric in the same place. If you do not get an answer from a local priest, you should write to the church headquarters in one of these cities. (Do try to get your letters written in Romanian.)

RUSSIA

In one wild and historic assoluta the archives have leapt like the prima ballerina of the Bolshoi onto the world's genealogical stage—from the days of *nyet* to the heady days of *da*, from the gloomy stage of Ulanova to the bright lights of Rosarkhiv, the Federal Archival Service of Russia.

After twenty years of fruitless effort I can now produce a chapter that holds out hope for the Russian ancestor-hunter. No more futile interviews in Moscow and St. Petersburg, no more long-distance calls to nameless functionaries in Russian embassies and consulates around the world, no more letters in Russian or English, no more phone calls and faxes to faraway places—thanks to the personal charm and grim determination of two remarkable women, Patricia Kennedy Grimsted and Miriam Weiner, the first famed for her brilliant scholastic achievements and the latter for that strength of purpose inherited from her Jewish ancestry.

The word that opened the long-closed doors was "online," and then other incantations followed—Internet, E-mail, and web site. I must not let my enthusiasm lead you astray—I am naturally delighted to hear a creaking door after years of silence, but I must also tell you to restrain your ardor because there is a long road to travel, and there will be no easy task to open the door wider and gain access to the treasures of the Russian archives.

Let us talk about access to Russian archives by computer, and then later we can consider the probabilities of success by personal contact—correspondence, phone, fax, and personal visit. Your first point of computer contact is probably a web site maintained by the International Institute of Social History, in Amsterdam (**www.iisg.nl/**). This gives you access to the ArcheoBiblioBase directory and bibliographic database for Russian archives, which provides a listing of the current fourteen federal archives administered by the Federal Archival Service of Russia (Rosarkhiv); archives of major federal agencies that have the right by law to the long-term retention of their own records, including those of a more technical and specialized profile; and local municipal and oblast archives in Moscow and St. Petersburg (Leningrad Oblast). An English translation of the *Regulations for the Work of Reading Rooms of State Archives of the Russian Federation*, issued by Rosarkhiv in 1998, is now also provided at this web site.

At this point you had better become familiar with certain sets of initials. The Russians seem to like them and, of course, they are a simple and economical description of many sources with which you may be dealing:

ROSARKHIV (Federal'naia arkhivnaia sluzhba Rossii)
Federal Archival Service of Russia
103132, Moscow, ul. Il'inka, 12
Phone: 011-7-206-27-85. Fax: 011-7-95-206-55-87
E-mail: kinarch@online.ru

GARF (Gosudarstvennyi arkhiv Rossiiskoi Federatsii)
State Archive of the Russian Federation
119817, Moscow, ul. Bol'shaia Pirogovskaia, 17
Phone: 011-7-245-81-41. Fax: 011-7-95-245-12-87
E-mail: garf@glasnet.ru

TsIAM (Tsentral'nyi istoricheskii arkhiv Moskvy)
Central Historical Archive of Moscow
117393, Moscow, ul. Profsoiuznaia, 80
Phone: 011-7-128-67-86. Fax: 011-7-95-334-44-89

TsGIA SPb (Tsentral'nyi gosudarstvennyi istoricheskii arkhiv Sankt-Peterburga)
Central State Historical Archive of St. Petersburg
190008, St. Petersburg, ul. Pskovskaia, 18
Phone: 011-7-219-79-61

There is no shortage of archives in Russia: there are federation archives, state archives, oblast archives (county), and municipal archives. For example, there are over fifty archives in Moscow alone—covering such subjects as Army, Far East, Films, Security Services, and the Environment.

Also available is a new directory, in English, entitled *Archives of Russia: A Directory and Bibliographic Guide to Holdings in Moscow and St. Petersburg*, edited by Patricia Kennedy Grimsted (Armonk, NY, and London: M.E. Sharpe Publishers, 2000. Phone 800-541-6563. Fax: 914-273-2106. E-mail: mesinfo@usanet).

Let us now turn to personal contact with Russian archives. Rather than trying to make contact yourself, you may find it wiser—and in the end cheaper—to discuss your problems with the superb organization known as RAGAS (Russian American Genealogical Archival Service):

RAGAS
PO Box 1112, 1929 18th Street NW
Washington, DC 20009
E-mail: ragas@cityline.ru; ragas001@mail.ru

This organization was created in 1992 with the aid of several agencies, with the aim of creating a means of developing contacts for genealogical research in the Soviet Union. This coincided with *glasnost* and the creation of a new and independent Russia, Belarus, and Ukraine. RAGAS was instrumental in developing the co-operation of these three governments. The organization is now completely independent. Annual subscription is $50 US, and this brings you four copies of the *Ragas Report* each year—an invaluable publication, which keeps you quite up-to-date with information about archival service and developments in the three countries. The organization maintains an office in Moscow, directed by Vladislav Soshnikov.

If you decide to place an order with RAGAS, you will need to have specific information about your ancestor, including the patronymic, date of event (birth, marriage, death, location—location being most important because there is much duplication of place names in the area). The importance of the use of RAGAS is that the staff is familiar with the various archives and the material they contain. Often, genealogical records before the 1917 Revolution are in different archives from those since that time. Generally speaking, central and regional archives are most likely to be the place for civil registration, census returns, and church records.

Because of the wide dispersal of records, the variation in the places where they are kept, and the frequent closure of archives for indefinite periods, a search may take months.

In my experience the archival authorities in descending order of co-operation are in the following places—St. Petersburg, Minsk, Kiev, Lvov, Kharkhov, Moscow. However, this personal list of mine, based on my own experiences, may be totally out-of-date by the time you read this. Another factor to bear in mind is that the elderly archivists still around after *glasnost* are far less co-operative than the younger men and women still climbing the archival ladder.

I think I have told you enough to make it clear that winds of change are blowing down the corridors of the Russian archives, and when the next edition of this book appears in several years, there may be as many pages about Russia as there are in the German chapter.

My final advice to you is to join RAGAS and, at the same time, use the Internet as a valuable aid—but remember that the computer cannot think, but YOU can and so can the experts of RAGAS.

The situation in Russia is difficult to describe in any detail because any comments about accessibility of records, increasing computer contacts, methods of research, and so on may be completely out-of-date by the time you read this. I can give you precise and accurate information about conditions in 2000, but who knows about 2001? So much depends on Russia's financial situation, its relations with Belarus and Ukraine, and above all, with the rest of Europe.

So far as its immediate neighbors are concerned, the atmosphere burns hot and cold. When the Soviet Union fell apart the three countries formed what was called the CIS—the Commonwealth of Independent States—but now it is simply The Russian Federation. The three countries are bound together economically, geographically, and politically, but their individual relations with the rest of the world vary.

Possibly the most powerful player in the game is "Cyberia"—the area of the Internet which surely will prevent any country from withdrawing within itself as did the Soviet Union. For this reason, I am sure the next edition of this book will contain far more information about archives and make the search for our ancestors in Russia far easier. You will also be able to obtain additional information from the following web sites, which provide excellent profiles compiled by Dr. Patricia Grimsted. Each profile provides a summary of holdings, who has access, and who has contact information. There are also information papers, such as one by Dr. Grimsted on the effect of the Russian economic crisis on the archives. These sites are worth exploring: **www.iisg.nl/~abb/** (this is the site hosted by the International Institute of Social History in Amsterdam, mentioned earlier) and **www.huri.har vard.edu/abbukr/index.html** (Archives in Ukraine).

RUSSIAN CONSULAR RECORDS

A fabulous collection of Russian consular records, available on microfilm in Canada and the United States, may very well solve genealogical problems for many Canadians and Americans whose ancestors were Armenian, Estonian, Finnish, Georgian, Jewish, Latvian, Lithuanian, Mennonite, Polish, Russian, and Ukrainian who came to Canada from Czarist Russia before 1922. Many of them eventually joined relatives who were already in the United States.

At the time of the Russian Revolution in 1917 there were three Russian consuls in Canada: Serge Likacheff in Montreal, Constantine Regosine in Vancouver, and Harry Mathers in Halifax. All three lost their jobs when the new government in Russia ordered the closing of the consulates. However, the Canadian government, which did not recognize the new regime, offered them positions in the Immigration Service so that they could continue to meet the needs of Russian citizens in Canada. This arrangement continued until 1922, when the Canadian government officially recognized the government of the Soviet Union.

The files of the consulates contained records of immigration, settlement, military service in both Canada and Russia, education, Russian police permits, details of place of origin, and family histories. There were hundreds of thousands of photographs, letters, certificates, and a variety of other documents. The three consuls appear to have had a passion for collecting everything they possibly could about anyone with whom they had occasion to deal. For example, during the First World War the Russian government tried to get Russians overseas to return home to fight in the army. If a many had already done his military service under the conscription laws of the Czar, he was under no legal obligation to return. When he received his orders to do so, via one of the consulates, he would, of course, get in touch with the consul and produce his release papers and his police permit to leave Russia. The consul would apparently inform the Russian government and then retain the documents in his files.

In 1922 the consuls decided the Canadian government might send their files back to Moscow and, knowing that the U.S. government had not recognized the government of the USSR, they had them shipped to the Russian consulates in New York and Boston (the U.S. government did not recognize the USSR until 1933). From the consulates the records were sent to the Russian Embassy in Washington. When the first Soviet ambassador arrived, he insisted that the embassy building be cleared of all traces of "imperialism." His request was granted and everything was removed.

As time went by, all trace of the files was lost, but rumors circulated that this genealogical treasure was somewhere in an underground vault belonging to the National Archives of the United States. After some years of searching, and some very astute detective work by Canadian officials, files consisting of over a hundred large cartons were found in a subterranean repository and returned to Canadian custody in 1980.

The records, known as the Li-Ra-Ma Collection, were catalogued, copied, sorted (a mammoth task), and eventually microfilmed. The National Archives of Canada has the finding aid and nominal index, along with the contents of the Collection, on microfilm, which is available for inter-library loan. In 1989 the original material was returned to the United States National Archives, which had a similar collection of records. Both the Canadian and American original material was then returned to Moscow, where it is now housed in the Archives of the Foreign Ministry. However, the records were microfilmed by the LDS Church and can be accessed at their Family History Centers or at the U.S. National Archives in College Park, Maryland. Information about the consular records is also available in the book *Russian Consular Records Index and Catalog* by Sallyann Amdur Sack and Suzan Wynne (Garland Publishers, 1987).

It should be noted that, although the records stop in 1922, the information they contain goes back in many cases well into the nineteenth century. When considering the Canadian or U.S. records in relation to your own family you must remember that Russian immigrants who had acquired citizenship will not be mentioned from then on, as they would be under no legal obligation to have anything further to do with a Russian consulate.

SAN MARINO

This tiny independent country of about 32 square miles is located in the Apennine area of Italy. It is believed to have become an independent country in about 380, but there have been a number of occasions since then when it was occupied temporarily by its more powerful neighbors. It is governed by two elected regents and a general council.

All genealogical records are either in the local churches or in the State Archives (Archivio di Stato), Palazzo Valloni, Via Carducci 141, San Marino.

SLOVAKIA

Slovakia was joined with the Czech Republic to form Czechoslovakia until Slovakia became an independent country in 1993. See the chapter on the Czech Republic earlier in this book for a history of the area.

The rules and regulations governing genealogical research in Slovakia are, as of this writing, very similar to those of the Czech Republic; however, you should check ahead because laws in this new country might change over the next few years. Much of the information about the availability of records in the Czech Republic also applies to Slovakia, so be sure to read through the Czech Republic chapter as well. However, from a genealogical point of view, Slovakia had a very different history than the Czech Republic because it was ruled by Hungary for nearly a thousand years. For this reason, you should also check the chapter on Hungary for information about records.

In 1949 administrative districts were set up in Czechoslovakia. The three that are now in Slovakia are listed below, together with the name of the chief administrative city in each district:

Západoslovenský (Bratislava)

Středoslovenský (Bánská Bystrica)

Východoslovenský (Košice)

The three districts listed above each contain the following counties:

ZÁPADOSLOVENSKÝ: Bratislava-Mesto, Bratislava-Venkov, Duhajská Streda, Galanta, Komárno, Levice, Nitra, Nové Zámky, Senica, Topol'čany, Trenčin, Trnava.

STSSŘEDOSLOVENSKÝ: Bánská Bystrica, Čadca, Dolní Kubín, Liptovský Mikulaš, Lučenec, Martin, Považská Bystrica, Prievidza, Rimavská Sobota, Stara, Ždiar nad Hronom, Žilina, Zvolen.

VÝCHODOSLOVENSKÝ: Bardéjov, Humenné, Košice, Michalovce, Poprad, Prešov, Rožňava, Spišská Nová Ves, Trebišov.

A very useful book to consult is *Die Deutschen in der Tschechoslowakei, 1933–1947* by Vacloc Kral, which lists place-name changes from German to Slovak and Czech.

Language

Try to buy a good Slovak dictionary and study it. A good book about ancestor-hunting in the area is *Genealogical Research for Czech and Slovak Americans* by Olga Miller, which provides some first-rate information about the Slovak language.

Civil Registration

This started in 1894. The records are not available for search by an individual but the National Archives will supply copies of certificates for a fee. Application should be made in writing either to your nearest Slovakian embassy or consulate, or directly to the National Archives in Bratislava, the capital city of Slovakia (Odbor archívnictva a spisovej služby, Kriškova 7, 81104 Bratislava). You must supply the date and place of the vital event, but the archives will usually check over a period of five years to allow for error.

Church Registers

The churches of all denominations retain the registers in the original churches. Their responsibility to record vital events ended in 1894 with the introduction of civil registration, but they still continue to keep their own records.

Although some Catholic registers in Slovakia date back to 1650, not many church registers exist before 1800 because of destruction during the Turkish invasions, or Slovak revolts against the Hungarians. Slovakia was a stronghold of the Lutheran faith and this is reflected in the church records. There are more surviving Protestant registers than Catholic for this very reason. Up to 1720, entries in the registers were in Hungarian, and after that year in Slovak or Latin. In 1840 the use of Hungarian was again ordered and this lasted until 1868, when a choice of either Slovak or Hungarian was allowed, depending on local choice and the population balance.

The LDS Church has begun microfilming church registers of all religions in the former Czechoslovakia from 1599 to 1896. Check with your nearest Family History Center for up-to-date information.

Census Returns

In Slovakia censuses were held in 1809, 1880, 1890, and 1910, and then in 1920 and every ten years since. They are in the National Archives. Copies of the pre-1920 ones are in the National Archives of Hungary (Magyar Országos Léveltár, Bécsikapu tér 2-4, 1014 Budapest).

Wills

These date from the fifteenth century and are in the National Archives in Bratislava. They are open to public search.

National Archives

The National Archives are located in Bratislava, and the address is:

Odbor archívnictva a spisovej služby
Križkova 7, 81104 Bratislava
Phone: 011-421-7-397629, 396051-3. Fax: 011-421-7-394530

When you start on genealogical research in Slovakia, you will soon find that the country came lately into the archival field. During the nearly one thousand years of its inclusion in the kingdom of Hungary, it had no archives except for a few odds-and-ends of local records. Even after the creation of the new state of Czechoslovakia after World War I, the situation did not greatly improve—domination by Hungary was, from the Slovak point of view, merely followed by a similar situation by its union with the Czechs. Slovakia only became really independent in 1993. Since then, the national and district archives of Slovakia have much improved in organization and quality of service. So be patient in your dealings with them and understand their difficulties—not only with financing by the government but also in the training of the staff. One final note of cheer—there are good and helpful archives in Hungary for your Slovakian ancestor-hunting before 1919.

If you are dealing directly with the National Archives, it will be helpful if you can write in Slovak. You can visit the archives personally on a visit to Slovakia, but it will be wise if you apply beforehand, giving details of your Slovak ancestry and the areas you wish to visit. This application should be sent to the National Archives at the above address, or to the nearest Slovak embassy in your country. Allow a month for the reply.

The Archives contain land records, wills, and census returns. However, there are new acquisitions coming in, and you should write for information about the records in which you are interested.

Military Records

These may be of value to you because conscription was in force during the Hungarian regime. The address of the Military Archives is as follows:

Volensky historicky archiv (Military Historical Archives)
Univerz itné namestie
91800 Trnava

District Archives

The various district archives in Slovakia are listed below:

Štátný Oblastný archiv v Banskej Bystrici
Sládkovičova 77, 97604 Bánská Bystrica

Štátný Oblastný archiv v Bratislava
Kriškova 7, 81104 Bratislava

Štátný Oblastný archiv v Bytči
01435 Bytča-kaštiel

Štátný Oblastný archiv v Levoča
Mierové nám. 7, 05480 Levoča

Štátný Oblastný archiv v Nitre
Novozámocká ul. 388, 94908 Nitre

Štátný Oblastný archiv v Prešove
ul. Slovenskej Republiky rád 137, 08001 Prešov

Archiv hlavného mesta Bratislavy
Primaciálne nám. 2, 81471 Bratislava

Note: All the above archives are district archives except for the last one, which is confined to the city of Bratislava.

The Calendar

Before searching records, do not forget the changes in the calendar. In 1582 Pope Gregory XIII ordained that ten days be dropped from the calendar, and that the beginning of the year be changed from March 25 to January 1. Catholic churches observed the change almost immediately; Protestant ones were slower to follow. In Slovakia the year started on 1 November 1587.

Emigration

No lists have survived, except in a few unrelated places, but most Slovaks emigrated overseas through the German ports of Hamburg and Bremen. Although the latter records were destroyed during the Second World War, the Hamburg records exist for the period from 1850 to 1934 (except for Jan.–June 1853 and Aug. 1914–1919). You will find many more details about these records in the chapter on Germany.

SLOVENIA

This area was originally inhabited by the Celtic and Illyrian tribes but came under Roman control the last century BC. The South Slavs settled there in the 5th century AD but they were conquered by the Franks in 788. Slovenia was part of the empire of Charlemagne until 843, when it came under the control of the Duke of Bavaria. From 1335 until 1918 it was part of the Hapsburg estates and later of the Austro-Hungarian Empire.

After the collapse of the Empire in 1918, it became part of the newly created Kingdom of the Serbs, Croats, and Slovenes (Yugoslavia). During World War II it was divided among Germany, Italy, and Hungary. In 1945 the country was re-united and became a part of the newly formed republic of Yugoslavia. It was also awarded part of the Italian area of Venezia Giulia (basically the area surrounding the city of Trieste, without the city itself, which remained in Italy).

Slovenia was never happy under the increasing dominance of Serbia, and declared its independence in 1991. It was the most highly industrialized of the Yugoslav republics and realized its future lay with the countries of central Europe rather than in the Balkans. It has a population of some 2 million.

There are various archives in Slovenia of interest to ancestor-hunters of Slovenian descent. Some of the information I obtained from the archival authority may be of slight interest: In 1997 the archives were used by 992 people, 29,883 photocopies were made, and 909 printouts were supplied, 7,557 pieces of written material were used, as were 251 film titles.

The National Archives are in the capital, Ljubljana, and the address is as follows:

Arhiv Republike Slovenije
Zvezdarska 1, 1127 Ljubljana
Phone: 011-386-61-24-14-200. Fax: 011-386-61-24-14-269
E-mail: ars@gov.si
Web site: www.sigov.si/ars/index.html

The Provincial Archives

These are located in the three main centers outside Ljubljana:

Pokrajinski Arhiv Maribor
Glavni trg 7, 62000 Maribor
Web site: www.pokarh-mb.si/pamb.html

Pokrajinski Arhiv Koper
Goriska 6, 62000 Koper

Pokrajinski Arhiv Novi Gorici
trg Edvarda Kardelja 3, 65000 Nova Gorici

There are also a number of historical archives:

Azodovinski, Mestni trg 27, 61000 Ljubljana (headquarters);
    Web site: www.zal-lj.si
68000 Novo Mesta
64000 Kranj
64220 Skofja Loka
65280 Idrija
62250 Ptuj
63000 Celje

Church Registers

There are three ecclesiastical archives. Generally speaking, the registers are still in the original churches, but many were destroyed during various wars. Some had already been transferred to the archives to avoid loss or damage.

The country is predominately Catholic, and the local priests were responsible for the recording of vital events until 1926, when the government took over. When examining the registers, be prepared for entries in Latin and the use of patronymics instead of family names.

A recent development is that the National Archives have passed on to the Catholic Church the registers of the areas of historic Slovenia that now are outside the present boundaries, i.e., Italy. For further information consult the Catholic Archives in Ljubljana, Maribor, and Koper.

I have left the good news to the end. There is now a genealogical society in Slovenia: Slovensko rodoslov no društvo-SPD, Lipica 7, 64220 Škofja Loka. The society publishes a monthly bulletin.

SPAIN

Over the years Spain has suffered a succession of invaders and civil uprisings. These, plus its isolation on the Iberian Peninsula between the Pyrenees and the sea, have produced a unique race—proud, brave, deeply suspicious of strangers, and yet with a passion for exploration and the conquest of lands beyond the sea.

The Romans were the first conquerors of Spain, then the Vandals, the Visigoths, and most important, the Moors in 711. For four hundred years and more these warriors from North Africa occupied nearly all of the area of present-day Spain. At the time of the invasion and for many years after, Spain was a collection of small kingdoms: León, Navarre, Aragón, Castile, and so on. It was not until 1492 that the Moors were finally expelled and a united Spain was created, ruled by a single king. During the next three centuries the central government extended its control over the old kingdoms and semi-autonomous provinces, and then turned its eyes westward to the Americas.

In 1808 Spain was invaded by the French armies of Napoleon, who placed his brother Joseph on the throne for a few years. The Spaniards proved to be superb guerrilla fighters and by 1814, aided by the British Army under Wellington, they drove the French from the country. During the occupation and fighting, a number of local genealogical records were destroyed or damaged.

In the next one hundred years there were a number of rebellions, caused partly by poverty and oppression in some areas, and partly by a deep-rooted provincial patriotism in others. The great tragedy of the present century was the Civil War, 1936–39, with its great loss of life. More records were destroyed, too, but a surprisingly small number in proportion to the whole, even in areas of the fiercest fighting. There are, or were, 13,000 parishes in Spain and only a handful lost their registers.

Spain is divided into fifty provinces, but you will find many more references to the fifteen historical divisions based in the main on the original small kingdoms. You will find below a list of the fifteen regions, and under each one the names of the present-day provinces within that region. In this way, if you only know that your ancestor came from Catalonia, you will at least now know the names of the four provinces within Catalonia:

ANDALUSIA: Almeria, Cádiz, Córdoba, Granada, Huelva, Jaén, Málaga, Sevilla.

ARAGÓN: Huesca, Teruel, Zaragoza.

ASTURIAS: Oviedo.

BALEARES: Baleares.

BASQUE PROVINCES: Álava, Guipúzcoa, Vizcaya.

CANARY ISLANDS: Las Palmas, Tenerife.

CASTILE (OLD): Ávila, Burgos, Logroño, Santander, Segovia, Soria.

CASTILE (NEW): Ciudad Real, Cuenca, Guadalajara, Madrid, Toledo.

CATALONIA: Barcelona, Gerona, Lérida, Tarragona.

EXTREMADURA: Badajoz, Cáceres.

GALICIA: La Coruña, Lugo, Orense, Pontevedra.

LEÓN: León, Palencia, Salamanca, Valladolid, Zamora.

MURCIA: Albacete, Murcia.

NAVARRA: Navarra.

VALENCIA: Alicante, Castellón, Valencia.

Archives

In Spain there is an embarrassing richness of archives: national, regional, provincial, municipal, parish, military, governmental, and finally, those of private and noble families.

The major archives in these various categories are listed below, but I make no claim that the list is complete. I am sure it is not, because I doubt if anyone knows where all the Spanish archives are. My information was collected from a variety of sources in Spain and elsewhere over a period of several years. I have only listed the name of the archive in some cases, and in others have given the name of the city or town as well, but not the street address. There is a great deal of changing of location going on in Spain and any detailed list would soon be out of date. Every archive is, of course, well known in its own area and letter-writing or a personal visit will still be quite easy without an exact address.

Whatever you do, do not neglect the local city, town, or village archives. They are of much greater importance than in most other countries, where the tendency has been to centralize records in counties or provinces, or in central archives in the capital city. For over five centuries the Spaniards have been storing material in local archives and little attempt has been made to either centralize these records or even put them on microfilm or microfiche, and to lodge original material in major archives or in secure storage.

With the mass of archival material available at the local level, you have a good chance of being able to trace your Spanish ancestors back for 500 years. The key to it all is the knowledge of the place from which your ancestor emigrated—not the port from which he or she sailed, but his or her place of birth or origin.

So far as church registers are concerned, the vast majority are in the original churches, except in a few dioceses where an attempt is being made to collect all the registers into a diocesan archive. There is great local resistance to these projects even on such a limited and local scale. There are no registers in the main archives of the state.

There are eleven different National Archives, based in the main on the ancient divisions of what is now a united country:

Archivo Histórico Nacional
Serrano 115
28006 Madrid

Archiva General de Indias
Avenida de la Constitución 3
41071 Seville

Archivo General de Simancas
Miravete 8
47130 Simancas, Valladolid

Archivo de la Corona de Aragón
Almogavares 77
08018 Barcelona

Archivo del Reino de Valencia
Alameda 22
46010 Valencia

Archiva General de Navarra
37070 Pamplona
31001 Navarra

Archivo Regional de Galicia
San Carlos, La Coruña
15001 Galicia

Archivo del Reino de Mallorca
Ramón Llull 3
07801 Palma de Mallorca

Archivo de la Real Chancilleria
Plaza de la Chancilleria
47071 Valladolid

Archivo de la Real Chancilleria
Plaza Suarez 1
18009 Granada

Archivo General del
    Ministerio de Asuntos
    Exteriores
Plaza de la Provincial
28071 Madrid

For further information about the Spanish archive system, write or fax Archivo Histórico Nacional (Serrano 115, 28006 Madrid; Phone: 011-34-915-618-001; Fax: 011-34-915-631-199; Web site: www.mcu.es/lab/archivos/AHN.html)

There are some other sources in Spain that you may find useful:

Biblioteca Nacional, Paseo de Recoletos 20, 28071 Madrid; Phone: 011-34-91-580-78-23; E-mail: info@bne.es; Web site: www.bne.es

Instituto de Genealogia Salazar y Castro, Aniceto Marinas 114, 28008 Madrid

Real Academia Matritense de Heraldica y Genealogia, Quintana 28, 28008 Madrid

There are also important archives (Archivo Municipal) in all major centers as well as in smaller towns and villages. It is not possible to list all of these but the following major centers have excellent archives:

Alicante, Barcelona, Cáceres, Córdoba, La Coruña, Gerona, Guadalajara, Guipúzcoa, León, Madrid, Orense, Palencia, Pamplona, Salamanca, Santander, Segovia, Seville, Teruel, Vizcaya, and Zamora.

There are also archives in Mahón, in the Balearic Islands.

There are three types of very important records that will be found at the local level: civil registration, church registers, and notarial records. Let us talk about these in turn.

Civil Registration (Los Registros Civiles)

This started officially in 1870 and it is easy to discount its importance because it commenced so recently. However, to do that is wrong, because civil registration certificates will take you back another two generations so far as the births are concerned, and at least one more generation in the case of marriages and deaths.

Although the official starting date was 1870, it had already been in operation in a few municipalities for a number of years. The responsibility for organizing the new system was given to the local court, the Court of the First Instance (Juzgado de Primera Instancia), as it was called. All vital events—births, marriages, and deaths—had to be registered within eight days of the event.

The civil registers are still kept in the same courts. In large cities there may be several Juzgado and in underpopulated areas one office will serve a score of municipalities. The volumes in which the registers are kept are indexed by surname, but in the very early days of registration of births the indexes were by given, or Christian, name, and this can make searching a little hard at times.

When you write for a copy of an entry, be very sure you ask for a *full* copy, because if you don't you will receive an extract, and you will miss the fund of information contained in the original entry. The Spaniards are even more thorough than the Finns in the amount of detailed family information recorded.

The *birth* entries contain the usual day and date of birth, names, town and street address, and names, ages, and birthplaces of both parents, but in Spain this is only the beginning! You will also find the dates and places of birth of the grandparents, and the occupations or professions of the two generations, plus the names of the witnesses, and the signatures of all those present. Finally, there is full personal information about the person who registered the birth.

The *marriage* entries are less detailed. They give names of the bride and groom, addresses, ages, places of birth (in some cases the date of birth), names and addresses of the parents on both sides, and their places of birth.

The *death* entries give the names of both the deceased and the surviving spouse, with their addresses and places of birth; the full names of the parents of the deceased, and whether they are living or dead; the cause and place of death; the names of all surviving children; and the particular cemetery where the burial took place.

As I mentioned above, civil registration started in 1870, but be sure you always check whether it started earlier in the parish in which you are interested. There are a number of churches with records dating back to 1840.

There is no central index for civil registration, so you must know a place to start. The government department responsible for the administration of the system is the Ministry of Justice (Ministerio de Justicia), and the official directly concerned is the Director-General (Dirección General de los Registros y del Natariado), Madrid.

Church Registers (Registros de Parroquia)

The parish churches of Spain contain records that go back at least to 1650, and in many cases much earlier. The oldest baptismal entries found so far are those of Alcala de Henares, which date back to 1437. The earliest known parish papers are those of Solsona and are dated 1394. A guide to the various parishes was published in 1954 (*Guia de la Iglesia en España,* Vol. 4). Ninety percent of the parishes are listed. A few of the registers have been copied by the LDS Church.

Apart from the registers of baptism, marriage, and burial, the parish records also include confirmations, parish censuses, the church account books, inventories of parish property, and the minutes of meetings of the Cofradias (a society of laymen, which organizes social and religious events within the parish). The three most important records named above are usually each in a separate book, and confirmations are generally recorded in a separate section of the birth registers.

A **baptismal** entry contains a great deal of information from about 1760 to the present, but earlier registers will not contain as much information; for example, the names of grandparents did not appear much before 1780.

In recent times the baptismal entry will give the name of the child being baptized; paternal and maternal surnames; the date of the baptism; the names, addresses, and birthplaces of the parents and grandparents; the birth date and birthplace of the child; whether the child is legitimate or illegitimate; the names of the godparents, and their addresses and birthplaces.

A **marriage** entry contains the full names of the bride and groom; their marital status; their occupations; their addresses and birthplaces; their ages;

and the names, addresses, and birthplaces of the parents on both sides. Earlier marriage entries omit mention of the grandparents.

The **death** entry is by no means as detailed and there is tremendous variation from parish to parish as to the information given. Some mention the date of death, but not of burial—or vice versa. Usually, the entry will give details of name of the deceased, address at the time of death, age, birthplace, name of surviving spouse or of the spouse who had died earlier, names of the parents, names of the children, and a notation stating that the will was made before a lawyer (notario) or written down by the priest.

Confirmation, although a sacrament of the church, is treated quite differently in that it is not performed by the parish priest but by the bishop. Consequently a person might have to wait many years to be confirmed. In the present day, with ease of travel, such delays no longer exist. The confirmation entry will give the date it was performed, the name and address of the person, and the names of the parents.

The **Cofradias** records will not help you with your family tree, but if your ancestors were active in the church you will find out quite a lot about them; what their views were on different subjects, when they joined, how active they were, and when they died.

The **Padrones** or censuses were taken in parishes at various times and on various occasions. There was no particular pattern, or any regularity, but you may find in some parish archive a census entry for your family that tells you the place they came from and, suddenly and almost miraculously, a major problem has been solved.

You will also find the church account books, which contain details of payments received for masses for the dead, and this may give you the date of death of an ancestor, or you may find in the land records (capellanías) details of a gift of land from your ancestor to the church. You may also find copies of wills (testamentos) and petitions (expedientes). These latter were applications to the priest for a marriage, signed by bride and groom, usually including copies of their baptismal records—another valuable document in an unlikely location, judged by our present-day experiences.

You must always be prepared to find that church records have been destroyed, either in the French invasions at the end of the eighteenth century, or during the Civil War, or by vandalism or fire. In that case, you should try the archives of the diocese in which the parish is located; sometimes there are duplicate records or registers in the custody of the bishop, or diocesan censuses that may help you go further back. If you don't know the exact diocese, you should write to the headquarters of the Catholic Church (Conference Episcopal Española, Oficina de Estadistica y Sociologia, Alfonso XI 4, Madrid 14), give them the name and province of the village, and ask for the name of the diocese and the address of the diocesan office.

Civil Censuses (Padrones Civiles)

These records are kept in local municipal offices (Ayuntamiento) and are very complete. The name of each family member is listed, with date and place of birth and relationship to the head of the household, and length of time in present town or village. In addition, details are given of education and military service. The records are not indexed but in smaller places this is no great drawback, as one page in the register is devoted to one family, and it is just a question of turning the pages for a short time. The family name at the top of the page is usually quite legible. A search in a large city can be a monstrous chore, but it may be worth all the effort. Only you can decide.

Civil censuses have been held in various places at very frequent intervals since the 1500s. There is no official list of these censuses and I doubt if anyone knows how many there are. As dusty old documents are sorted in dusty old archives, dusty old census lists are always being discovered. All you can do is to check with the municipal offices (Ayuntamiento) or the provincial archives for information about early civil censuses in the area of your own interest. National censuses have been held since 1857 but the ones open to public search do not contain very much personal information. The most comprehensive census of them all was the one called Catastro del Marques de la Ensenada, in 1752. Copies are preserved in the appropriate archives throughout Spain and are readily available, and in some cases indexed.

Notarial Records (Protocolos)

Notaries are, of course, lawyers and they can be involved in almost every aspect of life (particularly Spanish life). If you know the exact place of origin of your emigrant ancestor, you may be able to make good use of the great mass of information contained in these records, assuming your ancestor had some reason to make use of the services of a notary. Notarial records include such items as wills, real estate sales, property transfers, marriage settlements and contracts, dowries, apprenticeship records and indentures, adoptions, guardianships, boundary disputes, inheritance disputes, building contracts, etc.—ad infinitum.

However, there are problems in searching for the records. They can be found in any one of a variety of archives—provincial, district, local, municipal, historical, ecclesiastical, governmental—and, of course, in notaries' offices. The law states that records over twenty-five years old must be given to the district notary, and that the district notary, in turn, must give all records over one hundred years old into the custody of the provincial archives. These regulations are not strictly enforced in all places, due to local resistance, and so these time periods should not be accepted without question. There is also a law that restricts access to the records younger than one hundred years except by a direct descendant. In this case you must produce sworn evidence of descent, fully documented.

Notarial papers are filed under the name of the notary. This means you must first discover the name of the notary in your place of ancestral origin. My advice is to forget the whole idea if your ancestor came from a city or a large town. If he or she came from a small place, the provincial archives will be able to give you the names of notaries who practiced in that place at that particular time, and for a small fee will search the lists for you for mention of any documents connected with your ancestors.

There is one very important aspect of notarial records, apart from those listed above. Until about the middle of the last century, anyone wishing to emigrate from Spain had to complete three documents before a notary. One was a certificate of permission to emigrate (if under twenty-five) from his or her father or elder brother; the second was a contract with the captain of the vessel on which he or she was to sail; and the third was a bond by which a relative or friend agreed to be liable for any unpaid debts of the emigrant. These documents may be found among the notarial records mentioned.

Passport Applications

Many of these are on file in the Archiva de Gobernación, in Madrid.

Military Records (Hojas de Servicio)

These records are in the Military Archives in Segovia (Archivo General Militar) and contain the complete personal records of every Spanish soldier and sailor from the early 1600s up to the present day. The lists have been published and indexed in the earlier years. Other records for the navy are in the Archives of the Ministry of the Navy (Archivo Central del Ministerio de Marina), and in the Naval Museum (Archivo del Museo Naval).

Passenger Lists (Listas de Pasajeros)

In Spain, as in many other European countries, genealogists have been searching in vain for records of emigrants sailing on passenger ships from their country. It is true there are lists of people sailing out of the port of Seville to the Americas in 1509–1701, but these are limited in value. They exist because Seville was the port from which emigrants and others always left. The people listed were, in very many cases, going overseas on government or private business and would eventually be returning to Spain.

The lists end in 1710, though records of licenses issued for travel continue to about 1790. Both types of records give details of the head of the family and his place of birth or residence. If your ancestors emigrated before the latter date, these records may be invaluable to you. They are located in Archivo General de Indias, in Seville. It must be remembered that the lists are not infallible; many emigrants went unrecorded, by accident or design. Some attempts are being made to index the very early lists. No emigration or passenger lists after 1790 are known to be in existence.

Genealogical Societies

There are believed to be two genealogical organizations in existence in Spain, but since no replies have been received from either of them to several letters, I do not know if they are still in existence:

Instituto Salazar y Castro
La Calle del Duque de Medinacelli 4, 28014 Madrid

Instituto Internacional de Genealogia
Apartado 12079, Madrid

As you will realize by now, the amount of genealogical material available for you in Spain is immense, but it is not centralized and is poorly organized. If you speak fluent Spanish and have plenty of time, you will accomplish a great deal with a very leisurely visit. If you have to depend on correspondence, be prepared for very long waits for answers. "Mañana" may even mean "Nunca."

SWEDEN

The Swedes, like the Danes and the Norwegians, are descended from the Vikings, but, unlike their neighbors who went west to conquer the British Isles, France, and the Low Countries, the Swedes turned east. For centuries the wars between Sweden and Russia left their marks on the populations of both countries. From time to time the Swedes also fought with the Danes and the Norwegians, with an occasional foray into Finland.

Sweden and Norway joined forces in 1319 and in 1397 Queen Margaret of Denmark united the three countries in the Kalmar Union and ruled from Copenhagen. Sweden became independent again in 1523. During the next century the Swedes conquered Livonia, Karelia, Pomerania, and parts of the area that is now Germany. In 1720 after the Peace of Westphalia they returned the conquered territory. In 1814 they lost Finland to Russia at the Congress of Vienna, but were given Norway as compensation. Norway then remained a separate kingdom in personal union with Sweden until 1905.

Ancestor-hunting in Sweden is probably easier than in any other country in Europe, with the exception of Switzerland. However, it is particularly important that you start off by researching within your family. First, try to find out the name of the parish from which your ancestor came; there are over 2,000 parishes in Sweden. Check your surname very carefully. Your emigrant ancestor may have anglicized it upon his or her arrival in the new country; many thousands did so. Olsson became Oliver, Persson became Perkins, Stalhammar became Steel. Check your family papers; you may find the official exit permit from Sweden issued by the pastor of your ancestor's church. It will give a full name, date and place of birth, and a character reference. This is called a flyttningsbetyg.

Superb as the records are, you will need to know the name of the place where your ancestor was born, or lived prior to emigration. Unless you know this you will have problems.

The country is divided into twenty-four districts or counties (län). Sometimes these län are identical with the province (landskap), although there may be more than one län in a landskap. In seven counties there are archives, known as Landsarkivet.

Each län is divided into smaller units known as fögderi. These, as well as the cities and towns, have their own separate administrations. From a judicial point of view, each län is divided into other units known as härad. Each län is further divided into smaller ecclesiastical units similar to parishes. These were originally known in Swedish as socknar, but are now called församlingar. There are over 2,000 of these, too many to list in this chapter.

The following archives are in existence in Sweden:

Riksarkivet (National Archives)
Fyrverkarbacken 13-17, PO Box 12541, 102 29 Stockholm
Phone: 011-46-8-737-6350. Fax: 011-46-8-737-6474
E-mail: registry@riksarkivet.ra.se
Web site: www.ra.se (please note this is the only Swedish archival web site in English)

Regional Archives

Landsarkivet in Östersund
Arkivvägen 1, 831 31 Östersund
Phone: 011-46-63-10-84-85. Fax: 011-46-63-12-18-24
E-mail: landsarkivet@landsarkivet-ostersund.ra.se
Web site: www.ra.se/ola/

Stockholms Stadsarkiv
PO Box 22063, 104 22 Stockholm
Phone: 011-46-8-508-283-00. Fax: 011-46-8-508-283-01
E-mail: stadsarkivet@ssa.stockholm.se
Web: www.ssa.stockholm.se

Värmlandsarkiv for the District of Värmland
PO Box 475, 651 11 Karlstad
Phone: 011-46-54-10-77-30. Fax: 011-46-54-100-77-31
E-mail: varmlandsarkivet@telia.com
Web site: www.ra.se/vla

Landsarkivet in Uppsala
PO Box 135, 751 04 Uppsala
Phone: 011-46-18-65-21-00. Fax: 011-46-18-65-21-03
E-mail: landsarkivet@landsarkivet-uppsala.ra.se
Web site: www.ra.se/ula

Landsarkivet in Vadstena
PO Box 126, 592 23 Vadstena
Phone: 011-46-143-1300-30. Fax: 011-46-143-1022-54
E-mail: landsarkivet@landsarkivet-vadstena.ra.se
Web site: www.ra.se/vala

Landsarkivet in Visby
Visbogsgatan 1, 621 57 Visby
Phone: 011-46-498-21-05-14. Fax:011-46-498-21-29-55
E-mail: landsarkivet@landsarkivket-visby.ra.se
Web site: www.ra.se/vila

Landsarkivet in Lund
PO Box 2016, 220 02 Lund
Phone: 011-46-46-19-70-00. Fax: 011-46-46-19-70-70
E-mail: landsarkivet@landsarkivet-lund.ra.se
Web site: www.ra.se/lla

Landsarkivet in Göteborg
PO Box 19035, 400 12 Göteborg
Phone: 011-46-31-778-68-00. Fax: 011-46-31-778-68-25
E-mail: landsarkivet@landsarkivet-goteborg.ra.se
Web site: www.ra.se/gla

Landsarkivet in Härnösand
PO Box 161, 871 24 Härnösand
Phone: 011-46-611-835-00. Fax: 011-466-611-835-28
E-mail: landsarkivet@landsarkivet-harnosand.ra.se
Web site: www.ra.se/hla

Other Archives

Krigsarkivet (Military)
115 88 Stockholm
Phone: 011-46-8-782-41-00. Fax: 011-46-8-782-69-76
E-mail: krigsarkivet@krigsarkivet.ra.se
Web site: www.ra.se

Statiskiska Centralbyran (Statistics Sweden)
Box 24300, 104 511 Stockholm
Phone: 011-46-8-506-940-00. Fax: 011-46-8-661-52-61
E-mail: swestat@scb.se
Web site: www.scb.se

Civil Registration

This does not exist in Sweden. The responsibility for recording births, marriages, and deaths rests with the ministers of the Lutheran Church, which became the official church in 1527. Since then it has also become the official recorder of the vital events of Sweden.

Church Registers

In 1571 a royal proclamation ordered that books should be kept in each church in which statistics could be recorded. In 1608 the church urged its ministers to obey the law and maintain the records. The clergy does not seem to have paid much attention to these royal and ecclesiastical urgings, because few registers exist before 1686, when a new law specified that a record be kept of all married couples, together with the names and addresses of parents; the births of all children, with the names of parents and witnesses at the baptism, the dates of birth and baptism, and the place of birth; the name of each dead person, with a short account of his or her life, and age at death; the name of those moving in or out of the parish, with details of where they came from, or where they were going; and, finally, a book containing the names of all parishioners being instructed in the catechism before being confirmed (this was called the katekismilängder).

There was still resistance to the law and many did not comply until the early 1700s. On the other hand, some started much earlier, for example, Skultuna, in the län of Västmanland (1607), and Holy Trinity Parish (Trefaldighets) in Uppsala city (1608).

Each parish maintained its own books. Some were kept in the church, some in the minister's house, and some in outbuildings. As a result many were lost, burnt, or damaged. In 1888 all the registers were transferred to the Landsarkivet. However, there was some opposition to this transfer, particularly in the län of Kopparberg. It was finally agreed that individual churches could retain their registers if certain standards of storage could be observed. Over the years many of these retained registers have been transferred and very few now remain in the churches. In the latter cases there are copies in the Landsarkivet. No exemptions have been granted since 1916. Churches, of course, retain the current registers.

The kinds of records that were, and are, maintained in the churches are births and baptisms, banns and marriages, deaths and burials; church accounts; catechism, confirmation, and communion records; records of arrivals and departures; and since 1750, house examination rolls (husförhörslängder).

The house examination rolls are invaluable—if only every country maintained such records! They are a record kept by the minister of his visits to his church members (in the days when clergymen, like doctors, made house calls). The rolls give details of the social status of the individuals, their education, their character, their occupation, their state of health, their journeys away from the parish, and the names of any visitors in the house when the minister called. In 1895 some changes were made in these records and they became known as församlingsböcker. These records are still kept up to the present day and do not differ in any substantial way from the husförhörslängder.

It should be noted that in 1860 the ministers started sending a copy of the entries in the parish registers to Statistics Sweden (see address on page 275). These records are filed by year, county, and parish and are still in operation. In cases where the original registers have been lost, the copies in Statistics Sweden will fill the gap.

Personal Records (Personakt)

In 1946 all Swedes were given personal records (personakt) that contain a précis of the information in their parish records. When they move, they take the records with them. If they die or leave the country permanently, the personakt is sent to Statistics Sweden. Here the records are divided into two sections, one for deaths and the other for emigration.

Censuses (Mantalslängder)

These started in 1620 in various places and at irregular intervals. The information contained in the early censuses varies a great deal. A good rule of thumb is, the later the census the more detailed the information. Copies are in the National Archives in Stockholm, and in the Landsarkivet.

Property Lists (Jordeböcker)

These date back as early as 1540 and record all transactions in property, together with tax information relating to the property. The names of all owners of property are given in great detail and the genealogical value can be very great. These records are also in the Landsarkivet.

Probate Records (Bouppteckningar)

These are inventories of the real and personal property of deceased persons. They date back to about 1660 and give details of birth and death, heirs and their relationship to the deceased, together with their ages and locations. They are to be found either in regional archives or district courts (Rådhusrätt).

Tax Lists (Boskapsräkningar)

These only existed for a short period (1620–42) before they were incorporated in other records, and they are located in the National Archives in Stockholm.

Court Records (Domböcker)

These very comprehensive records start in 1620 and continue to the present day. They include details not only of court cases and prosecutions, but also of real estate transfers, mortgages, guardianships, and marriage settlements. Recent records are in local courts, and earlier ones are in the Landsarkivet.

Trade Guilds (Skråhandlingar)

These cover the period from 1604 to about 1890 and are usually found in city archives (Stadsarkivet). In almost every European country the trade guilds were immensely powerful. They were the equivalent of today's trade unions and in each trade they regulated that particular craft or industry. Membership was a jealously guarded privilege, because only members could practice their trade in the city or community. To qualify for membership you had to be an upright and honest citizen of impeccable character; to have served your apprenticeship in the craft; to have passed an examination of your skills by a board of examiners; and, most important, to have an opening in the craft in your community available for you. Once in, you were a success in life. You were protected against competition and were a respected figure in your community. You were also told where you should live, and if you were single a marriage could be arranged for you with the daughter of another guild member. You had duties and responsibilities to your guild, but you obtained rights and privileges in return.

The guild records list full personal details about each applicant, including date and place of birth, and parents and their place of residence.

Emigration Records (Emigrationshandlingar)

I have left these most important records to the end. Nearly all emigrants from Sweden passed through the ports of Malmö and Göteborg, though a few emigrated overseas via Hamburg, Germany. (For information about the records there, see the chapter on Germany.)

All emigrants passing through the two Swedish ports had to register with the police, who recorded the names and addresses of the emigrants, age and sex, occupation, place of birth, and intended destination. These police records did not start until 1867, but most emigration from Sweden started after that date. In any case, do not forget that the parish records I mentioned earlier give details of people leaving a particular parish and their destination. The police records are almost completely indexed and are in the regional archives.

In addition, the national government also kept emigration records from 1851. These are in Statistics Sweden, and also in the Landsarkivet in Göteborg.

The Swedish Emigrant Institute (P.O. Box 201, 351 04 Växjö; Phone: 011-46-470-201-20; Fax: 011-46-470-394-16; Web site: www. svenskaemigrantinstitutet.g.se) has a manuscript collection consisting of original documents, microfilms, sound recordings, and photographs relating to Swedish emigrants. In addition, the Institute's Archives house microfilms of population census manuscripts, church archives from Sweden, passenger lists, registers for passport applications, and more.

Finally, there are all the records and correspondence of the Larsson Brothers, emigration agents in Göteborg. These date from 1876 to 1913 and are in the Landsarkivet there. They give not only details of emigrants and their families, but in many cases names and addresses of relatives who had emigrated previously.

From all these sources you should be able to find out all there is to know about your emigrant ancestor. Certainly no other country has such detailed records in this particular area of genealogical research. If, after searching all of them, you are still in need of information, there are still the records of passports issued. These are in the Military Archives in Stockholm and in the regional archives.

One final word about Swedish records. Be prepared for poor writing in many areas, and also for the fact that however good your spoken Swedish may be, you will be dealing with Swedish in a German script up to about 1790. Because of this you may need to employ an expert in Sweden on occasion; a list of researchers can be obtained from the archives in your area of interest.

Genealogical Societies

Sveriges Släktforskarförbund (The Federation of Swedish Genealogical Societies)
Box 30222, 104 25 Stockholm
Phone: 011-46-8-695-0890. Fax: 011-46-8-695-0824
Web site: http://www.genealogi.se/

The Federation of Swedish Genealogical Societies was founded in 1986. More than 120 genealogical societies in Sweden are members, and a list of these societies is available on the Federation's web site.

Genealogiska Föreningen
Box 6442, 113 82 Stockholm
Phone: 011-46-8-329-680
Web site: www.genealogi.net

In addition, there is an active organization in the United States:

Swedish Genealogy Society of Minnesota
5768 Olson Memorial Highway
Golden Valley, MN 55422
Web site: www.mtn.org/~mgsray/sgg/swedish.htm

Counties (Län)

The borders of the twenty-four counties have been almost unchanged since 1634. Nowadays, the counties are usually named by a letter instead of the full name, and this can be very confusing for genealogists. I list each county below with its letter equivalent. For example, Gotland is I-Län.

Älvsborg (Elfsborg)	P	Malmöhus	M
Blekinge	K	Norrbotten	BD
Gotland	I	Örebro	T
Gävleborg	X	Östergötland	E
Göteberg and Bohus	O	Skaraborg	R
Halland	N	Södermanland	D
Jämtland	Z	Stockholm	B
Jönköping	F	Uppsala	C
Kalmar	H	Värmland	S
Kopparberg	W	Västerbotten	AC
Kristianstad	L	Västernorrland	Y
Kronoberg	G	Västmanland	U

The Use of Patronymics

These were used by the working class until about 1860. The nobility, clergy, and guild members adopted surnames in the seventeenth century—in some places much earlier. Women often retained their surnames.

SWITZERLAND

The federal capital of Switzerland is Bern. In the early centuries the Swiss were conquered by the Romans, and later by the Franks and the Alamans. In 1291 three cantons—Uri, Schwyz, and Unterwalden—formed a confederation to protect themselves against attempts by the Hapsburg dynasty to control them. This was the period of the famous William Tell and his equally famous apple. Other cantons joined the confederation over the centuries, and in 1648 the independence of the Swiss Confederation was recognized in the Treaty of Westphalia. In 1815 the perpetual neutrality of the country was endorsed by the Treaty of Paris and the Congress of Vienna.

The country is divided into twenty-three cantons and six half-cantons. The latter are joined in pairs to form three full cantons. The list of the cantons is given below, together with the chief city of each. The German-speaking cantons are listed under their German names, with the French variation, if any, in parentheses; the reverse applies for the French-speaking cantons, and the only Italian-speaking one is listed in Italian, with the French and German variations. In the "Remarks" column is noted an additional appropriate language to use when writing.

German-speaking Cantons	Chief City	Remarks
Aargau (Argovie)	Aarau	
Appenzell—Ausser-Rhoden, Inner-Rhoden (Rhodes-Extérieures, Rhodes-Intérieures)	Herisau and Appenzell	
Basel—Basel-Stadt, Basel-Land (Bâle-Ville, Bâle-Campagne)	Basel and Liestal	
Bern (Berne)	Bern	also French
Glarus (Glaris)	Glarus	
Graubünden (Grisons)	Chur	also Romansch

German-speaking Cantons	Chief City	Remarks
Luzern (Lucerne)	Luzern	
St. Gallen (St. Gall)	St. Gallen	
Schaffhausen (Schaffhouse)	Schaffhausen	
Schwyz	Schwyz	
Solothurn (Soleure)	Solothurn	
Thurgau (Thurgovie)	Frauenfeld	
Unterwalden (Unterwald)—	Stans and	
Nidwalden, Obwalden	Sarnen	
Uri	Altdorf	
Zug (Zoug)	Zug	
Zürich (Zurich)	Zürich	

French-speaking Cantons	Chief City	Remarks
Fribourg (Freiburg)	Fribourg	also German
Genève (Genf)	Genève	
Jura	Delémont	
Neuchâtel (Neuenburg)	Neuchâtel	
Valais (Wallis)	Sion	also German
Vaud (Waadt)	Lausanne	

Italian-speaking Canton	Chief City	Remarks
Ticino (Tessin)	Bellinzona	also German

The Swiss Confederation deals with foreign affairs, transport and communications, and tariffs. All other matters are the responsibility of the individual cantons.

Generally speaking, unless you are writing in English, you will find the above guide to cantonal languages reliable. If, however, you are a fluent German speaker and are going to visit the German-speaking areas of Switzerland on an ancestor-hunt, a word of caution. Be prepared to find great difficulty in understanding and being understood. The Swiss-German dialect is an amalgam of Middle High German (1200–1500) and numerous regional dialects.

Civil Registration

Government registration of births, marriages, and deaths started in Switzerland on January 1, 1876. Before that date, such records had been the responsibility of the churches. When civil registration began, there were two types of registers kept. The first contained records of the *local* vital events; the second was a list of vital events affecting local people that occurred elsewhere. This system continued until 1928, when the second register was discontinued.

However, a second register was again started but in a very different form. The second register became a family register, recording and collating the vital events that occurred in each family. This information comes to the registrar from the first, or local, list and also from information from authorities in other areas. This information can be very complete. For example, a Swiss couple living in Canada will report the births of their children to the local Swiss consul. He, in turn, will pass on the information to the hometown of the couple and the entry will be made in the family register. Such records are invaluable, and they are signed, witnessed, and officially endorsed. Photocopies are obtainable for a small fee by writing to the Civil Registrar (Zivilstandsamt or Greffier Civil) of the particular district. All records for the pre-civil-registration period (1834–75) are also in the District Registry Office. Civil registration is based on a unique principle: Every Swiss has a "Bürgerort," a place of citizenship or hometown. This is NOT a place of birth, but a place of record of each generation. You can follow your ancestors at the same place back to 1876. It is vital to know this place to begin your search.

Church Registers

These are known by a number of names: Kirchenbücher, Pfarrbücher, Matrike, Kirchenrodel, or Rodeli. They include the usual entries of baptism (Taufen), marriage (Trauungen, Heiraten, Verehelichungen), and burial (Begräbnisse, Beerdigungen), but also confirmations (Konfirmationen) and, until 1875, the information now found in the civil registries. Generally speaking, the Protestant church records started in about 1550, but some early baptismal entries have been found that date back to 1481. The Catholic records start about 1580, but in fact the record-keeping in that church did not really come into full effect until about 1610. (In Zurich Canton the date is 1525 and in Basel Canton 1529.)

As you may imagine, the efficiency of the records depends very much on the efficiency and energy of the priest or pastor of the time. There are gaps; there is indecipherable writing; there are mysterious abbreviations (Xopher for Christopher, for example); and, of course, the entries are in German, French, Italian, or Latin.

Family registers (Familienregister) were started in many parishes in the late 1700s, but here again there are exceptions. Some have been found that date back to 1620 and others did not start until 1812. Be sure you check thoroughly to see if a family register is available for the parish in which you are interested. The great advantage of this register is that it was created from the church registers and includes all the entries in chronological order. You may find three or more generations on the one page, with the earliest member at the top and the most recent at the bottom. In other words, you will find a complete family tree spanning at least three generations, and you will also find references to other entries elsewhere in the register linking up with your family. Bear in mind, though, that you are exposed to human error and always try to cross-check with the church registers.

In church records you may also find citizen books (Bürgerbucher or Bürgerregister). To a large degree these duplicate the information in the family registers but they often contain details of emigration from the town or village to another place (either in Switzerland or overseas). A number of these have been published and you should always check for them with the local Standsamt (municipal office) or Archiv.

Population Registers (Bevölkerungsverzeichnisse)

These are also known as Burger Rolls or Status Animarum, and are found in the cantons of most of Switzerland, but particularly in the German-speaking areas. These records, like others, often duplicate information to be found in other places, like church registers and Family Books, but sometimes they include information left out of the other sources.

Censuses (Volkszählungen)

The first city census was taken in Bern in 1764, and the first federal census in the period April 1836 to February 1838. The latter is very incomplete. In 1841 the quality improved. In 1850 the census only included people with rights of residence and not the actual people present at a place during the census. In 1860 the census as we know it was instituted and has continued every ten years ever since. Copies can be obtained from both state and city archives.

Wills (Testamente)

The location of wills is a good illustration of the problems in a federated state. Because of the autonomous situation of the cantons, each has developed its own systems and ideas over the years. The earliest wills date back to the twelfth century and they can be found in state or city archives, or in local or district courthouses. Until 1912 the probating, or proving, of wills was entirely the responsibility of the cantons, but in that year the law was changed and the responsibility devolved on the federal government. In the case of death, the will has to be submitted to a judge, or other authority, who is dealing with matters of succession for proof of probate, regardless of whether the will has been retained in private hands or lodged in the office of a notary. Searching for wills, therefore, involves making contact with both courts and notaries. However, persistence pays off, and I know of several instances where wills have been eventually found as far back as 1600.

There are a variety of other records that you will need to search, some of them peculiar to Switzerland.

Notarial Records (Notariatsregister)

These date from the fourteenth century and include land records (Katasterbücher), which list the inheritors of land for several generations, together with details of their addresses, ages, and occupations; marriage contracts (Eheverträge), which were always drawn up when property was involved and give the full names of the couple, ages, names of parents, places of birth, and current residence; inventories (Bestandsaufnahmen), which list all property and possessions left by the deceased, together with name and age, address, occupation, and surviving family members; mortgages (Hypotheken), which list not only mortgages, but loans against property, contracts for real estate sales, and the full names and addresses of the parties involved.

The more recent of the above records are in the local courthouse (Kantonal- und Amtsgericht). Older records are in the canton and state archives and some of them have been indexed.

Genealogical City Registers (Genealogische Stadtregister)

Four localities have such registers: Bern, Glarus, Zürich, and Schaffhausen. The first three are in the state archives and the fourth in the city courthouse. The registers include pedigrees of local families, some of which date back for six centuries. These records, of course, are over and above the many printed genealogies you will find in local libraries. Always check with a local library for any information they have about your family. You may be astonished at what you will discover. My wife and I had quite an experience once in Scotland. We were working on her paternal grandmother's family, the Coplands. We knew that recent generations had come from the area of the city of Dumfries. While we were there we called in at the local library and found that they had, in manuscript form, a complete history of the family for 500 years, fully documented, and completed some fifty years ago by a member of the family. Our own research joined in with the manuscript material and saved us many, many hours of work. You see what can happen!

Military Records (Militärakten)

Each male citizen of Switzerland must spend time in the army and then go on the reserve. These records date from 1800 and are in the Military Department of the Federal Government (Eidgenössisches Militärdepartement, 3000 Bern).

University Registers (Universitätsmatrikeln)

If your ancestor graduated from a university (Basel, Geneva, Lausanne, Zürich) you will find him or her listed. The registers go back to the fifteenth century in Basel, to the sixteenth century in Geneva and Lausanne, and to 1832 in Zürich. Old records are in the state archives and more recent ones in the various university archives.

Guild Records (Zunftbücher)

In Switzerland, as in most other European countries, the trade guilds were powerful organizations, controlling who could enter a trade, where he could practice it, whom he married, and in which area he could live. These records cover the 300 years from the early sixteenth century and are in either state or city archives.

Passports (Passkontrollen)

A list of passports issued in the eighteenth and early nineteenth centuries up to 1848 is in the state archives; a list of passports after 1848 is in the Federal Office of Police (Bundesamt für, 8003 Berne). This gives very full personal information, including place of birth as well as current address and, usually, a list of family members traveling with the passport-holder. If you know your ancestor left the country in, say, 1842 but you don't know his or her place of origin, the passport records may solve your problem very easily.

Other Records

There are many other more specialized or localized records in the various state archives. These are listed below, together with major city archives and church archives. In addition, the LDS Church has microfilmed many parish registers in the cantons of Appenzell, Basel, Luzern, St. Gallen, Thurgau, Zürich, Geneva, and Vaud. It also has the research papers of a Swiss gene- alogist named Julius Billeter who traced the descent of over 1,200 families. These are also on microfilm and can be inspected in your nearest LDS Family History Center. The federal archives of Switzerland are located in Bern (Schweizerisches Bundesarchiv, Archivstrasse 4, 3003 Bern; Phone: 011-41-31-322-89-89; Fax: 011-41-31-322-78-23; E-mail: Bundesarchiv@ bar.admin.ch; Web site: www.admin.ch/bar), but because of the local na- ture of Swiss government the individual cantonal archives (see below) are much more useful.

State or Cantonal Archives
German-speaking Cantons

AARGAU:	Staatsarchiv
	5000 Aarau
APPENZELL (AUSSER-RHODEN):	Staatsarchiv
	9100 Herisau
APPENZELL (INNER-RHODEN):	Landesarchiv
	9050 Appenzell
BASEL (LAND):	Staatsarchiv
	4410 Liestal
BASEL (STADT):	Staatsarchiv
	4001 Basel

BERN:	Staatsarchiv 3012 Bern
GLARUS:	Landesarchiv 8750 Glarus
GRAUBÜNDEN:	Staatsarchiv 7000 Chur
LUZERN:	Staatsarchiv 6003 Luzern
ST. GALLEN:	Staatsarchiv 9000 St. Gallen
SCHAFFHAUSEN:	Staatsarchiv 8200 Schaffhausen
SCHWYZ:	Staatsarchiv 6430 Schwyz
SOLOTHURN:	Staatsarchiv 4500 Solothurn
THURGAU:	Staatsarchiv 8500 Frauenfeld
UNTERWALDEN (NIDWALDEN):	Staatsarchiv 6730 Stans
UNTERWALDEN (OBWALDEN):	Staatsarchiv 6060 Sarnen
URI:	Staatsarchiv 6460 Altdorf
ZUG:	Staatsarchiv 6300 Zug
ZÜRICH:	Staatsarchiv 8001 Zürich

French-speaking Cantons

FRIBOURG:	Archives de l'État 1700 Fribourg
GENÈVE:	Archives de l'État 1211 Genève 3
JURA:	Chancellerie de l'État 2800 Delémont
NEUCHÂTEL:	Archives de l'État 2001 Neuchâtel
VALAIS:	Archives de l'État du Canton 1951 Sion
VAUD:	Archives cantonales 1022 Chavannes-Renens VD

Italian-speaking Canton

TICINO: Archivio cantonale
                                     6500 Bellinzona

City Archives (Stadtarchiv)

Aarburg (Kanton Aargau)   Luzern (Kanton Luzern)
Arbon (Kanton Thurgau)   Mellingen (Kanton Aargau)
Baden (Kanton Aargau)   Murten (Canton de Fribourg)
Biel (Kanton Bern)   Olten (Kanton Solothurn)
Bischofszell (Kanton Thurgau)   Rheinfelden (Kanton Aargau)
Bremgarten (Kanton Aargau)   Schaffhausen (Kanton
Brugg (Kanton Aargau)   Schaffhausen)
Diessenhofen (Kanton Thurgau)   Steckborn (Kanton Thurgau)
Kaiserstuhl (Kanton Aargau)   Stein am Rhein (Kanton
Klingnau (Kanton Aargau)   Schaffhausen)
Laufenburg (Kanton Aargau)   Winterthur (Kanton Zürich)
Lausanne (Canton Vaudoise)   Zofingen (Kanton Aargau)
Lenzburg (Kanton Aargau)

Church Archives (Kirchliche Archiv)

Archiv des Kapuzinerklosters Appenzell
9050 Appenzell

Archives de l'Ancien Évêché de Bâle
2900 Porrentruy

Bischöfliches Archiv des Bistums Basel
4500 Solothurn

Stiftsarchiv Beromünster
6215 Beromünster

Bischöfliches Archiv Chur
7000 Chur

Stiftsarchiv Disentis
7180 Disentis

Stiftsarchiv Einsiedeln
8840 Einsiedeln

Stiftsarchiv Engelberg
6390 Engelberg

Provinzarchiv der Schweizerischen Kapuzinerprovinz
6006 Luzern

Klosterarchiv Mariastein
4115 Mariastein

Archiv Institut Menzingen
6313 Menzingen

Stiftsarchiv der Benediktinerabtei Muri-Gries
3910 Gries-Bozen

Stiftsarchiv St. Gallen
9001 St. Gallen

Archives de l'Abbaye de Saint Maurice
1890 Saint-Maurice

Genealogical Organizations

Swiss Genealogical Society
(Schweizerische Gesellschaft für Familienforschung)
Grabenweg 1, Füllinsdorf 4414
Phone: 011-41-61-901-41-72
E-mail: h.ochsner@dplanet.ch

There are also genealogical societies in various locations, and these are listed below, together with address and postal code, and the name of the secretary:

BASEL
Genealogisch-Heraldische Gesellschaft Region Basel
Dr. Hans B. Kalin
Steinbühlallee 189, 4054 Basel
Phone: 011-41-612-301-74-55. Fax: 011-41-61-301-74-51
E-mail: habekaelin@datacomm.ch

BERN
Genealogisch-Heraldische Gesellschaft Region Bern
Therese Metzger
3110 Münsingen
Phone: 011-41-31-721-09-45
E-mail: metz.thw@bluewin.ch

FRIBOURG
Institut Fribourgeois d'Heraldique et de Génélogie
Dominic Pédrazzini
Les Falaises, 1722 Bourguillin
Phone: 011-41-26-322-42-63

GRAUBUNDEN
Rätische Vereinigung für Familienforschung
August G. Müller
Campodelsweg 11, 7000 Chur
Phone: 011-41-81-353-21-72

JURA
Cercle Généalogique de l'Ancien Evêché de Bâle
François Kohler
34 rue de Bâle, 2800 Delémont
Phone: 011-41-32-422-18-84
E-mail: rais.fr@bluewin.ch
Web site: www.jura.ch/cgaeb

LUZERN
Zentralschweizerische Gesellschaft für Familienforschung
Eric Walthert
Werdstrasse 1 (Postfach 51)
8958 Dietikon
Phone: 011-41-1-741-42-97

NEUCHATEL
Societé Neuchâteloise de généalogie
Nicolas Junod
31b ch. des Jonchères, 2022 Bevaux
E-mail: sng@junod.ch
Web site: www.junod.ch/SNG

ST. GALLEN
Vereinigung für Familienkunde St. Gallen-Appenzell
Anton Rechsteiner
Buebenloostrasse 20, 9500 Wil SG
Phone: 011-41-71-911-46-31

TICINO
Societa Genealogical della Svizzera Italiano
Giovanni Staffieri
via Cantonale. la, 6900 Lugano
Phone: 011-41-91-923-36-39

VALAIS
Association Valaisanne d'Etudes Généalogiques
Philippe Terrettaz
1913 Saillon
Phone: 011-41-27-744-22-25
Web site: www.isuisse.com/aveg

VAUD

Circle Vaudois de Généalogie
32 rue de la Mouline
1022 Chavanne-prés-Renens
E-mail: peos@omedia.ch
Web site: www.ancestres.ch

ZURICH

Genealogische-Heraldische Gesellschaft Zürich
Werner Adams
Dammbodenstrasse 1, 8604 Volketswil
Phone: 011-41-1-946-18-13

UKRAINE

This country has existed since the twelfth century. It became part of Lithuania in 1386 and part of Poland in 1569. The name Ukraine came into general use in the sixteenth century. In 1654 the country came under the control of Moscow. As the result of a war in 1667 the country was partitioned between Russia and Poland. Russia took the left bank of the Dnieper River and Poland the right. The various partitions of Poland in the late eighteenth century resulted in Russia gaining control of the whole country. There were a number of unsuccessful revolts against the Russians in the next century. Ukraine finally gained independence in 1918 but the Red Army occupied Kiev and a Soviet Republic was declared in 1922. With Stalin's approval Ukraine annexed the Crimean Peninsula in 1954. This transfer is now under dispute between the two countries. Ukraine declared its independence in 1990.

Archives

In Ukraine there are two major archives with records on the national level, and several smaller ones for the various counties (oblasty) into which the country is divided. The records of the latter are very uneven so far as genealogical information and general service is concerned. If you know the area from which your family emigrated, by all means take a chance and write for information. If you write in Ukrainian and enclose a $5 US bill, and offer to pay for any further charges, you may be lucky. From my experience this approach will have doubtful results.

The reception you will receive from the two main archives is much more likely to produce results, but you must be prepared for a request to send $80 in advance with no guarantee of results. In my opinion this is a quite justifiable demand. The archivists are honest and helpful and will devote time to searching for useful information for you. Here are the addresses:

Central State Historical Archives
Solomenskaya 24, 252608 Kiev, Ukraine
Phone: 011-380-277-30-02. Fax: 011-380-277-36-55
E-mail: dga@archiv.freenet.kiev.ua

Central State Historical Archives
Soborno 3a, 290008 Lviv, Ukraine
Phone: 011-380-322-72-30-63. Fax: 011-380-322-72-35-08

Because of frequent address changes I hesitate to list any of the oblasty archives, but I will do so on the basis it can do no harm! I am listing three of them because they are the three from which the great majority of ex-Ukrainians in the United States and Canada are most likely to have their ancestral roots:

State Archives of Lviv Oblast, Pidvalna 13, Lviv
State Archives of Ternopil, Pecshoholtravnia 14, Ternopil
State Archives of Chernivtsi, Shevchenka 2, Chernivtsi

So far as the State Archive of Lviv is concerned, its records are now primarily about Western Ukraine in the years before the 1917 Soviet Revolution in Russia. It also includes the period when this part of Ukraine (then named Galicia) was under Austrian control (from 1772–1919). These include land records and some local government records. You will also find Orthodox and Catholic church records from when the area was controlled by Poland from 1919 to 1939. There are also some land records and family papers. All records are open to public search, but individuals must produce a letter of introduction in Ukrainian from their "sponsoring organization." I assume a letter on official letterhead from a church authority might meet the requirement—but this is only a guess on my part!

You can try a web site of an unofficial Ukrainian genealogical search organization I have seen listed, but I know nothing about it: It is **www.infoukes.com/genealogy**. Information on archives in Ukraine is available at **www.huri.harvard.edu/abbukr/index.html**.

YUGOSLAVIA

Many countries "grow" in size because of war or revolution, or friendly mergers. Yugoslavia is getting smaller and one day may disappear completely and become Serbia. It was created at the end of World War I by the Allied Powers—led by Wilson, Clemenceau, and Lloyd George, who cobbled it together from the odds and ends of places and people left over from the defeated Austro-Hungarian Empire. The creation of Yugoslavia must have seemed a good idea at that time—it solved a lot of messy little territorial problems, and they thought it might solve the "Balkan Problem." This had created two wars, several assassinations, a couple of civil wars, and some rather unpleasant revolutions—all within a century or so.

So the three wise men—supported by interested parties of various ethnic backgrounds—created a brand-new country and named it Yugoslavia. The people living in the area of the new state had little to say about it—they were poor, their economies were in ruins, and they were tired of all the fighting. Yes, it seemed like a good idea at the time. The name Yugoslavia meant the country of Serbs, Croats, and Slovenes—the majority of the people within its boundaries came from these three races, and no one really bothered very much about the others.

Thus were sown the seeds of hatred in the future, and nothing was done to solve the problems of the past. The Balkans, that disparate collection of ancient enmities, had been held together by ties of blood—the blood of other people, in an area constantly torn asunder by unreasoning hatreds.

So the Serbs, Croats, and Slovenes, who did not like one another very much, had their new country. They were joined in hope and fear by the Slavs, the Bosnians, the Macedonians, the Montenegrins, the Herzegovinians, the Dalmations, the Ystrians, the Kosovars, the Vojvodinians, and in a few scattered areas, some Hungarians, Austrians, and Italians left behind by the anonymous map-makers who drew the boundaries of the new state.

This grotesque melange managed—by some miracle—to cling together from 1919 to 1991, helped beyond question by World War II, which united most of them in resisting the German invaders. Acts of great courage and bitter suffering brought old enemies together, and for a few years after all seemed well. It was during this apparently halcyon period that my wife and I visited Yugoslavia many times. We saw no signs of ethnic hatreds, but everywhere the signs of growing prosperity. What went wrong?

You can hear a dozen reasons, but the basic reason appears to be an inherent fear of large government in Belgrade (Beograd), the capital of both Yugoslavia and Serbia, and a fear of Serbia's belief in its destiny as Greater Serbia. In 1991 Yugoslavia simply fell apart—Slovenia, Croatia, Macedonia, and Bosnia-Herzegovina all declared their independence. The newly independent countries went their separate ways and were all recognized by their neighbors and the rest of the world. There were some difficulties in Croatia stemming from Croatia's part in World War II, there was a full-scale civil war in Bosnia, and newly independent Macedonia had some trouble over recognition by Greece, which had its own ambitions in that area.

The Yugoslavia that remains consists of Serbia, Montenegro, and two autonomous areas of Serbia named Kosovo and Vojvodina. In 1999 Yugoslav forces attempted to deprive Kosovo of its self-governing rights and the resultant civil war was only stopped by the intervention of the armed forces of the UN. There was a bitter civil war in Bosnia, which remains under the UN intervention. Montenegro, although still allied with Serbia, is not happy with the situation.

All of this has had a major effect on genealogical research; the transfer of archives and other events complicate a search for your roots in the Balkan area. To a major degree the transfer of archives between Belgrade and the newly independent nations was a harmonious proceeding, but many records cannot be easily separated. For that reason you must be prepared to do your research in Belgrade as well as in the archives of the countries that are now independent. In addition, if your ancestors came from "Yugoslavia" or any of its former or present states, you will be aware of recent developments, which will cause difficulties for you—archives may have been destroyed, abolished, or located elsewhere. This may make it hard for you to obtain replies to letters or trace addresses, web sites, and fax and phone numbers. If you are planning a personal visit to Serbia, Bosnia, or Kosovo, I suggest you delay such arrangements in the interests of your own safety.

It has been necessary to explain at some length the political divisions of what is now Yugoslavia, and the history of the various regions over the centuries. Without this knowledge you will have difficulty in knowing just where to look for the records of your ancestors.

There is more to follow before we discuss specific records and their locations, because you must also know about the various religions and languages within Yugoslavia, two more factors that will have a great influence on your success or failure.

Religions

The major religion is Orthodox but there are large Muslim minorities in the south, especially in Montenegro and Kosovo, and Catholics in the north, especially in Vojvodina. It is a genealogical misfortune that these religions are not tidily assembled in particular parts of the country. If you do not know the religion of your Yugoslav ancestors you must tread with care and check all the religious sources available to you. It should also be noted that the religions are not confined to a particular area within a particular republic.

Language

The principal language of present-day Yugoslavia is Serbo-Croatian. Although *Serbs* and *Croats* speak variations of the same language and have no difficulty understanding each other, the Serbs use the old Cyrillic alphabet and lettering, and the Croats the Latin. The *Montenegrins* share the same language and alphabet as the Serbs and are regarded, historically, as of similar ethnic stock.

It should also be mentioned that there are over half a million Hungarians in the Vojvodina, some 70,000 Romanians in the same area, and about two million Albanians in Kosovo.

So much for the background; now for the details.

Church Registers

Many of these have been destroyed or lost during rebellions and invasions. There are some exceptions. In Dubrovnik, for example, there are baptismal records dating back to the early seventeenth century. Generally speaking, the Catholic registers go back further than the Orthodox or Muslim ones. The early church registers are in the various archives (national, regional, and municipal). Unfortunately, no central list of the parishes and the dates is available.

One further complication with the church registers is that in many areas of Yugoslavia surnames did not stabilize until about 1870. As a result, registers can show someone being born, married, and buried under three different names. However, a close search will usually show two names bracketed together, the patronymic and the earlier family name. This is particularly true of Catholic registers but also applies to most Orthodox ones.

There are also a number of surviving Church Books that record the life of the local church and its members, church meetings, and clergymen's visits within the parish. These are also in the various archives.

Civil Registration

Registration of births, marriages, and deaths did not commence in Yugoslavia until 1946; before that only the various churches recorded these events, and, as I mentioned, many of these church records are missing. Certificates of birth, marriage, and death are issued by the local registrar in small towns and villages. In the larger cities, registration is done on a ward or small-district basis. When applying for a copy of a certificate, you should write to the registrar (Maticar) in the small town or village, and also in the large city—there are over twenty maticars in Belgrade, for example, but your letter will reach the right one provided you give the address where the person was living at the time of birth, marriage, or death.

There are early civil-registration records available in the Dalmatian area (back as far as the sixteenth century, but with many gaps). Records for 1550 exist in Zadar, for example. Civil registration started in Vojvodina in 1895, when it was part of Hungary.

Census Returns

Modern census returns are located in the Federal Statistical Bureau (Savezni Zavod Za Statistiku, Kneza Milosa 20, 11000 Belgrade; Phone: 011-381-11-361-32-45). Earlier ones are in the various provincial archives.

Records of earlier censuses (and some go back to 1453 in Turkish-held areas) have suffered in the same manner as the church records. Many have been destroyed, and those that still exist are by no means complete; you will just have to hope you will be lucky in your particular area of interest. When you do find an entry, bear in mind that it was the custom to round off the ages of the people listed, so that 67 became 70, 43 became 40, and so on.

Once again we have to face the fact that there is no centralization of records, or even of information about those records. I can tell you a little about early censuses in the various areas but cannot guarantee that the records mentioned are in any way complete.

Serbia

There were censuses in this area as early as 1528 but only males were listed. The only complete census of earlier years is that for 1863 and this is in the Serbian Provincial Archives. Austria took a census of Belgrade in 1733–34. It was done by the various priests and gives full names, ages, and relationship. It also is in the archives. Serbian censuses were taken in 1890, 1895, 1900, 1905, and 1910, but most are missing or incomplete. The census of 1884 is complete but so far unpublished and not normally available for research.

Vojvodina

A census was held in this area in 1715 and there were later ones between 1855 and 1910 but only portions are in the archives.

Occupied Areas

The Turks held regular censuses from 1453, and they give personal names, relationship, unmarried mature males, and sometimes, widows who were heads of households. There are also Turkish Population Lists dating from the early nineteenth century, and many of these included physical descriptions; for example, in the Sarajevo (which is in present-day Bosnia) list of 1841 you will find "Selim, short and bearded, Pyotr, tall and no beard."

Some of the Turkish records are in the various archives and others are believed to be in the National Archives of Turkey in the Topkapi Palace in Istanbul.

Other census information is in the National Archives of Hungary, Austria, and Italy. However, some of this has recently been handed over to the appropriate Yugoslavian archive and has not yet been sorted and catalogued.

Wills

Early wills and probate records are in the various regional archives but the collections are small. Not many people had any money or possessions in the area we now call Yugoslavia. More recent ones are in the local municipal court.

Tax Rolls

There are some sixteenth-century Turkish Tax Rolls (Defter) and these have been published and indexed by the Belgrade Museum of History (1107 Novi Beograd, Palmira Toljatija 1).

Records of Serfs

Some records exist of serfs bound to nobles or religious institutions. For example, the archives in the Kosovo region have Serf Lists (or Chrysobulls) dating back to 1357.

Details of the history and records of the four separate parts of Yugoslavia follow:

SERBIA

The capital city is Belgrade (Beograd), which is also the capital of the Federal Republic. It was an independent kingdom by 1217, but in 1389 it fell under the control of the Ottoman Empire and became a Turkish province in 1521. There were frequent insurrections over the next centuries, and in 1878 its independence was assured by the Congress of Berlin. In the Balkan Wars of 1912 and 1913 the Serbs fought against both the Austro-Hungarian and the Ottoman empires in an effort to liberate the whole Balkan area from foreign domination. It also fought and won a short war against Bulgaria in order to secure a major part of the Macedonian area of that country. When a Serbian nationalist assassinated an Austrian archduke in 1914, the Austro-Hungarian Empire declared war on Serbia and precipitated the First World War. In 1915 the country was overrun by Austria-Hungary, Germany, and Bulgaria. The government and part of the army were evacuated to the island of Corfu (Kérkira), and in 1917 on that island representatives of Serbia, Croatia, Slovenia, and Montenegro proclaimed a Union of the South Slavs.

Archives

National Archives (Arhiv Jugoslavije), Vase Pelagica 33, 11000 Belgrade; Phone: 011-38-11-650-755; Fax: 011-38-11-652-740; E-mail: archiv@gov.yu; Web site: www.gov.yu/archiv

Archives of Serbia, Karnegijeva 2, 11000 Belgrade
Historical Archives of Belgrade, Palmira Toljatija 1, 11070 Novi Beograd
Archives of Bor, Jugoslovenske armije 18, 19210 Bor
Historical Archive of Valjevo, Pop Lukina 26, 14000 Valjevo
Historical Archives "31. Januar," Partizanska 17, 17500 Vranje
Historical Archives "Timočka Krajina," Nikole Paštića 160, 19000 Zaječar
Historical Archives "Srednje pomoravlje," Millana Mijalkovića 14, 35000 Jagodina
Historical Archives of Šumadija, 21. Oktobra 13, 34000 Kragujevac
Historical Archives of Kraljevo, Dositejeva 19, 36000 Kraljevo
Historical Archives of Kruševac, Miloja Zakića bb, 37000 Kruševac
Historical Archives of Leskovac, Dr Rade Svilara 25, 16000 Leskovac
Historical Archives of Negotin, Branka Perića 13, 19300 Negotin
Historical Archives of Niš, Tvrdjava bb, 18000 Niš
Historical Archives "Ras," Oslobodjenja 41, 36300 Novi Pazar
Historical Archives of Pirot, Laze Lazarevića bb, 18300 Pirot
Historical Archives of Požarevac, Dr Voje Dulicá 10, 12000 Požarevac
Historical Archives "Toplice," Tatkova 2, 27000 Prokuplje
Historical Archives of Smederevo, Kralja Petra I br. 2, 11300 Smederevo
Historical Archives of Smederevska Palanka, Trg Heroja 5a, 11420 Smederevska Palanka
Historical Archives of Užice, Dimitrija Tucovi a 52, 31000 Užice
Historical Archives of Čačak, Gospodar Jovanova 2, 32000 Čačak
Historical Archives of Šabac, Vojvode Mišića 18a, 15000 Šabac

MONTENEGRO

This area of the Balkans was originally the Principality of Zeta within the Serbian kingdom. By the end of the fifteenth century, it was occupied by Turkey and Venice—except for a very small section that remained within Serbia. In 1515 it came under the control of the Prince-Bishop of Cetinje, and so it remained until 1851. During the whole of this period the inhabitants, though heavily outnumbered, fought almost continually against the Turks and any other invader. It was not until 1799 that Turkey recognized it as an independent state. In 1878, at the Congress of Berlin, Montenegro was given back its lost territories and its boundaries were recognized by its neighbors.

In World War I it invaded Albania to obtain more territory and, with great bravado, declared war on the Austro-Hungarian Empire. It was, of course, occupied at once by the forces of the Empire and of Germany.

After the war it joined with Serbia and the other Balkan states to form the Kingdom of Yugoslavia. This association with Serbia continued to the present day, but with Montenegro becoming an increasingly unhappy partner. At the time this book was written Montenegro appeared to be planning for independence, but the harsh reality of economic and security ties with Serbia may prevent it. In addition, if it did become independent, Serbia would become a completely landlocked state.

Montenegro's capital was renamed Titograd after World War II as a tribute to the leader of Yugoslavia in the war against Germany. However, it has now reverted to its original name of Podgorica.

Archives

Like the other Balkan countries the archives suffered greatly from the war, but there are now four in the country and they are gradually collecting registers and documents together, and so are the churches (which are predominantly Orthodox). The archives are located at the following addresses:

State Archives of Montenegro, Njegoševo 100, 81250 Cetinje
Archives of Budva, Cara Dušana 13, 85310 Budva
Archives of Herceg Novi, Marka Vojnovića 9, 85340 Herveg Novi
Archives of Kotor, Njegoševa 208, 85330 Kotor

Kosovo

This area is in southeast Yugoslavia and the capital city is Priština. From the fourteenth century until 1913 it was part of the Ottoman Empire. It was then partitioned between Serbia and Montenegro, and incorporated into what is now Yugoslavia in 1918. The population is mainly Albanian, with some Serbian and Montenegrin minorities.

In 1999 Yugoslav forces invaded Kosovo in an attempt to expel all the inhabitants of Albanian descent. Forces of the European Community, and the U.S. Air Force came to the defense of the inhabitants and after some weeks of air attacks on Serbian targets Yugoslav forces withdrew. (Montenegro took no part in the Serbian invasion of Kosovo and, in fact, received many thousands of refugees from Kosovo.) Some refugees received safe haven in Albania and Macedonia, and others were airlifted to the United States, Canada, the United Kingdom, and several European countries. Most refugees have now returned to Kosovo—there are no Yugoslav forces remaining in the region. Legally, the province remains in Yugoslavia.

Archives

There are six archives in Kosovo:

Archives of Kosovo and Metohija, Bolničko neselje bb, 38000 Priština
City Archives of Priština, Cara Dušana bb, 38000 Priština
Historical Archives of Gnjilane, Kralja Petra I Karadordevica bb, 38250
   Gnjilane
Historical Archives of Kosovska Metroviča, Kralja Petra 10, 38220 Kosovska
Historical Archives of Pec, Bore Vucmirovica 13a, 33800 Pec
Historical Archives of Prizren, Ivo Lola Ribar bb, 38400 Prizren

Note: These addresses were sent to me during the fighting in Kosovo. It is not known what damage was done to the Archives, but it is believed to be considerable in both Priština and Prizren.

Vojvodina

This is in northeast Yugoslavia and the capital is Novi Sad. It was part of Hungary and Croatia before its conquest by the Turks in the sixteenth century. It was restored to Hungary in 1699 and the whole area was resettled by Croats and Serbs from the Ottoman Empire, and a little later by German colonists. As a result, the population is a very mixed one, including Serbs, Croats, Magyars, Romanians, and Slovaks. The region was ceded to Yugoslavia under the terms of the Treaty of Trianon in 1920, and became autonomous in 1946. There are three sections to the region: the Srem, in the southwest, which was part of Croatia-Slavonia until 1918; the Backa, in the northwest, which was part of Hungary; and the western part of the Banat of Temesvar, which had also been Hungarian. (The eastern part of the Banat went to Romania.)

Archives

Following are the addresses of archives in the area:

Archives of Vojvodina, Dunavska 25, 21000 Sad
Historical Archives of Novi Sad, Tvrdjava, 211131 Petrovaradin
Historical Archives of Bela Crkva, Prvog 40, 26340 Bela Crkva
Historical Archives of Pančevo, Nermanjina, 26001Pančevo
Historical Archives of Zrenjanin, Trg slobc, 23000 Zrenjanin
Historical Archives of Kikinda, Trg srpskiholjaca 21, 23300 Kikinda
Historical Archives of Senta, Trg Maršala T, 24400 Senta
Historical Archives of Sombor, Trg Cara La, 25000 Sombor
Historical Archives "Srem," Vuka Karadžića, 22000 Sremska Mitrovica
Historical Archives of Subotica, Trg slobode, 24000 Subotica

BIBLIOGRAPHY

This is a very short bibliography because of limitations of space. I could have included an additional several hundred books but (a) very many of them would have been in one of the European languages and (b) most of them would have referred to certain specific areas within a particular country. There is also the problem that although your ancestors came from Europe you may not speak the language that they spoke. In that case, a list of genealogical books in Bulgarian, or Hungarian, or Swedish would be of little use to you.

After much soul-searching I have decided to include only a representative collection. You can find out what other books are available (either in English or in your ancestral language) by writing to one or all of the following:

1. The National Archives of your ancestral country.
2. The National Library of the same country.
3. The Genealogical Society of The Church of Jesus Christ of Latter-day Saints, Salt Lake City, Utah.
4. A genealogical organization (if one exists) in the country in which you are interested.
5. A genealogical organization in North America that concentrates exclusively on the one country (some of these are listed at the end of this section, but I cannot guarantee the addresses, since the secretaries may have changed since I compiled the list).

Be sure you enclose a self-addressed airmail envelope and return postage (three International Reply Coupons with any overseas mail).

AUSTRIA
Finsterwalder, K. *Tiroler Namenkunde.* Innsbruck, 1978.
Senekovic, D. *Handy Guide to Austrian Genealogical Records.* Logan, Utah, 1979.

BELGIUM
Belgian Government. *Het Rijksarchief (De Vlaamse Provinciën).* Brussels, 1975.

————————. *Les Archives de l'État (Provinces Wallonnes)*. Brussels, 1975.

————————. *Registres Paroissiaux (Brabant)*. Brussels, 1976.

Sabbe, P.D., and L. Buyse. *Belgians in America*. Tielt, 1960.

BULGARIA

Tosheva, Snezhina. *Spravochnik na Bibliotekitev Bolgariya*. Sofia, 1963.

CROATIA

Prpic, G. *Croatian Immigrants in America*. New York, 1971.

CZECH REPUBLIC AND SLOVAKIA

Kral, Vacloc. *Die Deutschen in der Tschechoslowakei*. Prague, 1964.

Miller, Olga K. *Genealogical Research for Czech and Slovak Americans*. Detroit, 1978.

Procházka, R. *Genealogisches Handbuch Erschlosener Böhmischer*. Neustadt, 1973.

Society for the History of Czechoslovak Jews. *The Jews of Czechoslovakia*. Philadelphia, 1968.

DENMARK

Baisler, B. *History of the Danish Jews*. Copenhagen, 1932.

ESTONIA

Penmar, Parming, and Rebanc. *The Estonians in America, 1627–1975*. Dobbs Ferry, N.Y., 1975.

FINLAND

Brenner, A. *Staktforskning: Practisk Handbok*. Helsinki, 1947.

Kolehmainen, J. *The Finns in America*. New York, 1947.

FRANCE

Audin, Margaret. *Barking Up That French Tree*. Utica, N.Y., 1980.

Beattie, W. *The Waldenses or Protestant Valleys of Piedmont*. London, 1938.

Beaucarnot, J.-L. de. *Chasseurs d'Ancêtres*. Paris, 1980.

Durye, Pierre. *Genealogy*. New Orleans, 1977.

Fleury, M., and L. Henry. *Des Registres Paroissiaux*. Paris, 1956.

Hézelles, N., and Nadine Vigier. *La Généalogie*. Paris, 1979.

Levy, P. *Les Noms des Israélites en France*. Paris, 1960.

Reaman, G. E. *The Trail of the Huguenots*. Toronto, 1963 (republished with corrections Baltimore, 1966).

Tupigny, J. de. *Guide des Recherches Généalogiques aux Archives*. Paris, 1956.

GERMANY

Anderson, S. Chris, and Ernest Thode. *A Genealogist's Guide to Discovering Your Germanic Ancestors*. Cincinnati, Ohio, 2000.

Bahlow, H. *Deutsches Namenlexicon*. Munich, 1967.

Baxter, Angus. *In Search of Your German Roots*. 4th ed. Baltimore, 2001.

Brandt, Edward R. *Germanic Genealogy: A Guide to Worldwide Sources and Migration Patterns*. St. Paul, Minn., 1995.

German Genealogy Research Guide, CD-ROM. Fremont, Calif., and Baltimore, Md., 1999.

Hansen, Kevan M. *Finding Your German Ancestors: A Beginner's Guide*. Orem, Utah, 1999.

Henning and Ribbe, *Handbuch des Genealogie*. Neustadt, 1972.

Jensen, L.D. *Genealogical Handbook of German Research*. Pleasant Grove, Utah, 1980.

Jones, George F. *German-American Names*. Baltimore, 1995.

Kessler, G. *Die Familiennamen der Juden in Deutschland*. Jerusalem, 1935.

Minerva Handbücher. *Archiv in Deutschsprachigen Raum*. Berlin, 1974.

Smith, C. and A. *Encyclopedia of German-American Genealogical Research*. New York, 1976.

Thode, Ernest. *Address Book for Germanic Genealogy*. 6th ed. Baltimore, 1997.

Thode, Ernest. *German-English Genealogical Dictionary*. Baltimore, 1992.

Wright, Raymond S. *Meyers Orts- und Verkehrs-Lexikon des Deutschen Reiches. With Researcher's Guide and Translations of the Introduction, Instruction for the Use of the Gazetteer, and Abbreviations*. In Three Volumes. Baltimore, 2000.

GREECE

Saloutos, T. *Greeks in the United States*. Cambridge, Mass., 1964.

HUNGARY

Brandt, Edward Reimer. *Contents and Addresses of Hungarian Archives*. Baltimore, 1993.

Judák, Margit. *Egyházi Anyakönyvek Mikrofilmmásolatai*. Budapest, 1977.

Kempelen, D. *Magyar Forangu Csaladok*. Budapest, 1931.

Pamlenyi, E. *A History of Hungary*. Budapest, 1973.

Suess, Jared. *Handy Guide to Hungarian Genealogical Records*. Logan, Utah, 1980.

Szeplaki, J. *The Hungarians in America*. Dobbs Ferry, N.Y., 1975.

ICELAND

Jonasson, E. *Tracing Your Icelandic Ancestors*. Winnipeg, 1974.

Lindal, W. *The Icelanders in Canada*. Winnipeg, 1967.

Ólason, P.E. *Íslenzkar Aeviskrár.* 5 vols. Reykjavik, 1940.

Thorgeissen, O. *Almanach Fyrir.* Reykjavik, 1895.

ITALY

Carmack, Sharon DeBartolo. *Italian-American Family History.* Baltimore, 1997.

Cole, Trafford R. *Italian Genealogical Records: How to Use Italian Civil, Ecclesiastical, and Other Records in Family History Research.* Salt Lake City, 1995.

Colletta, John Philip. *Finding Italian Roots.* Baltimore, 1993.

Fucilla, J.G.S. *Our Italian Surnames.* Evanston, Ill., 1949.

Musmanno, M. *The Italians in America.* Garden City, N.Y., 1965.

Preece, P.P., and F.S. Preece. *Handy Guide to Italian Genealogical Records.* Logan, Utah, 1978.

Roth, C. *Stemmi di Famiglia Ebraice Italiane.* Jerusalem, 1967.

LATVIA

Akmentińs, O. *Latvijas Ideja Amerika.* Boston, 1969.

LITHUANIA

Michelsonas, S. *Lietuviu Išeivija Amerikoje.* Boston, 1961.

LUXEMBOURG

Bruck, A. *Fondations des Bourses d'Études Instituées en Faveur des Luxembourgeois.* Luxembourg, 1928.

Krieps, R. *Luxemburger in America (1609–1974).* Boston, 1975.

MALTA

Xuereb, P. Catalogue of Books and Articles in the University of Malta Library. Malta, 1974.

NETHERLANDS

De Jong, G.F. *The Dutch in America.* Boston, 1975.

Van Resandt, W. Wijaendts. *Repertorium DTB* (Dutch Parish Registers). The Hague, 1969.

NORWAY

Andersen, A.W. *The Norwegian-Americans.* Boston, 1974.

Norlie, O. *History of the Norwegian People in America.* New York, 1973.

POLAND

Chorzempa, Rosemary A. *Polish Roots.* Baltimore, 1993.

Lewanski, R.C. *Guide to Polish Libraries and Archives.* Boulder, Col., 1974.

Weinryb, B. *The Jews in Poland, 1100–1800.* Jerusalem, 1975.

PORTUGAL

Cardozo, M.S.S. *The Portuguese in America.* Dobbs Ferry, N.Y., 1976.
De Sousa, A.C. *Indice General da História Genealógica.* Coimbra, 1955.
Mattos, A. *Manuel de Genealogica Portuguesa.* Pôrto, 1943.
Tavares, B.E. *Portuguese Pioneers in the U.S.A.* Fall River, Mass., 1973.

ROMANIA

Bodea, C., and V. Cândea. *Heritage and Continuity in Eastern Europe: The Transylvanian Legacy in the History of the Romanians.* Boulder, Col., 1982.
Wertsman, V. *The Romanians in America.* Dobbs Ferry, N.Y., 1975.

RUSSIA

Stumpp, Karl. *The Emigration from Germany to Russia, 1763–1862.* Lincoln, Neb., 1978.
Wertsman, V. *The Russians in America, 1727–1970.* Dobbs Ferry, N.Y., 1977.

SPAIN

Baer, Y. *A History of the Jews in Christian Spain.* Philadelphia, 1961.
Catholic Church. *Guia de la Iglesia en España.* 4 vols. Madrid, 1954–57.

SWEDEN

Furtenbach, B. *Slaktforskning for alla.* Stockholm, 1971.
Hildebrand, B. *Hand Bok i slakt-och personforskning.* Stockholm, 1961.
Johanssen, Carl-Erik. *Cradled in Sweden.* Salt Lake City, 1972.
Olsson, Nils William. *Tracing Your Swedish Ancestry.* Sweden: Swedish Institute, 1982.
Ottervik, Gösta. *Libraries and Archives in Sweden.* Stockholm, 1964.
Royal Ministry of Foreign Affairs. *Tracing Your Swedish Ancestry.* Uppsala, 1977.

SWITZERLAND

Editions Polygraphiques. *Familiennamen Buch der Schweiz.* Zürich, 1968–71.
Faust, A., and G. Brumbaugh. *Lists of Swiss Emigrants in the Eighteenth Century to the American Colonies.* 2 vols. Washington, D.C., 1920, 1925 (repr. Baltimore, 1968).
Suess, Jared H. *Handy Guide to Swiss Genealogical Records.* Logan, Utah, 1978.
Von Grüninga, J.P. *The Swiss in the United States.* Madison, Wis., 1940.

UKRAINE

Wertsman, V. *The Ukrainians in America, 1627–1975.* Dobbs Ferry, N.Y., 1976.

YUGOSLAVIA

Govorchin, G. *Americans from Jugoslavia.* Gainesville, Fla., 1961.

Jovanovic, S., and M. Rojnic. *A Guide to Jugoslav Libraries and Archives.* Columbus, Ohio, 1975.

Rojnic, M. *Jugoslav Libraries.* Zagreb, 1954.

Vujnovich, M. *The Yugoslavs in America.* Minneapolis, 1977.

JEWISH (GENERAL)

Beider, A. *A Dictionary of Jewish Surnames from the Kingdom of Poland.* Teaneck, N.J., 1996.

Beider, A. *A Dictionary of Jewish Surnames from the Russian Empire.* Teaneck, N.J., 1993.

Fraenkel, J. *Guide to Jewish Libraries in the World.* London, 1959.

Gorr, S. *Jewish Personal Names.* Teaneck, N.J., 1992.

Gruber, R. *Jewish Heritage Travel.* New York, 1998.

Kagan, B. *Sefer Hapremumerantin.* New York, 1975.

Kurzweil, A. *From Generation to Generation.* Rev. ed. New York, 1994.

Kurzweil, A., and M. Weiner. *The Encyclopedia of Jewish Genealogy.* Northvale, N.J., 1991.

Mokotoff G., and S. Sack. *Where Once We Walked.* Teaneck, N.J., 1991.

Sack, S., and the Israel Genealogical Society. *A Guide to Jewish Genealogical Resources in Israel.* Rev. ed. Teaneck, N.J., 1995.

Stern, M. *First American Jewish Families.* 3rd ed. Baltimore, 1991.

Weiner, M. *Jewish Roots in Poland: Pages from the Past and Archival Inventories.* Secaucus, N.J., 1997.

Wynne, S. *Finding Your Jewish Roots in Galicia: A Resource Guide.* Teaneck, N.J., 1998.

Zubatsky, D., and I. Berent. *Sourcebook for Jewish Genealogies.* Teaneck, N.J., 1996.

GENERAL

National Archives of the United States. *Guide to Genealogical Research in the National Archives.* 3rd ed. Washington, D.C., 2000.

GENEALOGICAL SOCIETIES AND WEB SITES

This is a partial list of genealogical societies in Canada and the United States whose members concentrate their research on a particular country or group of countries in Europe. It has been difficult to put it together for a variety of reasons. Some of the organizations do not publicize their existence. Some grow steadily over the years—others die on the vine. Some addresses are constant, others change with the election of a new president or secretary. Some have web sites and others do not. In other words, I do not guarantee accuracy. If any reader with knowledge of organizations, or their phone or fax numbers, cares to write to me I will be delighted and will include the information—after checking—in the next edition of *In Search of Your European Roots*. I have also included some web sites of special interest to a specific country.

ALBANIA
Free Albania Organization, 397b North Broadway, South Boston, MA
    02127
Genealogy Forum: www.genforum.com/albania
Albanian Research List: feefhs.org/al/alrl.html

BELARUS
Belarus Genealogy Page: feefhs.org/by/frg-by.html
Belarus Genealogy Forum: www.genforum.com/belarus/

BELGIUM
Belgian Institute for Genealogy, Avenue Charles Theilmans 93, 1150
    Brussels; Phone: 011-31-2-772-500-27
Genealogy in Belgium: win-www.uia.ac.be/u/pavp/sdv/index.html

BULGARIA
Bulgaria National Front, PO Box 59240, Chicago, IL 60659
Bulgaria.com: www.bulgaria.com/index.html

CROATIA
Croatian Genealogical Society, 2527 San Carlos Avenue, San Carlos, CA
94070; Phone: 415-592-1190
Croatian Genealogy Network, PO Box 4327, Davis, CA 95617-4327
Croatian Ethnic Institute, 4851 S. Drexel Boulevard, Chicago, IL 60615
Croatian Institute for Culture and Information: www.croatia.hr/
contents.html

CZECH REPUBLIC
Czechoslovak Genealogical Society, PO Box 16225, St. Paul, MN
55116-0225; Phone: 612-739-7543; E-mail: PaulMCzech@aol.com
Czech Republic Home Page: www.czech.cz/

DENMARK
Denmark Mailing Lists: www.rootsweb.com/~jfuller/gen_mail_country-
den.html
Danish-American Genealogy Group, c/o Minnesota Genealogy Society,
5768 Olson Memorial Highway, Golden Valley MN 55422; Web site:
www.mtn.org/mgs/branches/danish.html

ESTONIA
Estonian American National Council, 243 E. 43rd Street, New York, NY
10016
Estonian Educational Network: www.eenef.ee

FINLAND
Finnish-American Heritage Society, PO Box 252, Canterbury, CT 06331;
Phone: 860-546-6671
Family History Finland: www.open.org/rumcd/genweb/finn.html

FRANCE
FranceGenWeb: francegenweb.org/

GERMANY
German Genealogical Society of America, 2125 Wright Avenue, Suite
C9, La Verne, CA 91750-5818; Phone: 909-593-0509; E-mail:
German_Genealogical._Society_of_America@hotmail.com; Web site:
www.feefhs.org/ggsa/frg-ggsa.html
Germanic Genealogical Society, PO Box 16312, St. Paul, MN 55116-
0312
Genealogy.net: www.genealogy.net/gene/
Germany GenWeb: www.rootsweb.com/~wggerman/

HUNGARY
Hungarian-American Friendship Society, 2811 Elvyra Way, Sacramento,
CA 95821-5865; Phone/Fax: 916-489-9599; E-mail:
73524.3664@compuserve.com

Hungarian Genealogical Society, 124 Esther Street, Toledo, OH 43605-1435

Hungarian Home Page: www.fsz.bme.hu/hungary/homepage.html

ITALY

Italian Genealogical Group, PO Box 626, Bathpage, NY 11714-0626

Italy GenWeb: www.rootsweb.com/~itawgw/index.html

LATVIA

Latvia SIG, PO Box 3581, Granada Hills, CA 91394-3581

American Latvian Association, PO Box 4578, Rockville, MD 20849-4578

LITHUANIA

Lithuanian-American Genealogical Society, 6500 Pulaski Road, Chicago, IL 60629-5136

Lithuanian Genealogy Forum: www.genforum.com/lithuania

MONTENEGRO

The Montenegrin Association of America: www.montenegro.org/

NORWAY

Emigrant Society of Norway, 10129 Goodrich Circle, Bloomington, MN 55437; Phone: 612-831-4409

POLAND

Polish Genealogical Society, 984 Milwaukee Avenue, Chicago, IL 60622-4199; E-mail: schmidtSR@aol.com

PORTUGAL

American-Portuguese Genealogical and Historical Society, PO Box 644, Taunton MA 02780-0644; www.tauntonma.com/apghs/

ROMANIA

Romanian Heritage Center, 2540 Grey Tower Road, Jackson, MI 49201; Phone: 517-522-8260

Romanian Internet Sources: www.indiana.edu/~reeiweb/romania.html

SLOVAKIA

Slovak Genealogical Research Center, 6862 Palmer Court, Chino, CA 91710-7343; Phone: 909-627-2897

SLOVENIA

Slovenian Genealogical Society, 52 Old Farm Road, Camp Hill, PA 17011; E-mail: LRFM15A@prodigy.com

(Canada Chapter) 1385 Maple Bay Road, RR5, Duncan, DC V9L 4T6 Canada

Genealogy and Heraldry in Slovenia: genealogy.ijp.si/default.htm

SPAIN

Hispanic Genealogical Society, PO Box 231271, Houston, TX 77223-1271

SWEDEN

Swedish Genealogy Group, 5768 Olson Memorial Highway, Golden Valley, MN 55422

SWITZERLAND

Genealogy in French-speaking Switzerland: www.unige.ch/biblio/ses/jla/gen/swiss-e.html

UKRAINE

Ukrainian Genealogical Society, 573 NE 102nd Street, Miami Shores, FL
Ukrainian Genealogical Society, RR#2, Cochrane, AL TOL 0W0 Canada

INDEX